100

SAINT-SIMON AT VERSAILLES

SAINT-SIMON

AT

VERSAILLES

SELECTED AND TRANSLATED FROM THE
MEMOIRS OF M. LE DUC DE SAINT-SIMON BY
LUCY NORTON

WITH A PREFACE BY
NANCY MITFORD

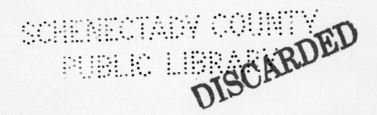
HARPER & BROTHERS *Publishers* NEW YORK

First published in Great Britain, 1958
by Hamish Hamilton Ltd
90 Great Russell Street London WC1

Copyright © 1958 by
Hamish Hamilton Ltd
and Harper & Brothers

PRINTED IN GREAT BRITAIN
BY WESTERN PRINTING SERVICES LTD BRISTOL

CONTENTS

Preface by Nancy Mitford		vii
Translator's Note		xvii
List of books used in compiling the selection		xxi
List of Illustrations		xxiii
1691	CHILDHOOD	1
1692	MARRIAGE OF M. LE DUC DE CHARTRES	3
1693	MADEMOISELLE DE MONTPENSIER	11
1693	THE FATHER OF SAINT-SIMON	13
1694	THE PRINCESSE DE CONTI DISMISSES MLLE CHOIN	17
1695	MARRIAGE OF SAINT-SIMON	21
1695	THE DUC DU MAINE AT THE FRONT	25
1695	MUCH BICKERING AMONG THE PRINCESSES	30
1696-7	THE LITTLE PRINCESSE OF SAVOY	32
1696	MME DE CASTRIES	36
1697	THE KING AND THE PRINCE OF ORANGE	37
1698	AN ENVOY FROM ENGLAND	38
1698	MANOEUVRES AT COMPIÈGNE	43
1698	THE IGNORANCE OF BRETEUIL	51
1699	COISLIN'S REVENGE	53
1699	INCREDIBLE ROBBERIES	54
1700	LE NÔTRE	57
1700	THE DUC D'ANJOU BECOMES KING OF SPAIN	59
1700	DEPARTURE OF PHILIP V	68
1701	ROSE, THE KING'S SECRETARY . .	69
1701	DEATH OF MONSIEUR	74
1702	SAINT-SIMON LEAVES THE ARMY	80
1703	THE FUSS OVER THE OFFERTORY	85
1703	MADAME DE CHARLUS	91
1704	SAINT-SIMON IS BLED	92
1704	THE GRIGNAN FAMILY	94
1704	SKETCH OF PUYSIEUX	95
1705	THE MASKS	96

A*

1705	CALAMITY TO FARGUES	97
1705	SINGULAR CHARACTER OF NINON, CALLED DE L'ENCLOS	100
1705	RAISING THE MILITIA	103
1706	THE EMBASSY TO ROME	104
1706	THE DUC DE VENDÔME	109
1706	MY RELATIONSHIP WITH M. LE DUC D'ORLÉANS	116
1707	THE KIDNAPPING OF BERINGHEN	122
1707	THE 'PARVULO' AT MEUDON	125
1707	THE DUC DU MAINE AND THE COMTE DE TOULOUSE	128
1707	MADAME DE MONTESPAN	130
1707	DEATH OF THE DUCHESSE DE NEMOURS	137
1708	MISHAP TO MME LA DUCHESSE DE BOURGOGNE	139
1708	SAMUEL BERNARD THE BANKER	141
1708	DEATH OF MANSARD	143
1709	THE FEARFUL WINTER OF 1709	145
1709	FALL OF THE DUC DE VENDÔME	151
1709	THE SILVER IS TAKEN TO THE MINT	153
1709	WHY I WISHED TO RETIRE FROM THE COURT	157
1711	DEATH OF MONSEIGNEUR	161
1712	DEATH OF MME LA DUCHESSE DE BOURGOGNE	185
1712	DEATH OF MGR LE DUC DE BOURGOGNE	195
1712	THE KING IS BORED	205
1713	BRISSAC PLAYS A PRANK	206
1714	THE KING'S WILL	208
1715	CHARACTER OF M. LE DUC D'ORLÉANS	216
1715	CHARACTER OF MME LA DUCHESSE D'ORLÉANS	225
1715	A HIGHLY DUBIOUS AMBASSADOR FROM PERSIA	229
1715	DEATH OF THE KING	232
1715	CHARACTER OF LOUIS XIV	245
1715	LOUIS XIV AND THE COURT	252
1715	MME DE MAINTENON	266
1715	AFTER THE DEATH OF THE KING	285
1715	THE SESSION OF THE PARLEMENT	289
1719	THE BED OF JUSTICE	297

Genealogical Tables: I. The Family of Louis XIV   facing page 16
     II. Louis XIV's Descendants   facing page 48

Index   305

Preface

LOUIS XIV, the Sun-King, lived in his golden palace and the whole French world revolved around him. The ablest man, according to Lord Acton, to be born in modern times on the steps of a throne, he never did anything without a purpose. Versailles was built to be a cage where he could keep the French nobility under his eye, away from their estates and the sources of their own power.

When he was a child[1] the lords and Princes of the Blood had revolted against the crown in the civil war known as the Fronde (1648–53). They had no other objective than their own aggrandisement, and did not hesitate to call on the Spanish enemy for help when it suited them. Louis XIV never forgot or forgave the shameful episodes of the Fronde; he never trusted the nobles or allowed them to take part in the government; his ministers were magistrates of the Parisian bourgeoisie. His method of holding down the proud feudal chiefs was simple and cunning. Playing upon the French love of fashion, he managed to establish the fact that, while Versailles was the hub of the universe, the provinces were dowdy and ridiculous. Anybody who displeased the King was sent, as a punishment, to his own estates. Paris was out of bounds; in any case, the day at Versailles was so arranged, with too many duties crammed into too little time, that there was no opportunity to go there. This policy prevented any danger of another Fronde, but it left a difficult heritage for the heirs of Louis XIV, who were much less clever than he.

The best descriptions of the curious, enclosed life at Versailles are those of Madame, the King's sister-in-law, and of the Duc de Saint-Simon. They both deal with the end of the seventy-two years' reign, Saint-Simon with the last twenty years. By the time of which he was writing the system was well established; the King, long past his youth, had come to be regarded with a

[1] Louis XIV, born 1638, reigned 1643–1715.

religious awe, worshipped by the courtiers who were exceedingly frightened of him. They had reason to be; he had done some frightening things. People spoke in whispers of the Man in the Iron Mask, of a pamphleteer shut up in the very cage used by Louis XI to punish his enemies, of the sudden fall and disappearance of the apparently all-powerful minister, Fouquet. Louis XIV had always inspired fear. His sister-in-law, Henrietta of England, dreaded 'the mortal coldness of the King' when they were both in their 20's. The only people who ever dared to stand up to him were Madame, who succeeded Henrietta as his sister-in-law; the Grande Mademoiselle; Madame de Maintenon; and the Duchesse de Bourgogne. The courtiers were abject. 'The rain at Marly is not wet.' (Marly was his favourite country house.) They made up for this moral servitude by endless squabbles amongst themselves, mostly to do with precedence. The King was always ready to arbitrate, since authority in these matters was part of his hold over them, but in his eyes all his subjects were equal. His valet-de-chambre, Molière, had the full authority of the master to mock his other servants, whether dukes or marquises, doctors or ministers. Like Queen Victoria, whom he resembled in many ways (Louis XIV, aged one and a half, had the same face in the same bonnet as Queen Victoria when old), he firmly believed that not only kings and queens but also royal princes were on a higher plane than the rest of the human race. He seems to have regarded the Almighty as a sort of superior fellow-king. 'How could God do this to me, after all I have done for him?' he said, on hearing of the battle of Blenheim. He imposed this point of view on his subjects, and it was taken for granted by rich and poor, educated and ignorant alike. Fénelon saw no difference between a republican and a thief. Massillon thought it necessary to begin his funeral oration on the King's death with the words: 'Only God is great', as though his listeners had long ago forgotten this truth. Louis XIV's extraordinary generosity to his deposed cousin, James II, is accounted for by the fact that James was the Lord's Anointed like himself. He supported him and his odious, squabbling band of English and Scotch exiles in royal state at the Palace of Saint-Germain-en-Laye; his indulgence went so far as to allow James to touch for King's Evil *in his capacity of King of France* (a claim which the English crown had never abandoned).

The King, at Versailles, lived in full view of his subjects.
There was no cosy family life behind the scenes, as at Windsor.
He had special names for his own relations, certainly, but not
such names as 'Ducky', 'Missy', or 'Tootsey-Boy'. The palace
was open to all, nobody was excluded, and people wandered
freely about the house and gardens. When the King appeared,
which he did at certain hours with a clockwork regularity, anybody could present a petition. His morning progress from his
bedroom to the chapel took a long time as he was then beset
by petitioners. To each one he made the same reply: 'I will
see', and he always did see. None was ever ignored or forgotten.
Louis XIV was one of the most polite men who ever lived, as
well as one of the most exact.

The royal family, at the time of which Saint-Simon writes,
consisted of the King's brother, the Duc d'Orléans; the King's
unacknowledged second wife, Mme de Maintenon; his only
surviving (legitimate) child, the Dauphin; his three grandsons,
the Ducs de Bourgogne, Anjou, and Berry; his bastard daughter
by Mlle de la Vallière, the dowager Princesse de Conti; and his
four surviving bastards by Mme de Montespan: the Duc du
Maine, the Comte de Toulouse, the Duchesse de Bourbon, and the
Duchesse de Chartres. The Queen had died in 1683. She was
Marie-Thérèse, daughter of the King of Spain, whom Louis
XIV had married, for reasons of state, at a time when he was
deeply in love with Marie Mancini. He was not faithful to his
wife, a poor, simple, unattractive creature, but he treated her
respectfully and slept in her bed. She never learnt to speak
French properly, she said 'eschevois' for horse and called the
King's mistresses 'les putes du roi'. She was one of the many
victims of the dreadful Court doctors; they killed five of her six
babies and finally killed her, says Madame, 'as surely as if they
had pierced her heart with a sword'.

The King's brother, the Duc d'Orléans, was known as Monsieur. He was a wretched little creature, painted, coquettish,
mincing, covered with ribbons and jewels. The courtiers rather
liked him; he had a certain charm when he wanted to please,
and was good at arranging parties. He lived at Saint-Cloud in
a splendid palace (burnt down by the Germans in 1871) and at
the Palais-Royal in Paris. As time went on and the Kings of
France were seen less and less in the capital, the Parisians came
to prefer the d'Orléans branch of the royal family, who lived

among them. More interesting than Monsieur were his two
wives. Henrietta, the first Madame, was a typical Stuart, ugly,
charming, and unlucky. Monsieur did not care for women; he
was entirely governed, all his life, by the Chevalier de Lorraine
and the Marquis d'Effiat. This sinister pair were supposed to have
murdered Henrietta, though in view of her medical history, it
is quite as likely that she died of peritonitis (1670). She left two
daughters, the Duchess of Savoy and the Queen of Spain. Monsieur married secondly Princess Elizabeth-Charlotte (Liselotte),
daughter of the Elector-Palatine of Bavaria, who described herself as 'a noisy, rough and wayward girl'. She liked outdoor
life, and hated court ceremonial. Somebody once asked her
little son, the Duc de Chartres, if he was fond of parties and
dressing up. He replied, 'I do not hate them as much as
Madame, but neither do I love them nearly as much as
Monsieur does.'

Madame had a better claim to the throne of England than
her cousin George I, and had she not married a French prince
and turned Roman Catholic she might have become our Queen.
It is perhaps fortunate that she did not, since she had no opinion
of the English: 'deceitful, untrustworthy, republicans at heart'.
As Germans do, she also loathed the French and never had a
good word for them, but all her life she was in love with Louis
XIV. Madame's hobby was letter-writing; she wrote, in German, three or four long letters every day, sometimes amounting
to fifty pages. She was not such a great writer as Saint-Simon,
but an excellent journalist with a nose for news; she evolved
an organization for obtaining it which was useful to Saint-Simon
since Madame often passed on pieces of information to him.
In youth, her chief correspondents were her aunt, the Electress of Hanover, and her two step-daughters; when these were
all dead, she wrote to her own daughter, the Duchesse de Lorraine, and to Caroline of Anspach, the Princess of Wales. Her
letters confirm Saint-Simon's statements in most respects, and
on the whole she and he shared the same likes and dislikes.
They were both obsessed by the King, and felt an exaggerated
loathing for Mme de Maintenon, whom Madame generally
referred to as 'die alte Zote' (the old whore). Madame saw
much less of the King after Mme de Maintenon's rise to favour;
also she blamed her for the Duc de Chartres' marriage in 1692
to the King's bastard daughter. Chartres, later Duc d'Orléans,

Regent of France, was Saint-Simon's greatest friend at Versailles. He was a mixture of vice and virtue: famous for his debaucheries, capable of real goodness, intelligent and brave, incurably slothful. Poor Madame minded her son's *mésalliance* more than anything that happened in the whole of her life. Monsieur, very naturally, did not much care for it, but the King obtained his consent by bribing the Chevalier de Lorraine with the Order of the Saint-Esprit. After that, Madame could do nothing. Chartres' own feelings were not taken into account; as the 15-year-old bride herself remarked, 'It doesn't matter if he loves me or not, what matters is that he should marry me.' In fact, the marriage did not turn out too badly. The Duchesse de Chartres had much of the charm of her mother, Mme de Montespan; she was vicious, lazy, and very amusing; her husband knew her by heart and rather loved her. She conducted her own affairs discreetly, and never interfered with his.

After the Chartres marriage, Madame's haunting terror was that her other child, Elizabeth Charlotte, would be married to the King's favourite bastard, the Duc du Maine. According to her, the King was only prevented from forcing this second disgrace on his brother's family by Parisian opposition, strongly expressed in the lampoons and libels of the day. She was ever grateful to the citizens of Paris for saving her daughter, who finally married the Duc de Lorraine: their son was the father of Marie-Antoinette.

The Dauphin, known to history as le Grand Dauphin, although he had no single quality of greatness, was called Monseigneur at Versailles. Drowned in fat and apathy, he was despised by all; Saint-Simon was not the only Frenchman who dreaded the day when he would come to the throne and give power to the worthless set of sycophants by which he was surrounded. He had a German wife with whom he was happy for a while, but his half-sister, the Princesse de Conti, put him against her. The courtiers were unkind to her, the royal family neglected her, and finally she shut herself up in two little dark rooms with her Italian maid and they both died, perhaps of poison. Some think that Monseigneur then secretly married his mistress, Mlle Choin, lady-in-waiting of the Princesse de Conti. He lived partly in his own sumptuous ground-floor rooms at Versailles, and partly in his palace of Meudon, situated between Versailles and Paris. He predeceased his father (1711).

The Dauphin had three sons, the Ducs de Bourgogne, Anjou, and Berry. After his death, Bourgogne succeeded him as Dauphin, and was then addressed as Monsieur, spoken of as Monsieur le Dauphin, and written to as Monseigneur. He is one of the most touching characters of French history. 'In all his life,' says Madame, 'he never harmed a single person.' Michelet, the most anti-Bourbon of historians, says of Saint-Simon's great passage on his death: 'A hundred and fifty years after the event we weep as we read the harrowing pages in which Saint-Simon describes his passing. . . . History is disarmed before his memory.' It is now nearly two hundred and fifty years after the event; we still weep, as Michelet did. Bourgogne was adored by his contemporaries; his charming wife, though never in love with him, loved and respected him greatly. She was a princess of Savoy, the granddaughter of Monsieur and Henrietta. When she arrived at Versailles, aged twelve, she introduced an element of natural gaiety which had not existed there since the days of her grandmother. All were bewitched by her, not least the King, whom she could twist round her little finger. Saint-Simon does not say, and perhaps never knew, that she regularly sent state secrets to her father when he was at war with France. The King knew it: '*la coquine, elle nous a trahi*,' ('naughty little creature, she has betrayed us,') but forgave her. Mme de Maintenon went so far as to say that her death may have been a good thing for France. Her sister was the Queen of Spain; they both inherited the bad luck of the Stuarts, dying, like poor Henrietta, young and mysteriously.

The Grand Dauphin's second son, the Duc d'Anjou, became King of Spain. When Cardinal Mazarin forced Louis XIV to marry the Infanta Marie-Thérèse, he had expected thus to unite the thrones of France and Spain. He had not foreseen that her father, Philip IV, would marry again and produce a sickly heir, Charles II, to succeed him when only a baby. Mazarin's plan was thus postponed for a whole generation. In 1700, Charles died, bequeathing Spain and her dependencies to the Duc d'Anjou. After some doubt and hesitation, Louis XIV accepted the inheritance on behalf of his grandson. This gave rise to the War of the Spanish Succession (1701–14), in which England and the Empire were allied against France and Spain, a war marked by the brilliant victories of Marlborough and Prince Eugene. Nevertheless, d'Anjou, now Philip V, remained firmly on his throne, and Spain was ruled by his descendants until 1931.

The third brother of Bourgogne and d'Anjou was the charming Duc de Berry, who lived for pleasure. Saint-Simon helped to arrange his marriage to a daughter of the Duc de Chartres, and Mme de Saint-Simon became their lady-in-waiting. This gave the Saint-Simons a coveted apartment at Versailles. The Duc de Berry died of a hunting accident in 1714. Madame, who mourned him with all her heart, said, however, that the widow, her granddaughter, was in no way to be pitied. Had she not the highest rank of any lady in France (since the death of the Duchesse de Bourgogne), about £300,000 a year, and fantastic jewellery? How could she possibly be unhappy? This lucky duchess, who, as well as a young husband, had lost both of her babies, shared her father's intemperate life, and died having an illegitimate child. (It was perhaps as well that she did, since she seems to have been going mad.) 'She was his beloved child,' says Madame, recording the event not without emotion.

In about 1683 (the exact date is not known, but soon after the death of the Queen) Louis XIV married Mme de Maintenon. She had been brought to Versailles by his mistress, the Marquise de Montespan, as governess to the royal bastards. That so pedestrian, so unattractive, so truly governessy a person should have supplanted the superb Marquise is one of those tricks by which real life sometimes confounds us. Mme de Montespan was born Mortemart; she and her sisters stole the limelight wherever they appeared, they were beautiful and clever, and had such an original way of talking that it was almost like a special language. The King adored her for years. However, when they had had six children his passion began to cool. As Voltaire says, 'he reproached himself for his liaison with a married woman, and when he was no longer in love his conscience made itself felt more keenly.' After many humiliations at the hands of Mme de Maintenon, Mme de Montespan retired from the court, living in hopes that the King would send for her again. He never did. Furthermore, her children loved Mme de Maintenon like a mother; this must have been very hard to bear. Mme de Maintenon's life, however, was no bed of roses in spite of the position to which she was elevated by her marriage. The King was as selfish and autocratic to her as he was to everybody else. When they were both over 70 (she was five years his senior) he still insisted on his conjugal rights, sometimes twice a day, regardless of her feelings. On his death bed he annoyed her considerably by saying that no doubt, at her age, she would soon be joining him in the next world. Few people liked Mme de Maintenon and many hated her. Her enemies used to say, with some truth, that she was not even an efficient governess. All her charges were thoroughly unsatisfactory; the only one of Mme de Montespan's children to turn out well was the Comte de Toulouse, and he had never been looked after by Mme de Maintenon.

The Duc du Maine was Louis XIV's favourite child; Mme de Maintenon, too, loved him devotedly. He was an amusing talker, like all his family, but there was nothing else to be said for him. Crooked in mind as in body (he had infantile paralysis as a child), he was a coward, which was particularly unfortunate, since at Versailles all forms of eccentricity were tolerated except that. He married the daughter of the Prince de Condé, and had seven children but no grandchildren. The Duc and Duchesse du Maine lived at Sceaux, where they kept great state.

The Comte de Toulouse married, for love, a Noailles. They lived at Rambouillet and in the splendid house which is now the Banque de France. They had one son, the Duc de Penthièvre, an ancestor of the present French royal family.

The Princes of the Blood were Bourbon-Condé and Bourbon-Conti; both families descended from the Duc de Vendôme, an uncle of Henri IV. The head of the Condés was known either as Monsieur le Duc or Monsieur le Prince, according to the King's decree. The great Condé and his son were both called Monsieur le Prince; Louis III de Bourbon-Condé, who married Louis XIV's daughter, was Monsieur le Duc. They lived at Chantilly and at the Hôtel de Condé on whose site the Odéon was subsequently built, in Paris. The head of the Contis was always a Prince, and had no special form of address. The Monnaie (Mint) occupies the site of their town house.

Another royal family which figured at Versailles was that of Lorraine. Its innumerable members all descended from two brothers, Antoine, Duc de Lorraine (1490–1544), and Claude, Duc de Guise, both married to Bourbon princesses. Guise was the grandfather of Mary, Queen of Scots. The Lorraines, it was said, paid their court to the King of France, but their hearts were

with the Empire. They were notorious double-dealers, and
Prince Eugene and other enemies of France got much information from them. There was a running fight over precedence
between cadets of this family and the French dukes.

The Duc de Saint-Simon was born in 1675. When he was a
child, his favourite treats were royal funerals and requiem
masses. He would also listen entranced while his elders discussed questions of usage. He was determined to become the
chronicler of his age, and confided this ambition to M. de
Rancé, during a retreat at La Trappe. The great and holy man
entirely approved, and Saint-Simon dedicated his life to this purpose. Like a journalist, he had a passion for news; unlike a
journalist, he reported it and put it away. 'He who would write
the story of his times truthfully and with no respect for persons,'
he said, 'should never show it to anybody. He should leave it to
ripen under lock and key.' His subject was the Court of France,
at a time when the Court was France, but Saint-Simon was by
no means a typical courtier. He knew that the King ought to be
treated 'like a god, like a father, like a mistress', but he never
could bring himself to do so. He could not cringe, and when he
felt strongly about something he would burst out. Louis XIV
was for ever telling him to hold his tongue; he was often half in
disgrace. Luckily for him, the King was fond of Mme de Saint-
Simon, and it was probably due to her that they were never
actually exiled from the Court. His bone of contention with the
King was the powerlessness to which the French aristocracy had
been reduced. It was the obsession of his life, and the theme
which runs through his *Mémoires*. His concern over what seem
to us silly, trivial matters, who should hand round the offertory
bag in the chapel, for instance, is really part of his effort to keep
some responsibility in the hands of the nobles, and prevent
them from turning into the elegant, unreal figures described by
Proust. Privilege, in his eyes, was the outward and visible
sign of power. He did not realize quite how successful Louis
XIV had been, not only in his undermining of the power of the
nobles but also of their will to power. Saint-Simon himself was
capable of energetic action. Almost single-handed, he defeated
the Duc du Maine in his attempt to seize the person of the little
King after Louis XIV's death. He then persuaded his friend, the
Regent, to restore aristocratic government in France. It was too
late; the dukes no longer wanted to lead except in war, and the

chance for them to do so never came again. Saint-Simon failed
as a politician, through no fault of his own.

But as a writer his success was paramount. He was lucky to
have such interesting people to write about. There has seldom
been a dull Bourbon. Licentious or bigoted, noble or ignoble,
they were nearly all odd, original men with strong passions,
unaccountable in their behaviour. Louis XIV casts a dazzling
glare on the pages of all the writers of his day; he was the most
extraordinary member of this extraordinary family. Saint-
Simon was able to observe him like a specimen under a micro-
scope, and made the most of his opportunity. He hated the King,
but he was not unfair to him. Indeed, his prejudices were usually
justified. His most violent was that against the Duc du Maine;
he raged at the false, proud, cowardly, ambitious, club-footed,
devilish bastard to such effect that, although we live at a time
when rehabilitations are the fashion, no French writer has ever
attempted to rehabilitate him. It would be no good telling us
not to believe Saint-Simon's verdict, we cannot help believing
it, and, in fact, it seems hardly to have been too severe. Madame
entirely agrees with it. Passionately as Saint-Simon felt about
legitimized royal bastards, who, in his view, were a danger to
the State, he had nothing but praise for the Comte de Toulouse.

Everybody has heard of the *Mémoires* of Saint-Simon; very
few people have read them all through. Indeed, they have
never been printed in full. The manuscript covers 2,700 folio
pages in a minute handwriting with no stops, chapters, or divi-
sions of any sort. Lord Macaulay, who read them in the (highly
inaccurate) first edition of 1830 and again in 1854, and some of
whose own most living passages are taken from them, said, 'I
am more struck with the goodness of the good parts than ever.
To be sure, the road from fountain to fountain leads through a
very dry desert.' Miss Norton takes us, in her admirable
selection, from fountain to fountain, but the desert road has its
charms too. Only those who have the courage to walk it will be
rewarded by what Lytton Strachey calls 'the enormous pano-
rama, magnificent, palpitating, alive'.

NANCY MITFORD

Translator's Note

WHEN you translate the work of a famous writer you can take one of two courses. You may regard his words, phraseology, and punctuation as sacred and never to be departed from. Faithfulness, you may say, is all. This is my author; this is how he wrote in his own language at his own period; here he is in English. Let him be ponderous, verbose, slangy, or obscure; let his sentences run on for half a page or more, packed with strings of adjectives and relative clauses; his is the responsibility, I must follow him blindly into whatever morass he leads. But the translator has also a duty to the reader, and with Saint-Simon such writing would be virtually unreadable. In long parts of the Memoirs where he consciously composed, a literal translation would read like the following:

'A situation so harsh and so general, emanating necessarily from so many contradictory phrases given successively to the finances under the false idea of repairing the chaos and ruin in which they were found on the death of Louis XIV, did not allow the public to regret the man whom it considered to be its author.'

What reader, for pleasure, nowadays, would read thousands and thousands of such sentences, paragraphs, and pages?

The other way is to try to translate with broader truth to the author's style, spirit, and intention, for the enjoyment of those who cannot or will not read him in the original. It means trying to learn to know your author so well that when you reproduce his sense, you write, as it were, holding his pen in your own language and century, in harmony with his thought, you hope, but not slavishly bound to every word and comma. This is the course which I have tried to pursue.

Of course Saint-Simon did not always write in the style of the above quotation. Had he done so his Memoirs would not be remembered. When he reported conversations or described the exciting historical scenes which he witnessed, his words poured out like a torrent, disdainful of grammar or style. He could not write quickly enough to crowd onto his paper all that he had to say. At such moments he becomes most fascinating and vehement, but also most colloquial and slangy, seizing the vivid, homely expressions that come first into his head, and providing his would-be faithful translator with an even greater problem.

At the end of his Memoirs Saint-Simon wrote: 'Shall I say a word about my style, the negligences, the repetitions of the same word at close intervals, the too many synonyms, the sense obscured by lengthy sentences, repetitions, and grammatical errors? I felt these faults. I could not help them, for I was always carried away by the interest of the matter and was very little attentive to the manner of rendering it, except so as to explain it well.'

But to translate Saint-Simon into ungrammatical English would be unbearable, and the French slang which he wrote two hundred years ago was not necessarily the English slang of that period, nor would modern slang endure for more than a very short while. I have therefore avoided slang and bad grammar and have tried to convey his often colloquial, racy style in good English so far as I am able.

It must not be thought that because so much of the translation reads in the idiom of today, there has been any attempt to modernize the language. That was how Saint-Simon wrote. Even his slang has a ghostly familiarity. 'The Maréchal', he says, 'mopped up (*essuyait*) a good many reprimands'; 'I gave it to him good and proper' (*Je lui en donnais belle*); and when an impertinent duchess sat on a stool above her station in the line of duchesses at the King's supper, Monseigneur intervened to protect her from the royal anger, but 'washed her head for her properly' (*lui lava bien la tête*) after the Monarch withdrew.

In the same way, the abrupt transitions are not the result of abridgment. They are characteristic of Saint-Simon, who was often in such a hurry that he leaped in the most disconcertingly sudden way from topic to topic. The headings are Saint-Simon's own. His manuscript was not divided into chapters, he simply noted the topic in the margin. In some cases, notably under his heading 'The Duc du Maine at the Front', I have included parts of an earlier passage, in order to explain what had been happening.

I have never consciously put into Saint-Simon's mouth words that are not in the manuscript, or changed his intention by my omissions, but I have constantly had to make cuts in order to bring the selection to manageable proportions, and I have straightened out some parts where 'the sense is obscured by lengthy sentences'. I have omitted altogether long dissertations on rank and precedence, and genealogies (sometimes extending to bastard second cousins) which often fill several pages at a time.

In this selection much has had to be sacrificed. I have thought it best to omit all mention of certain subjects that do not come within the chosen scope of *Saint-Simon at Versailles*. Thus, Spain, alas, has had to be passed over altogether, with much that is most fascinating. Wars have gone; the Church, very regretfully, has gone, along with Fénelon, Port-Royal, and the Jesuits. The Princesse des Ursins and her intrigues at the Spanish Court have gone, so has Lauzun, with his dangerous, abominable conduct in hiding under the King's bed through the whole of one night, in order to hear his future debated with Mme de Montespan. So much delectable gossip I have had to abandon, including the tale of the eccentric Mme de Saint-Hérem, who found the Seine too cold for agreeable bathing and had kettles of boiling water poured round her, thereby developing scalds which kept her in bed for a week.

Nevertheless, what is included is the best of all: Saint-Simon's life at the Court, in the extraordinary, terrifying world of Louis XIV at Versailles and Marly, some most brilliant portraits of the men and women who were its inhabitants, some of the historical scenes where Saint-Simon becomes most absorbing, and some of the gossip.

My aim has been to try to give the essence of the Memoirs, so that many who know Saint-Simon only as a name may find new pleasure, and some, perhaps, be led to discover for themselves greater delight along the enchanting 'desert road' of the great original.

LUCY NORTON

List of books used in compiling the selection

Mémoires du duc de Saint-Simon. Ed. Chéruel & Adolphe Régnier fils. Preface by Sainte-Beuve. Paris, Hachette, 1873–1886, 22 vols.

Mémoires de Saint-Simon. Ed. A. de Boislisle. Paris, Hachette, 1879–1928, 43 vols.

Memoirs of the Duc de Saint-Simon. Translated and abridged by Katharine Prescott Wormeley. London, Heinemann, 1899, 4 vols.

Saint-Simon par lui-même. François-Régis Bastide. Paris, Editions du Seuil, 1953.

Saint-Simon Mémoires. Ed. Gonzague Truc. Paris, Bibliothèque de la Pléiade, Gallimard, 1953.

Saint-Simon et sa Comédie Humaine. La Varende. Paris, Hachette, 1955.

NOTE

The footnotes in this volume are by Nancy Mitford and Lucy Norton.

List of Illustrations

Louis, Duc de Saint-Simon *frontispiece*

facing page

Marie-Adélaide de Savoie, Duchesse de Bourgogne 32

The Camp at Compiègne 33

The Duc d'Anjou as King Philip V of Spain 64

Louis XIV 65

Anne-Marie de Bourbon, Princesse de Conti 96

Raising the Militia: 22nd December 1705 97

Madame de Maintenon, with her niece, Françoise 128
  d'Aubigné

Louis-Auguste de Bourbon, Duc de Maine 129

Louis-Joseph de Bourbon, Duc de Vendôme 129

L'Homme de Village 168

Louis XIV and his heirs 169

Louis, Duc de Bourgogne 192

Philippe, Duc d'Orléans, later the Regent 192

Louis XIV and his family 193

1691

Childhood

I was born on the night of January 15th, 1675, son of Claude, Claude, Duc de Saint-Simon, Peer of France, by his second wife, Charlotte de l'Aubespine, the only child of that marriage. By my father's first wife, Diane de Budos, he had had no sons and one daughter, whom he had married to the Duc de Brissac, the only brother of the Duchesse de Villeroy. She died without issue in 1684, and in her will she made me her residuary legatee.

I bore the title of Vidame de Chartres, and much care and thought was lavished on my upbringing, for my mother, a most virtuous lady, vastly sensible and intelligent, took endless pains over my education. She did not want me to share the fate of many young men who think their fortunes made, when they become independent too soon, and my father, who had been born in 1606, seemed unlikely to live long enough to spare me that misfortune. She therefore constantly reminded me that I urgently needed to train myself for some position since I should be entering the world alone and unprotected, the son of Louis XIII's favourite, whose friends were dead or in no position to aid me. As for her, she had been brought up in the house of her kinswoman, the old Duchesse d'Angoulême, and had married an elderly man. Thus she had made no friendships with people of her own age, and, what is more, had no uncles, aunts, or cousins. I should be thrown entirely upon my own resources, which made it doubly necessary to make the best possible use of myself, for I could expect no other support.

My mother accordingly did her utmost to encourage me to overcome this major handicap, and she succeeded in giving me a great desire to do so, although the fact that I cared little for learning did not assist her. I had, however, a natural love for reading and history, and I improved my mind by trying to emulate the great men of whom I read, which made up for my

B

dislike of the classics. Indeed, I have sometimes thought that had I made the former my serious study and wasted less time upon the latter, I might perhaps have become something.

My reading of history, especially the memoirs of my own times and the period immediately after the reign of François I, gave me the idea of writing down my own observations, in the hope that by learning all I could of current affairs I might fit myself for some high position. I foresaw the dangers of such a course, but a firm resolve to keep my undertaking secret seemed to meet all possible objections. In July 1694, therefore, I began my Memoirs, being at that time colonel of a cavalry regiment in my own name, encamped at Guinsheim in the Vieux-Rhin, part of the army commanded by the Maréchal the Duc de Lorges.

In 1691, I had been studying philosophy and equitation at the Académie des Sieurs de Mesmont et Rochefort, but was beginning to be tired of masters and study. I became very eager to enter the army, for the King himself had commanded at the siege of Mons in the early spring of that year, and most of the young men of my own age were serving in their first campaign. What moved me most, however, was that M. le Duc de Chartres[1] was there also. He was my elder by eight months; we had been brought up together, as it were, and, if youth will excuse the expression between men so unequal in rank, we were friends. Such considerations determined me to extricate myself from the schoolroom, but I shall not enlarge upon all the ruses I used in order to succeed. I first spoke to my mother; but soon realized that she would only laugh at me; I then went to my father and managed to persuade him that as the King had laid one great siege that year he would rest in the next; I deceived my mother, who only discovered my plot on the eve of its execution, and I worked upon my father so that he should not weaken.

The King always insisted that everyone who entered his service, except the Princes of the Blood and his bastards, should spend a year in one of his two companies of musketeers. Then, before they were allowed to buy a regiment, they had to go for training, for a varying period, either as captains of cavalry, or as junior officers in his own artillery regiment. My father therefore took me with him when he went to Versailles. He made his

---

[1] Philippe d'Orléans (1674–1723), son of Monsieur. Later, M. le Duc d'Orléans. Became Regent of France in 1715.

bow, and presented me as wishing to become a musketeer, on St. Simon and St. Jude's Day, at half-past noon, at the time when the King was leaving the Council.

His Majesty did him the honour of embracing him three times, but when it came to me, he thought me puny and delicate-looking and said that I was still exceedingly young. My father answered that I should have all the longer to serve him. Then the King asked in which company my father wished to place me, and he chose the first, because his friend Maupertuis was captain, and he knew that I should be well looked after. He also knew that the King always questioned the two captains minutely, and especially Maupertuis, about the young men of quality in their companies, and that their reports influenced his first impressions, on which so much depended. As it turned out, my father was not mistaken, for I have reason to attribute the King's early good opinion of me to Maupertuis' kind offices.

1692

Marriage of M. le Duc de Chartres

THE King had been busy providing establishments for his bastards, whom every day he advanced in rank and honours. Two of his illegitimate daughters he had already married to Princes of the Blood. Mme la Princesse de Conti,[1] his only daughter by Mme de la Vallière, was a widow without children, the other, his eldest daughter by Mme de Montespan, had married Monsieur le Duc. For a long time past Mme de Maintenon, even more than the King, had thought of nothing but their further aggrandisement. Now, both wished to marry Mlle de Blois, the King's second daughter by Mme de Montespan, to M. le Duc de Chartres, his only legitimate nephew, far above even the Princes of the Blood, by his rank as a Grandson of France and by the Court of Monsieur, his father.

The King well knew the shocking scandal that had been created by the marriages of the Princes of the Blood, and he could imagine the effect of one which society would consider

---

[1] She had been widowed in 1685 and was known as the Princesse de Conti, *douairière* (dowager).

infinitely more improper. Nevertheless, he had been turning the matter over in his mind during the past four years and had already begun to make the first moves. These he had found all the more difficult because Monsieur was inordinately proud in anything that touched his rank, and Madame came of a nation that abhorred bastardy and misalliances.

In this dilemma he consulted his crony, Monsieur le Grand,[1] desiring him to win over his brother the Chevalier de Lorraine, an exceedingly good-looking man who ruled Monsieur in everything. Indeed, the latter, who had no taste for women (a fact which he did not even try to disguise), had taken the Chevalier for his master and remained true to him for the rest of his life. These two brothers asked for nothing better than to please the King in a matter that touched him so closely, and, like the clever men that they were, they turned it to their own advantage. The first move was made in the summer of 1688. Only about a dozen chevaliers of the Order[2] still remained, and everyone knew that promotions could not be long delayed. The two brothers now demanded the honour for themselves and claimed to be given precedence of the dukes. The King, who had never yet given the Order to any Lorraine on such an assumption, was reluctant to agree, but the brothers stood firm. They triumphed; and thus, having received payment in advance, the Chevalier de Lorraine answered for Monsieur's consent and the means to bring Madame and the Duc de Chartres to agree to the marriage.

Now the young Duc de Chartres when he left the nursery had been placed in the care of Saint-Laurent, a man of no standing, an assistant to the head of the protocol in Monsieur's household, of humble appearance, but for all that a gentleman and well-fitted to educate a prince and form a great King. He was a friend of the curé of Saint-Eustache, who had a valet named Dubois,[3] a most intelligent man, whom he had encouraged to study the classics and even history. This Dubois had been no more than a servant in the curé's employ, but he had pleased his master, who passed him on to Saint-Laurent to act as a secretary in the education of M. le Duc de Chartres. They made him take orders

---

[1] Customary title of the Grand Ecuyer de France, then Louis de Lorraine, Comte d'Armagnac. The position was similar to that of Master of the Horse in the royal household.

[2] Always refers to the Ordre du Saint-Esprit.

[3] Guillaume Dubois (1656–1723). When his pupil Chartres (Duc d'Orléans) was Regent of France, Dubois was chosen as Prime Minister.

to rub off his rough corners and gradually introduced him into the prince's schoolroom to help in preparing his lessons, copying his essays, looking up words for him in the dictionary, and generally making his work easier. I used often to see Dubois when I went to play with M. le Duc de Chartres. Later, when Saint-Laurent grew old, Dubois set the lessons and did it very well and at the same time managed to make himself agreeable to the young prince. After Saint-Laurent's sudden death he was temporarily appointed to the post of tutor.

The Chevalier de Lorraine and the Marquis d'Effiat, Monsieur's first equerry, had become interested in Dubois when he was training for the priesthood, and they now tried to have him confirmed in the appointment. This they were not able to achieve at first, but by obstructing all other nominations they finally managed to stampede him into the post. Never have I seen a man so happy as Dubois, nor with better reason. Gratitude and a desire to keep his job made him loyal to his patrons, and it was therefore to him that the Chevalier applied when they wished to persuade M. le Duc de Chartres to accept the marriage.

Dubois, as I have explained, was in the prince's confidence; it was not hard for him to teach one so young and inexperienced to dread the anger of the King and Monsieur and to regard any alternative as heaven itself. None the less, in spite of all his efforts, the best he could do was to prevent a flat refusal, but that was enough to ensure success. Monsieur's consent had already been gained, and as soon as the King received the word he made haste to dispose of the business. A day or two earlier, however, Madame had got wind of it, and with the forcefulness which she never lacked she had spoken to her son and had extracted a promise that he would never agree. Thus, M. de Chartres, weak with his tutor and weak with his mother, hating the one course and fearing the other, found himself utterly discomfited.

One afternoon, very early, as I was passing through the upper gallery, I saw M. le Duc de Chartres come out of the back door of his apartment looking monstrously wretched and harassed, attended by an officer of Monsieur's guard. As I happened to be in his way, I asked him where he was going in such a hurry, to which he replied that the King had sent for him. I did not think it politic to accompany him, so I turned to my tutor and said that there might be some question of his marriage and that the news would soon break. There had been rumours of angry scenes for some days past, and my curiosity made me very watchful and attentive.

M. de Chartres found the King alone with Monsieur in his study, where he had little expected to see the latter. His reception was most loving, for the King said that he wished to provide an establishment for him, and that since the war deprived him of suitable foreign princesses and there were no Princesses of the Blood of his own age, he could show him no greater love than to give him his own daughter, both of whose sisters were already married to Princes of the Blood. Such a marriage, said the King, would make him a son-in-law as well as a nephew, but, although he was eager to arrange it, he would not compel him, but would leave him full liberty to decide for himself. This proposal, delivered with the terrifying majesty that was the King's natural manner, and addressed to a prince who had no answer ready, upset M. de Chartres completely. He tried to shirk the question by putting the responsibility upon Monsieur and Madame, stammering out that the King was master, but that his own wishes depended on his parents. 'That is very right and proper,' replied the King, 'and since you have no objection, your father and mother will not stand in your way.' Then, turning to Monsieur, he continued, 'Is that not true, brother?' Thereupon Monsieur agreed, as had already been arranged between them, and the King immediately sent for Madame, saying that only she remained to be consulted. He then began a conversation with Monsieur and both of them pretended not to notice M. de Chartres's nervousness and low spirits.

As soon as Madame made her appearance, the King said that he felt sure she would not oppose an arrangement which Monsieur welcomed and M. de Chartres approved, namely his marriage to Mlle de Blois. He admitted that he himself was most anxious for it and shortly repeated what he had been saying to M. de Chartres. All this was done with a commanding air, yet as though he never doubted that she would be otherwise than delighted, which he very well knew was not the case. Madame, who had counted on her son's refusal because he had given his promise (and he had really done his best to keep it by hesitating and looking embarrassed), was left speechless and cornered. Darting two furious glances at Monsieur and M. de Chartres, she said that since they were determined, she had nothing further to say and, dropping a very brief curtsey, she returned to her apartments. Her son followed her instantly, but she did not give him a moment to explain and drove him from the room with a torrent of tears and abuse.

Shortly afterwards, Monsieur went to her, but except that she did not actually turn him out, she spared him no more than her son, and he came out looking abashed, not having had the chance to utter a single word. The entire scene was over by four in the afternoon, and that evening there was 'Appartement', as used to happen three times a week in wintertime. On the other three evenings there was a play, and on Sundays, nothing.

What they called 'Appartement' was a reception for the entire Court in the great suite of rooms that runs from one end of the long gallery to the ante-chamber of the chapel. It lasted from seven until ten in the evening, when the King sat down to supper. At first there was music, and then tables were prepared for all kinds of games. There was one for lansquenet,[1] which Monseigneur and Monsieur always played, and another for billiards; in a word there was freedom to do as one pleased, to make up card-parties and to call for more tables when necessary. Beyond the room used for billiards there were refreshments, and each room was beautifully illuminated. In the beginning, the King used to appear and played for a time, but latterly he ceased to come, although he liked others to attend regularly, and everyone went because they were anxious to please him. He used to spend his own evenings in Mme de Maintenon's apartments working with the different ministers, one after another.

That evening, shortly after the end of the concert, the King sent for Monseigneur and Monsieur, who had already sat down to lansquenet, for Madame, who had taken up her position by a game of hombre but was scarcely giving it a glance, for M. de Chartres, who was gloomily playing chess, and for Mlle de Blois. The latter [aged 15] had only just begun to appear in society, and was marvellously over-dressed, although she knew nothing of what was happening. Being naturally timid and horribly frightened of the King, she thought she was being sent for to receive a scolding, and trembled so violently as she

---

[1] A card game, of German origin.

entered, that Mme de Maintenon took her upon her lap and
held her in her arms, but even so she could not entirely calm her.

After all this bustle of the royalty being summoned to Mme
de Maintenon's apartments and Mlle de Blois with them,
rumours of a marriage spread through the Appartement at the
same time that the King was announcing it to his family. The
commotion lasted only a few minutes and the news was made
public as soon as the royal persons returned. That was the
moment at which I arrived to find the Court all in a huddle
together, and astonishment pictured on every face. I soon
learned what was the matter, but was not surprised because of
my encounter with M. de Chartres earlier in the day.

In the long gallery, Madame was marching up and down
with Châteautiers, her favourite. She strode about handkerchief in hand, weeping unrestrainedly, speaking rather loud,
gesticulating, and looking for all the world like Ceres after the
rape of Proserpine. Everyone made way for her respectfully, and
only passed her when they wished to reach the Appartement.
Monseigneur and Monsieur went back to their lansquenet.
The former appeared quite as usual, but no one has ever looked
more ashamed of himself than Monsieur, nor more embarrassed,
and he remained in this condition for several weeks. M. de
Chartres looked utterly miserable, and his intended was in a
state of great distress and unhappiness. She was very young
and the marriage a marvellous one for her, yet she could see
and feel the effects of it and dreaded the consequences. Indeed,
the dismay was pretty general, except amongst a few. As for
the Lorraines, they triumphantly rejoiced in their success, and,
having no shame, they had good reason.

On the surface, that Appartement seemed duller than usual,
on account of the situation, but in reality it was very lively and
interesting and, to me, it seemed shorter than usual. It ended
with the King's supper, where I resolved to let nothing escape
me. The King seemed perfectly composed. Madame sat next
M. de Chartres, but never so much as glanced at him, nor at
Monsieur. Her eyes were full of tears, which fell from time to
time, and every now and then she wiped them away, looking
around all the while to see how others were affected. M. de
Chartres's eyes also were very red, and neither he nor his
mother ate much. I observed how courteously the King offered
Madame the dishes that were placed before him and how

ungraciously she refused, which did not in any way disturb his air of polite attention. It was much remarked that after they had left the table, the King made Madame a particularly low and impressive bow, at which she performed a pirouette so neat and swift that all he could see as he straightened himself, was her back retreating towards the door.

Next day, the entire Court called upon Monsieur, Madame, and M. le Duc de Chartres, but nothing was said. People merely made their bows and everything passed off in perfect silence. Afterwards, everyone waited as usual in the long gallery for the Council to rise and the King to pass on his way to mass. Madame was there too, and when her son came up to her to kiss her hand, she dealt him such a resounding box on the ear that it could be heard some distance away. Receiving this, as he did, in the presence of the whole Court, the poor prince was covered with embarrassment and the vast crowd, myself included, were prodigiously amazed. On that same day the details of the bride's enormous dowry were announced, and on the following, the King visited Monsieur and Madame. It was all very unhappy. After that, no one thought of anything but the wedding.

On Shrove Sunday, the King gave a state ball. That is to say, one that began with a *branle*,[1] after which everyone danced. I paid a call on Madame in the morning, and she could not resist telling me in a sour disagreeable voice that I seemed delighted about the balls but that was because I was young, for her part, she was older and wished that they were over. Monseigneur le Duc de Bourgogne danced that evening for the first time, and opened the *branle* with Mademoiselle. This was also the first time that I danced at a state ball, and I led out the provost marshal's daughter, Mlle de Sourches, who danced exceedingly well. Everyone was vastly fine.

On Shrove Monday, all the royal party and the bride and bridegroom in splendid attire went to the King's study and thence to the chapel, which was arranged as it usually is for the King's mass, except that they had placed two cushions between his stool and the altar for the bridal pair, who thus had their backs turned to the King. Cardinal de Bouillon came out of the sacristy wearing his vestments, and said mass after performing the ceremony. After this, they all went at once to dinner.

---

[1] A processional dance.

B*

There was a horseshoe table. The Princes and Princesses of the Blood sat to right and left according to precedence, ending with the King's two bastards, and next them, for the first time, the widow of the Duc de Verneuil (the bastard of Henry IV), who thus, long after his death, became a Prince of the Blood, which he would certainly never have expected. This the Duc d'Uzès thought so comical that he marched up and down in front of her, crying, 'Room, room, for Mme Charlotte Séguier!'[1] No duchesses paid their court at this dinner, except the Duchesse de Sully and the Duchesse du Lude, the daughter and daughter-in-law of Mme de Verneuil, which all the others thought so improper that they dared not return afterwards.

In the afternoon the King and Queen of England[2] came to Versailles with their suites. There was a gala concert and cards, with the King present nearly all the time, vastly delighted and very magnificent, wearing his blue ribbon over his coat, as he had done on the previous evening. Supper was like dinner, King James having his Queen on his right hand and the King on his left, and each with their *cadenas*.[3] Later the bridal pair were led to the apartments of the new Duchesse de Chartres. The Queen of England presented the shift to her, and the King of England gave the one to the Duc de Chartres, but he refused it at first, saying that he felt too miserable. Cardinal de Bouillon performed the rite of blessing the bed. He kept them waiting for a quarter of an hour, which everyone thought unbecoming in a man who had just returned from a long period of exile (he had been disgraced for refusing to pronounce the nuptial blessing over Madame la Duchesse without being invited to the royal banquet).

On Shrove Tuesday, there was a full dress reception in Mme de Chartres's apartments, with the King and Queen of England present, and the King and the entire Court. Mass followed, and then dinner, as on the previous day. Mme de Verneuil was sent back to Paris that morning. It was considered that there had been enough of her. After dinner, the King was closeted with the King and Queen of England, and later a gala ball was held like the earlier one, except that the new Duchess was led out by Mgr le Duc de Bourgogne. Everyone wore the same coat and danced with the same partner as before.

[1] Surname of the Duchesse de Verneuil, whose father was the Chancellor, Pierre Séguier, who died in 1672.

[2] James II and his second wife, Mary of Modena.

[3] Cases containing forks and spoons.

1693

Mademoiselle de Montpensier

MADEMOISELLE, La Grande Mademoiselle (so-called to distinguish her from Monsieur's daughter), or, to give her her proper title, Mlle de Montpensier, eldest daughter of Gaston d'Orléans[1] and only child of his first marriage, died at her palace of Luxembourg on Sunday, April 3rd, at the age of sixty-three, after suffering long from retention of urine. She was the wealthiest single princess in Europe. The King had visited her during her last illness, when she had strongly recommended that M. de Joyeuse should be made a Marshal of France, on the grounds that he was her kinsman; for she claimed kinship with, and advanced, and interested herself keenly in all those who had the honour of belonging to her household, and in this particular, although very haughty, she differed vastly from what the Princes of the Blood have latterly become. In the same way, she was meticulous about wearing mourning for all her relations, however distant or unimportant, and she would tell how and why they were related. Monsieur and Madame scarcely left her during her last illness; for beside the attachment that had always existed between her and Monsieur, he fluttered around her rich inheritance and did, in fact, succeed in becoming her residuary legatee, although the plumpest morsels escaped him.

The princess's published memoirs clearly show her partiality for M. de Lauzun and his folly in not marrying her as soon as he had obtained the King's permission, because he wished for greater pomp and splendour. When the King withdrew his consent, their despair was extreme, but the gifts in the marriage contract had already been made, and were confirmed by other deeds. It was Monsieur, prompted by Monsieur le Prince, who persuaded the King to retract, but Mme de Montespan and M. de Louvois had even greater influence and on them had fallen the full blast of Mademoiselle's fury and the rage of her lover—for M. de Lauzun was certainly that.[2] The

[1] This brother of Louis XIII had no son and his title, Duc d'Orléans, went to Monsieur, the brother of Louis XIV.

[2] It is not, in fact, quite certain that Lauzun was her lover in the full sense of the term,

affair did not last long, for he let fly more than once at the King, and still more often at his mistress, and gave the minister concerned many excellent opportunities to ruin him. Finally, he succeeded in getting himself arrested and sent to Pignerol, where he remained for ten years, being very harshly treated by Louvois's orders. Mademoiselle's love did not at all cool during his absence, but advantage was taken of it to make a splendid settlement on M. du Maine at her expense and that of M. de Lauzun, who by this means bought his freedom. Eu, Aumale, Dombes, and several other properties were handed over to M. du Maine to Mademoiselle's deep regret. It was on the pretext of showing gratitude for these gifts, and because he wished to raise their status, that the King made his bastards take Mademoiselle's livery, which used to be that of Monsieur Gaston. Mademoiselle resented her compulsory heir, and was always on the defensive about her remaining estates, lest the King should extract them also for the benefit of this most favoured son.

M. de Lauzun's incredible exploit[1] in rescuing the Queen of England and the Prince of Wales brought him back to favour, but by that time he had quarrelled with Mademoiselle, who was jealous and refused to see him, even on her deathbed. He had retained her gift of the estates of Thiers and Saint-Fargeau, on the excuse that the marriage had taken place, and he appeared before the King wearing a black mantle, which the King took very ill. After the period of mourning he refused to revert to his former liveries, but had new ones specially designed of darkest brown, with blue and white lace, as a witness to his abiding sorrow for the loss of Mademoiselle, whose portraits were everywhere in his house.

The histories of the civil wars[2] and Mademoiselle's personal memoirs make it unnecessary for me to comment on her part in them. The King never forgave her for St. Anthony's Day, when she turned the Bastille cannon upon his troops. I once heard him reproach her for it in jest, but pretty sharply, when they were at supper. She seemed slightly embarrassed, but extricated herself fairly well on the whole.

The funeral ceremonies were carried out with great pomp

[1] Lauzun happened to be in England when the Revolution broke out in 1688. He managed to effect the escape to France of the Queen (wife of James II) and of their son, the 'Old Pretender'.

[2] The Fronde.

and circumstance in every detail, and a guard of honour was mounted over the body for several days. Every two hours a duchess, or a princess, and two ladies of quality changed the guard, all wore mourning cloaks and were notified in advance by the King, through the grand master of ceremonies. This differs from the custom with Daughters of France, who have twice as many ladies, as well as bishops in rochets and hoods; also with that for Princesses of the Blood, whose servants alone mount guard. The Comtesse de Soissons refused to attend at first, but the King grew angry, threatened to dismiss her, and forced her to obey.

A ridiculous incident occurred during the funeral service. In the middle of the proceedings, in the presence of the entire Court, the urn containing the entrails, which was on a credence table, exploded with a deafening report and a sudden, intolerable stench. On the instant, all the ladies were swooning or in flight. The heralds and the psalm-singing monks blocked the doors with the rest of the escaping crowd. There was utter confusion, but most people managed to reach the garden and forecourts. The explosion had been caused by the fermentation of the entrails, which had been inadequately preserved. Everything was perfumed and put to rights and the scare provided a laugh. Finally, the entrails were taken to the Convent of the Celestines, and the heart to Val-de-Grâce. The body was escorted to Saint-Denis by the Duchesse de la Ferté, the Princesse d'Harcourt, and ladies of quality.

1693

The Father of Saint-Simon

A FEW days later, on May 3rd, at ten o'clock in the evening, I had the misfortune to lose my father. He was eighty-seven years old and had never fully recovered from his serious illness at Blaye, two years earlier. For the past three weeks, he had ailed a little with the gout, and my mother, seeing him weakening, had suggested that he should dispose of certain family matters, to which, like a good father, he consented. She also persuaded him to agree to resign his high rank of duke and peer in my favour. He had been dining with friends that evening, for he still enjoyed good talk, and when night fell had gone to bed without pain or mishap. While they were still conversing with him, however, he had suddenly heaved three deep sighs in quick succession, and was dead before they could cry out that he was ill. There had been no more oil in his lamp.

I heard the sad news as I was returning from the King's *coucher* (he was taking physic next day), and I gave myself up that night to my private grief. On the following day, I went early in the morning to see Bontemps, the King's valet, and, later, to the Duc de Beauvilliers, who had been my father's friend and whose year of service[1] it was. He assured me of much good feeling on the part of the princes and promised that when he drew the King's curtains, he would ask him to grant me my father's titles. The King consented at once, and Bontemps, who was much attached to my father, hurried to where I waited in the tribune and informed me of it. M. de Beauvilliers then came himself, bidding me be in the gallery at three o'clock, when he would admit me through the private rooms as the King's dinner was removed.

I found the crowd dispersing in the King's bedroom. As soon as Monsieur, who was standing by the pillow, caught sight of me, he cried out in a loud voice, 'Ah! here is M. le Duc de Saint-Simon!' I then approached the bed and uttered my thanks, bowing very low. The King questioned me closely about my misfortune, saying many kind things about my father and myself, for he well knew how to sweeten his favours. He went on to speak of the sacraments, which my father had had no time to receive, and I told him that very shortly before his death he had made a retreat at Saint-Lazare, where he was in the habit of going to confess and say his prayers, and I added something about the godliness of his life. The conversation lasted some little time, and ended with the King exhorting me to continue in virtue and good behaviour and promising me his protection.

High birth and fortune do not always go together. My branch of the family had been ruined in the wars and my ancestors were left with little wealth or glory in exchange for their services. My grandfather, after serving in all the campaigns of his time,

---

[1] The King had four gentlemen of the bedchamber, who served their year of office in turn.

was forced to retire to his estates, where lack of fortune obliged him to send his elder sons as pages to the late King, a service which included the greatest names.

Louis XIII was inordinately fond of hunting in the open country, without the crowds of huntsmen, the huge packs of hounds, laid on in relays, and all the other elaborations added by the present King. My father soon noticed the King's impatience at the delays caused by changing to fresh horses, and he conceived the idea of bringing up the new horse nose to tail with the one on which the King sat. By this means, an active man could swing himself from one to the other without dismounting, and all was over in a moment. The King was vastly pleased, asked always to have the same page when he changed horses, made inquiries about my father, and gradually grew fond of him, so that when Baradat, the first equerry, became intolerably arrogant, the King dismissed him and promoted my father to his place. Later, after the death of Blainville, he made him a first gentleman of the chamber.

The King loved my father well, but he could also rebuke him soundly, and my father told me of two such occasions. The Duc de Bellegarde, master of the horse and a first gentleman of the chamber, had been exiled. My father was his friend, also a first gentleman and first equerry, and at the height of his favour with the King. This last fact, as well as his official duties, required his constant attendance, so that for want of other leisure he began a letter to M. de Bellegarde while he waited for the King to go hunting. Just as he was finishing, the King appeared and caught him, as it seemed, in the act of rising hastily and endeavouring to hide a paper. Louis XIII liked to know everything, especially where his favourites were concerned; he noticed the movement and asked what the paper was. My father, embarrassed and cornered, admitted that he had been writing to M. de Bellegarde. 'Show it to me!' said the King, taking the letter and reading it. 'I see no harm,' he said, 'in your writing to your friend, even though he is in disgrace, for I am very sure that you would write nothing improper. What I think very bad is that you should fail in the respect you owe to a duke and a peer, and that because he is exiled, you should not address him as " Monseigneur", which is his right.' Then, tearing the letter in half, he said, ' Here, take your letter; it is a very good one. Rewrite it after the hunt, and give him his " Monseigneur", as you should.' My father went on to say that although he was much ashamed at this reprimand, given, as it was, while the King was walking before the whole Court, yet he felt thankful to have escaped so lightly. He had been mortally afraid of receiving worse for writing to a man in deep disgrace and hopelessly out of favour.

The other reprimand concerned a far graver matter. The King had fallen deeply in love with Mlle d'Hautefort.[1] He visited the Queen more often on her account, and talked much with her. He also spoke of her constantly to my father, who saw clearly that he was smitten. My father was young and gallant at that time, and he could not understand the King being so much in love, so little able to conceal it, and yet going no further in the matter. He judged that timidity must be the cause, and one day when the King was talking passionately about the lady, he acted on that assumption and offered his services as ambassador, to bring the affair to a successful conclusion. The King let him speak; then, looking very stern, said, 'It is true that I am in love, that I am sensible of the fact, that I enjoy speaking of her, and think of her still more often. It is also true that all this happens in spite of myself, because I am a man and therefore weak in this respect. But since my position as King makes it easy for me to gratify my passion, I must be doubly careful to avoid sin and scandal. I forgive you this time because of your youth, but never let me hear you speak like this again, if you wish me to continue to be your friend.' This speech descended on my father like a thunderbolt, and the scales fell from his eyes. The idea that the King was timid in love vanished in the light of his pure, triumphant virtue. This was the lady whom the King appointed lady-in-waiting to the Queen, and caused to be addressed as Mme d'Hautefort. In the end she became the second wife of the last Maréchal de Schonberg, by whom she had no children. Since that time, spinster ladies-in-waiting have always been given the title of Madame.

My father never recovered from the death of Louis XIII, never spoke of him without tears in his eyes, never referred to him but as 'the King, my master', and never missed going every year on May 14th to his memorial service, at Saint-Denis, or having a solemn mass said for him at Blaye, if he happened

[1] She had been maid of honour to the Queen-Mother, Marie de Médicis, and, later, to Anne of Austria.

to be there. He expressed his veneration, gratitude, even his love for the late King every time that he spoke of him, and delighted in expatiating on his virtues and courage. He took me to Saint-Denis one 14th of May, before he had presented me to the King.

After paying the last honours to my father, I set out for Mons to join the Royal-Roussillon, in which regiment I held a captaincy.

1694

The Princesse de Conti dismisses Mlle Choin

DURING the campaign, various adventures had been happening to the 'Princesses', a distinctive title, intended solely for the King's three daughters.[1] Monsieur had quite reasonably requested that the Duchesse de Chartres should call the other two 'Sister', but that they should never address her as anything but 'Madame'. That was correct, and the King so ordered it, which annoyed the other two excessively. The Princesse de Conti submitted with good grace, but Madame la Duchesse, as sister by the same mistress, took to calling Mme de Chartres '*mignonne*'. Now nothing was ever less pet-like than the face, figure, and general appearance of Mme de Chartres. She dared not show how much she disliked the name, but when Monsieur came to hear of it, he realized its absurdity and the ruse to avoid saying 'Madame', and let fly in anger. The King very sternly forbade Madame la Duchesse to be so familiar, which annoyed her exceedingly although she did not allow it to appear.

On one of the excursions to Trianon the Princesses slept there and, being young, took to walking about at night and amusing themselves with letting off fireworks. Whether by mischief on the part of the two elder or by mischance, they exploded some under Monsieur's windows, so that he woke up and thought very ill of them. He then went and complained to the King, who apologized deeply and scolded the Princesses severely, but nevertheless had much trouble in pacifying him. Monsieur kept his anger in the family. Mme de Chartres bore the brunt for a

[1] The dowager Princesse de Conti, Madame la Duchesse, and the Duchesse de Chartres.

long time, but I do not know that the other two were much disturbed about that, and Madame la Duchesse was even suspected of writing a set of verses on the subject. However that may be, in the end everything was smoothed over. Monsieur entirely forgave Mme de Chartres after Mme de Montespan, to whom he was much attached, had visited him at Saint-Cloud. She also reconciled her daughters to one another, for she still had some authority over them, and they greatly respected her.

Mme la Princesse de Conti had a different adventure, which created a huge scandal and had important consequences. The Comtesse de Bury had been given her as lady-in-waiting at her marriage. She was very virtuous, gentle, well-bred, intelligent, and decorous. She had been Eurre d'Aiguebonne and, in 1666, had been left the childless widow of the younger Rostaing, brother of old Mme Lavardin, mother of the Chevalier de l'Ordre,[1] who was ambassador to Rome. Mme de Bury sent into the Dauphiné for her niece, Mlle Choin, whom she placed with Mme la Princesse de Conti as a maid-of-honour. Mlle Choin was a stout, untidy-looking girl, brown-haired, plain, snub-nosed, but with intelligence and a love for intrigue. She saw Monseigneur daily, for he never quitted Mme la Princesse de Conti; she amused him and, almost imperceptibly, wormed herself into his confidence. Mme de Lillebonne and her two daughters,[2] who also never left the princess's house and were intimate with Monseigneur, noticed what was happening and rapidly made friends with the Choin. M. de Luxembourg,[3] with his keen nose, also smelled it out. He was a man whom the King disliked and only employed when necessary, a fact which he knew and resented and which attached him wholly to Monseigneur, but the King was beginning to learn something of his schemes with regard to that prince.

Monseigneur had also taken a liking for Clermont, a young man belonging to a branch of the de Chattes family, an ensign in the Guards. He was a tall, fine-looking man, with nothing to recommend him but honour, courage, and a certain love of intrigue, and he had attached himself to M. de Luxembourg

---

[1] L'Ordre: see p. 14, note 2.

[2] Mme de Lillebonne was Anne de Lorraine (1639–1720), an illegitimate daughter of Charles IV. She married François de Lorraine, Prince de Lillebonne. Her daughters were Mlle de Lillebonne and Mme d'Espinoy.

[3] Maréchal de Luxembourg (1628–1695), known as 'Le Tapissier de Notre Dame' because of all the enemy flags he had hung there.

because he was related to that gentleman. The latter was pleased to take him under his protection and introduced him into the house of Mme la Princesse de Conti, where he played the lover with some success. With her support, he rapidly became a favourite with Monseigneur, aiding all M. de Luxembourg's plans to gain an ascendancy over Monseigneur's mind and thus rule the kingdom after his accession.

With that end in view, Clermont was persuaded to attach himself to the Choin, become her lover, and seem willing to marry her. They told him what had been discovered with regard to her and Monseigneur, and advised him that such a course would lead to making his fortune. Clermont, who owned nothing, was glad enough to consent. He made advances, and the Choin was not unkind. His pretended love, most freely given, won her confidence; she did not hide from him that Monseigneur also loved her, and very soon Monseigneur, too, made no secret of his feeling for the Choin. The Princesse de Conti thus became their dupe. At that point everyone left for the front, where Clermont received all the rewards that M. de Luxembourg could bestow upon him.

The King, who was disturbed at the plots being hatched over the head of his son, allowed them to go, but did not fail to breach the secrets of the post. Private couriers robbed him of much good fruit, but indiscretion in not keeping everything for couriers finally proved their undoing. The King obtained some of their letters, discovered the plan of marriage between Clermont and the Choin, their love-affair, and the plot to rule Monseigneur both then and after his own death. He also discovered how deeply M. de Luxembourg was involved in the matter and the great future which he was designing for himself. He learned at the same time how little the Choin and Clermont esteemed the Princesse de Conti, whose letters Clermont had enclosed in the self-same packet which the King had intercepted, along with one wherein he spoke of the princess with no respect and referred to Monseigneur as 'our fat friend'. The King thereupon decided that he had had enough and, one evening when the weather was too bad for him to go out, he sent for the Princesse de Conti to come to his study. He had her and Clermont's letters in which their love was most explicitly stated, and letters from Clermont and the Choin mocking her.

Like her sisters, the Princesse de Conti never approached the King except between his supper and his *coucher*, apart from ceremonies like sermons or meets of the hounds, and she was astounded by the message. She went to the King, much concerned to know what he wished, for he was dreaded by his family, even more than by his subjects, if that were possible. Her lady-in-waiting remained in one of the ante-rooms and the King took her alone into his study. There, he told her that he knew all, making it useless for her to attempt to hide her partiality for Clermont, adding that he had their letters, and, so saying, drew them from his pocket. 'Do you recognize these handwritings?' he said, showing first her own and then Clermont's. At such an opening, the poor princess swooned away and the King, seized with compassion, brought her round as best he could, afterwards giving her the letters on which he had been sermonizing, but in a kindly way. Later, he told her that that was not all, for he had others to show her, from which she would see how unwisely she had given her love, and to what rival she had been sacrificed. This new blow was possibly even more afflicting than the first, and the princess was again knocked flat. The King again revived her but, this time, it was to punish her cruelly, for he insisted upon her reading in his presence her own abortive letters as well as those of Clermont and the Choin. At that point she thought she would die. She flung herself at the King's feet, all bathed in tears, and almost incapable of speech. After that, there was nothing but sobs, pleas for pardon, despair, fury, and demands for justice and vengeance. She was soon settled. The Choin was dismissed on the following day. M. de Luxembourg received orders to send Clermont to the nearest fortress, which happened to be Tournai, to give up his command, retire to the Dauphiné, and remain in that province. The King then sent word to Monseigneur telling him about his interview with his daughter, thus making it impossible for him to protect the two wretches.

Monseigneur's feeling for the Choin had also appeared in the letters, so that the Princesse de Conti was obliged to keep up appearances in some sort. She sent the Choin in one of her own coaches to the Abbey of Port-Royal, in Paris, gave her a pension and carriages to remove her furniture. The Comtesse de Bury, who had known nothing of the affair, was inconsolable and applied for retirement shortly afterwards.

Mme de Lillebonne and her daughters made haste to visit the Choin, but most secretly. They knew that that would be a sure means of endearing themselves to Monseigneur, but wished to run no risks with the King or the Princesse de Conti, whom they had every sort of reason to cherish. They were themselves princesses [of the House of Lorraine], but often were literally hard put to it to find clothes or bread, through the negligence of M. de Lillebonne. M. de Louvois had frequently helped them in the past, and it was Mme la Princesse de Conti who had brought them to the Court. She fed them, gave them presents continually, procured all kinds of pleasures for them, and to her they owed their presentation to Monseigneur, which had led first to his friendship, and then to his most marked and proclaimed affection.

The lampooners finally commemorated this unhappy tale of the Princess and the Confidante.

1695

Marriage of Saint-Simon

THE day of my marriage was now fast approaching. During the previous year, there had been some talk of an alliance with the eldest daughter of the Maréchal de Lorges, but the idea had been dismissed almost as soon as entertained. Now, on both sides, there were great hopes of renewal. The Maréchal had been ruined in the wars, his only reward having been his marshal's bâton. As soon as he had received it, however, he had married the daughter of Frémont, the keeper of the King's jewels, who amassed a vast fortune under M. Colbert and was considered the ablest and most consulted financier of his day. Immediately after his marriage, the Maréchal had been appointed captain of the bodyguard, a post left vacant by the death of the Maréchal de Rochefort, and had earned a reputation for honour, courage, and ability in that service.

The Maréchal de Lorges's integrity and candour had much pleased me when I had had the opportunity of observing him closely during the campaign which I fought under his command. The love and esteem in which he was held by the whole army, his high reputation at Court, his magnificent establishment and

extremely noble birth, his distinguished connections that offset
the inferior marriage which he was first of his line to be obliged
to contract, all made me earnestly desire the match. His eldest
brother, moreover, was greatly esteemed and, by a strange
coincidence, held similar honours, offices, and establishments.
The devoted affection between them and, indeed, throughout
the entire large family, most of all, the goodness and sincerity
of the Maréchal himself, so rare, so real in him, made me very
eager. I hoped to find everything that I lacked to sustain me
and advance my interests and to enable me to live agreeably
amid noble connections and a pleasant family.

What is more, in the irreproachable virtue of the Maréchal's
wife, and her sagacity in reconciling her husband with M. de
Louvois and thus gaining him a dukedom, I found everything
that I could desire for training a wife whom I wished to appear
at Court. There the Maréchale was universally praised and
respected for the elegant, wise, and dignified manner in which
she kept open house to the highest society, without admixture,
conducting herself with perfect modesty, yet never forgetting
the position due to her husband's rank. By this means she had
made her inferior birth forgotten by the Maréchal's family, the
Court, and society in general, where her character had earned
her general esteem. Nevertheless, she existed only for her husband, who trusted her in everything and lived with her and all
her relations in a mutual affection and respect that did him much
credit.

They had one son, a boy of twelve whom they loved to distraction, and five daughters. The two elder had spent their
childhood with the Benedictines, at Conflans, and for the past
three years had been living with their grandmother, Mme
Frémont, whose house communicated with that of the Maréchale
de Lorges. The elder girl was seventeen, the second, fifteen
years old. They had never been allowed out of their grandmother's sight, for she was a woman of great good sense and
perfect virtue, who, in her youth, had been exceedingly handsome and still retained some traces of her former beauty.
She was a most pious lady, active in good works, and entirely
devoted to the upbringing of her two granddaughters. For a
long time past her husband had been afflicted by paralysis and
other diseases, but his mind was clear and he managed his own
affairs. The Maréchale lived with them all, busy with all

manner of duties and charities, and they respected her and loved her dearly.

Mme Frémont secretly preferred Mlle de Lorges, whereas the Maréchale's favourite was the second daughter, Mlle de Quintin. Indeed, had it depended only on her mother's wishes, the elder would have been sent to a convent in order to give her sister the chance of a better marriage. The latter had dark hair and beautiful eyes; Mlle de Lorges, on the other hand, was fair, with a perfect figure and complexion. She had a most pleasing expression, was very modest, yet stately in her bearing, and there was something about her that I thought very gracious because it came from natural goodness and gentleness. I liked her infinitely the better of the two when I first saw them together; there was no comparison for me, and I hoped that she would make my life's happiness, as she has done, solely and absolutely. As she is now my wife, I shall abstain from saying more, except that she has proved far above all that was promised me and beyond my own fondest hopes.[1]

My mother and I were informed of all the necessary details by Mme Frémont's sister-in-law, a fine handsome woman, on excellent terms with them all and better used to good society than is usual with people of such inferior birth. She negotiated the marriage contract, and skilfully but honestly steered matters to a successful conclusion, in spite of the obstacles that invariably beset life's most important occasions. Finally, however, all the difficulties were smoothed away for a consideration of four hundred thousand livres, cash down (with no concessions), and living expenses for an indefinite period at Court and with the army.

When the arrangements were at last completed, the Maréchal de Lorges spoke to the King, on my behalf as well as his own, to avoid trouble. His Majesty was gracious enough to say that he could not do better for his daughter, and went on to speak most kindly of me—the Maréchal enjoyed telling me of this.

Thus it was that on the Thursday before Palm Sunday we signed the preliminary articles. Two days later, however, after we had taken the contract to the King and I was beginning to visit the Hôtel de Lorges every evening, the match was suddenly broken off on an ill-defined pretext, which everyone

---

[1] The Saint-Simons had two intensely dreary sons, known at Court as 'Les Bassets' (dachshunds).

persisted in interpreting after his own fashion. Luckily, just as
we had reached a deadlock, with everyone pulling in a different
direction, d'Auneuil,[1] the Maître des Requêtes, the Maréchale's
only brother, arrived from the country where he had been on
circuit and removed the obstacle at his own expense. (This is
an obligation which I must repay and for which I shall ever be
deeply grateful.) God sometimes uses the most unexpected
means to carry out His will. The whole venture thus almost
miscarried, but the marriage was at last celebrated at the Hôtel
de Lorges, on April 8th, which I have always regarded, and
with good reason, as the happiest day of my life. My mother
behaved like the best of mothers. We proceeded to the Hôtel
de Lorges on the Thursday before Low Sunday, at seven in the
evening. The contract was signed and a grand banquet was
given for the nearest relations on both sides of the family. At
midnight, the curé of Saint-Roche said mass, and we were married in the private chapel. On the previous evening, my mother
had sent forty thousand livres' worth of jewels to Mlle de
Lorges, and I a corbeille containing six hundred louis and the
elegant trifles usually given on such occasions.

We slept that night in the state bedroom, and on the following day M. d'Auneuil, who lodged over the way, gave a great
dinner for us, after which the bride received in her bed[2] at the
Hôtel de Lorges. The highest society of France came in great
numbers out of civility and curiosity, and the first to arrive was
the Duchesse de Bracciano[3] and her two daughters. My mother
was still in half-mourning, her apartments were draped with grey
and black, which was why we preferred to receive the company
at the Hôtel de Lorges. Only one day was devoted to these
visits, and on the following, we went to Versailles. In the evening the King graciously asked to see the bride in Mme de
Maintenon's apartments, where she was presented by my
mother and by hers. The King joked with me about my marriage
on the way, and was so obliging as to receive the ladies with
much praise and distinction.

Afterwards they attended the King's supper, and the new
duchess had her tabouret.[4] As he came to the table, the King

---

[1] He was Nicolas Frémont, Seigneur d'Auneuil.
[2] At that time it was fashionable for ladies to receive in bed.
[3] Princesse des Ursins.
[4] The stools without arms on which duchesses were allowed to sit in the King's
presence.

said to her, 'Madame, pray be seated.' He looked up as his napkin was being unfolded, and seeing all the duchesses and princesses still standing, he half-rose from his chair and said to Mme de Saint-Simon, 'Madame, I have already asked you to be seated,' whereupon all those who had the right sat down, and Mme de Saint-Simon sat between my mother and hers, who came after her in order of rank. Next day, she received the entire Court, in her bed, in the apartments of the Duchesse d'Arpajon, as being most convenient because they were on the ground floor. The Maréchal de Lorges and I were present only for the visit of the royal family. On the day after, they went to Saint-Germain and on to Paris, where I gave a grand dinner at my house for the whole wedding party. On the following day I gave a private supper to those remaining of my father's old friends, to whom I had been careful to announce my marriage before it was made public, and whom I always took great pains to cultivate until the day of their death.

1695

The Duc du Maine at the Front

THE Maréchal de Villeroy[1] was pressing M. de Vaudémont as closely as he could,[2] and the latter and by far the weaker was using every endeavour to escape. Both commanders felt that the entire campaign was in their hands. Vaudémont believed that the success or failure of the siege of Namur depended upon the safety of his army, and Villeroy that victory for him would seal the fate of the Low Countries, bring peace with glory, and all the personal consequences of so great an event. He therefore

[1] Later tutor to Louis XV.

[2] The accession to the English throne of the Prince of Orange, in 1688, had destroyed Louis XIV's carefully built-up alliance with England, a corner-stone of his foreign policy. In 1695 Louis was at war with the Empire, Holland, Spain, England, and Sweden. In spite of such a formidable alliance against her, France won all the battles on her northern front until the death of the Maréchal de Luxembourg (1695). He was replaced by the Maréchal de Villeroy, irresistible to women, but not to the enemy, who was greatly hampered by the presence, as one of his commanders, of the Duc du Maine.

The opposing general was an illegitimate scion of the House of Lorraine called Vaudé-mont. Saint-Simon himself was serving with the French army during the events which he describes. The war terminated in 1697 with the Treaty of Ryswick by which Louis XIV was obliged to acknowledge the heretic William as King of England.

made the preliminary moves with the greatest care, and by the evening of the 13th [of July] was so near to M. de Vaudémont that the latter seemed to have no possible hope of escaping on the 14th. He then sent a courier to inform the King.

By dawn of the 14th everything was ready. Monsieur le Duc commanded the right wing, M. du Maine the left, M. le Prince de Conti all the infantry, and M. le Duc de Chartres the cavalry. It fell to the left to open the battle because that wing was nearer to the enemy. Vaudémont, in an exposed position and with the French so close, had not dared to retreat during the night, for his enemies were far superior in numbers and quality, and all his best troops were engaged at the siege. Neither had he dared to give battle without cover of any kind. Thus the only course that remained for him was to march by daylight, taking every precaution against being attacked on the march, but with the prime object of moving forward towards the broken wooded country that lay three good leagues ahead.

At the first ray of light, the Maréchal de Villeroy sent orders for M. du Maine to attack and open the engagement. He intended to bring up the entire army in support, but needed time for that operation and relied on the left wing to delay the enemy and prevent him from beginning his march. When nothing resulted from this order, he grew impatient and sent again to M. du Maine, five and even six times. M. du Maine wished to reconnoitre, then to confess, then to reorganize his wing, although that had been ready for a long time and the men were burning to be off. During this delay, Vaudémont was marching away as quickly as caution would permit. The general officers on our left wing were fuming, and Montrevel, the senior lieutenant-general, could no longer restrain himself as he saw what was happening. He pressed M. du Maine, reminding him of the repeated orders he had received from the Maréchal de Villeroy, the sure and easy victory, the consequence to his reputation and to the siege of Namur, the glorious outcome of success there, and the resulting panic and defencelessness of the Low Countries, when the only army capable of succouring them had been defeated. He spoke to him as man to man. He could not withhold his tears. Nothing was refused or denied, but all his efforts were useless. M. du Maine stammered and procrastinated, and continued in this way for so long that the chance was lost and M. de Vaudémont was allowed to escape from the most perilous situation in which any army could be placed. He would have been utterly destroyed had his enemy, who could see and count every man, made the slightest movement to attack him.

The French army were in despair, and no man attempted to withhold the words that patriotism, anger, and the evidence suggested to their minds. Even the common soldiers and mounted troopers said what they thought; in a word, the officers and men were even more outraged than astounded. The best that the Maréchal de Villeroy could do was to detach three regiments of dragoons to attack the enemy's rear. They captured one or two flags and created some slight disorder among the last troops, who formed the rearguard of all that army.

No one was more outraged than the Maréchal himself, but he was too good a courtier to shift the blame to another's shoulders. Relying upon the support of the entire army, upon all that the soldiers had seen and heard, and the outcry which they had not attempted to suppress, he sent an officer to the King to report that contrary to his almost certain expectations, Vaudémont's swiftness in retreat had saved him. He entered into no details, but resigned himself to take the consequences, whatever those might be.

The King had been counting the hours throughout the past day and night as he waited for news of a great victory. He was therefore more than astonished to see only this private gentleman come with dispatches, instead of some high dignitary, and was deeply concerned when he learned how quietly the day had passed. The Court, anxious for news of sons, husbands, and brothers, was left in suspense, and the friends of the Maréchal de Villeroy felt intensely embarrassed. So general and brief a dispatch, making so little of a grave and crucial situation, disquieted the King considerably, but he decided to wait until time should bring an explanation.

In the meanwhile he made it his business to see all the gazettes from Holland. In the very first that appeared, he read of a great battle on the left flank and fulsome praise for the courage of M. du Maine, whose wounds were said to have prevented a victory and allowed M. de Vaudémont to escape. It was added that M. du Maine had been borne off the field on a stretcher. The King was irritated by this colossal piece of irony, but was still more annoyed when the next copy of the gazette retracted its previous description, saying that M. du Maine had not received so much as a scratch. All of which, with the total silence that had reigned since the day of battle, and the Maréchal de Villeroy's terse dispatch offering no excuses, combined to make him nervous and suspicious.

Vienne, a highly fashionable bathing attendant of Paris, had been taken into the King's personal service at the period of his love-affairs,[1] had gained credit by prescribing various drugs which gave the King opportunities of greater satisfaction, and by this road, had risen to become one of the four head-valets. He was a very good honest fellow, but a peasant, coarse and plain-spoken to a degree, and because of this very quality in a truthful man, the King had fallen into the habit of asking him things which other people would not tell him, always provided that the matter lay within his compass. The events mentioned above led to a visit to Marly, where Vienne was questioned. He looked intensely embarrassed, because, being taken un-awares, he was unable to hide his feelings, which increased the King's curiosity until finally he issued commands. Then Vienne dared no longer hold back. He told the King that which he would gladly have gone through his life without knowing and which drove him to the verge of despair, for he had over-come so many difficulties and jealousies, had taken so much pleasure in giving M. de Vendôme[2] command of an army, solely because it meant advancement for M. du Maine. His entire object had been to hasten that promotion by using the rivalry between the Princes of the Blood as an excuse to be rid of them. The Comte de Toulouse[3] was already an admiral; his future was assured. It was therefore upon the Duc du Maine that the King's whole mind was fixed. At that moment he saw all his hopes dashed, and his distress was more than he could bear. He felt the weight of the army's contempt for that much cherished son, and the mockery in the gazettes taught him what was being said abroad. His chagrin was great.

On this one occasion, Louis XIV, that prince who appeared so equable, who was always master of his smallest movements,

---

[1] 'Il rendait des services d'un ordre tout particulier à Louis XIV, comme le dit en termes décents Saint-Simon.' M. Gonzague Truc, Ed. Bibliothèque de la Pléiade. Vienne was also renowned as a ladies' hairdresser.

[2] M. le Duc de Vendôme (1655–1727), illegitimate grandson of Henri IV.

[3] Louis-Alexandre de Bourbon (1678–1737), son of Louis XIV and Madame de Montespan.

even in tense situations, succumbed to his emotions. As he was leaving the table at Marly, with all the ladies and in the presence of the Court, he happened to notice one of the dessert-waiters in the act of pocketing a sweet biscuit. That instant, forgetting his royal dignity, cane in hand, for it had just been returned to him with his hat, he rushed at the footman who, like those whom the King thrust out of his way, expected anything but that, beat him, abused him, and ended by breaking the cane across his shoulders. As a matter of fact, it was bamboo and very brittle. Then still holding the broken end and cursing at the footman, who was well away by that time, he crossed the little salon and another ante-room into Mme de Maintenon's apartment, where he spent nearly an hour, as he often did after dinner at Marly. On leaving there to go to his own rooms he happened to meet Père de La Chaise,[1] and directly he perceived him standing among the courtiers, he exclaimed in a loud voice, 'Mon Père, I have beaten a rascal soundly and have broken my stick on his back, but I do not think that God will be displeased,' and then and there he described the so-called crime. All those present were still shaking with fright at what they had seen or learned from onlookers, and their terror increased at this fresh bout. Some of the more intimate began to murmur against the fellow, and the unhappy priest made noises of approval through his closed teeth, so as to prevent the King from becoming even angrier in public. You may imagine all the talk to which this gave rise, and the general consternation because no one could guess the cause, although all were aware that this provoking incident could not be the real matter. At last the truth became known, as word was gradually spread from one friend to another that it was Vienne, at the King's command, who had been the reason for this unparalleled and most unseemly display.

To cut a long story short, let me end by relating the witticism of M. d'Elbeuf. Good courtier though he was, he must have been nauseated by the sudden rise of the bastards, for when the campaign drew to a close and the princes were leaving he asked M. du Maine before the whole company where he meant to serve in the next campaigning season. He said that wherever the duke went he meant to accompany him. When he was quizzed to give his reasons, he answered that anyone who

---

[1] The King's confessor (1624–1709). The famous cemetery of Père Lachaise was built on land belonging to him.

stayed close to the duke could be sure of preserving his life. This devastating remark provoked a great stir. M. du Maine stared at the floor and dared not say anything. No doubt that he remembered it against M. d'Elbeuf for a long time to come; but the latter and all his family were on excellent terms with the King, and that would have caused him no disquiet.

1695

Much Bickering among the Princesses

A FEW days later, we were included in a Marly excursion (the first for me, as it happened), during which a most extraordinary scene took place. Morning and evening, the King and Monseigneur each had their tables set at the same time and in the same room. The ladies divided impartially between the two, except that Mme la Princesse de Conti always went to Monseigneur's table, and her two sisters to that of the King. In a corner of that same room, five or six other places were laid, where, in the same way, people might sit at random, but no one sat at the head. The King's table stood nearest to the large drawing-room, the other near the windows and the door through which the King went to Mme de Maintenon's apartments after dinner. At that period she often ate at the King's table, sitting opposite to him, for the tables were round. She never dined except at that table and supped alone in her own room. It was necessary to describe this scene in order to explain what followed.

The Princesses were only just on speaking terms, as I have already said, and Mme la Princesse de Conti was boiling inwardly at Monseigneur's partiality for Mlle Choin,[1] whom she could not ignore and dared not snub. At dinner one day when Monseigneur was out hunting and his table was headed by Mme la Princesse de Conti, the King was pleased to amuse himself with Madame la Duchesse and, to the huge surprise of the assembled company, forsook that immense dignity which he almost never relaxed, and began to play at olives with her.[2] This pastime caused Madame la Duchesse to drink several glasses

1 See pp. 18–21.   2 Presumably to see who could furthest spit the stones.

of wine, the King pretended to take one or two, and the game lasted until dessert was over and they left the room. As the King passed Mme la Princesse de Conti, he must have been annoyed by her severe expression, for he said rather tartly that her sobriety hardly matched their drunkenness. The princess, more than a little piqued, let the King go, and turning to Mme de Châtillon in that moment of chaos, when everyone is rinsing out his mouth, said that she would prefer to be a sobersides than a chronic boozer. She was referring to certain somewhat prolonged repasts which her sisters had lately enjoyed together. This remark was overheard by Mme la Duchesse de Chartres, who retorted loudly in her slow, quavering voice, that for her part she would sooner be a wine-skin than a tart, referring to the many guards officers who had been dismissed or banished on the princess's account. There was no answering this monstrous piece of cruelty, which soon spread all over Marly and on to Paris and elsewhere. Madame la Duchesse, so witty and clever, so brilliant in writing comic verses, made up some terrible rhymes in the same vein, and Mme la Princesse de Conti was driven to despair, for she had not the same skill and did not know how to extricate herself. Monsieur, ordinarily the king of mischief-makers, intervened when he thought that things had gone far enough, and Monseigneur assisted him. He gave a dinner-party for them at Meudon, to which Mme la Princesse de Conti went by herself and arrived first. Then the other two were brought by Monsieur. They said very little to each other, the atmosphere was frigid, and they returned to their homes in exactly the same mood as they had come.

The end of that year was very stormy at Marly. One evening, Mme la Duchesse de Chartres and Madame la Duchesse who had been brought together by the enmity of Mme la Princesse de Conti, settled down to an impromptu meal after the King's *coucher*, in Mme de Chartres' room at the château. Monseigneur was playing cards very late in the salon. On his way up to bed, he went into the princess's room and found them both smoking pipes, which they had sent for from the Swiss Guards. Monseigneur, realizing the consequences if the smell of tobacco were to spread, told them to stop that experiment at once, but the smoke had already betrayed them. Next morning the King gave them a harsh reprimand, which made Mme la Princesse de Conti exultant. But the bickering continued, and the King, who had hoped that it would end of itself, finally grew vexed. That evening at Versailles, when they were all assembled in his study after dinner, he spoke very severely to them and ended by threatening that he would hear no more of their nonsense. They each had country-houses and he would send them there for a very long time and think himself well quit of them. This threat had its effect, for calm and decorum returned, and good manners took the place of mutual affection.

1696–1697

The Little Princess of Savoy

I RETURNED to Paris on the evening before the King brought the little princess[1] from Montargis to Fontainebleau and I attended him at his carriage door. In this way, I hoped to conceal the fact that I had been absent for a short time.

The princess's new French household waited for nearly three weeks at Lyons, until she was taken to Pont-Beauvoisin, where she received them. She arrived there early on the morning of Tuesday, October 16th, accompanied by the Princesse de la Cisterne and Mme de Noyers, of the Court of Savoy. The Marquis de Dronero had been responsible for her journey, and to him and to the rest of her old household many valuable presents were distributed on behalf of the King.[2] A house had been prepared for her on the Savoy side of the town, and there she rested and dressed. She then went to the bridge that belongs solely to France, received her new household at the entrance, and was escorted to her lodgings on the French side. She remained there for two days, after which she bade farewell to her Italian household without shedding a tear. Only one of her tiring women and her doctor remained with her; but they were not intended to stay long in France and were, in fact, sent back almost immediately.

[1] Princess Marie-Adélaide of Savoy, a granddaughter of Monsieur by his first wife, Henrietta, was nearly eleven years old at that time. She came to France in order to be married to M. le Duc de Bourgogne, and the marriage was celebrated a year later.

[2] The presents were: a diamond rose for the Princesse de la Cisterne, a box containing fifty diamonds for M. de Dronero, a set of bracelets for Mme de Noyers, and silver for officers and servants of her household.

MARIE-ADÉLAIDE DE SAVOIE, DUCHESSE DE BOURGOGNE

From the portrait by J. B. Santerre

Within the engraving:

LE CAMP DE COUDUN
PRES DE COMPIEGNE
OU
L'ART DE LA GUERRE ENSEIGNE PAR LE ROY A MESSEIGNEURS
LES PRINCES ENFANTS DE FRANCE

THE CAMP AT COMPIÈGNE

On Sunday, November 4th, the King, Monseigneur, and Monsieur went separately and early to Montargis, so that when the princess arrived at six o'clock, the King was ready to receive her at the door of her coach. He led her to the apartments that had been prepared for her in the house where he was lodged, and presented Monseigneur, Monsieur, and M. le Duc de Chartres. They say that everyone was surprised by her graciousness, her pretty, lively remarks, and her easy, yet respectful manner, and that the King was charmed from the first. He did nothing but pet and praise her and sent off a courier in great haste to Mme de Maintenon to tell her of his delight. Afterwards he dined with the ladies of the suite and had the little princess placed between himself and Monseigneur.

Next day the King called for her to go to mass, dined as he had supped on the previous evening, and straightway got into his coach. The King and Monsieur sat on the back seat, Monseigneur and the little princess in front, and the Duchesse du Lude by the door on his side. The Duc de Bourgogne met them at Nemours and was made to take the door-seat on the other side. At four o'clock in the evening they all arrived at Fontainebleau, in the Cour du Cheval Blanc. The entire Court was assembled waiting to receive them on the horseshoe staircase, with the crowd standing below, a magnificent sight. The King led in the little princess, who seemed to be emerging from his pocket, walked very slowly along the terrace and then to the Queen-Mother's apartments, which had been allotted to her, where Madame and her ladies were waiting. He himself presented the first of the Princes and Princesses of the Blood, asked Monsieur to name the others and to be sure to see that she was greeted by all who had that right, and then went to rest. Monseigneur went out with him, the latter to Mme de Maintenon's apartments, the former to Mme la Princesse de Conti, who was not dressed because a wen had been removed from above her eye, which she had come near to losing.

Monsieur was thus left with the princess, both standing. He presented to her all those, men and women, who had come to kiss the hem of her dress, and told her whom she should kiss, that is to say, Princes and Princesses of the Blood, dukes and duchesses and other tabourets, and Marshals of France and their wives. This ceremony lasted a good two hours, after which the princess dined alone in her apartments, where Mme de

c

Maintenon and Mme la Princesse de Conti visited her privately. On the following day, she called on Monseigneur and Mme la Princesse de Conti, and received many presents of jewellery and precious stones. The King sent all the crown jewels to Mme de Mailly,[1] her lady-in-waiting, so that she might wear as many as she wished.

The King gave a ruling that she should be styled simply 'La Princesse', that she should dine alone attended by the Duchesse du Lude, that she should hold no courts as yet, and that Mgr le Duc de Bourgogne should visit her only once a fortnight and MM. his brothers[2] only once a month. On November 8th, the Court returned to Versailles, where the princess was allotted the late Queen's apartments, and afterwards, those of Madame la Dauphine. When she arrived, everyone of importance who had stayed in Paris was presented to her, in the same way as at Fontainebleau. The King and Mme de Maintenon made a pet of her, for her pretty, coaxing ways and good manners pleased them vastly, and she gradually became familiar with them in a way that none of the royal children dared to attempt. M. de Savoie must have informed himself very thoroughly about the ways of our Court, for he had instructed his daughter well, but the marvel was that she understood his teaching so perfectly and was so graceful in everything that she did. Nothing ever equalled the charm with which she bewitched Mme de Maintenon. She called her 'ma tante', and showed her as much respect and obedience as though she were her mother and a queen, and all with such an air of freedom and affection that Mme de Maintenon was enchanted and the King also.

His Majesty delighted more and more in the princess, who was incomparably more intelligent and agreeable than is usual at her age, and he fixed the day of the marriage for December 7th,[3] which fell on a Saturday, being determined to lose no time after her twelfth birthday. He let it be known that he wished the Court to be very magnificent on that occasion and he himself, who for a long time past had dressed most simply, ordered some more resplendent coats. This was enough for all who were not priests or lawyers to disregard questions of means, or even of rank. Each one tried to surpass the rest in magnificence and originality. There was scarcely enough gold and silver

---

[1] She was, incidentally, Mme de Maintenon's first cousin.
[2] The dukes of Anjou and Berry.   [3] Of the following year, 1697.

to go round and the shops were emptied in a very few days. In short, the wildest extravagance reigned throughout the Court, and in the town as well, for there was an immense crowd of spectators. Things went to such a pitch that the King was sorry he had ever made the suggestion, and said that he failed to understand how husbands could be so foolish as to allow themselves to be ruined for their wives' clothes—or for their own, he might have added. But he had loosened the reins and there was no time to remedy matters. Indeed, I believe that in his heart of hearts the King would not have wished it otherwise, for he thoroughly enjoyed seeing the fine clothes. One could see that the display of rich materials and curious workmanship pleased him vastly and that he delighted in praising the most sumptuous and tasteful of the costumes. He put in his word for the sake of policy, but was enchanted to find that it went unheeded.

This was not the first time that such a thing had happened, for he loved magnificence of any kind, especially on state occasions, and anyone who had listened to what he said would not have been wise. In any event, there was no possibility of being wise in the midst of such extravagance, for so many new clothes were required. As for Mme de Saint-Simon and myself, it cost us twenty thousand francs between us. There were not enough craftsmen to have everything finished in time.

On Saturday morning, December 7th, [1697] the entire Court went early to the apartments of Mgr. le Duc de Bourgogne, after which the duke went to visit the princess. She was already dressed, but very few of her ladies were there, for most had gone to the tribunes and stands erected for spectators in the chapel. The royal family had already seen her and were waiting in the King's study, where the bridal pair presented themselves shortly after noon. The King immediately led the way to chapel. The procession and all the details were just as they had been for M. le Duc de Chartres, except that Cardinal de Coislin began with the betrothal and everybody knelt during the pause between the betrothal service and the marriage.

It was a dull day on the whole. The King and Queen of England came to dinner and the Queen sat between the two Kings. On leaving the table, the ladies went to see the bride's *coucher*, but the men were rigidly excluded by the King's command. The ladies remained with her and the Queen of England presented the nightgown, which was handed by the Duchesse du Lude.

Mgr le Duc de Bourgogne undressed in the ante-room, seated on a folding stool, attended by the King and all the princes. The King of England presented the shirt, which was handed by the Duc de Beauvilliers.

When Mme la Duchesse de Bourgogne was in bed, Mgr le Duc de Bourgogne entered and got into bed on the right-hand side, in the presence of the King and the entire Court. Immediately afterwards the King and Queen of England departed, the King retired to bed, and everyone left the chamber except Monseigneur, the princess's ladies, and the Duc de Beauvilliers, who stayed with his pupil, while the Duchesse du Lude stood at the other side. Monseigneur remained chatting for about a quarter of an hour, after which he made his son get up, telling him to kiss the princess, in spite of the Duchesse du Lude's objections. It turned out that she was right, for the King thought it very bad, saying that he did not wish his grandson to kiss so much as the tip of his wife's little finger until the time came for them to live together. He dressed again in the ante-room because of the cold, and went back to sleep in his own bedroom in the usual way. The little Duc de Berry, so naughty and bold, thought very ill of his brother's meekness in this respect. He said that he should have remained in bed.

1696

Madame de Castries

WHEN we returned from the army, we found the Marquise de Castries established as lady-in-waiting to Mme la Duchesse de Chartres in place of Mme de Mailly.

Mme de Castries was a scrap of a woman, a kind of *biscuit manqué*,[1] well-proportioned, but so extremely tiny that you might have passed her through a ring of medium size; no bottom, no bosom, no chin, monstrously plain, always looking

---

[1] A *biscuit manqué* is an innocent-looking sponge cake full of rum. Here is the recipe:
Stir 1 lb. sugar with 18 egg-yolks in a basin until the preparation is white and light. Add 3 tablespoonfuls of rum, 13 oz. sifted flour, and 10 oz. melted butter, carefully poured. Mix, raising it with the spatula in so doing. Set this preparation in buttered and dredged moulds, filling the latter only half full. Bake in a moderate oven. (Escoffier's recipe.) *A Guide to Modern Cooking*, Heinemann, 1957.

anxious and bewildered, yet, withal, a face sparkling with intelligence and giving even better than its promise. She knew everything—history, philosophy, mathematics, the dead languages—yet she never appeared to do more than speak good French, which she did with eloquence, grace, and aptness, even in the most everyday matters, and with that unique turn of phrase which only the Mortemart[1] family possess. Agreeable, diverting, grave, and gay, she could be all things to all men, fascinating when she wished to please, genuinely droll, brilliantly and apparently quite unconsciously witty, and delivering her sallies in a manner that made them unforgettable. She was imperious; liable to be shocked at a thousand things in a plaintive tone that would bring the house down. She could be cruelly cutting when she chose, but was a very good friend, cultivated, kind, always ready to oblige, not a coquette, but sensitive, and delighting in other people when she found them to her liking. She had a charming talent for story-telling, and when she pleased to invent some impromptu romance, everyone was amazed by her inspiration, variety, and humour. For all her pride, she thought herself well-married because she was fond of her husband. She expatiated on everything concerning him and was quite as vain about him as about herself. He returned the compliment and treated her with every care and consideration.

1697

The King and the Prince of Orange

I PERCEIVE that I have not mentioned the private reasons which made it so bitter for Louis XIV to recognize the Prince of Orange as King of England. These are they.

The King was very far, when he first had bastards, from wishing to give them high rank, as he increasingly did in later years. The Princesse de Conti's birth, however, was the least distasteful,[2] she was also the eldest, and the King decided that she would make a splendid match for the Prince of Orange. He proposed it at a time when the prince's prospects and position in Europe had

---

[1] Mme de Montespan also was born Mortemart. Mme de Castries was her niece.
[2] Since her mother, Mlle de La Vallière, was not married.

persuaded him that the marriage would be viewed as an honour and a great advantage. He was wrong. The Prince of Orange was the son of a daughter of King Charles I of England, and his grandmother had been the daughter of an Elector of Brandenburg. The prince recalled this fact with considerable haughtiness and added shortly that the Princes of Orange were accustomed to marry the rightful daughters of great kings, not their bastards. Louis XIV was so nettled by this remark that he never forgave it, and took peculiar pains, even against his own interests, to show that the insult had cut him to the quick.

The prince did everything possible to appease him. Respect, concessions, peace-offerings, patience under insults and personal injuries, renewed overtures, all were treated with contempt. The French ministers in Holland were given express instructions to thwart him at every turn, not only in affairs of state, but in all personal and private matters, to incite as many burghers as possible against him, to lavish money at elections so as to return opposing magistrates, to protect openly his declared enemies, in short, to do him all the harm and show him all the discourtesy that they could devise. Never, until the beginning of the war, had the prince ceased, both in public and private, in his efforts to allay the King's anger, and never once did the King soften towards him. Finally, in despair, hoping that his departure to England and the formidable League which he had made against France would have their effect, he said openly that all his life he had tried in vain to win the King's friendship, but that he hoped now to be more successful in gaining his respect. You may imagine his triumph when he had compelled the King to recognize him as King of England, and what it cost Louis XIV to do so.

1698

An Envoy from England

KING WILLIAM of England was gratified beyond measure when at last he had received recognition from King Louis and was in peace upon the throne. Nevertheless, usurpers are never truly satisfied nor in peace, and this one bitterly resented the fact that the rightful King and his family were still living at Saint-Germain. It was too close to the King of France and to England for his comfort. At Ryswick, he had made every effort to have them banished from the country or at least from the Court, but he had found the King inflexible. He now decided to stake everything on one throw and see whether by making no conditions (he had already won so much), but showering Louis XIV with proofs of his regard and respect, he could not gain his point by sweetness.

With this end in view he sent a Knight of the Garter, the Duke of St. Albans, as a special envoy to convey his congratulations on the marriage of Mgr le Duc de Bourgogne. He could hardly have chosen a greater man for so unimportant a mission and, indeed, it was a wonder that the duke accepted, for as the bastard of Charles II, the elder brother of King James, he would have had an excellent reason for refusing. As a matter of fact, he did try to obtain ambassadorial privileges on account of his rank, but the authorities were politely determined to treat him as an ordinary envoy from England. Dukes of that country have no ranking over here and French dukes have none in England. Our King did indeed make the Duchess of Portsmouth and her son, the Duke of Richmond, a duke and duchess of France, and he did casually grant a tabouret to the Duchess of Cleveland, the mistress of his friend, Charles II, but these were special cases and had no bearing on the general rule.

The Duke of St. Albans was the precursor of a new English ambassador, the Earl of Portland, after whose arrival he left. No one more splendid could possibly have been nominated. He was attended by a vast and magnificent suite, and his expenditure on his table, horses, liveries, carriages, furniture, dress, and silver was most princely and all in exquisite taste. Everything then seemed to happen at once, for no sooner was the earl in his coach, on his way from Calais, receiving all manner of military and civil honours, than a great fire broke out at Whitehall, during the course of which the biggest and most hideous palace in the whole of Europe was burned almost to the ground. It has not yet been rebuilt, and the Kings are now lodged pretty miserably in St. James's Palace.

Portland's first audience with the King was on February 4th, and he remained in France for four months. His arrival was an immense personal triumph, for people were overcome by his exquisite courtesy, his perfect bearing at Court and in society, his gallantry and amiability. Moreover, he was exceedingly dignified, even haughty, but tactful, very sound in all his judgments, and he did nothing rash. The French, who love novelty, good food, and magnificence, were delighted with him. He wooed them with discretion, like one who had studied the ways of our Court and desired only the best and most exclusive society. Soon it became the fashion to visit him, to give entertainments in his honour and be received at his house. What was most astonishing was that the King, who at heart was still greatly vexed with King William, should also have welcomed him, for he gave fêtes for him and did more for Portland than he had done for any previous ambassador. He may perhaps have wished to compensate him for the disappointment which he must have felt on realizing that his mission was doomed to failure from the beginning.

Portland spoke of the expulsion of King James and his family at his very first meeting with Torcy, the secretary for foreign affairs, even before he had been to Versailles. Torcy very wisely cut him short once and for all, saying that the point had been discussed often and thoroughly during the conferences at Ryswick and that the subject was closed and done with. He said further that he knew that the King would never change his mind and would be exceedingly vexed if the matter were mentioned again. Portland, he said, might rest assured that King Louis was ready to play his part fully and sincerely in the alliance that was forming between himself and the English King, and would treat the ambassador with every mark of distinction, but one word on the subject of Saint-Germain might ruin everything and render Portland's mission a sad and sorry affair. If he might offer a word of advice, added Torcy, it would be to say nothing whatsoever on the matter, either to the King or his ministers, for the King's mind was finally made up. Portland listened and complied, but as you shall see he was not best pleased. On the other hand, the King thoroughly approved of Torcy for having silenced him from the start. Great pains were taken to prevent any of the English at Saint-Germain from coming to Versailles or Paris, or within range of the ambassador, and it was all arranged most carefully.

Portland went hunting with Monseigneur, and twice went from Paris to Meudon for the wolf-hunting. On both occasions

Monseigneur kept him to supper. One evening the King called him to hold the candlestick at his *coucher*, which was a signal favour, only granted to the most distinguished people. Ambassadors are scarcely ever on terms of sufficient intimacy to come to Court at such times, and even when they do they are rarely granted this honour. Thus, laden with favours, fêtes, and courtesies of every kind, Portland had his farewell audience with the King on May 20th. The Maréchal de Villeroy then took him to Marly by the King's command and showed him the château, for he liked to see everything of interest and was especially pleased with Fontainebleau, which he said he preferred to all the other royal houses. After his formal audience, he went back to pay his court to the King, who happened to be taking physic. He was allowed in after the King had taken it, which was a monstrously great honour, and to cap everything he was admitted inside the balustrade, where no foreigner, no matter how distinguished, ever penetrates, except at the state audiences for the corps of ambassadors.

After leaving the King, Portland again attended Monseigneur out hunting and was invited for the third time to sup with him at Meudon. Monsieur himself wished to show him Saint-Cloud and Madame especially absented herself for the occasion. He was given a great banquet which Monseigneur attended with a vast number of guests. This was an honour indeed.

Nevertheless, amid all these roses strewn in his path, he did find a few thorns, chief amongst which was the continued presence of the rightful King of England. Once, for instance, when he went to hunt at Meudon, just as they were about to start and Portland was drawing on his boots, Monseigneur was informed that the English King was coming to the meet. He at once explained the situation to Portland, asking him to wait for another day, whereupon the Earl was forced to remove his boots and return to Paris.

Portland was a keen hunter, and whether because he really wished to ride after the King's hounds, or because he was vexed with the Duc de La Rochefoucauld[1] (the master of the royal hunts) for showing him no civilities beyond a bow when they happened to meet, he repeated over and over again that he longed to go with the King's pack. He said this so often in the hearing of so many people that he felt certain it had

---

[1] Son of the author of the Maxims. Le Grand Veneur.

c*

reached the duke's ears; yet there was no response. At last, he could endure it no longer, and stopping M. de La Rochefoucauld as they left the King's *lever*, he asked him point-blank. La Rochefoucauld, not in the least put out, answered rather shortly that although he had the honour to be master of the royal hunts he did not make the arrangements. He took his orders, he said, from the King of England, who often hunted and never announced until the last moment whether or not he intended to come. A stiff bow followed immediately, and Portland was left standing, very much annoyed, but with nothing about which to complain. M. de La Rochefoucauld was the only great nobleman who never pandered to Portland. His answer had been made purely out of chivalry towards King James, who did indeed have the disposal of the royal hounds, although he rarely hunted. M. de La Rochefoucauld could easily have granted Lord Portland's request, but he felt vexed because society was fawning upon the Earl in full view of the Court of Saint-Germain, and he would not deny himself the pleasure of snubbing the usurper's triumphant ambassador. None the less, everyone was conquered by Portland, not even excepting M. de Lauzun, in spite of the latter's promises and his attachment to the English King and Queen. Yet Lauzun gained nothing but contempt for slavishly following the fashion and trying to curry favour with King Louis.

Finally, laden with every honour, Portland made up his mind to go home. Indeed, he was becoming anxious because the Duke of Albemarle was increasingly popular in England. On his way back, Monsieur le Prince invited him to stay at Chantilly and gave him a magnificent fête, in that perfect taste which is so typical of the Condés. He then continued his journey by way of Flanders, where the King not only granted him permission to inspect the fortifications, but sent engineers to explain them. Everywhere he was received with full honours and a captain and fifty guardsmen were always in attendance. He returned to England after this scintillating mission to find himself supplanted at the Court by a new and younger rival, so that he had no comfort but in the memory of past favours, and many regrets that his absence had allowed a new favourite to take his place.

Before leaving Paris, he most carefully spread it abroad that so long as King James remained at Saint-Germain the queen would not receive the dowry granted her by the Peace of Ryswick, and he kept his word.

1698

Manœuvres at Compiègne

PEOPLE talked of nothing but Compiègne, where sixty thousand men were assembled under canvas. In one way, it was the marriage of Mgr le Duc de Bourgogne all over again, for the King let it be known that he expected the regiments to be very splendidly equipped and that they should compete against one another. This was enough to provoke a rivalry among the individual officers which they had good reason to repent of later. Not only were all the troops very fine in themselves, indeed it would have been hard to distinguish any particular corps for excellence, but their commanders added to their military lustre, arms, horses, harness, and all the splendours of the Court, while the junior officers ruined themselves still further by purchasing uniforms grand enough for a state occasion.

The colonels and many of the captains gave free meals to all who came, of the most abundant and delicious refreshments. Six lieutenant-generals and fourteen brigadiers were particularly noticeable for their open-handed expenditure, but the Maréchal de Boufflers astounded everyone by his spending, his perfect organization of the ample provisions, his exquisite taste, his magnificence, and his supreme courtesy during all the time that the camp lasted, day and night, at all hours, so that he gave an example to the King himself on how to give a really sumptuous entertainment. Monsieur le Prince was excellent in this line, but the Maréchal showed even him what true elegance, ingenuity, and perfect good taste could achieve. No spectacle has ever been more glorious nor, indeed, more grandiose, yet in the midst of it all, nothing could have surpassed the serenity of the Maréchal and all his household in distributing this universal hospitality. Nothing was ever more silent and smooth-running than this tremendous undertaking, or more easy, modest, and seemingly carefree than this great general, who made all the arrangements and continued to supervise, although to all appearance he was wholly concerned with commanding the army.

Innumerable tables were constantly replenished and meals were served as soon as people presented themselves. Officers, gentlemen of the Court, spectators, even the merest sightseers, were all received as honoured guests by the eager courtesy of his vast staff. All manner of hot and cold beverages were served, everything, in fact, that could possibly be included in a list of liquid refreshments. French and foreign wines and the choicest liqueurs were offered to everyone, and the arrangements were so perfect that immense quantities of game and venison continually arrived from all directions, and the seas around Normandy, Holland, England, Brittany, and even the Mediterranean, furnished day after day all that was most costly and exotic, delivered in small post-chaises at exactly the right moment by a prodigious number of couriers. Even the very water, which, it was feared, might become exhausted or muddy with so many mouths to feed, was brought from Sainte-Reine, the Seine, and other famous sources. It is impossible to imagine anything not provided, for the poorest chance arrival as well as for the honoured and invited guest.

Wooden guest-houses had been built, furnished like the most comfortable Parisian mansions, all newly constructed with perfect taste to serve this very purpose, and vast tents were set up, sufficient to provide a camp in themselves. There were kitchens arranged, and butteries, and an innumerable staff of servants for the uninterrupted service of the tables, pantries, and cellars; and all this array provided a scene of such smooth-running order, serenity, punctuality, speed, and perfect decorum that it excited universal delight and admiration.

This camp was the first excursion on which the ladies overcame their natural fastidiousness in a way which no one would have liked to propose. So many of them wished to be of the party that the King relaxed his rule and allowed them all to go to Compiègne if they so desired. That, however, was not their ambition, for they all wished to be nominated and commanded, not merely permitted, to make the journey, and that is why they played every trick in the pack to cram themselves into the princesses' carriages. Until then, the King had always chosen the ladies who followed the Queen or Madame la Dauphine in the carriages of the 'first princesses', as the King's bastards were called. They, however, had friends of their own, to whose presence they made the King consent, and these ladies travelled in their personal carriages, which they thought a fine thing, for they liked being placed on that footing. On this particular occasion, however, anything served provided that they went. There were no ladies in the King's coach, except the Duchesse du Lude, attending on the princesses. Monsieur and Madame remained at Saint-Cloud and Paris.

The gentlemen of the Court came in great numbers, and for the first time, dukes were billeted in couples. I shared with the Duc de Rohan a fine large house belonging to the Sieur de Chambaudon, where we and our servants were perfectly comfortable.

All the ambassadors were invited and going to Compiègne until old Ferreiro of Savoy put it into their heads to demand the privilege of the *pour*, which he insisted had been given to him on his first embassy to Paris. The Portuguese ambassador said that following the King's example, Monsieur had made the stewards give it to him when he had stayed at Montargis. The nuncio maintained that the Nuncio Cavallerini had had it before he was made a cardinal. All the masters of ceremonies protested that such a thing was impossible; that no ambassador had ever claimed it before, and that there was nothing about it in the records—but you know how much reliance should be placed on records. The fact of the matter was that the ambassadors realized the King's desire to impress them with the splendours of the camp and hoped to extract something for themselves in the shape of a new privilege. The King remained firm, however, so that the argument continued until the actual day of the journey, and in the end none of the ambassadors went. The King was so much vexed about it that I myself heard him say at supper—he, usually so silent and restrained—that he had a good mind to forbid their ever coming to Court except for audiences, as is the custom in other countries.

I am indeed ignorant of the origins of the *pour*, but as a distinction it is really utterly nonsensical. It consists in writing in chalk upon the doors of apartments, either '*pour* M. So and So', or merely 'M. So and So'. When the stewards of the King's household mark the rooms assigned to different people on such journeys, they add the *pour* for Princes of the Blood, cardinals, and foreign princes. M. de La Trémoille also had it, and the Duchesse de Bracciano (afterwards the Princesse des Ursins). I say that the distinction is foolish because it conveys no better nor more honourable lodging. Cardinals, foreign princes, and dukes are all lodged alike, without any distinction whatsoever.

The whole matter is in the word *pour*, which has absolutely no significance.

The Court set out on Thursday, August 28th. The King went by way of Saint-Cloud, slept at Chantilly, stayed there for one day, and arrived at Compiègne on the Saturday. The Maréchal de Boufflers' headquarters were in the village of Coudun, where houses had been erected as well as tents. The King had a wonderful meal there accompanied by Mgr le Duc and Mme la Duchesse de Bourgogne, and they viewed all the arrangements that I have mentioned with much wonder and admiration. When they reached Compiègne, the King told Livry (his high steward), that Mgr le Duc de Bourgogne must not dine as had been arranged, but that when he went to the camp he must dine with the Maréchal de Boufflers, for despite Livry's best endeavours, nothing could compare with what he had just seen.

During the reviews, an amusing trick was played on the Comte de Tessé, colonel-general of the dragoons. Two days earlier, M. de Lauzun had asked him in that friendly unassuming manner he so often adopted, whether he had everything proper to salute the King at the head of his dragoons. Thereupon the Comte had launched into a long description of his horse, uniform, and staff. After congratulating him, M. de Lauzun said guilelessly, 'But your hat; I did not hear you mention a hat?' 'Oh! no,' said the other, 'I expect to wear a cap.' 'A cap!' exclaimed Lauzun, 'what can you be thinking of? Caps are all very well for the others; but a colonel-general in a cap! Monsieur le Comte, you cannot be serious!' 'What do you mean?' said Tessé. 'What else should I wear?' Lauzun kept him on tenterhooks, making him repeat the question again and again on the grounds that he must be joking. Finally, in response to entreaties, Lauzun said that he could not allow him to make such a terrible mistake. He knew the etiquette because the post had been created especially for him, and the most important rule was that the colonel-general should wear a grey hat when the king reviewed the dragoons. Tessé was dumbfounded, admitted his total ignorance and poured out his thanks to M. de Lauzun for his timely warning. He then hurried home and sent one of his servants to Paris to buy a hat. The Duc de Lauzun had been careful to draw Tessé on one side, for he did not wish to be overheard; he knew that Tessé would be too much ashamed of his ignorance to tell anyone, and he himself did not breathe a word.

On the morning of the review, I went to the King's *lever* and happened to notice that M. de Lauzun stayed in the room, although, having the grande entrée, he usually withdrew when the rest of the Court entered. I also noticed Tessé, strutting about and parading a grey hat, with a black plume and a vast cockade. What seemed to me most extraordinary was the colour of the hat, for the King had a particular aversion to grey and no one had worn it for several years past. It therefore struck me as odd and made me look at him attentively, for he was standing opposite me, and M. de Lauzun was fairly near him and a little behind. After the King had been given his shoes and had spoken to one or two people, he suddenly noticed the hat and in his astonishment asked Tessé where he had got it, to which Tessé smugly replied that he had sent for it to Paris. 'For what purpose?' said the King. 'Sire,' said Tessé, 'Your Majesty does us the honour to review us today.' 'Well!' said the King, still more astonished. 'What has that got to do with a grey hat?' 'Sire,' replied Tessé, beginning to feel embarrassed, 'it is the colonel-general's special privilege to wear a grey hat on review days.' 'A *grey* hat,' said the King, 'where the devil did you learn that?' 'From M. de Lauzun, Sire; you created the post for him, and he told me.' At that moment M. de Lauzun burst out laughing and vanished. 'Lauzun was fooling you,' said the King, rather crossly. 'Believe me, you had better send that hat at once to the prior-general of the White Friars.' Never have I seen a man more abashed than Tessé, as he stood with downcast eyes staring at the hat, looking so thoroughly miserable and ashamed of himself that he made a perfect spectacle. No one could help laughing, and those nearest and most intimate with the King said something smart, until at last Tessé pulled himself together sufficiently to leave the room. But the entire Court let him know what they thought, and asked him whether he had not yet learned to know M. de Lauzun, who chuckled whenever it was mentioned. Tessé did not dare to take offence and the incident passed as a joke, although it was really a bit steep; but he was tormented about it for a long time and was very much discomfited.

Nearly every day during the camp, the Sons of France dined with the Maréchal de Boufflers, and sometimes Mme la

Duchesse de Bourgogne and the princesses and ladies-in-waiting dined with them; but more often they picnicked. The quality and quantity of the silver services, enough for everyone and all marked with the Maréchal's crest, were wonderful, and even more so was the punctuality of the meals, not only to the hour, but to the very minute, everywhere. Nothing was ever wanting, nothing dragged. In serving the least of the bystanders, or even the lackeys, it was the same as for the greatest lords. There was something at all hours and for all comers. For ten miles around Compiègne, every village and farm was full to overflowing with visitors, both French and foreign, they could not have held another person; yet everything proceeded in orderly fashion. The gentlemen and servants belonging to the Maréchal were hosts in themselves, all most civil and obliging in their duty of welcoming all comers and serving them with whatsoever they needed, from five o'clock in the morning until ten or eleven at night, without stinting, and doing all the honours assisted by a vast staff and a great number of pages. I find that I repeat myself, but no one who witnessed it can ever forget that sight or cease to admire the abundance, splendour, and efficiency, which never failed for a single moment or at any point.

At Compiègne, the King wished to give an example of everything that happened in war, so that regular siege was laid to the town, with all the proper procedure, lines, trenches, batteries, mines, etc., but much simplified. An ancient rampart ran round the château on the side facing the open country; its top, raised on a level with the King's apartment, overlooked the entire plain. At its foot and stretching a little beyond stood an old wall and a windmill; the rampart, itself, had no buttress nor supporting wall.

Saturday, September 13th, was the day appointed for the assault. The King, followed by all the ladies and in the loveliest weather imaginable, went out onto the rampart, where crowds of people were assembled and all the distinguished foreigners. Standing there, one could see the entire plain and the disposition of all the troops. I was in the semi-circle, very close to His Majesty, not more than three paces away, and no one was in front of me. It was the most superb sight, that great army, and the crowds of spectators on foot and on horseback keeping at a proper distance so as not to be in the way. The movements of the attacking force and the defence were plain to see because, there being no reason for the manœuvres, except display, neither side needed to conceal themselves unless the precision of their movements required. There was, nevertheless, one other spectacle which forty years hence I shall be able to describe as vividly as I do today, so forcibly did it strike me, and that was the spectacle which the King presented from the top of the rampart to his whole army, and to the enormous crowd of onlookers of every degree, both in the plain and on the rampart itself.

Mme de Maintenon[1] sat there, facing the plain and the troops, in her sedan-chair, behind its three glass windows. On the front left-hand shaft sat Mme la Duchesse de Bourgogne, and standing behind her in a semi-circle were Madame la Duchesse, Mme la Princesse de Conti, and all the ladies, flanked by a group of courtiers. The King was by the right-hand window of the chair, standing, and behind him, a semi-circle of the most distinguished gentlemen. The King's hat was off for most of the time, and at every moment he bent down to speak to Mme de Maintenon through the window, explaining what she was seeing and the reason for every manœuvre. Each time that he did so, she was polite enough to lower the glass four or five inches, but never as far as halfway, for I particularly noticed, and I must admit to having been far more interested in this scene than in the movements of the troops. She sometimes opened the window herself to ask the King a question, but it was nearly always he who bent down to inform her, without waiting for her to address him; and sometimes, when she was not paying attention, he rapped on the glass to make her open. He spoke to no one else, save to give orders, in a few words and very seldom, and occasionally to answer Mme la Duchesse de Bourgogne, who made efforts to persuade him to speak to her. Mme de Maintenon pointed things out to her and spoke in sign language from time to time through the front window, but without opening the glass, and the young Princess screamed back a few words in reply. I closely examined the faces of the onlookers. They all had expressions of ill-concealed nervous and shamefaced astonishment, and those in the semi-circles behind the chair gazed far more attentively at Mme de Maintenon than at the army, and all looked acutely alarmed and embarrassed. The King frequently laid his hat on the roof of the chair when he spoke into it, and

[1] The King had married her secretly soon after the Queen's death.

the continual bending must have tired his back very considerably. Monseigneur was in the plain, on horseback, with his younger sons, and Mgr le Duc de Bourgogne was with the Maréchal de Boufflers, who commanded the entire operation. The time was five o'clock in the afternoon and the weather as fine as the heart could desire.

Directly in front of the sedan-chair, a steep path invisible from above led downhill, and an opening had been made at the end of the old wall, so that a messenger could come from below to take the King's orders, should it prove necessary. Such an event occurred when Crenan sent Canillac, the colonel of one of the defending regiments, to receive the King's commands on some detail or other, I know not what. Canillac came up the path, and had reached the point when his head and shoulders were beginning to appear above the level of the rampart (I see him now, as clearly as I saw him then). As his head gradually emerged, he suddenly perceived the chair, the King, and all the onlookers, whom he had hitherto neither seen nor suspected, because his post had been below, at the foot of the rampart, and he could not observe what was happening above. The sight completely bowled him over, so that he stopped short, staring, with mouth open and eyes glazed, and on his face an expression of the most utter astonishment. No one could have missed it, and the King saw it so plainly that he exclaimed with some heat, 'Come along, Canillac; hurry up!' Canillac stayed where he was, and the King said again, 'What is the matter, man? Come on up.' Canillac then did manage to come up and approached the King very slowly, trembling in every limb, and looking to right and left, thoroughly bewildered. I have already said that I was standing three paces from the King. Canillac passed directly in front of me and stammered out something in a very low voice. 'What's that?' said the King. 'Speak up, man!' He never managed to recover himself, but brought out some sort of mumble which the King failed to understand. Then, seeing that Canillac could do no better, he answered curtly, adding in a vexed tone, 'Go away, sir!' Canillac did not have to be told twice; he went back to his path and disappeared. 'I do not know what is wrong with Canillac,' said the King, looking round as soon as the latter had gone, 'he seems to have taken leave of his senses; he has forgotten what he had to say to me.' Nobody answered.

Just before the surrender, it appeared as though Mme de Maintenon asked leave to withdraw, for the King cried out, 'Bearers for Madame!' and they came and carried her away. Less than a quarter of an hour afterwards the King retired, followed by Mme la Duchesse de Bourgogne and almost the entire company. Many of the spectators were eyeing and nudging one another as they went and whispering, but very low, for people could not get over the sight which they had just witnessed. It was the same with the spectators in the plain; even the soldiers were asking about the sedan-chair into which the King was continually bending, so that it became necessary to silence the officers discreetly and stop the troops from asking questions. You may imagine the effect that it had on the foreigners and what they said about it. All Europe heard of it, and the incident was as much talked of as the camp itself, for all its pomp and splendour.

At other times Mme de Maintenon appeared very little at the camp, and always in a carriage with three or four intimate friends. She went once or twice to see the Maréchal de Boufflers and the marvels of his extraordinary lavishness. At last, after attacks on the trenches, displays of mimic warfare, and interminable reviews, the King finally left Compiègne on Monday, September 22nd, and travelled with the same people in his coach as far as Chantilly, where they spent the Tuesday night. On the Wednesday they arrived at Versailles, with as much relief on the part of the ladies as there had been eagerness to join the expedition at first. They had not eaten with the King at Compiègne, and had seen as little of Mme la Duchesse de Bourgogne as at Versailles. Nevertheless, they had been obliged to go to the camp every day and the fatigue had seemed to them greater than the pleasure, and far greater than any distinction which they might have hoped to gain.

The King was exceedingly pleased with the fine appearance of the troops, who had worn full-dress uniform with every embellishment that their officers could devise. As he left, he ordered six hundred francs to be given to each cavalry and dragoon captain, and three hundred to each infantry captain. He gave as much to the majors of every regiment, and distributed a few favours among his household. To the Maréchal de Boufflers, he presented one hundred thousand francs. Altogether, this must have cost him a good deal, but it was a drop in the ocean to the individuals concerned. There was not a single regiment that was not ruined for many years to come, both corps and officers. As for the Maréchal de Boufflers, I leave you to imagine how far one hundred thousand francs would go towards defraying the cost of a display so magnificent, so fantastic to those who saw it. All Europe trembled at the reports of the foreign observers, who day after day could scarcely believe their eyes.

1698

The Ignorance of Breteuil

WHEN the King returned from Fontainebleau, Breteuil[1] was given the post of head of the protocol. He was a man not lacking in intelligence, but he had a passion for the Court, ministers, people of high rank or in the best society, and especially loved making money by offering his services in negotiating government contracts. People bore with him and mocked him. He had been one of the King's readers and was brother of Breteuil, the councillor of state and administrator of finances. He often pushed his way into M. de Pontchartrain's house, to which he had been introduced by his friend and kinsman, Caumartin. Breteuil liked to pose as a know-all, although he was very servile, and people loved to torment him.

One day when he was dining with M. de Pontchartrain, he began to hold forth, and laid down the law in a monstrously foolish way before a large company. Mme de Pontchartrain took him up, and in order to silence him said that for all he was so well-informed she wagered that he could not tell who composed the Paternoster. Breteuil tried to laugh it off, but Mme de Pontchartrain kept pressing the point, challenging him, and harking back to the subject. He defended himself as best he might and managed to temporize until they left the table, when Caumartin, seeing his predicament, caught him as they were entering the drawing-room and kindly whispered in his ear the word 'Moses'. Breteuil, who had been completely at a loss, now felt much comforted, with the result that when the coffee

---

[1] Baron de Breteuil, the father of Mme du Châtelet.

was brought in he returned to the charge and appeared exultant. This time Mme de Pontchartrain had no difficulty in persuading him, and Breteuil, after reproaching her for pretending ignorance and avowing his shame at being obliged to mention anything so trite, announced that as everyone knew, Moses had composed the Paternoster. There was a great burst of laughter and poor Breteuil, utterly disconcerted, could hardly find his way to the door. Everyone said something witty about the brilliance of his intellect. He was angry with Caumartin for a long time afterwards, and the incident of the Paternoster was not soon forgotten.

His friend, the Marquis de Gesvres, prided himself on being equally well-read and indeed, he sometimes remembered a sentence here and there, which he loved to slip into his conversation. In the King's apartments one day, he was holding forth like any connoisseur in praise and criticism of the fine pictures, that included several Crucifixions by great masters. He maintained that a great number had been painted by the same artist, and all in that particular gallery. People began to mock him, pointing out the various painters and how they might be recognized by their personal styles. 'Nonsense,' exclaimed the Marquis. 'The painter of all of them was called "INRI", cannot you read his signature?' You may imagine the silence that followed this gross blunder, and what became of the ignoramus.

1699

Coislin's Revenge

GENTLEMEN of the Court mourned the loss of a real cynic, who lived and died a member of the Court and society, and would brook nothing that displeased him in either of those worlds. His name was the Chevalier de Coislin, and he was the brother of the duke and the cardinal of that name. He was in every way a gentleman and a brave man, and although poor, his brother, the cardinal, allowed him to lack for nothing. He was a most unordinary type of man, very liverish and irritable, most awkward to deal with. He scarcely ever left Versailles but he never saw the King, indeed, he made such a point of avoiding him that I and many others have seen him deliberately turn away if he found himself in the King's path. M. de Louvois went out of his way to victimize him, until he left the army, and for the rest of his life he never forgave either the minister or his Master, who bore with his rudeness for the sake of his brothers. Coislin lived in the cardinal's apartments and dined at his table, where there was always good company. If anyone happened to bore him, he ate something in his own room, or if someone he disliked arrived while he was at table, he would throw down his napkin and go off to sulk or to finish his dinner alone. No one was wholly safe from his onslaughts, and his brother's house was more frequented after his death—although most of those who went there were much like himself. His bad manners almost drove his brothers to desperation, especially the cardinal, whom he bullied.

One story will tell you the whole of him. It happened that he went with his brothers and a fourth (I know not whom) on one of the King's excursions, for he followed the King everywhere, although he would not see him, in order to be with his brothers and their friends. Now the Duc de Coislin was devastatingly polite, so much so that people became bored to tears in his company. He had a habit, when on these journeys, of making endless flowery speeches to the people with whom he lodged, while the chevalier nearly exploded with impatience. On this occasion, they were assigned rooms in the house of a certain gentlewoman, who was lively, well-bred, and handsome. There were long civilities in the evening, and still longer speeches next morning. M. d'Orléans,[1] who was not then a cardinal, implored his brother to have done; the chevalier raged; the duke continued to pay his compliments. Coislin, knowing his brother and guessing that there would be no sudden end to the business, decided to relieve himself and wreak his revenge very prettily at the same time.

Later, when they were some ten miles upon their journey, he began to speak of their charming hostess and of all his brother's compliments; then, overcome by laughter, he told the coach party that he had a notion the lady would not feel gratified for

[1] M. d'Orléans. The usual way of referring to bishops (here the Bishop of Orléans) after their cathedral towns.

long. There was the Duc de Coislin, much puzzled, unable to imagine why, and anxiously asking questions. 'Do you really want an answer?' said the chevalier brutally. 'Your fine speeches drove me past all bearing, so I went up into the room where you slept and planted an enormous stool plumb in the middle of the floor. At this precise moment, our lovely hostess is in no doubt but that it was you with all your fine compliments who left her that token.' The other two began to laugh heartily, but the duke was furious, wishing to stop the coach, take one of the servants' horses, and ride back to expose the real villain and again hold forth in shame and apologies.

It was raining hard, but they had all the trouble in the world to prevent him, and still more to heal the breach. They told the story to their friends that evening. It made one of the pleasantest tales of those journeys. To those who knew them, it was the best of all.

1699

Incredible Robberies

A MOST daring robbery was committed on the night of June 3rd in the great stables[1] at Versailles, when the King himself was in residence. All the hammercloths and harness were taken to the tune of more than a hundred and fifty thousand francs' worth, and the thieves planned so well that although the house was full of people and the night a very short one, no one heard a sound. Everything was removed and nothing more was ever heard of it. Monsieur le Grand and his staff appeared in a fury, messengers were sent by all the roads, and searches were instituted in Paris and Versailles but without result.

That reminds me of an even more outrageous theft that occurred shortly before I began to write my memoirs. The furniture in the state apartments, which ran from the gallery to the chapel, was upholstered in crimson velvet with gold braid and fringes. One morning, it was discovered that all this trimming had been cut off and removed, an incredible thing to have

---

[1] La grande écurie: one of the two buildings designed by François Mansard (1679–1685), opposite the Château of Versailles, on the further side of the Place d'Armes. The stables stood either side of the Avenue de Paris.

happened in a place where people were passing in and out all day long, and which was locked and guarded all night. Bontemps searched everywhere in desperation and had every possible inquiry made, but it was all quite useless.

Five or six days later, I attended the King's supper. There was no one but d'Aquin, the Royal physician, between me and the King, and no one at all between me and the table. Just as the entremets[1] were being served, a monstrous big blackish object came sailing through the air over the table. It went so fast that I had no time to examine or point to it before it landed just in front of where Monsieur and Madame's covers were usually laid. On that day they happened to be in Paris, but they always sat at the end of the table, on the King's left, with their backs to the window overlooking the courtyard. The noise it made was prodigious and the weight seemed likely to break the table. The plates jumped but luckily nothing was upset, for the object fell upon the cloth and not among the dishes. The King half-turned his head at the sudden crash and said without the slightest trace of alarm, 'I expect those are my fringes.' And indeed, it was a package rather larger than a priest's hat with the edges flattened out, about two feet high, shaped like an ill-made pyramid.

It had been thrown from some distance behind where I was standing, through the middle door of the two ante-chambers, and a piece of fringe had become detached in mid-air and had fallen on the King's wig; but Livry, the high steward, who was on his left, noticed and removed it at once. Livry then went to the end of the table and verified that the object was indeed the fringes, done up into a bundle, and we all saw them at the same time and there was a hum of voices. He was just about to pick it up when he saw that there was a note attached, which he took, leaving the bundle where it was. At this, the King stretched out his hand, saying, 'Let me see'; but very rightly, Livry would not allow this. Taking a step backwards, he read it to himself and then passed it behind the King's back to d'Aquin, where I read it as he held it in his hand. The note was written in a disguised hand, long, like a woman's, and it read: 'Take back your fringes, Bontemps, they were not worth the trouble. Give my respects to the King.' It was folded, but not sealed.

[1] Dishes of stew served between the roast and the dessert.

The King again tried to take the paper from d'Aquin, but the latter drew back, smelt it, rubbed it, turned it over, and showed it to the King but would not let him handle it. The King then told him to read it aloud, and read it himself at the same time. 'This is most insolent!' he said, but in a calm almost bored voice. Then he told them to remove the package. It was so heavy that it was all Livry could do to lift it, and he quickly handed it to one of the blue-coated footmen. After that the King did not mention the incident again and no one else dared say anything, at least not aloud, and the rest of that supper passed as though nothing untoward had happened.

Apart from the incredible insolence of the theft, what an appalling risk to have taken! How could anyone, unless he were surrounded by accomplices, have hurled a package of that weight and size for such a distance, especially during the King's supper, when the crowd is so dense that one can scarcely move in the outer rooms? Even had there been a group of accomplices, how could the wide gesture needed to throw with such force possibly have passed unnoticed? It was the Duc de Gesvres's year of service, but until the King had risen, neither he nor anyone else thought of shutting the doors. You may imagine whether the culprits were likely to remain, when they were given three-quarters of an hour in which to escape. At last the doors were shut, but only one stranger was discovered, whom they immediately arrested. He said that he was a gentleman from Saintonge and acquainted with the Duc d'Uzès, the governor of that province. As the duke happened to be at Versailles, they sent to beg him to come, which he did, although he was about to go to bed. He recognized and vouched for the gentleman, who was set free with apologies. Nothing further has ever been discovered about this theft, and the strange manner of its return.

1700

Le Nôtre

LE NÔTRE[1] died at about this time. He had lived in perfect

[1] André Le Nôtre (1613–1700), contrôleur-général des bâtiments, the creator of French landscape gardening. The Avenue des Champs-Elysées and St. James's Park, London, were laid out by him.

health for eighty-eight years and retained his faculties, excellent taste, and capability until the last. He was celebrated for designing the fine gardens that adorn all France and have so lowered the reputation of Italian gardens (which are really nothing by comparison) that the most famous landscape architects of Italy now come to France to study and admire. Le Nôtre was honest, honourable, and plain-spoken; everybody loved and respected him, for he never stepped out of his place nor forgot it and was always perfectly disinterested, working for private patrons as for the King himself, and with the same care and industry. His only thought was to aid nature and reveal true beauty at as low a cost as possible. There was an artlessness about him, a simple-hearted candour that was perfectly delightful. On one occasion, when the Pope had obtained the King's permission to borrow him for a few months, Le Nôtre entered his room, and instead of falling to his knees, ran towards him, and putting his arms round his neck kissed him on both cheeks, exclaiming, 'Ah! Holy Father, how well you look! How rejoiced I am to see you in good health!' The Pope, Clement X, Alfieri, laughed heartily. He thoroughly enjoyed this informal kind of greeting and treated Le Nôtre with much kindness.

After he returned, the King took him into the gardens of Versailles and showed him all that had been done in his absence. When they reached the colonnade, Le Nôtre did not utter a word until the King pressed him for his opinion. 'Well, Sire,' said he, 'what would you have me say? You have turned a stone-mason into a gardener (he was referring to Mansard[1]) and he has treated you to one of the tricks of his trade.' The King said nothing and everyone smiled, for indeed, although it pretends to be one, the colonnade has little resemblance to a fountain and is vastly out of place in a garden.

A month or so before he died, the King, who enjoyed seeing and talking to him, again took him into the gardens and because of his great age had him put into a chair, which a footman wheeled beside his own. Thereupon Le Nôtre exclaimed, 'Alas! my poor father,[2] had he but been alive to see this poor

---

[1] Jules Hardouin-Mansard (1646–1708), chief architect to Louis XIV. He built the châteaux of Marly and Dampierre, the chapel of the palace of Versailles, the Grand Trianon, and the Place Vendôme. His little house at Marly still remains. He was the great-nephew by marriage of François Mansard (1598–1666), the designer of the mansard-roof.

[2] Jean Le Nôtre, landscape gardener and head-gardener at the Tuileries.

gardener, his own son, riding in a chair beside the greatest king on earth, his happiness would have been complete.'

He was superintendent of the royal residences and lived at the Tuileries, where he had charge of the palace and the gardens, which he had designed. All that he did is still considered far better than anything done since, although many have taken the greatest pains to imitate and follow him as far as they were capable. About ornamental flower-beds, he used to say that they were only good for nursemaids who were tied to their charges and could look down upon them from second-storey windows. Nevertheless, he excelled in designing them, as well as all other parts of a garden; but he did not care for them, and he was right, because no one ever walks in those parts.

1700

The Duc d'Anjou becomes King of Spain

No sooner had the King of Spain[1] expired than there arose the question of opening his will. A council of state was held, at which all the grandees then in Madrid were present. Curiosity to witness so extraordinary a scene, affecting so many millions, drew all Madrid to the palace, where the crowds in the rooms adjoining that in which the will was read were so great that there was grave danger of suffocation. The foreign ministers thronged about the door in their anxiety to be the first to know the late King's choice and the first to inform their respective Courts. Blécourt (the French Ambassador) was there with the rest, knowing no more than they, and the Comte d'Harrach, the Emperor's envoy, who hoped and believed that the will would favour the Archduke,[2] stood next him by the door, wearing a look of triumph. Everyone grew impatient. Finally, the door opened and closed again. The Duc d'Abrantès, whose wit was pleasant but much to be dreaded, entered, apparently wishing to have the pleasure of announcing the successor as soon as the grandees and the council were agreed. He was instantly

---

[1] Charles II, King of Spain (1665–1700), bequeathed his throne to the Duc d'Anjou.
[2] The Archduke Charles, second son of Leopold II, Emperor of Austria, who had a claim to the Spanish throne through his mother.

surrounded. Casting a glance around the assembly, he remained gravely silent. Blécourt stepped forward, at whom he looked fixedly, then turned away appearing to search among the by-standers, an action that surprised Blécourt, who thought that it boded no good for France. Suddenly the Duc d'Abrantès made as though he had just perceived the Comte d'Harrach. A look of joy came over his face, he flung his arms about his neck and said loudly in Spanish, 'Monsieur, it is with much pleas-ure . . . ,' then, after a pause for further embraces, 'Yes, Mon-sieur, it is with the greatest joy . . . ' (still another pause for embraces) 'and satisfaction that I take leave of you for the re-mainder of my life and bid farewell to the Royal House of Aus-tria.' He then made a dash through the crowd, who all ran after him to know the name of the successor. The Comte d'Harrach's surprise and indignation effectually stopped his mouth but fully appeared upon his countenance. He remained rooted to the spot for several minutes, allowed his underlings to inform him of the news when the council rose, and then went to his house in a state of confusion, all the greater from having been duped by the Duc d'Abrantès's embraces and the cruel mockery of his compliments.

Blécourt did not wait to hear more. He hurried home to write the news and dispatch his courier, and while he was so doing Ubilla[1] sent him an extract from the will itself, so that he had only to include it in the packet, which was carried straight to the King, at the Conseil des Finances, on the morning of Tuesday, November 9th.

The King had arranged to shoot on that day, but he counter-manded the hunt and dined as usual *au petit couvert*, showing nothing by his expression, merely announcing the death of the King of Spain, that he should wear mourning, and that there would be no Appartement, plays, nor other diversions at the Court during the whole of the winter. When he returned to his study, he summoned the ministers to assemble at three o'clock in Mme de Maintenon's room. By this time Monseigneur had returned from wolf-hunting, and he, too, went to Mme de Maintenon's room at three o'clock. That council lasted until seven in the evening, after which the King continued working until ten o'clock. Mme de Maintenon was present all the time that the council was sitting and during all the work that followed.

[1] Secretary of the council.

On the following day, the usual council of state was held in the morning in the King's study, and when he returned from hunting he held another in Mme de Maintenon's room, from six in the evening until ten. Although the Court had grown accustomed to the vogue for Mme de Maintenon, they were not used to see her openly taking part in state affairs, and there was great astonishment when two councils of state were held in her apartment on the gravest and most important matter that had come under discussion during that long reign or, indeed, in many others.

The King, Monseigneur, the chancellor,[1] the Duc de Beau-villiers, and Torcy (no other ministers of state were present) were the only ones who debated this great matter, and Mme de Maintenon sat with them, but was silent out of modesty until the King asked for her opinion after all had expressed theirs with the exception of himself. The speakers were divided in their opinions; two were in favour of the Treaty of Partition,[2] the other two were for accepting the will.

These two opinions, of which I have given the barest summary,[3] were much amplified by both sides and discussed at length many times over. Monseigneur, usually so deeply imbedded in fat and apathy, appeared a different man, to the intense surprise of the King and his counsellors. When the time came for him to speak, he expressed himself strongly in favour of accepting the will, recapitulating some of the chancellor's finest arguments, then, turning respectfully but firmly towards the King, he added that, having given his opinion like the rest, he took the liberty of claiming his inheritance, since he was in a position to accept it. The crown of Spain, he said, had been the rightful property of the Queen his mother, consequently it was now his, or, for the sake of the peace of Europe, that of his second son to whom he gladly ceded it. But, he added, he would not yield a single inch of that land to anyone else, for his claim was just, in conformity with the King's honour and the interests and majesty of the throne, and he hoped that it would not be rejected. All this he said, scarlet in the face, to the great astonishment of everyone present.

The King listened attentively and then said to Mme de

---

[1] Pontchartrain.
[2] By which the Spanish Empire was to be divided between France and Austria.
[3] Six pages of explanation omitted in this translation.

Maintenon, 'And you, Madame, what is your opinion?' She
made a show of reluctance but after being urged, even ordered,
to speak her mind, produced a few words expressing becoming
diffidence, a sentence or two in praise of Monseigneur, whom
she both feared and detested (as he did her), and added that she
advised acceptance.

The King ended the council without disclosing his own
opinion. He said that he had listened well and understood that
there were powerful arguments on both sides; it would be better
therefore to sleep upon the matter and to wait for twenty-four
hours, to see what might more come from Spain and whether
the Spaniards were of the same mind as their late King. He
then dismissed the counsellors, ordering them to assemble on
the following evening at the same place. The next day, Thursday, between his *lever* and mass, the King gave an audience
to the Spanish ambassador, at which Monseigneur and Torcy
were present; the ambassador presented him with an authentic
copy of the will, on behalf of the Queen[1] and the Junta. None
of us doubted that the King, without committing himself, had
then given the ambassador strong hopes of his acceptance, for
after his departure Mgr le Duc de Bourgogne was sent for and let
into the secret. The chancellor went off to Paris and the other
ministers were given leave of absence until Versailles, so that
everyone knew that the matter was decided one way or another.

The necessity of continuing so interesting a tale without
breaking the thread has not allowed me to pause. Now, however, I must retrace some of my steps. At Madrid, Blécourt's
amazement, at a proposal which surprised him no less than it
did the Comte d'Harrach, was unparalleled. That of King Louis
and his ministers was inconceivable. Neither he nor they could
believe what they read in Blécourt's dispatches, and several
days were needed before they had recovered sufficiently to deliberate that vital matter. The news, when it was published,
had the same effect upon the Court. Foreign ambassadors spent
whole nights conferring together, meditating on the King's
probable decision and the interests of their masters, yet extern-
ally preserving strict silence. The courtiers did nothing but
argue, but nearly all favoured acceptance. The manner of so
doing was much discussed in all the councils, and it was even

---

[1] Mariana of Neuburg. The first wife of Charles II of Spain had been the daughter of
Monsieur and Henrietta.

proposed to spring a surprise upon the world by allowing the Duc d'Anjou to disappear and as suddenly to reappear in Spain under the auspices of the nuncio Gualterio. I heard of this plan and thought of being one of the party. But it would have been a shabby trick and was instantly rejected, partly from shame at so furtive an acceptance of the proffered crowns and partly because it was necessary to throw off the mask in order to support a Spain too weak to be left unprotected.

Since no one at Court talked of anything but the course to be followed, the King amused himself one evening by asking the Princesses for their advice. They answered that M. le Duc d'Anjou should be sent forthwith to Spain, and that such was the opinion which they heard from every side. 'I am sure,' said the King, 'that plenty of people will blame me whatever I decide to do!'

This occurred on Saturday, November 13th. Next morning, the day before the Court left Fontainebleau, the King was closeted for a long time with Torcy, who then warned the Spanish ambassador to be at Versailles on the following evening. When this became generally known, it threw everyone into a state of ferment. Those in the know also discovered that on the preceding Friday the King had had a long conversation with M. le Duc d'Anjou in the presence of Monseigneur and Mgr le Duc de Bourgogne, an event so extraordinary that people were sure of an acceptance. On that very same Sunday, moreover, a Spanish courier from the Comte d'Harrach had stopped at Fontainebleau on his way to Vienna, had seen the King at his supper, and had said publicly that they were waiting impatiently at Madrid for M. le Duc d'Anjou, and that four grandees had been nominated to escort him to the capital. M. le Duc d'Anjou, when approached, only expressed his gratitude to the late King, and behaved so calmly that it appeared as though he neither knew nor expected anything until the moment of his proclamation.

On Monday, November 15th, the King left Fontainebleau between nine and ten in the morning, his coach containing only Mgr le Duc de Bourgogne, Mme la Duchesse de Bourgogne, Mme la Princesse de Conti and the Duchesse du Lude. He ate a morsel without leaving the coach and arrived at Versailles about four o'clock. Monseigneur went to Meudon to dine and spend a few nights, and Monsieur and Madame to Paris. The

Spanish ambassador received another courier while he was on the way, bringing fresh orders and urging him to be zealous in asking for M. le Duc d'Anjou. The Court at Versailles was very large, curiosity having brought them there even before the King's arrival.

On Tuesday, November 16th, immediately after his *lever*, the King summoned the Spanish ambassador to his study, which the Duc d'Anjou had already entered through the back way. The King then pointed to the Duke, telling the ambassador that he might salute him as his King, at which he fell to his knees in the Spanish fashion and made a longish address in that language, whereupon the King said that since the prince, his grandson, did not yet understand Spanish, he would answer for him.

Immediately afterwards, against all custom, the King had the double doors of his study flung wide open, and commanded the company, which almost amounted to a crowd, to enter. Then casting a most majestic glance over that numerous assembly, he announced, pointing to the Duc d'Anjou, 'Messieurs! Behold the King of Spain! His birth has called him to that throne, also the will of the late King. The entire nation desires him and claims him from me. This is Heaven's command, and I accede with pleasure.' Turning to his grandson, he continued, 'Be a good Spaniard, that is your first duty now; but remember that you were born a Frenchman and foster the unity between the two nations. That is the way to make them happy and to preserve the peace of Europe.' Then again pointing with his finger, he said to the ambassador, 'If he follows my advice, you will be a great noble, and that very soon. He cannot do better at present than be guided by you.'[1]

When the first excitement among the courtiers had subsided a little, the two other Sons of France stepped forward and all three embraced tenderly, again and again, with tears in their eyes. Zinzendorf, the Emperor's envoy (who has since amassed a vast fortune at Vienna), had asked for an audience at that time in complete ignorance of all that was happening, and was waiting below in the ambassadors' ante-room until the head of protocol should send for him to announce the birth of the Emperor's grandson.[2] He went upstairs knowing nothing of what had

---

[1] It was at this moment, according to Voltaire, that Louis XIV exclaimed, 'There are no longer any Pyrenees!'

[2] Leopold Joseph, son of the Archduke Joseph and Wilhelmina of Hanover. He died a few months later.

Louvre

THE DUC D'ANJOU AS KING PHILIP V OF SPAIN
From the portrait by Rigaud

LOUIS XIV
From the portrait by Rigaud

occurred. The King sent the King of Spain and the Spanish ambassador into one of the back offices, before summoning Zinzendorf, who learned only after his audience of the awkward moment that he had chosen. The King then went to mass, as usual, and the King of Spain walked beside him at his right hand. In the royal gallery, the whole royal family—that is to say, all down to and including the Grandsons of France and no others—hurriedly arranged themselves in a row upon the King's foot-rug. Unlike the time of prie-dieu,[1] they all leaned with him upon the carpeted balustrade, but the King was the only one to have a hassock. The rest knelt on the same step, which was also covered with the rug, but there were no hassocks for them. When they entered the gallery, only one hassock was provided, which the King took, and offered to the King of Spain, and when he refused it, it was put on one side and both heard mass without hassocks. Afterwards, there were always two hassocks when they both attended the same mass, which happened very often.

On their return, the King stopped in the great bed-chamber of the state apartments, and told the King of Spain that that should henceforth be his room. He slept there that same night and received the whole Court, who came in crowds to pay their respects. Villequier, the first gentleman of the King's bed-chamber, was given orders to wait on him, and the King gave up two rooms leading out of the state bedroom, so that he might be private, and communication uninterrupted between the two wings of the palace, for the only way was through the state rooms.

After that day, it became known that the King of Spain would leave on December 1st and that the two princes, his brothers,[2] would go with him to the frontier. M. le Duc de Beauvilliers was given authority over the princes and courtiers during the journey, and sole command over the troops, officers, and suite. He had the ordering of everything. The Maréchal the Duc de Noailles was appointed with him, not to interfere in any way, nor to give orders in his presence, although he was a Marshal of France and Captain of the Bodyguard, but in case of his illness or absence from the princes. All the youth of the Court received permission to make the journey and many went, either in their

---

[1] The King's short prayer, after dressing and before leaving the bedroom.
[2] The dukes of Bourgogne and Berry.

D

own coaches or in those of the suite. We heard, too, that after the separation at Saint Jean-de-Luz, the princes would make a tour of Provence and the Languedoc, passing through part of the Dauphiné and returning by Lyons, and that their excursion would take four months. An hundred and twenty men of the guards, under a lieutenant and an ensign, and a number of police, were detailed to escort them, and MM. de Beauvilliers and de Noailles each had fifty thousand livres for their expenses.

Monseigneur, who knew the hour which the King had fixed for the proclamation, told those at Meudon. Monsieur was told the secret on leaving Fontainebleau and was so impatient to announce it that he stood under the clock for several minutes before the appointed time, and could not refrain from informing his Court that they were going to hear great news as soon as the hand touched the hour that allowed him to speak. Mgr le Duc de Bourgogne, M. le Duc d'Anjou, and the Spanish ambassador had known since the preceding Friday, but they guarded the secret so well that nothing appeared in their manner or expressions. Mme la Duchesse de Bourgogne had been told when she arrived at Fontainebleau, M. le Duc de Berry on the Monday morning. They were all delighted, but felt the sadness of the separation, for they were devoted to one another, and when youth and high spirits sometimes caused quarrels between the eldest and youngest brothers, it was always the second, with his calm, virtuous, reserved nature who patched them up again.

Immediately after the proclamation, the King sent word to the King and Queen of England, by the first equerry.[1] In the afternoon, the King of Spain called on Monseigneur at Meudon, who received him at the door and led him in. He made him walk in front, gave him 'Your Majesty', and everywhere in public remained standing with him. Monseigneur, indeed, appeared quite beside himself with joy, often repeating that no one had ever before been in a position to say, 'The King my father, and the King my son'. Had he, however, known the prophecy made at his birth, 'Son of a king, father of a king, never king himself', he might not have been so delighted. After the proclamation, the King of Spain was treated in the same manner as the King of England, with an armchair at dinner at

---

[1] Jacques Louis, Marquis de Beringhen (1651–1723). Le premier écuyer, known as Monsieur le Premier, Master of the Horse at the smaller stables of Versailles.

the King's right hand, and his own cadenas.[1] Monseigneur and the rest of the royal family had folding-stools, as usual, at the end and side of the table, a goblet and a covered glass to drink from, and a taster,[2] like the King. They met in public only at chapel, on the way there and back, and at supper, after which the King accompanied him as far as the door of the great gallery. He saw the King and Queen of England at Versailles and Saint-Germain, and was treated in every way as an equal, but the three Kings never went anywhere together. In private, that is to say in the offices and in Mme de Maintenon's room, he behaved to the King as though he were still only Duc d'Anjou, indeed, at the first supper, the former turned to the Spanish ambassador and said that he felt as though it had all been a dream. He made only one formal call on Mme la Duchesse de Bourgogne and on Messeigneurs her brothers-in-law, and received only one from them, the visit being like those paid to the King of England, and it was the same when he went to Paris to call on Monsieur and Madame. Whenever he went in or out the guards beat the general salute—in fact, complete equality with the King. When they passed through the state apartments together, going to or coming from mass, the King walked on the right, but when they reached the last chamber he ceded that position to the King of Spain, as being no longer on his own territory. The evenings were spent in Mme de Maintenon's apartments, in different rooms from that in which she sat with the King, and there he played all kinds of games, generally childish games like touch-last, with Messeigneurs his brothers, Mme la Duchesse de Bourgogne who worked hard to amuse him, and the small circle of ladies who were permitted to be present.

The nuncio and the Venetian ambassador broke through the crowd immediately after the proclamation and went to congratulate the King and the new monarch, a fact that was noted with great interest. The attitude of the other foreign ministers was much more reserved, indeed, embarrassed. As for Zinzendorf, who remained in the drawing-room for some time after his audience, his state of mind was vastly interesting and curious. I think that he would gladly have paid handsomely for prior information that would have kept him in Paris.

[1] The case containing his knife and fork.
[2] The wine and water was always tasted before it was offered to the King.

1700

Departure of Philip V

ON Saturday, December 4th, the King of Spain went to the King before anyone else was admitted and stayed a long time. He then called on Monseigneur, with whom he was also a long time alone. They then all heard mass together, amidst a great throng of courtiers. After mass, they at once got into their coach, Mme la Duchesse de Bourgogne at the back between the two Kings, Monseigneur in front between Messeigneurs his two other sons, Monsieur by one door, and Madame by the other. They were surrounded by a far greater escort of guards than usual, as well as by mounted militiamen and light-horse. The whole road as far as Sceaux was lined with carriages and people. They arrived there shortly after midday, to find it full of ladies and courtiers and guarded by two companies of musketeers. When they left the coach, the King walked quickly through the lower apartments and entered the last room alone with the King of Spain, leaving the rest of the company in the salon. A quarter of an hour later he sent for Monsieur, and shortly afterwards for the Spanish ambassador to bid his royal master farewell. The King then summoned Mgr and Mme la Duchesse de Bourgogne, M. le Duc de Berry, Monsieur and Madame, all together, and, after a short interval, the Princes and Princesses of the Blood. The double doors were thrown wide open and from the salon they could be seen all weeping bitterly.

The King then said to the King of Spain, presenting the princes, 'Behold the princes of my blood and yours! From now onwards the two nations must regard themselves as one, their interests must be the same. I therefore desire that these princes shall be as closely attached to you as to myself, you could have no better nor more faithful friends.' This scene took up an hour and a half. At the close of it they were obliged to separate, the King conducted the King of Spain to the end of the state apartments and embraced him many times, holding him long in his arms, and Monseigneur did the same. It was a most touching sight.

The King then retired to recover his composure, Monseigneur got into his carriage alone, and the King of Spain, his brothers, and M. de Noailles drove away together and slept at Chartres. The King went for a drive in an open carriage with Mme la Duchesse de Bourgogne, Monsieur and Madame, and afterwards they all returned to Versailles. Various officers of the household followed on the journey to Spain, Desgranges, as master of ceremonies, as well as secretaries and equerries. Hersent, as keeper of the wardrobe and La Roche as head valet, were to remain in Spain with some servants and a few other people in the way of dentists and doctors.

M. de Beauvilliers, who had stuffed himself with quinine in the effort to check a persistent fever, accompanied by most distressing diarrhœa, took his wife, with Mmes de Cheverny and de Rasilly as her companions, for the King had absolutely insisted that he should start and attempt to make the journey.

Let them go, and let us marvel at the ways of Providence that so disposes of the thoughts of men and the fates of nations. What would Ferdinand and Isabella have thought, or Charles V, or Philip II, who so often attempted to invade France, and were accused of aspiring to world-monarchy? Or Philip IV himself, with all his precautions at the marriage of the King and the Peace of the Pyrenees? What would he have said at seeing a Son of France become King of Spain, by will of the last of his line and by the unanimous desire of all Spaniards, without French plots or intrigue, indeed, quite unknown to our King and his ministers, who felt only trouble in deciding and sorrow in acceptance? What deep, what grave thoughts such ideas provoke! But they would be out of place in these Memoirs. Let us now return to what was actually happening, for I am unwilling to interrupt so unusual and interesting a tale.

1701

Rose, the King's Secretary

AT this time, Rose, another of the King's private secretaries, died. He was eighty-six or eighty-seven years old, in perfect mental and bodily health until the last, and had held the pen for the past fifty years. He was also president of the Chambre des Comptes, vastly wealthy, vastly avaricious, and unequalled for his witty sallies and repartees. He had a good knowledge of literature, possessed an admirable memory and was a perfect mine of information about the Court and public affairs. He was merry, lively, bold, often deliberately impudent, but to those who took no liberties with him he was always polite and respectful, keeping in his proper place, very much after the manner of the old Court. Formerly, he had been in the service of Cardinal Mazarin, who placed entire confidence in him and made a friend of him. This had earned for him a similar and enduring relationship with the Queen Mother and the King, so that he was courted and considered by all, even by the ministers. His official duties brought him into close contact with the King and he was sometimes concerned in matters of which the ministers knew nothing.

To *hold the pen*, as they call it, is to be a kind of public forger, and to do in the course of duty what would cost other men their lives. The work consists in imitating the King's handwriting so perfectly that there is no difference, and by this means writing all manner of letters, which the King either should or would wish to write himself were no labour involved. Many monarchs and foreign princes employ such amanuenses, and some of their subjects, such as army generals, philanthropists, and other great men use them for their private correspondence. No man could have given utterance to a great king with more dignity than Rose, or in words better adapted to each different matter and recipient. The King signed these letters with his own hand, and the handwriting of the rest was so much like his own that no one could have discerned the least difference. Thus an immense number of vastly important matters had passed through Rose's hands, and still continued to involve him from time to time. He was exceedingly faithful and secret, and the King trusted him absolutely. Among the four private secretaries, the one who holds the pen has all the privileges and the three others have none, except their entrées. After Rose's death, Callières held the pen.

Rose, that honest man, was shrewd, cunning, clever, and dangerous to cross. Endless numbers of stories are told about him, but I shall relate only two or three that serve particularly well to portray him and those who had dealings with him. He had a fine estate very close to Chantilly, with a good house upon it, which he was very fond of and often visited. He was very careful to pay proper respect to his great neighbour, Monsieur le Prince[1] (I am speaking of the late duke), but at the same time was ever on the watch to safeguard his independence. As time went on, Monsieur le Prince, or more probably his hunt-servants, began to feel cramped for space and suggested that Rose should give up his property, a suggestion which he refused to entertain on any account. At last, driven to desperation, Monsieur le Prince began to lay traps for him, with the idea of wearying him into breaking his resolution. When one ruse after another had been tried without success, he collected three or four hundred foxes from different parts of the country and loosed them over the wall into Rose's park. You may imagine the damage which they did, and the utter stupefaction of Rose and his servants at that sudden swarm of foxes that had appeared overnight.

The good secretary, however, knew the ways of Monsieur le Prince and was in no doubt about who had sent him that unwanted gift; he was also angry and fiery-tempered. He went straight to the King in his study and boldly begged permission to ask a somewhat peculiar question. The King, knowing Rose and his jests, for he was very humorous and amusing, asked what was the matter. 'The matter, Sire,' said Rose, 'is that I would have you tell me whether we have two kings in France or one.' 'And what does that mean?' said the King, turning red himself. 'It means,' retorted Rose, 'that if Monsieur le Prince is also king, I must bow my head in tears beneath his yoke, but if he is only premier Prince of the Blood, I demand justice, Sire, for that you owe to all your subjects, and you should not suffer one of them to be victimized by Monsieur le Prince.' Then he told the King how they had tried to persuade him to sell his estate, and then to compel him by persecution, and so came to the story of the foxes. The King promised to speak to Monsieur le Prince so that Rose should be left in peace. Indeed he commanded him to have every last fox removed from Rose's park at his own expense, without any damage being done, and to repair the harm that had been done already. The King was so peremptory regarding the future that Monsieur le Prince, as servile a courtier as he was ungentlemanly, tried to conciliate Rose, who for a long while kept his distance, and never afterwards dared to

[1] Henri-Jules de Bourbon (1643–1709), son of Le Grand Condé and father-in-law of Madame la Duchesse.

cross him in the slightest matter. Although in the end Rose
was bound to accept his advances, he never forgave Monsieur
le Prince and was always delighted when he could make a fool
of him. I and fifty others witnessed one such occasion.

On the days when the Council met, the ministers used to
assemble in the King's room after mass, so as to be ready to
enter the study when they were summoned, for the King always
went from the chapel straight through the great gallery into
his business room. There were always courtiers about at such
times in the King's bedroom, either because they had business
with the ministers and could speak there more informally when
they had not much to say, or merely because they wished to
converse with them. Monsieur le Prince was often present,
speaking to all the ministers without any particular matter to
discuss, and looking for all the world like some hanger-on
seeking favours. Rose, who let nothing escape him, chose a time
when most of the best people were present and Monsieur le
Prince had been fawning on the ministers with gross flattery and
servility. He made straight towards him, shutting one eye, with
a forefinger pressed against his nose—a favourite gesture—and
said loudly, 'Monsieur, I have noticed for several days past that
you are having a game with these gentlemen, and acting with a
purpose. I have known the Court and courtiers for a long time,
and you cannot fool me. I know what is in your mind.' All this
was said in a meaning high-pitched tone that caused Monsieur le
Prince acute embarrassment, although he made every effort to
defend himself. The conversation brought ministers and other
great persons crowding around them, and when Rose saw that
they were well and truly encircled and that the Council was
about to be summoned, he took Monsieur le Prince very respectfully by the tip of the elbow, and said with a sly smile, 'Tell me
now, Monsieur, are you not anxious to be addressed as 'Premier Prince of the Blood'? and immediately, turning on his heel,
he melted into the crowd. Monsieur le Prince was left aghast,
and the bystanders were in fits of uncontrollable mirth. That
was one of Rose's most audacious pranks, which provided the
Court with amusement and gossip for several days. Monsieur le
Prince was furious, but he dared not do or say anything. This
incident happened only a year before Rose's death.

Rose never forgave M. de Duras[1] for an act that was really a

---

[1] The Maréchal de Duras, brother of Saint-Simon's father-in-law the Duc de Lorges.

monstrous piece of cruelty. It occurred during one of the Court journeys, when Rose's carriage was out of action for one reason or another and he had mounted a horse in his impatience to be off. He was a bad rider, and before very long he and his horse were engaged in a quarrel which ended with the horse falling over with him into a muddy ditch. M. de Duras, passing by in his coach, heard Rose crying out for help from beneath his horse in the ditch. The coach was moving very slowly on account of the mud, but all that M. de Duras did in the way of succour was to stick his head out of the window and call out laughing that it must be a dainty horse to roll on *roses*. Then he continued on his way. Soon afterwards the more charitable Duc de Coislin appeared and helped Rose to his feet, but so furious was the latter, so beside himself with rage, that it was some time before the travellers learned what had occurred. The worst, however, was at the King's *coucher*. M. de Duras feared no man and had a tongue as sharp as Rose, he had already told the story and the King and the Court were highly diverted. This, Rose found so monstrous that he never again spoke to M. de Duras, and never spoke of him without losing his temper, but he was never able to mock him in front of the King, who always laughed and began to talk of muddy ditches.

At the end of his life, Rose married his granddaughter, already immensely wealthy and with expectations of even greater riches when he died, to Portail, who died long since, when he was a premier président of the Parlement in Paris. It was not a harmonious marriage, for the young lady, who was aware that she had been a great catch, despised her husband and was wont to say that instead of marrying into good society, she had remained at the *portail*. At last matters went so badly that the father-in-law, an old conseiller de grand-chambre, and his son came to protest formally to Rose. At first he paid little attention then when he saw that they were about to begin all over again, he promised to speak to the girl but did nothing about it. In the end, growing weary of their complaining, he exclaimed angrily, 'You are perfectly right, she is a baggage, a piece of impudence, there is no doing anything with her. If I hear another word about her I shall disinherit her, I am resolved upon it.' That was the end of the matter for him.

Rose was a little man, neither fat nor thin, with a clever, rather handsome face and keen eyes that sparkled with intelligence.

D*

He dressed like the clergy in a short cloak, with a satin skull-cap on his nearly white hair, and wore white bands like those of an abbé. He always carried his handkerchief between his coat and waistcoat, for he said that worn in that way it was nearer to his nose. He took a liking to me and used to poke fun at the foreign princes with all their different ranks and claims to rank. He always addressed those dukes whom he knew as 'Your Ducal Highness', as a gibe against other so-called Highnesses. Until the very last he was hearty, hale, and of excellent under-standing. He was a real character.

1701

The Death of Monsieur

On Wednesday, June 8th, Monsieur came to Marly from Saint-Cloud to dine with the King, and entered the study as usual as soon as the council of state was over. He found the King exceedingly angry because M. de Chartres had been deli-berately annoying his daughter and he did not care to take the matter up with him directly. The fact was that M. de Chartres had fallen in love with Mlle de Séry,[1] one of Madame's maids of honour, and was pursuing the affair in a tactless, high-handed manner. The King took this occasion to heap bitter reproaches on Monsieur for the conduct of his son. Monsieur, in the state that he then was, needed no excuse to vex him and answered tartly that fathers who lived certain kinds of lives were in no position to issue reprimands. The King could not help seeing the point of this remark, but returned to his daughter's wounded feelings, saying that such things ought to be kept out of her sight. By this time, however, Monsieur had fairly got the bit between his teeth and reminded the King pretty sharply that he had paraded his own mistresses before the Queen, even going to the extent of making them sit beside her in his coach. Much incensed, the King returned the compli-ment, and they were soon at it hammer and tongs.

---

[1] She was later called Mme d'Argenton and had a son by the Duc d'Orléans (1702). He was known as the Chevalier d'Orleans and became the Grand Prieur. See also 'My Friendship with M. le Duc d'Orléans'.

At Marly, the four apartments on the ground floor were similar and each contained three rooms. The King's study opened out of a smaller drawing-room which, at that time of day, was always full of courtiers waiting to see him go to dinner. By one of those customs which, for no known reason, have developed differently in the different palaces, the door of the King's study at Marly was kept open, except during the council. There was nothing but a curtain which an usher drew back to allow entrance. This usher, when he heard the quarrel, went in and told the King that he was distinctly audible from the drawing-room, and Monsieur, too; then he immediately retired. The King's inner study opened out of the first, but with neither door nor curtain in between, and this room led into another small withdrawing-room, which had been reduced in width to make a place for the King's night-commode. The indoor footmen always stood in this inner drawing-room, so that they, too, must have heard the whole of the conversation as I have described it.

The usher's warning made them lower their voices but did not stop the recriminations, and at last, Monsieur, flying into a rage, told the King fairly that when the Duc de Chartres married he had promised him the moon and the stars and that so far all he had extracted had been a governorship. Monsieur said that he wished his son to have employment to divert him from love-affairs and that M. de Chartres also desired it keenly, as the King well knew, since he had again and again asked it as a favour. It had been refused him persistently, however, and Monsieur did not intend to prevent the young man from finding consolation in his pleasures. He added that at the time of the marriage he had justly been warned that he would get nothing but shame and contempt and reap no profit whatsoever. The King, becoming more and more furious, retorted that the war would soon make him economize and that since Monsieur had shown himself so disobliging, his pensions should go first, before the King touched his own pocket.

At that point dinner was announced and they left the room to go to table. Monsieur was scarlet, his eyes sparkling with anger, so that some of the ladies remarked that he looked in great need of bleeding. Dinner passed off as usual, Monsieur eating prodigiously as he always did at his two meals, not to mention the copious draughts of chocolate every morning and all that he swallowed at other times of day, in the way of fruit, sugar biscuits, and such titbits as filled his pockets and the drawers of the tables and cabinets. When they rose from table, the King walked out alone, and Monsieur returned at once to Saint-Cloud.

After supper that evening, the King was still in his study, with Monseigneur and the princesses, when an attaché arrived from Saint-Cloud bearing a message from M. de Chartres. He was admitted to the study, where he told the King that Monsieur had been seized with acute exhaustion at supper, but that he had been bled and now felt better and that they had given him an emetic. It appeared that he had been supping as usual with the ladies and that when the entrées were being served he had poured a glass of wine for Mme de Bouillon, had seemed to stammer something, and had pointed with his finger. He used occasionally to speak Spanish, so that some of the ladies asked what he was saying, while others cried out in alarm. It was all over in a moment and he fell down in an apoplectic fit into the arms of M. de Chartres. They carried him to his bedroom, where they shook him, walked him up and down, bled him copiously, and gave him a strong emetic, without awakening more than the faintest signs of life.

The King, who usually rallied to Monsieur's side at the smallest provocation, went instead to Mme de Maintenon's apartments and had her woken up. After spending a quarter of an hour closeted with her, he returned to his own rooms at about midnight, ordered the carriages to be harnessed, and sent the Marquis de Gesvres back to Saint-Cloud with instructions to return and wake him should Monsieur grow any worse. Then he went to bed. I think that on account of the quarrel the King suspected a plot to relieve the tension between them, and that he had gone to consult with Mme de Maintenon because he preferred to fail in the proprieties rather than be duped.

Mme de Maintenon disliked and feared Monsieur. He seldom visited her and, in spite of his nervousness and more than deferential attitude, he sometimes allowed himself a sneer at her relations with the King, thus showing that he despised her and respected public opinion. She was therefore in no hurry to urge any sign of affection towards him. Still less was she ready to encourage the King to travel through the night, lose his sleep, and witness a pathetic scene that might touch his heart and cause him to examine his conscience. She may also have hoped that if all were quickly over the King might be spared some pains.

After the King had gone to bed, one of Monsieur's pages came to say that he was now better and had sent to ask M. le Prince de Conti for some Schaffeuse water, which is excellent in cases of apoplexy. About an hour and a half later, however, an officer arrived from M. de Chartres. He woke the King, to report that the emetic had had no effect and that Monsieur was now *in extremis*. Whereupon the King rose and left for Saint-Cloud, meeting M. de Gesvres upon the road.

It is impossible to describe the tumult and disorder of that night at Marly, or the horror that reigned in that pleasure-palace of Saint-Cloud. Everyone at Marly rushed as fast as they could to Saint-Cloud, taking any carriage that came to hand, without permission or any regard for good manners. Monseigneur travelled with Madame la Duchesse, in a great state of alarm because he, too, had lately been seriously ill with an attack of indigestion. It was as much as his equerry could do to half-drag, half-carry him trembling to his coach. The King arrived shortly before three in the morning to find that Monsieur had not regained consciousness for a single moment. There had been a glimmer of life when his confesssor, le Père du Trévou, was about to say mass, but it had not lasted.

In the most awe-inspiring scenes there are often ridiculous incidents. Le Père du Trévou, at that moment had turned round and shouted into Monsieur's ear, 'Monsieur, don't you recognize your own confessor? Don't you know dear old Père du Trévou?' which made those who were least moved laugh in rather a shocking manner.

The King himself appeared much affected. He was naturally prone to weep and therefore burst into tears. Indeed, he had never had cause to do other than love Monsieur, and although they had been on bad terms for the past two months, these sad moments must have reminded him of their old affection. It may be that he blamed himself for precipitating Monsieur's death by that morning's quarrel. Perhaps he may have felt uneasy because Monsieur was his junior by two years and had seemed as healthy as himself, if not more so. He remained at Saint-Cloud long enough to hear mass at eight o'clock, then, as his brother was past human aid, Mme de Maintenon and Mme de Bourgogne persuaded him to wait no longer and they

all returned together to Marly. When he was about to leave, he
said a few kind words to M. de Chartres, both of them weeping bitterly; whereupon the young prince clasped his knees,
crying, 'Alas, Sire, what will become of me?' I have lost Monsieur, and I know that you do not love me.' The King, who was
surprised and deeply touched, embraced him and spoke most
affectionately.

After the King left, the crowd gradually melted away,
so that Monsieur, dying upon the day-bed in his study, lay
exposed to the view of the lackeys and lower servants, most of
whom were much distressed, either out of love or self-interest.
The upper servants and others who were about to lose their
situations rent the air with their cries, while the women ran
hither and thither shrieking, their hair loose, as wild as Bac-
chantes.

In the meantime, Madame, who never had much affection
or regard for her husband but felt her loss of position most
keenly, remained in her own apartments, crying out at the top
of her voice, 'No convent for me! Let no one speak to me of
convents! I will not go to a convent!' She was not out of her
senses. She remembered that by the terms of her marriage
contract she must choose between a convent and retirement at
the Château de Montargis. It may well be that she saw better
hope of escaping from the one than from the other, or else,
knowing how much cause she had to dread the King,[1] although she did not yet know the whole matter and he had
paid her the civilities usual on such occasions, she may well
have feared a convent most. When Monsieur was dead,
she immediately entered her coach with her ladies and drove to
Versailles, followed by M. and Mme la Duchesse de Chartres
and their entire households.

On the following morning, which was Friday, M. de Chartres
went to the King, who was still in bed and who spoke very
kindly, bidding him look henceforth on him as a father and
promising to protect his honour and interests and to forget all
the petty vexations of the past. He hoped that M. de Chartres
also would forget, and that these protestations of affection
would persuade him to return the love which the King offered.

[1] In letters to her aunt, the Electress of Hanover, Madame had openly criticized the
government of France, and had sneered at Mme de Maintenon, all of which the King
knew. See also Preface, p. x.

You may be sure that M. de Chartres knew how to answer in a proper spirit.

After so awe-inspiring a spectacle, such tears, such demonstrations of love, everyone believed that the remaining three days of that Marly excursion would be exceedingly dull. However, when the ladies went at midday to Mme de Maintenon's apartments on the morning after Monsieur's death, they found the King already there with Mme la Duchesse de Bourgogne, and heard them from the ante-room singing the prologues to several operas. Shortly afterwards the King perceived that Mme la Duchesse de Bourgogne was sitting in a corner of the room, looking very miserable. He seemed surprised, asked Mme de Maintenon what had upset her, and then had tried to divert her by playing with her and some ladies whom he sent for to entertain them. That was not all. When they came out from dinner, that is to say, shortly after two o'clock, only twenty-six hours after Monsieur's death, Mgr le Duc de Bourgogne invited the Duc de Montfort to play a hand of brelan. 'Brelan!' exclaimed Montfort in utter astonishment. 'You cannot have forgotten! Monsieur is not yet cold.' 'Indeed,' said the prince, 'I know it very well, but the King will have no one bored at Marly. He has ordered me to start everyone playing and to set the example myself.' They then sat down to a hand of cards and before long the drawing-room was full of gaming tables. . . .

Although it would have been hard to find anyone meeker or more submissive than Monsieur with the King, even down to flattering his ministers and mistresses of former days, he took great pains to preserve, albeit with great respect, the easy relationship of a brother when they were in private. Thus he took many liberties, for instance, he always sat boldly down in an armchair without waiting to be invited, although, after the King's supper, no other prince ever sat in the study, not even Monseigneur. Nevertheless, in public, and when he approached or left the King, no subject ever showed more profound deference, and his most casual gestures were naturally graceful and dignified. At intervals he was assiduous in attendance on the King, but never for long, and when his gambling and the upkeep of Saint-Cloud and his favourites, began to cost more money than the King allowed him, he gradually ceased to make an appearance. To Mme de Maintenon he could never bring himself to show respect, nor refrain from having a sly dig at her when speaking to the King, and an occasional sneer in public. It was not that he minded her being a favourite, but he could not tolerate the idea of La Scarron[1] being his sister-in-law.

He was intensely vain, not haughtily so, but exceedingly sensitive and proudly conscious of his rights and dignities. He was a little pot-bellied man, whose heels were so high that he seemed to walk on stilts. He decked himself out with rings, bracelets, and other jewellery like any woman, wore a long black and powdered wig, spread out in front, and ribbons everywhere. He covered himself with all manner of perfumes and was the very pattern of elegance. They said that he used a touch of rouge. A monstrous long nose, a fine mouth and eyes, a face plump, but very much on the long side; all his portraits are good likenesses. I used to be vexed at seeing them, for they reminded me of the portraits of his father Louis XIII, that great prince, whom in merit he so little resembled.

1702

Saint-Simon Leaves the Army

AFTER the Peace of Ryswick, the reorganization of the army was exceedingly thorough and most strangely conducted, for no attention was paid to the varying excellence of the different regiments, their officers or colonels. Barbezieux, the war minister, was young and impulsive and the King gave him a free hand. I myself had no personal acquaintance with him. My regiment was reformed, and, because it was a very good one, parts were allocated to the Royals and the remnants to Duras' regiment; my own company was incorporated with that of the Comte d'Uzès, Barbezieux's brother-in-law. It was no consolation to me to know that others shared my fate, for colonels of the reformed companies were placed at the bottom of the list of their new regiments, and I had been seconded to that of Saint-Mauris, a gentleman of the Franche-Comté, whom I had never seen in my life.

After a time, some colonels junior to myself were given back

---

[1] Mme de Maintenon's first marriage was to the poet Paul Scarron.

their commands, but this seemed only reasonable, since they were all veterans, who had obtained their appointments through length of service. Rumours were current about a general promotion, but I attached little importance to them, for at this time birth and rank counted for nothing and special promotions were given only for actions on the field; moreover, I had too many above me to entertain any hopes of becoming a brigadier. My whole heart, therefore, was set on having a regiment and commanding it in the campaign that was about to open, so as to avoid the humiliation of acting as a kind of supernumerary aide-de-camp to Saint-Mauris.

The general promotion was made at last and everyone was astonished at the length of the list, for nothing had ever approached it in numbers. As I eagerly searched through the names of the new cavalry brigadiers, vainly hoping to find my own, I was humiliated to see five of my juniors included in the list. My pride was so deeply hurt that I could never forget their names, Ourches, Vendeuil, Streiff, the Comte d'Ayen, and Ruffey. Nevertheless, I kept silence, for fear lest in my vexation I might say something foolish. The Maréchal de Lorges was as indignant upon my account as upon his own, and his brother-in-law[1] not less so, and they both insisted that I should leave the service. I myself felt so angry that I was greatly disposed to do so; but my age, the opening of the campaign, the thought of renouncing all ambition in my chosen profession, the boredom of idleness, the sad summers when all conversation would be of war and partings, the advancement of men who by distinguished conduct gained high rank and reputation, were all powerful deterrents. I accordingly spent two months in mental anguish, resigning from the army every morning, and every night reversing my decision.

At last, driven to an extremity of doubt, I resolved to take the advice of impartial judges, selected from different walks of life, and I chose the Maréchal de Choiseul, M. de Beauvilliers, the chancellor [Pontchartrain], and M. de La Rochefoucauld. These gentlemen already knew how I was placed and were indignant at the injustice done to me; moreover, the last three were of the Court. This was just what I wished, for I was seeking to know what would be approved by the best people, the men of substance near to the King. Above all, I sought

[1] The Maréchal de Duras.

for the kind of advice that would not leave me a prey to uncertainty, rash impulses, or afterthoughts. The verdict, given unanimously and most forcibly, was that I should leave the service. They all said that it would be a shame and indefensible for a man of my rank, who had served with honour and distinction at the head of a fine regiment, to return to battle without regiment, troops, or even a company under his command, and with no other function than to act as aide-de-camp to Saint-Mauris. They added that no duke and peer of my condition should consent to serve as a mere soldier of fortune while other and lesser men gained employment and commands.

It was with no idea of pondering their advice that I had taken them as my arbiters. My course of action was now clear; but although I knew that they were right I still hesitated, and three months passed in a torment of doubt before I could bring myself to act. Finally, I did so, and when it came to procedure, I again followed the advice of the same judges. I was very careful not to display any personal feelings, for I was content to leave to public and especially to military opinion my omission from the list of promotions. The King's anger was inevitable; my friends warned me of it, and I fully expected it. Need I say that I dreaded it? He always took offence when people left his service, calling it desertion, especially where the nobility were concerned. What really nettled him, however, was that a man should leave him for a grievance, and anyone who did so felt his displeasure for a long time, if not for ever. My friends, nevertheless, allowed no comparison between the outcome of resignation which, after all, at my age, would eventually cease to affect me, and the disgrace of continuing to serve under such conditions. At the same time, they thought that respect and prudence demanded that I should act with all possible circumspection.

Accordingly, I wrote a short letter to the King, not in any way complaining, not mentioning my disappointment nor even hinting at regiments and promotions, but merely regretting that my health obliged me to leave his service. I added that my one consolation was my devotion to his person, for I now should have the opportunity of paying my court and attending on him more continuously. My friends approved my letter, and I gave it to the King myself, on the Tuesday in Holy Week, at the door of his study, as he returned from mass. I then went straight to see Chamillart,[1] with whom I was not then acquainted. He was just leaving to go to the council, but I stopped him and told my story, without allowing my disappointment to appear in any way. I then went to Paris, at once. I had already set several of my friends, both men and women, to discover anything, no matter how trivial, that might escape the King on the subject of my letter. For eight days I stayed in Paris and only returned on Easter Tuesday, when I learned that the chancellor had found the King reading it when he went in and that he had called out angrily, 'Well, sir! Here is another deserter!' and thereupon had read my letter aloud, word by word. On that same evening of Holy Tuesday, as he came out from supper, I attended on him for the first time since he received my letter. I should indeed be ashamed of relating the following trifle were it not that, in the circumstances, it sheds light upon the King's character.

Although the dressing-room was extremely well lit, the chaplain for the day, who held the lighted candle at evening prayers, always handed it to the chief valet to carry before the King when he went to his chair. The latter would then look around the room and call out the name of one of those present and the chief valet would give him the candlestick. This was considered a favour of some importance, thanks to the King's skill in giving weight to the merest trifles. He usually presented the candlestick only to the noblest and most distinguished persons, and sometimes, but very rarely, to lesser men, when their age or position justified the honour. He often gave it to me, hardly ever to ambassadors, except to the nuncio and, latterly, to the Spanish ambassador on some occasions. One removed one's glove, one took a step forward, one held the candlestick during the time of the *coucher*, which was not long; then one handed it back to the chief valet, who selected some other person to take it for the *petit coucher*. On this particular evening, I had purposely kept in the background, and was therefore much astonished, as were the onlookers, to hear my name called. On the following days, I had the candlestick almost

---

[1] Michel Chamillart (1652–1721), at that time Minister of State and Secretary for War. Louis XIV and Mme de Maintenon were devoted to him. Saint-Simon thought him a very good friend, honourable and patriotic, but crassly stupid. He says, 'The extraordinary thing was that his very incapacity endeared him to the King. He admitted it at every step, and the King loved directing and teaching him; so much so indeed that he thought of Chamillart's successes as his own, and forgave him every blunder.'

as often as before. It was not as though many other men of high
rank were not present at that *coucher*; but the King was so much
vexed with me that he did not wish others to perceive it.

That, however, was the only favour which I received from
him for three consecutive years, and he never lost the smallest
opportunity (for want of a greater one) to make me feel how
much I had angered him. He never spoke to me nor looked at
me, except by chance. He never mentioned my letter nor the fact
that I had left his service. He no longer invited me to Marly,
and after a few excursions I ceased to give him the satisfaction
of refusing to see me there.

I must put an end to this sad tale. Fourteen or fifteen months
later, he paid a visit to Trianon, where each of the Princesses
was allowed to name two ladies to be present at his supper,
and he never interfered with that privilege. After a time, however, he grew bored with constantly seeing new faces and
took to making a list (a very short one it was) of the ladies
whom he wished to see at his evening meal. Every day he sent
the Duchesse du Lude to notify them.

This particular Trianon visit lasted from a Wednesday to a
Saturday—thus three suppers—and Mme de Saint-Simon and
I were doing as we usually did when he went to Marly, that is
to say, dining with the Chamillarts at l'Étang, with the intention of driving on to Paris to sleep. Just as we were sitting down
to table, Mme de Saint-Simon received a message from the
Duchesse du Lude, to say that she was on the King's supper list
for that day. We were much astonished and immediately returned to Versailles. Mme de Saint-Simon discovered that she
was the only lady of approaching her own age at the King's
table, although Mme de Chevreuse was there, with Mme de
Beauvilliers and the Comtesse de Gramont, as well as three
or four duenna kind of persons, the usual palace ladies, and
no others. On the Friday, she was again summoned, and
thereafter the King always sent for her on his rare visits to
Trianon. I soon discovered the reason for this distinction and it
struck me as comic. He never sent for Mme de Saint-Simon at
Marly, because there husbands had the right to attend when
their wives were invited. He intended to show me that his dis-
favour was for me alone and that my wife was not included.

None the less, we persevered in our usual attendance, but
never sought an invitation to Marly. We lived among our

friends pleasantly enough and Mme de Saint-Simon continued to enjoy all the entertainments to which the King and Mme la Duchesse de Bourgogne were in the habit of inviting her, although she might not share them with me.

I have chosen to deal with the entire subject here. It is of interest because it throws a light upon the King's nature.

1703

The Fuss over the Offertory

THE year ended with another affair in which I played a more prominent role. On certain feast-days when the King went to high mass and vespers a lady of the Court always handed round the bag for the poor. The Queen, or when there was no longer a Queen, the Dauphine, nominated the ladies for each occasion, and in the interval between the two Dauphines, Mme de Maintenon took upon herself the duty of selecting somebody. So long as there were maids of honour, one of them was invariably chosen, but after these posts were abolished, one of the young ladies of the Court was appointed, as I have explained above.

The Lorraines, whose high rank was gained solely by the exploits of their family at the time of the League, and who had adroitly maintained and improved their position by constant care and intrigue, were ever on the watch to grasp the smallest opportunity. They began stealthily to avoid the duty of handing round the bag, so as to make it their right and privilege to abstain and thus, as in their marriages, to insinuate themselves onto the level of the Princesses of the Blood. A long time passed before anyone noticed or suspected what they were at, but at last the Duchesse de Noailles, her daughter, the Duchesse de Guiche, and the Maréchale de Boufflers discovered what was happening. Others gradually began to realize and then to speak of it, and they spoke to me also. Mme de Saint-Simon happened to be in full dress at the King's vespers one day during the Feast of the Conception, when there had been no high mass and Mme la Duchesse de Bourgogne had forgotten to appoint a lady. Mme la Duchesse de Bourgogne had accordingly thrown the bag to her and she had handed it round when it was time for the collection. At that moment, we had no idea that the Lorraine princesses would make that an excuse to abstain when their turns came.

After I had been warned, I determined that the other duchesses should be equally crafty until the occasion arrived to make things level. The Duchesse de Noailles spoke to the Duchesse du Lude, but she, being weak and frightened of everything, merely shrugged her shoulders. There was always some new and ignorant, or poor-spirited, duchess ready to collect from time to time. At last, the Duchesse du Lude was fairly hunted by Mme de Noailles until she agreed to speak to Mme la Duchesse de Bourgogne, who herself resolved to see just how far the Lorraine princesses intended to go. Accordingly, at the next feast-day, she had Mme de Montbazon[1] notified. This lady was young, pretty, often at the Court, and in every way fit to give the lead to others, but she happened to be in Paris, where it was the fashion to go before the Christmas holidays. She sent her excuses, saying that she was ill, although in fact she was perfectly well, spent half a day in bed, and then went about as usual. After that, nothing more was needed to show the plot. The Duchesse du Lude dared not pursue the matter further, nor did Mme la Duchesse de Bourgogne, although she was piqued, but the result was that from that time onwards no duchess had either will or courage to collect. The other ladies of suitable rank then perceived what was on foot. They felt that the duty of collecting was being left entirely to them and they, too, began to avoid it, so that after a time it fell into all sorts of hands and was sometimes altogether omitted.

The matter was pushed until eventually the King grew so angry that he was on the point of making Mme la Duchesse de Bourgogne take the bag round herself. This I heard from the palace ladies, who wished to prevent us going to Paris, and tried to frighten me by saying that the King had not forgiven me for leaving the service and that the storm would break over my head. Indeed, I was still not going to Marly and was still in the same position regarding him as I have earlier described. They then flattered me by saying that this might well prove to

---

[1] The Duc de Montbazon was a Rohan, which family claimed precedence, with the foreign princes, above French dukes.

be my opportunity. I consented to stay on condition that my wife was not required to collect, but since no such assurance could be given me, we went to Paris. The Maréchale de Cœuvres next refused, on the grounds that she was a grandee of Spain, and the Duchesse de Noailles sent her daughter as a substitute. On another feast-day Chamillart's two daughters,[1] both duchesses, were appointed and both refused although they were unable to leave Versailles. Then the rocket went up.

The King had been exasperated by all this intriguing. He ordered Monsieur le Grand [Louis de Lorraine] to make his daughter collect in church on the first day of the new year, 1704. Early next day I was warned by the Comtesse de Roucy, who had been told by Mme la Duchesse de Bourgogne, who was present at the time, that the King had gone to Mme de Maintenon looking very grave, saying that he was extremely vexed with the dukes because they showed less obedience than the princes, and that although none of the duchesses would collect, Monsieur le Grand had consented for his daughter as soon as he was asked. He added that there were two or three dukes, whose behaviour he would never forget. Mme la Duchesse de Bourgogne would not name them out loud, but whispered to Mme de Dangeau and a moment later begged her to warn me to be careful. This we heard at the chancellor's house, he being a third party to the conversation, and neither of us had any doubt that I was one of the three dukes mentioned. I then told them what had happened and asked the chancellor for his advice, which was to do nothing whilst I was still in the dark.

Very early next day I went to see Chamillart. He told me that at Mme de Maintenon's apartment on the previous evening, even before he had had time to open his portfolio, the King had asked him angrily what he thought of dukes who were less dutiful than princes, and had added hastily that Mlle d'Armagnac[2] had agreed to take the collection. Chamillart replied that such matters never reached his department and that he had only heard of the affair on the evening before. He knew, he said, that the dukes were distressed because the King blamed them for not guessing his wishes, and that the princes were delighted at

---

[1] The Duchesses de la Feuillade and de Quintin-Lorges; the latter was Saint-Simon's sister-in-law. He was very fond of her and used to call her 'ma grande biche' (my big sweetheart).

[2] Charlotte de Lorraine, demoiselle d'Armagnac, daughter of Monsieur le Grand.

receiving credit for what the dukes would gladly have done had the King spoken as frankly to them as he had done to Monsieur le Grand.

The King then muttered to himself and said that it was very strange, but since I had left his service I thought only of my rank and privileges and of picking quarrels with everybody; that I was the chief instigator of this pother, and that he had a good mind to send me so far that I should be prevented from annoying him for a long time to come. Chamillart answered that I concerned myself in such matters because I was abler and more intelligent than the rest, and that since the King himself had granted me my rank and precedence he should be pleased to see me striving to maintain them. Then, smiling a little, he had added soothingly that of course the King could send anyone where he pleased, but that it seemed scarcely worth while when a single word would have the desired effect. This did not mollify the King. He merely answered that what had annoyed him most of all was the refusal of Chamillart's daughters-in-law (especially the younger), through their husbands and apparently at my suggestion. To this Chamillart replied that one of his sons was absent and the other had merely made his wife conform. The King, however, still went on grumbling until at last they settled down to work. Chamillart advised me to speak to the King at the earliest possible opportunity about the dukes' point of view regarding the church collections, and then to say something on my own behalf.

After I left Chamillart, I went to consult the chancellor. He too advised me to see the King without delay. He said that to wait would merely increase his irritation, and that in speaking to him I must be careful not to get angry. He bade me have faith in the outcome, ask for an interview in the study, and if the King stopped and wished to hear me then and there, to say that I could see he did not wish to grant me an audience then, that I hoped it might be for another time, and instantly retire. It was indeed no small matter for me, young and out of favour, as I was, to go and engage the King in conversation.

I usually did nothing without the advice of the Duc de Beauvilliers. Mme de Saint-Simon, however, did not wish me to hear it now, for she was sure that he would tell me to write, which would have been less tactful and less effective than speaking; besides which, letters are never answered. She also thought that Beauvilliers' advice might embarrass me if it were contrary to that of the two ministers. I agreed, and went to wait for the King to pass on his way from dinner to his study, where I asked permission to follow him. Without answering, he made a sign for me to enter and walked over to one of the window-recesses.

Just as I was about to speak, I saw Fagon[1] and other members of the household crossing the room, so I waited until they had gone and I was alone with the King. Then I told him that I had heard he was vexed with me in the matter of the church collection, that I was deeply anxious to please him and could not bear to delay in entreating him to hear my side. At this he looked very stern and said nothing. 'Sire,' I continued, 'it is true that after the princesses had refused to hand the bag, I avoided the duty for Mme de Saint-Simon in the hope that all the duchesses would abstain, and some of them, indeed, I prevented, thinking that would be Your Majesty's desire.' 'But,' interrupted the King angrily, 'refusing the Duchesse de Bourgogne is failing in respect. It is refusing Us!' I answered that the manner in which the ladies were appointed gave us reason to believe that Mme la Duchesse de Bourgogne had no hand in the matter, and that the Duchesse du Lude or, more frequently, the first gentlewoman-in-waiting chose whom she pleased. 'But, Monsieur,' the King again interrupted in the same haughty, angry tone, 'you have been speechifying, have you not?' 'No, Sire.' 'What? Are you saying that you have not talked? . . .' And he ran on in this furious manner until I, also, had the courage to interrupt in a voice louder than his own. 'No, Sire,' I said, 'I have already explained, and had I said any such things I should have told Your Majesty, just as I have admitted avoiding the collection for my wife and preventing the other duchesses. I always believed, and with good reason, that since Your Majesty expressed no wishes in this matter, you were either ignorant of what was happening, or knowing, did not care. Let me entreat you most earnestly to believe that had any of the dukes, more especially myself, any reason to think that Your Majesty desired it in the very least, all the duchesses would have been eager to take the collection, and Mme de Saint-Simon with them, on all feast-days. If that were not enough to show my anxiety to please you, I would gladly have handed the bag myself, like any country churchwarden.

[1] The King's doctor.

'How, Sire,' I continued, 'could Your Majesty suppose that
we should think any duty beneath us that was performed in
your presence, especially one which the duchesses and princesses do every day in the Paris churches, as a matter of course?
The truth is, Sire, that the princes are so quick to snatch special
privileges that we are obliged to be on the watch, particularly
in this matter of refusing to hand round the bag.' 'But they did
not refuse,' said the King, somewhat mollified, 'they were never
asked.' 'Indeed, Sire,' I answered stoutly, 'they did refuse.
Not the Lorraines, but others (by whom I meant Mme de
Montbazon). The Duchesse du Lude may have informed you,
or she should have done so, for that was what decided us to act.
We know that Your Majesty is plagued by discussion and decisions and we hoped that our evading the collection would
suffice to prevent the princes from taking an advantage. As I
have already said, Sire, we believed that Your Majesty neither
knew nor cared since you made no sign.' 'Oh! very well,
Monsieur,' said the King quietly. 'The matter will not arise
again because I have already told Monsieur le Grand that I
wish his daughter to collect on New Year's Day, and I am
glad that she sets the example, for I love her father well.'

Then, looking straight at the King, I entreated him, for my
own sake and that of the other dukes, to believe that he had no
more dutiful subjects than ourselves. For we knew that all our
dignities came from him and that all our lives were enriched
by his bounty. He was our King and universal benefactor, the
absolute master of our ranks and privileges; it was for him alone
to raise or lower them, to treat them as his own, in the hollow
of his hand. Then, most graciously, with an air wholly kind
and gentle, he said several times that that was a very proper way
of thinking and speaking, and that he was well pleased with me.
I seized the occasion to tell him how much it grieved me that
no matter how hard I tried to please him, some people never
failed to do me the worst of ill turns, which I confessed I
could not forgive. I added that I could not help but suspect
Monsieur le Grand, for he had not forgiven me since the affair
of the Princesse d'Harcourt.[1] 'But,' I said, 'Your Majesty saw
then that I spoke the truth, whereas Monsieur le Grand did

[1] There had already been a quarrel about precedence between the Princesse d'Harcourt
(a Lorraine) and the Duchesse de Rohan, in which Mme de Saint-Simon had innocently
become involved.

not. I think that Your Majesty remembers, so I shall not weary you by repetition.'

The King answered that he remembered perfectly, and I believe that he would have listened to me patiently had I repeated the story, for his manner was both kind and considerate, but I did not think it wise to detain him any longer. I therefore concluded by imploring him to be so gracious as to tell me if ever he heard ill spoken of me, for he would see that such a favour would be followed by a justification, or else by a confession and a plea for forgiveness. After I had finished speaking, he remained silent for a moment, as though waiting to see whether I wished to say more. Then he left me with a slight, but most gracious bow, saying that all was now well and that he was satisfied. I retired, bowing very low, feeling mightily relieved and at the same time most thankful that I had managed to put the whole matter before him, about the dukes, the princes, and especially about Monsieur le Grand. The fact that the King remembered the affair of the Princesse d'Harcourt and his silence over Monsieur le Grand convinced me that it was to the latter I owed what I had once again circumvented.

As I left the King's study looking well content, I encountered Monsieur le Duc and some other gentlemen waiting to attend at the King's *botter*.[1] They stared hard as I passed, for they were surprised by the length of my audience, which had lasted for half an hour. It was exceedingly rare for private persons to be granted any audience at all, and none lasted more than half the time of mine. I then went to my apartment and relieved Mme de Saint-Simon of her anxiety.

1703

Madame de Charlus

THE Marquise de Charlus, Mézières's sister, and mother of the Marquis de Levis, who has since been created duke and peer, died old and rich. She always got herself up like an old-clothes woman and encountered many snubs because people failed to recognize her, which she thought monstrously ill-bred. As a

[1] The ceremony of putting on the King's boots.

relief from more serious matters, I propose to tell an anecdote
about her of a very different kind.

Mme de Charlus was greedy and a great gambler. She used
to spend whole nights wildly doubling against increasing odds,
for at that time they played lansquenet for high stakes, at the
house of Mme la Princesse de Conti, the sister of Monsieur le
Prince. One Friday night, Mme de Charlus was supping there
with a large company. She was ill-dressed as usual, but for once,
most fashionably, wearing one of those headdresses called com-
modes, that were not fastened in any way to the ladies' heads.
They were vastly high constructions and were removed or put
on just as men take off and put on their wigs and nightcaps.

Mme de Charlus was sitting next to Le Tellier, the Archbishop of Rheims. As she was removing the top of a boiled egg,
she leaned forward to take the salt and accidentally stuck her
head into the flame of a neighbouring candle. The Archbishop, seeing her on fire, hurled himself at the headdress and
flung it to the ground, whereupon Mme de Charlus, in amazement and fury at finding herself thus dis-wigged for no
apparent reason, threw her egg into the Archbishop's face, and
it ran down all over him. He did nothing but laugh, and the
entire company was in fits at seeing the ancient grey, dirty head
of Mme de Charlus, and the omelet she had made on the Archbishop. Especially comic was her rage and abuse, for she imagined that she had been insulted and would hear no excuse,
and then suddenly perceived that she had been left bald before
all the world. By this time, the headdress had been burnt and
Mme la Princesse de Conti had sent for another, but before it
could be placed upon her head there was plenty of time to contemplate her charms, and for her to continue with her furious
protests.

Gambling was again forbidden, under threat of severe
penalties.

1704

Saint-Simon is Bled

About this time I met with an unfortunate accident and allowed
myself to be bled because the blood was rushing to my head.

The operation seemed to me vastly well done. During the night, however, I felt a pain in my arm which Ledran, the well-known surgeon, who had performed the blood-letting, assured me was due to a tight bandage. To make a long story short, in two days' time the arm had swollen bigger than my thigh and I was in great pain and feverish. They kept me for two days longer with applications over the wound to draw out the poison, following the advice of the most renowned Paris surgeons. M. de Lauzun, rightly thinking that I was very ill indeed, insisted upon my seeing Maréchal, the King's surgeon, and himself went to Versailles to ask the King's permission, for without it Maréchal could not come to Paris and rarely slept away from the King. He was allowed to come and to spend the night and even to remain with me, and as soon as he arrived, he opened the arm from end to end. It was high time, for the abscess had spread to the body and was manifesting itself by fits of snivering. Maréchal stayed for two days, then came to see me every day, and afterwards, every two days. The skill and speed with which he performed the operation and dressings, and the pains he took to make me comfortable, pass all description. He made this accident an excuse to speak to the King on my behalf, who overwhelmed me with kindness after my recovery. A short time before this happened, Chamillart had managed to mend matters somewhat between us and what Maréchal said finally healed the breach.

On the day that I was bled I had strained my arm slightly, to which I attributed my accident, and during the course of the operation I asked Ledran to bleed me again, so that I might not lose the use of it. Maréchal and Fagon thought that a tendon might have been damaged, but they put weights upon my arm so that it remained its natural length and I felt no ill-effects. Every day and night the best surgeons of Paris were by my bed, relieving one another by turns. Tribouleau, surgeon to the French guards and a man with a high reputation, said that he supposed M. de Marsan[1] must be a dear friend of mine, for he had stopped him in the street to inquire after me and seemed greatly concerned to hear every detail. The fact was that he was after my governorship [of Blaye] and had actually applied for it; but the King asked him whether I had no son, which silenced and embarrassed him. Chamillart, in case I

[1] Chevalier de Lorraine-Armagnac, Comte de Marsan.

should not recover, had secured the post for my son without being asked, and lost no time in doing so. I afterwards pretended to know nothing of M. de Marsan's manœuvre. In any case I had no truck with him, nor with any of the Lorraines.

1704

The Grignan Family

I HAVE lost a friend who shared my upbringing, a man of honour and great promise. He was the only son of the Comte de Grignan and of that Mme de Grignan, who is the daughter so constantly praised in Mme de Sévigné's famous letters, which would be perfect did they not eternally harp on that one theme.

The Comte de Grignan (Chevalier de l'Ordre in 1688) was ruined by his service in Provence, where he had been only lieutenant-general. He and his wife therefore arranged a marriage for their son with the daughter of an immensely rich fermier-général.[1] When Mme de Grignan presented her daughter-in-law in society, she apologized for the marriage in her mincing, simpering fashion, casting languishing glances out of her little eyes and saying that from time to time it became positively necessary to manure even the best soil. She appeared hugely delighted with this witticism, although most people rightly thought it ill-bred, since she had made the match herself, and especially as she said it almost aloud in her daughter-in-law's presence.

Saint-Amans, the girl's father, who had accommodated them in all their debts, eventually heard the remark and was so much offended that he turned off the tap, but his unhappy daughter was none the better for that. She did not have long to suffer, however, for her husband, who distinguished himself at the battle of Hochstedt, died early in October at Thionville, of what was reported to be the smallpox. He already had command of a regiment and was about to be promoted. His widow was left childless and a saint, the saddest, quietest saint that I ever met. She shut herself up in her house and spent the rest of her life, perhaps a matter of twenty years, never going out, except to church, and seeing nobody.

[1] Arnaud de Saint-Amans.

1704

Sketch of Puysieux

HE was a little man, vastly stout and rather hunch-backed, but full of intelligence, character and fun; entirely gay, gentle, courteous, honourable, and the best of good fellows. He was also very learned, with excellent taste and much humility; an admirable companion, with a fund of amusing anecdotes. Everyone liked him. He served his country as best he could, but M. de Louvois took a dislike to him and pulled him up short in his career. He became a maréchal de camp[1] after having been governor of Huningen and was on excellent terms with the King, who always remembered his grandmother[2] with affection for the good times that he had had as a boy, playing in her home among her grandchildren. After the death of Louvois, Puysieux served in Alsace and was eventually promoted to lieutenant-general. He then found the Swiss embassy available and admirably suited to him. He obtained the post through M. de La Rochefoucauld and did marvellously well there. When, at intervals, he returned to France, the privilege of old acquaintance with the King and M. de La Rochefoucauld secured him private audiences, such as were never granted to other ambassadors. Indeed, Torcy was the only other minister whom M. de La Rochefoucauld treated on terms of intimate friendship. All these preliminaries are necessary in order to understand what follows.

Puysieux, arriving home on leave from Switzerland after the Court had returned from Fontainebleau, was most amiably received by His Majesty. He was in high spirits and because he knew the King well, thought that he would boldly try his luck. When therefore the King expressed affection for him and commended him on his work, he asked whether His Majesty were really pleased, or merely making an official speech. On the assurance that every word was meant, Puysieux assumed a quizzical expression and said that for his part he could not be equally satisfied with His Majesty. 'Puysieux, why not?' said the King. 'Why, Sire? Because although I am the most honest

---

[1] *Maréchal de camp*, a rank now obsolete, equivalent to brigadier-general.
[2] Mme de Puysieux, a great friend of the Queen-Mother.

man in your kingdom, you do not mind breaking your promise
to me these fifty years.' 'How, Puysieux?', said the King,
'How do you make that out?' 'Sire,' said Puysieux, 'you have
a long memory, you cannot have forgotten. Does not Your
Majesty remember that when I had the honour of playing
blindman's buff with you at my grandmother's, you put
your blue ribbon on my shoulder so that you should not be
recognized, and when I returned it, you promised me one for
myself when you became master? It is a long time now since
you have been master, no doubt of that, but I am still waiting
for my blue ribbon.' The King remembered, began to laugh,
admitted that Puysieux was perfectly right, and said that he
would keep his word and would call a special meeting of the
Order before the end of the year, so that Puysieux might be
admitted before New Year's Day. Indeed, that very day, he
appointed a date for the meeting, announcing that it was to be
for Puysieux.

This was not important, but it was an amusing thing to have
happened. It was most extraordinary with a prince as grave and
dignified as Louis XIV. Such little anecdotes about the Court
do have their interest.

1705

The Masks

LIEUTENANT-GÉNÉRAL BOULIGNEUX and Maréchal de Camp
Wartigny were both killed at the siege of Verua.[1] They were
very gallant officers, but most sinister characters.

During the previous winter, several portrait-masks had been
made of the people at Court. They were worn under other
masks, and when the time came to uncover people mistook the
second mask for the face; yet all the time the person's real
face was underneath. It was a good trick and caused much
amusement. The following winter, when they wished to repeat
the joke, it was found to the general amazement that, whereas
the other masks had remained as fresh and life-like as when they
were packed away after the carnival, the masks of Bouligneux
and Wartigny were pale and haggard as though moulded from
the dead body.

[1] A town on the River Po, besieged at the end of 1704.

ANNE-MARIE DE BOURBON, PRINCESSE DE CONTI

From a portrait by an unknown artist at Versailles

RAISING THE MILITIA: 22 December 1705

See page 103

Bibliothèque Nationale

They were seen like this at a ball, and so horrified every-body that an attempt was made to improve them with rouge; but the rouge faded instantly, and the haggard look could not be removed. This incident seems to me so extraordinary that I think it worth mentioning. I should have been very careful about reporting it had not the entire Court also witnessed several times, with intense astonishment, this most strange phenomenon. In the end, those two masks were destroyed.

1705

Calamity to Fargues

MME DE LAMOIGNON (for the 'de' has been adopted by many successful magistrates who only lately were earning their livings at the bar), Mme de Lamoignon, I say, was a Potier, daughter of secretary of state Ocquerre, brother to that Bishop of Beauvais who for a short time after the death of Louis XIII hoped to become prime minister, but was driven out by Mazarin. She was the mother of Lamoignon, president of the high court in Paris; of Baville, the administrator, or rather, the king of Languedoc; of Mme de Broglie, and of the late wife of Harlay.

Lamoignon, her son, handsome, agreeable, and vastly know-ledgeable about society and the latest intrigues at Court, with every apparent good quality, had shone in the post of maître des requêtes. His charm, amiability, and the pains he took to make himself popular with bar and bench, his liberal hospitality, so different from the stinginess of his predecessors, his polite-ness to men of learning, whom he asked to his house on certain days and honoured, whatever their birth, won him a reputation which still endures and has been of good service to his children. None the less, it must be said that the corruption in his office dates from his time and has continued ever since. As for the man's real character I shall relate one story concerning him because it is both true and revealing.

There was once a great hunt from Saint-Germain. In those days the deer were hunted with hounds, not driven by beaters, and the great paraphernalia of hounds, horses, huntsmen,

E

grooms, relays, and rides cut through the forests, were still unknown. On this occasion, the hunt led towards Dourdan, and
lasted so long that the King returned home very late, leaving the
others still following. The Comte de Guiche, the Comte (later
Duc) du Lude, Vardes, M. de Lauzun (from whom I had the
story), and some other gentlemen, became separated from the
rest and when darkness fell, realized that they were lost. Urging
their tired horses towards a distant light, they at last arrived at
the door of a kind of château. They knocked, they shouted, they
called out their names, they begged for hospitality. It was
towards the end of autumn, between ten and eleven at night.
The door was opened, the master of the house himself came
out to greet them, saw to it that their boots were removed,
that they were warmed, their horses led off to the stables, and,
in the meantime, had a supper prepared for them, which they
badly needed. The meal was not long in coming, and when it
appeared, was excellent, as was the wine of several different
varieties. The host was courteous and considerate, neither formal nor gushing, but in everything with the air and manners of
the highest society. They learned that he was called Fargues,
and his house, Courson; that he had lived retired from society
for several years past; that he sometimes entertained friends,
but was a bachelor, without children. His staff of servants
seemed well-trained and the whole house had an appearance of
modest wealth and comfort.

After they had supped Fargues led them straight to bedrooms where they were all most comfortably lodged, each man
with a room to himself, and Fargues's valets attended to their
wants. Being very tired they slept late next morning. As soon
as they were dressed, they found an excellent breakfast ready
prepared for them and when they left the table their horses
were saddled and waiting, and as much refreshed as themselves. Fargues's civility and his kind welcome touched all their
hearts, so that before setting off for Saint-Germain, they made
offers to do him every possible service.

These gentlemen were the élite of the Court, the very flower
of chivalry, and all were favourites with the King. Their absence
caused much talk, and their night's adventures still more
after their return. They told the King of the marvels of their
reception and were loud in praise of the master of the house,
his table, home, and servants. The King asked his name, and

when he learned it, said, 'What! Is Fargues so close to us here?'
The courtiers redoubled their praises and the King said no
more, but going in to the Queen-Mother he repeated the story,
whereupon they both concluded that Fargues was monstrously
bold to live so near the Court, and that it was indeed strange
that he should have been there so long without their knowledge.

At the time of the Fronde, Fargues had played a prominent
part in all the plots against the Court and Cardinal Mazarin.
That he had not been hanged was not for want of the desire to
punish him, but because he had been protected by his party and
explicitly included in the general amnesty. At the same time,
he had aroused considerable hatred, which he fully expected to
cause his death, and had thought it more prudent to avoid further offence by leaving Paris and retiring to his country house
where, until then, he had lived unnoticed. Cardinal Mazarin was
dead, old offences were forgotten, but as a marked man, he
feared some new accusation and therefore lived very quietly, at
peace with his neighbours, secure in the knowledge that his
past was protected by the terms of the amnesty.

The King and the Queen-Mother, however, had pardoned him
only because their hands were forced. They sent for Lamoignon
and required him to pick secretly into Fargues's life and conduct, and to examine well in case some means might be found
of punishing his past insolence and causing him to repent of
flaunting his comfortable life so near the Court. They told
Lamoignon of the hunting misadventure through which his
whereabouts had become known, and expressed an ardent desire for some legal method by which he might be destroyed.

Greedy for gain and an excellent courtier, Lamoignon resolved
to give them every satisfaction and glean something for himself into the bargain. He made inquiries, verified facts, and
sifted so diligently and so fine that he managed to implicate
Fargues in a murder, committed in Paris when the troubles
were at their height. Thereupon he had him secretly indicted
and, one morning, sent officers to arrest him and take him to the
Conciergerie. Fargues, very certain that he had done nothing
in the slightest degree reprehensible since the general pardon,
was much astonished; but he was even more so when he learned
the matter at his interrogation. He defended himself ably
against his accusers, pleading that the said murder had been
committed in Paris itself during the revolt, and that the amnesty,

which had wiped out all memory of those days, covered many things that could not be enumerated in the case of every individual, following the usual and hitherto never-questioned custom with general pardons.

The distinguished gentlemen who had received so much kindness from this unfortunate made every kind of representation both with his judges and with the King, but all in vain. Fargues's head was very promptly cut off, his property was confiscated and given, by way of reward, to First President Lamoignon, which suited that gentleman admirably for it became the portion of his second son, Administrator Baville. From Baville to Courson is less than one league.

1705

Singular Character of Ninon, called de l'Enclos

NINON, the famous courtesan, who called herself Mlle de l'Enclos when age had forced her out of business, is a shining example of the triumph of vice, when directed with intelligence and redeemed by a little virtue. The disturbances that she made, and worse, the dissipations into which she led the noblest and most brilliant young men of her day, taxed even the patience of the Queen-Mother, who was usually very lenient (not without good reason) to persons of easy and more than easy virtue. Finally she commanded her to retire into a convent. An officer of the Paris police brought the lettre de cachet, which Ninon read, noticing that no particular Order was mentioned. 'Monsieur,' she said, quite undismayed, 'the Queen has had the immense goodness to allow me to choose my cloister. Pray tell her that I should prefer to live with the Franciscan monks in their Paris monastery,' and she handed him back the letter with a sweeping curtsey. The policeman was struck dumb by the brazen impudence of the reply, but the Queen wa sso much amused that she left her in peace.

Ninon always had crowds of adorers but never more than one lover at a time, and when she tired of the present occupier, she said so frankly and took another. Yet such was the authority of this wanton, that no man dared to fall out with his successful rival; he was only too happy to be allowed to visit as a familiar friend. She sometimes remained faithful to one lover, if he pleased her greatly, for the entire duration of a campaign.

La Chastre boasted that he was one of those favoured few, when he set off for the wars. But apparently Ninon had made no definite promise, for he was foolish enough (indeed he was very foolish, and presumptuous into the bargain) to ask her to give it him in writing, which she did and he crowed over the paper. But the promise that it contained was ill-kept, and every time that she slipped, 'Oh! the note!' she cried. 'Oh! La Chastre's dear little note!' In the end, her new lover asked what she meant. She explained; he repeated; and La Chastre was overwhelmed with ridicule, which pursued him even to his post in the army.

Ninon made friends among the great in every walk of life, had wit and intelligence enough to keep them and, what is more, to keep them friendly with one another, or at least not openly at loggerheads. Everything about her was done with seemliness and that outward show of modesty, which is often lacking, even with high-born princesses in their frailties. For this reason, she numbered among her acquaintances the noblest and most fastidious men at Court, so that it became the fashion to be received at her house. Indeed it was much to be desired, because useful connections were formed there. There was never any gaming, nor vulgar laughter, nor quarrelling, nor mocking at religion and politics; but much witty, polished talk of matters old and new and of the latest love-affairs, and all without scandal-mongering, for the tone was always light, well-mannered, and restrained. She knew how to begin a conversation and was well able to maintain one, because she was intelligent and well-versed in the affairs of every period.

The respect (strange to relate) and the number and quality of her friends and acquaintances did not diminish when she no longer attracted society by her beauty, and when good taste and changing fashion forbade her to unite physical with spiritual charms. She knew all the intrigues of the old Court and the new, both serious and otherwise. Her conversation was a delight, not self-centred but loyal, secret, safe to the last degree. Indeed it may truly be said that, frailty excepted, she was full of goodness and integrity. She often placed her purse and credit at the service of her friends and entered into important negotiations on their behalf, very honestly keeping the considerable monies and secrets which they entrusted to her. All of which caused her to be held in an esteem and respect, altogether remarkable.

She had been an intimate friend of Mme de Maintenon when the latter was living in Paris. This lady did not like her to be mentioned in her presence, but dared not disown her, and wrote cordial letters to her from time to time, until the day of her death. L'Enclos, as Ninon called herself after she abandoned the profession of her youth which was protracted, was not so distant with her old friends, and when she was strongly interested in anyone or anything (which she was judicious enough to make a rare event) she wrote to Mme de Maintenon, who obliged her promptly and efficiently. After the latter grew so great, they met but seldom, and then in secret.

L'Enclos was wonderfully quick at repartee. Two remarks, especially, which she made to the Maréchal de Choiseul, will never be forgotten. The first was an admirable rebuke; the second is a sketch from life. Choiseul, one of her oldest friends, had in his youth been gallant and handsome. He had fallen out of favour with M. de Louvois and was complaining of his ill-fortune when, in spite of the minister, the King gave him the Order in the general promotion of 1688. Choiseul did not in the least expect it, although he was nobly born and one of the best of the lieutenant-generals. He was therefore highly delighted and could be seen gazing at himself in the mirrors, decked in his blue ribbon. L'Enclos found him doing so on one or two occasions and at last lost patience. 'Monsieur le Comte,' she said loudly before the whole company, 'if I catch you doing that again, I shall tell you the names of your fellow-members.' And indeed some members of the Order were enough to make one weep, yet even they were better by birth and character than some of those made in 1724, and later.

This Maréchal was the very pattern of virtue, but he was dull company and not over-intelligent. After one very long visitation, l'Enclos yawned, looked at him, and then exclaimed: 'Oh, God! How you do make me hate virtue!' which is a line from some comedy or other, I forget the name.[1] You may imagine the laughter and the tittle-tattle. None the less, even this sally did not provoke a quarrel between them.

[1] See Corneille: *La Mort de Pompée*, III, iv, 1072.

L'Enclos lived to be well over eighty, sound in mind and body to the end and much sought after and respected. Her last years she gave to God, and her death made news. I have spread myself upon her portrait because she was a very remarkable woman.

1705

Raising the Militia

THE losses in Germany and Italy, greater in the hospitals than on the field of battle, made the authorities resolve to increase each company by five men and to raise a levy of twenty-five thousand militiamen. By so doing they brought much poverty and distress to the provinces. The King was fooled into believing that the people were willing and eager to enlist by being shown a few hand-picked samples, two, four, and five men, whom he passed on his way to mass at Marly. He was told stories of the men's cheerfulness and valour. I heard such tales myself, more than once, and I heard the King later repeat them in self-congratulation. Yet, from my personal knowledge of my own estate and from what I heard people say there, I knew the despair that this levy was causing, even to the point when men were mutilating themselves in order to gain exemption. There was weeping and crying out loud that they were being taken to their deaths, and indeed it was true, for nearly all had been sent to Italy and none had ever returned. Everyone at Court knew the truth. They looked another way when they heard the lies and saw the King's credulity, and afterwards whispered to one another what they thought of this outrageous flattery.

At the same time permission was given to raise a number of new regiments, and a vast crowd of new colonels and their staffs had to be paid for, which was a very great error. Instead of new battalions and squadrons being added to existing regiments, so that they became imbued with the regimental traditions, there was the disadvantage of having raw troops formed into small regiments, which were promptly destroyed, simply because they were small.

1706

The Embassy to Rome

FOR the past five years, Cardinal de Janson had been in charge of the King's affairs in Rome. He had filled the post with dignity, although more like a good Frenchman than a cardinal, which had pleased neither the Pope nor his Court. Indeed, he had not been on good terms with the Pope, and was thoroughly disapproved of by the Court, which always expects obedience from everybody. Cardinal de Janson had been seriously ill for some time and had been asking for leave to return, which was finally granted him, but there being no suitable cardinal to replace him, the Abbé de la Trémoïlle was made chargé d'affaires after his departure, for want of a better man. Then came the question of sending an ambassador as soon as possible, for none had been appointed since the Duc de Chaulnes's sudden mission to attend the election of a new Pope, after the death of Innocent XI.

It was the Nuncio Gualterio who first broached the subject to me. He was a Frenchman at heart and it was of great importance to him to be able to rely upon the friendship of the French Ambassador. But I was only thirty years of age at that time, and the idea of my being appointed an ambassador seemed utterly fantastic, in view of the King's known aversion to young men and his determination never to employ them. Callières, the King's secretary, also mentioned it, and I said the same to him, pointing out the difficulty of having any success in Rome without becoming a bankrupt in the process, and adding that in my situation the embassy was unlikely to bring further promotion.

On Tuesday, March 11th, just eight days after the nuncio had spoken, about one o'clock in the afternoon, he entered my room with arms outstretched, beaming with pleasure and, hugging and kissing me, he begged me to lock the door and the door of the ante-room as well, lest anyone should notice his liveries. He then informed me that he was as glad as could be, because I was indeed about to be appointed ambassador to Rome. I made him repeat this twice, for I could not believe my ears, and I told him that his wish must be father to his thought, because the whole thing seemed to me impossible. He then joyfully and impatiently swore me to secrecy, saying that Torcy had just told him in confidence that the thing had been decided at that morning's council, but that the King had forbidden him to announce it until after the next meeting. If one of the portraits in my study had opened its lips to speak, I could not have been more surprised. Gualterio did all that he could to persuade me to consent; then, it being time for the dinner to which he was bidden, he left me and I went instantly to tell the news to Mme de Saint-Simon, who was as much amazed as myself.

I must admit to feeling flattered at being chosen so unexpectedly, at my age, and for so important a post, for no one had recommended me, and at that time I had no acquaintance, not even the slightest, with Torcy. M. de Beauvilliers was far too cautious to have proposed me without first ascertaining whether my circumstances would permit the expense, the chancellor was out of range, and Chamillart would have done nothing without my consent, besides which, being on none too good terms with Torcy, he would never have risked interfering in his department.

After the King's death, Torcy and I became firm friends, so that I was able to ask him how I came to be chosen. He protested that he was ignorant of the matter, save that at the time of the Council the King had already decided to send someone, and was weary of aspirants for a dukedom which he did not intend to create. He had interrupted Torcy as soon as the latter had begun to read the dispatches from Rome, saying that the time had come to appoint an envoy, that he wanted a duke, and that all that remained to do was to read down the list until he came to a suitable name. He then took a small almanac and began to read out the names. My seniority soon brought him to mine, whereat he paused and said, 'What about this one? He is young, but he is capable, etc.' Monseigneur wished for d'Antin and therefore said nothing, but M. le Duc de Bourgogne supported me, and so did the chancellor and M. de Beauvilliers. Torcy commended their judgment, but suggested continuing down the list. Chamillart thought no one better could be found. The King thereupon closed the almanac, saying that there seemed little point in pursuing the matter further since he had already

E*

decided on me, and he ordered them to say nothing for the time being, until he should desire them to have me informed. That was all that happened. Torcy went on reading his dispatches, and there was no more argument. This was told me more than ten years later by that honest man, who had no possible reason for concealing anything.

Beauvilliers and Chamillart each separately examined my circumstances, debts and revenues as compared to the expenses and emoluments of an embassy. The former they learned from our account books, which Mme de Saint-Simon fetched and considered with them; the rest they computed by guesswork. Both gentlemen concluded that I should accept. The duke was satisfied that I could afford the post without being ruined and said further, that if I refused it, especially after having left the service, the King would never forgive me. He would henceforward regard me as an idler by preference, would be sure to make me feel his displeasure on every possible occasion, and would refuse me things that I might really need. All of which would be more harmful to my interests, present and future, than any failure in an embassy.

In the end they did so persuade me, and I accepted. That is to say, I resolved to accept, and with great pleasure, as I am bound to admit. As for Mme de Saint-Simon, wiser and more prudent than I, and sad at the idea of separation from her family, she also gave her consent, but less gladly. Here I cannot deny myself the pleasure of relating what these three ministers, each separately and of their own accord, said to me of that young woman of twenty-seven (as she then was), whom they had known well in Court and family affairs, for they had been our advisers at every step of our married lives. They all three most earnestly counselled me to have no secrets from her in all the embassy matters, to seat her at the end of my table when I read and wrote my dispatches, and to consult her judgment in everything. I have rarely listened to advice so gladly, and I hold it an equal merit in her that she both deserved their praises and lived ever afterwards as though she had not heard them. But hear them she did, from my lips, and afterwards from theirs.

As it happened, I had no chance of following their counsel in Rome, for I never went there, but I had practised it at home long before that time, and for the rest of our lives I continued to hide nothing from her. I cannot resist adding that I never found advice more wise, prudent, and useful than hers, and that she saved me from many disasters, both small and great. I took advantage of it in everything, without reserve, and it was of inestimable benefit to me in my personal conduct as well as in the part that I played in foreign affairs, which, during the last years of the King's life and throughout the Regency, was not insignificant. She provided a most rare and sweet contrast to those idle women who are forbidden to accompany ambassadors or to share their secrets, and whose chief occupation is to entertain prodigally and run up accounts. How different are the latter from those few able women who make their influence truly felt, but with perfect discretion, very quietly and gently, and who, far from being self-righteous, always seem unconscious of the justice of their opinions throughout a lifetime of modest amiability and virtue.

Notwithstanding the King's injunction, it gradually became known that the choice had fallen on me. Torcy, however, still said nothing, and I scarcely knew what to tell my friends as I was dragged from one meeting of the Council to another. We returned to Versailles; we went on another excursion to Marly; people ceased to be guarded; indeed, at one of the balls, M. de Monaco, the son of an earlier ambassador, offered to provide me with what remained in Rome of his father's furniture and carriages, and all the time that we were dancing, Mme de Saint-Simon and I heard people exclaim, 'There is the new ambassador', or 'the new ambassador's wife'. The situation became so embarrassing that I implored Torcy (through a friend) to put an end to the affair in one way or another. He felt the impropriety of the thing itself, and the awkwardness for me, but did not dare to hurry the King. The real reason for the delay was that some hope had arisen of persuading the Pope to accept the Abbé de la Trémoïlle, and to press on with the nominations for the nineteen empty hats,[1] a matter that was setting all Rome in a fever, and that could not long be postponed on account of the great number of the vacancies. Yet postponed it was, so that in spite of not having been announced, my own nomination gradually became public property both in Rome and Paris.

When we were at Marly, M. le Duc de Bourgogne secretly congratulated me, even although we were not then on familiar

[1] The nomination of nineteen Cardinals.

terms. He thought that there had been too long a delay, and when I answered modestly, he encouraged me, saying that I had better begin to train myself for foreign affairs and high offices. He added that he was very glad I had resolved to accept the post, especially as the King would never forgive me if I refused.

Whilst I was thus in the limelight, the Comtesse de la Marck died of the smallpox, in Paris. She was the daughter of the Duc de Rohan, and a very dear friend of Mme de Saint-Simon, for they had been school-fellows at the same convent. Her goodness made her deeply regretted and Mme de Saint-Simon wept bitterly for her; I myself was much moved. Five or six hours after learning of this death, we had to go to a ball, although the eyes of Mme de Saint-Simon and her sister were red and swollen with weeping, and no excuses to offer. The King had little understanding of the laws of nature or the sentiments of the heart; his own were directed entirely towards affairs of state and the most trivial pleasures. He made the Duchesse de Duras dance at Marly in the first days of her widowhood, and we have already seen how, when Monsieur died, he showed little consideration or respect for the most honoured conventions.

To end this long-drawn-out story of my Roman embassy, matters dragged along in this fashion until the middle of April, when I at last learned how my fate had been decided. We were then at Marly, lodged in the same pavilion with Chamillart, whom I had begged, when he returned from the council, to come to my apartment before going up to his own, and to tell me privately what was to be done with me. He accordingly came to me in Mme de Saint-Simon's room, where we awaited him impatiently. 'You are going to be much relieved,' he said, 'and I am very sorry, for the King is not now sending an ambassador to Rome. The Pope has at last consented to make the Abbé de la Trémoïlle a cardinal, and to proceed with the other nominations, which have been so long delayed by his refusal to include the Abbé. The new cardinal will have charge of the King's affairs, without any ambassador.' Mme de Saint-Simon was indeed delighted. It almost seems as though she foresaw the discredit into which the King's Italian affairs would fall, and all the subsequent financial embarrassments, as well as the grievous situation to which these misfortunes would have reduced us had we gone to Rome.

1706

The Duc de Vendôme

AT that time, the Court and Paris witnessed the most extra-ordinary spectacle. M. de Vendôme had not left Italy since he had succeeded the Maréchal de Villeroy after the disastrous affair at Cremona.[1] His victories (such as they were), the for-tresses he had taken, the power he had seized, his borrowed reputation, his unbelievable success with the King, his powerful friends, all made him anxious to return to the Court and assume a brilliant role which, in the event, surpassed anything that he had the right to expect. But before describing the arrival of one who was to cast so strange a spell and whom, until now, I have mentioned only in passing, it would be well to describe the man himself, and even to include some details of a shocking nature because they were characteristic of him.

He was of ordinary height, rather stout, but strong, hearty, and active. He appeared handsome and well-bred, had the grand manner, and was naturally graceful in speech and bearing. Born with an intellect that was never cultivated, quick of tongue, with an audacity that gradually turned to downright rudeness, he had a vast knowledge of the world, the Court, and its various personalities and, beneath an air of carelessness, hid a very keen eye to his own advantage. Above all he was a most polished courtier and managed to escape the consequences of his worst excesses because of the King's respect for his noble birth.[2] When it suited his convenience he was artfully courteous, but with measure and discrimination, and was insolent beyond all bounds when he could be so with impunity. With the common people he affected a hearty familiarity that fed his vanity and made him popular with the vulgar. At heart he was eaten up with a pride that governed all his actions. As he rose in rank and favour, his arrogance and self-will rose in proportion, to a point where he became impervious to advice of any kind, and refused to listen to any but a very small number of intimates and to his

[1] On February 1st, 1702, Villeroy was surprised and taken prisoner by Prince Eugène at Cremona. In spite of this disaster the French garrison succeeded in throwing back the Imperial army.

[2] Vendôme's father was a bastard of Henri IV.

servants. Praise, flattery, and, finally, adoration were the only channels by which one might approach this demi-god, who flaunted ridiculous opinions, with which no one dared to disagree, let alone contradict.

Better than any man living he knew and took advantage of the servile instincts of the French, and gradually accustomed his junior officers and then the whole army to call him 'Monseigneur' and 'Votre Altesse'. As no one opposed him, this gangrene spread to lieutenant-generals and other distinguished persons, who followed one another's example like sheep. Not one of them dared to address him otherwise, so that after a time the improper title became a right and anyone who had ventured to do differently would have seemed deliberately insulting.

It is most extraordinary that the really filthy nature of his private life never seemed to disturb the King who, although he himself had been free with women, was horrified at the idea of unnatural vice. Yet there is no doubt that the King knew of his perversions. Vendôme himself was quite frank about them, and behaved as though he were conducting trivial and normal love-affairs. His servants and junior officers pandered to his tastes and were known to do so, and many used them to curry favour, in the hope of gaining promotion. I have already described the blatant manner with which he twice retired to take the grand cure.[1] Indeed, he was the first man who ever dared to obtain leave for that express purpose, so that his condition was a general topic at the Court, for the King himself set the example by condoning conduct which he would never have tolerated in one of the Sons of France.

M. de Vendôme's idleness was inconceivable. More than once he was nearly captured by the enemy because he refused to leave headquarters that were comfortable, but isolated, and he often hazarded the success of an entire campaign because he would not move from a camp when once he had settled there. In the field he saw little for himself, relying for information on his staff, whom he more often than not disbelieved, indeed, his daily routine, which he would not alter, scarcely allowed him to be more active. He was excessively filthy in his habits and boasted of them; the fools around him said that he was a child of nature. His bed was full of his dogs and bitches, that sometimes pupped beside him, and he relieved the needs of nature wherever

[1] The mercury cure for syphilis.

he happened to be. One of his favourite sayings was that everyone else acted in the same way but had not the honesty to admit
it. He upheld this proposition one day to Mme la Princesse de
Conti, the daintiest and most fastidious person in the world.

When he was with the army, his custom was to rise rather
late and at once to take his seat upon his chaise-percée, and in
this curious position he wrote his dispatches and issued his
orders for the day. Anyone who had business with him, even
general officers and distinguished visitors, found that the best
time to talk with him. He gradually accustomed the entire army
to that indecent habit and, still sitting there, would consume
an enormous breakfast with two or three boon companions,
eating, talking, and issuing orders, with a large audience of
bystanders. He evacuated copiously and the pot was carried
away in front of the entire company. On the days when he
shaved, the same pot was used. He called this a good honest
custom, worthy of the Romans, and a fine contrast to the finical
ways of some other army commanders. When he had finished,
he would dress and play piquet or hombre for high stakes, then
if it were really necessary to make a reconnaissance he would
mount his horse, but once he had given the order to return, the
day's work was over for him. He supped hugely with his intimates, for he was a great eater, no judge of good food, but
with a monstrous fondness for fish, and he preferred the stale
and often the stinking to the fresh. His table conversation consisted in airing his opinions and quarrelling, while from all
around came praises, flattery, and adulation, from morning to
night, and from every quarter.

He never forgave criticism, wished to be considered the
finest soldier of the age, and spoke slightingly and improperly
of Prince Eugène and all the other commanders. It was an
offence to contradict him. The common soldiers and lower
officers adored him because he was familiar with them and
allowed them to take liberties in order to win popularity; but
he lost credit in other directions because of his unbearable arrogance towards anyone of rank or breeding. When he was in
Italy he treated the distinguished men who came to treat with
him in the same insolent manner.

That was how the celebrated Alberoni came to make his fortune. His master, the Duke of Parma, having matters to negotiate with M. de Vendôme, first sent the Bishop of Parma, who

was shocked beyond measure at being received by the duke seated upon a chaise-percée, and was still more so when the latter stood up and turned round to wipe himself. He returned to Parma without further ado, declaring that nothing would induce him to have further dealings with such a monster. Alberoni was a gardener's son, who, being clever beyond the average, had taken minor orders so as to gain an entrée into circles where a peasant's smock would have been unacceptable. He was a clown, but he amused the Duke of Parma, who thought him sufficiently intelligent to be capable of employment. The sight of M. de Vendôme upon his chaise-percée was hardly likely to affect him unduly, and therefore the Duke of Parma decided to make him finish the work which the bishop had left undone.

Alberoni had no dignity to lose. He knew Vendôme for what he was and resolved to please him at any personal cost, in order to advance his master's affairs and himself into the bargain. He was received in the usual way by M. de Vendôme and leavened his arguments with much flattery and praise, and with several jokes that made the general laugh even louder than usual. Vendôme, behaving in exactly the same way as to the bishop, eventually rose and began to wipe himself without ceremony; but when Alberoni saw the exposed portions of the ducal posterior, he exclaimed, '*Oh! culo de angelo!*' and rushed to embrace them. Nothing could have served him better than this despicable action, for the Duke of Parma was constantly having to negotiate with the Duc de Vendôme, and when he saw how well Alberoni had begun, continued to employ him regularly as his envoy. Alberoni made himself pleasant to M. de Vendôme's household and managed to prolong his visits. He took the trouble to make cheese soups and other special dishes which the general enjoyed exceedingly, and was often asked to share his meal.

Gradually, he became so comfortable in that household that he began to imagine himself doing better there than at the Court of Parma, where his qualities, as he thought, were not fully appreciated. He accordingly acted so as to get himself dismissed and persuaded M. de Vendôme that he had sacrificed his whole future for the latter's sake. He thus changed masters and, shortly afterwards, without relinquishing his post as court jester and concoctor of exotic soups and stews, he began to pry in M. de Vendôme's correspondence with so much success that

he became principal private secretary and confidant. The rest of
M. de Vendôme's staff were not pleased and at last jealousy
rose to such a pitch that Magnani, one of the other secretaries,
chased him with a stick for more than a hundred yards, before
the whole army. M. de Vendôme was annoyed, but did nothing
about the matter. Alberoni, however, was not the man to give
up for so little in a good cause. He managed to turn the incident
to good account with his master, who liked him all the more
for it, made him a party to all his plans and treated him thence-
forth as a trusted friend rather than a servant, so that even the
intimate circle and the smartest officers had to reckon with him.

I have already described how artfully M. de Vendôme fed the
King with exaggerated reports of his plans and actions in the
field. Small skirmishes were blown up into battles, real, but
indecisive battles were proclaimed as victories with an effron-
tery that defied contradiction. A continual succession of couriers
brought news, and the King was pleased to be duped by them
and believed all that Vendôme desired, for he was supported
and praised by the inner council, opposed by no one, and protected, as I have said, by that constant stream of couriers from
Italy. Nothing was heard of him, except the acclamations which
his rank and influence evoked from the army. In such favourable
circumstances, he decided that, since Prince Eugène was in
Vienna, the time had come for him to return and harvest the
fruits of his labour, and he received permission to visit the
Court.

Vendôme came straight to Marly, where we also were, on
February 12th. There was an appalling racket when he arrived,
postillions, chair-carriers, and all the court footmen left their
posts to surround his coach. He had hardly reached his rooms
before the entire Court came flocking to welcome him. The
Princes of the Blood were the first to arrive, they who had been
so piqued by his promotion above them in the service and by
many other things. I leave you to imagine whether the bastards
kept him waiting. Ministers rushed to attend on him, and so
many of the courtiers that only ladies remained in the salon.
M. de Beauvilliers was away at Vaucresson; as for me, I was
content to observe events and did not go to adore the idol.

The King and Monseigneur sent for him, and as soon as he
was allowed to change his coat he was almost borne upon the
shoulders of the crowd to the salon, where Monseigneur had

the music stopped in order to greet him. The King was with
Mme de Maintenon, working with Chamillart. He summoned
Vendôme again, and came out of the little inner room into the
large study, embraced him many times, spent several minutes
talking to him, and said that he would see him at leisure on the
following day. Indeed, he did then converse with him for more
than two hours in Mme de Maintenon's apartment.

Chamillart carried him off to L'Etang on the pretext of working with him in more peaceful surroundings, and gave a most
magnificent fête that lasted for two whole days. Following this
example, Pontchartrain, Torcy, and many of the greatest nobles
thought fit to treat him in the same way, and outrivalled one
another in entertainment. People schemed to secure him;
they intrigued to be invited where he was asked. No triumph
ever equalled his, and he made fresh conquests every day. It is
not too much to say that everyone else seemed to pale beside
him; Princes of the Blood, ministers, the high nobility, served
only to set off his brilliance. Even the King himself appeared to
rule for the sole purpose of raising him still higher. They flocked
after him to Versailles and to Paris, when he went, ostensibly
to the opera, but really to bask in his incredible popularity. He
was mobbed in the streets. His presence was advertised in advance, the entire house was sold out, packed so that it was
stiflingly hot, and the price of the seats was doubled as for a
first performance.

Vendôme received these tributes with apparent calm, but inwardly he was astonished at the enthusiasm. He had never intended to stay long at the Court, but fearing that his popularity
might not last, he asked for permission to go to Anet between
two Marly excursions, in order to make himself precious. He
therefore spent only two days at Versailles, broken by a night's
visit to Meudon, in order to please Monseigneur. No sooner
was he established at Anet with a few boon companions, than
Versailles became a desert and the village of Anet crammed to
the very attics. Monseigneur went there to hunt, as did the
Princes of the Blood and the ministers. Anet became the height
of fashion and everyone made it a point of honour to go there.
Vendôme's pride was swollen by so much adulation; he behaved
towards the company as though they were his courtiers, and
they were base enough to accept this treatment without com-
plaint, saying it was country manners. Even the King, who

usually took offence if he were neglected for any reason whatsoever, delighted at Versailles' being abandoned for Anet, and
continually inquired whether people had been there, or intended
to go.

Everything points to the fact that Vendôme was quite deliberately made into a hero, that he realized what was happening
and took advantage of his situation, for he seized on that moment to renew his demand to rank as commander-in-chief over
all the marshals of France. He had been set up as the god of
war; how could he be refused command over the marshals? A
warrant as marshal-general was granted to him secretly, drawn
up in the same terms as that which was given to M. de Turenne,
since whom none had claimed such rank. It was not a suitable
position for M. de Vendôme, nor even for M. du Maine, and
was only offered in order to avoid something which the King
never intended to grant. It was a temporary expedient to provide some distinction for a man with royal blood in his veins.
Vendôme, however, insisted that his original claim to superiority
over the marshals should be written into the letters patent,
as granted to M. de Turenne. I do not know how the Maréchal
de Villeroy got wind of this proposal, but he certainly heard
of it in time to remonstrate with the King who, by then,
was ready to listen to reason. The Maréchal was in favour,
he won his point, and M. de Vendôme was informed that
nothing new would be added to the warrant, which would in
every way correspond with that granted to M. de Turenne. He
then took umbrage and refused it, a most rash action, but M. de
Vendôme well knew with whom he had to deal and the power
of his friends. He had been categorically refused the authority
to command the marshals who were appointed after he had
taken over the armies in Italy, but he disobeyed the
King's repeated orders and avoided the consequences with
remarkable dexterity. It now seemed to him that it had been a
longer step to this appointment as marshal-general than it
would be to the granting of his original demand. Indeed, events
proved him right, during that very same year.

His brother, Philippe de Vendôme, the Grand Prieur,[1] was
out of favour and went to Anet to seek M. de Vendôme's help,
although they had not been on good terms. Vendôme offered

[1] Le Grand Prieur de France. The highest national rank conferred by the Order of
Malta.

to present him to the King and to obtain for him a pension of ten thousand écus, but the impudent fellow would not be satisfied with anything less than a return to Italy and command of an army. He left Anet in a vile temper, and when Vendôme went back to the Court, he returned to rage and fume at his château at Clichy.

This Philippe de Vendôme had all his brother's vices. In debauch he was even worse in that all was fair game to him. Moreover he had the advantage in that for the past thirty years he had never been to bed at night without being carried there dead drunk, a custom to which he adhered faithfully for the rest of his life. He had none of the qualities of a good general, for his known cowardice was accompanied by a most sickening rashness. More conceited even than M. de Vendôme, his manner verged on insolence, and for that very reason he saw none but underlings. Liar, swindler, rogue, thief (as he demonstrated by his management of his brother's affairs), dishonest to the very marrow of his bones, a perfect coxcomb, and extraordinarily servile and flattering to those whose help he needed, ready to do and put up with anything for the sake of money, withal the most dissolute, and the greatest waster in the world. He had much wit and, in his youth, a fine appearance and a singularly handsome countenance. In short, he was the vilest, the most contemptible, and at the same time, the most dangerous creature imaginable.

1706

My Relationship with M. le Duc d'Orléans

ALTHOUGH the time has not yet come to speak of the character of M. le Duc d'Orléans, I can no longer refrain from describing the terms on which I stood with him after our reconciliation, which I have mentioned elsewhere. His friendship and his trust in me were great, and I always held him in sincere affection. I saw him alone in his study almost every afternoon at Versailles. He would reproach me if I were unable to visit him regularly, and he always allowed me to speak freely. No subjects were barred. He discussed everything with me and liked me to conceal nothing about himself. I saw him only at Versailles and Marly, that is to say at the Court. I never called on him in Paris, for one thing, I seldom went there, and when I did go for one or, very occasionally, for two nights, I had duties or business to transact. His pleasures, the company that he kept, and the life which he led in the city, did not attract me, and I had settled from the very beginning to have nothing to do with anyone from the Palais Royal, nor with his friends or mistresses. Neither did I desire any greater intimacy with Mme la Duchesse d'Orléans, whom I saw only on state occasions, or when I called formally upon her at long intervals, staying only for a moment, and I never in any way meddled with what went on in their houses. I always believed that to act in any other manner would be extremely vexatious and lead only to mischief-making, and thus I would never listen to gossip about them.

On that evening, when he was appointed general for Italy, I followed him out of the salon into his own room, where we had a long talk together. He told me that orders had been sent to the Maréchal de Marsin, who was still in Flanders with re-inforcements for the Maréchal de Villeroy (who had not waited for them to arrive before attacking), to proceed at once to take personal command of the armies on the Rhine. Other orders had gone to bid Villars leave that army and go by way of Switzerland to Italy, where he was to command under M. le Duc d'Orléans. M. de Vendôme was not to leave until both had arrived and had conferred with him. M. le Duc d'Orléans said further that he had been appointed general only on condi-tion that he did nothing without the Maréchal de Marsin's advice, no matter how much he might disagree, and the King had extracted from him a promise to that effect. But he said that he minded the restraint less than he felt the pleasure of attaining his lifelong wish, without asking, and at a time when he had ceased to hope or even to dream of it. M. le Prince de Conti held himself under firm control and behaved very well all that evening in the salon, but Madame la Duchesse who was playing cards when the appointment was announced, did not trouble to leave the table or go up to M. le Duc d'Orléans. She merely called out as he was passing that she congratulated him, and looked hurt while doing so. He did not answer her. Monsieur le Duc had not yet returned from Burgundy.

In the days that followed he was anxious to discuss all

manner of things with me and listened in a friendly, pleasant way to everything that I said. He explained his orders at great length, and the advice which he had received, asking me to write often and freely offer my suggestions.

He had been in love for a long time with Mlle de Séry, a young lady, well-born but without property, a pretty, lively, unruly, impulsive girl, with a roguish look that gave as good as it promised. Mme de Ventadour, her cousin, found a place for her as one of Madame's ladies, and it was while she was in that household that she became pregnant and bore a son[1] to M. le Duc d'Orléans. This caused her dismissal, but M. le Duc d'Orléans grew more and more attached to her. She was overbearing and let him know it, but he only loved her the more. Many things at the Palais Royal were ordered by her, she gathered a small court about her, and made many friends. Mme de Ventadour, for instance, in spite of her cult of repentance and moral views, continued to be a close friend and did not attempt to conceal their intimacy. Mlle de Séry apparently had good advisers, for she took this opportunity when M. le Duc d'Orléans was radiant with success to make him acknowledge and legitimize her son, and not content with that, she avowed that it was unseemly to be acclaimed publicly as a mother and addressed as Mademoiselle. There was no precedent for calling her anything else, for Madame is an honour reserved for Daughters of France and daughters of duchesses in their own right, but that did not deter either the mistress or her lover. He presented her with the lands and estate of Argenton, and took advantage of the King's favour, albeit with much hard work, to have her granted letters patent with permission to bear the title of Madame, and Comtesse d'Argenton. The thing was unheard of. It was feared that there might be difficulties over the registration by the Parlement, but M. le Duc d'Orléans, although he was on the eve of departure and overwhelmed with affairs of state, went himself to the Premier Président and the Procureur Général and the registration was effected. His appointment to Italy had been received with general applause in Paris and at the Court; this news somewhat abated the rejoicings and caused a good deal of grumbling, but a man when he is much in love thinks only of contenting his mistress and gladly sacrifices all for her sake.

[1] Jean-Philippe, Chevalier d'Orléans (1702–1748), Grand Prieur de France (1719).

Everything regarding this matter was set, sealed, and de-livered without a word of it passing between us. I was angry about the act in itself, and angry that he should have spoiled the brilliance of his departure by so public and improper a breach. But that was all. I remained firm to the decision I had taken when I first was reconciled with him, never to speak to him of his household or his mistresses. He knew very well that I disapproved of what he had been doing for this one, and was exceedingly careful to keep his mouth shut.

This much, however, he did tell me in the salon at Marly, one day when he had just arrived from Paris and was about to start for Italy. The very strangeness of his story, and the fact that it was verified by future events which he could not have fore-seen, forbid that I should omit it. M. le Duc d'Orléans was interested in all kinds of arts and sciences and, despite his superior intellect, had suffered all his life from that failing which is so common among the descendants of Henri II, and which was brought from Italy with other evils by Catherine de Médicis. He had tried his best to call up the devil on several occasions but, as he told me himself, had never succeeded. He was curious about the supernatural and keenly desired to know the future.

La Séry had a little girl of eight or nine years old living in her house, who was born there and had never been away, and who had all the ignorance and innocence of children of that age and upbringing. One of the many rascally dealers in mystery whom M. le Duc d'Orléans had encountered during his life was a cer-tain man who professed to be able to make events visible in a glass of water. This man, having been produced at Mme de Séry's apartment, asked for some young and innocent person to look into the glass and the little girl was accordingly sent for. The company then diverted themselves by asking what was happening in distant lands, and the child looked and reported whatever she saw.

M. le Duc d'Orléans had so often been tricked by similar experiments that he determined to check this one. He quietly whispered to one of his servants to go to Mme de Nancré's apartment next door, to see who was there, notice the position of the furniture and the nature of it, and all that was happening, and then, without losing a moment or speaking to anyone, to return and report into his ear. All of which he did unobserved upon the instant and whilst the little girl still remained in the

room. Then M. le Duc d'Orléans asked the child to see who
was at Mme de Nancré's apartment, and to tell him what they
were doing, and she related word for word what the messenger
had seen, even to describing the faces, figures, and dress of all
the people there, their positions in the room, those who were
playing cards at two different tables, the onlookers, whether
they were standing or sitting, the arrangement of the furniture, in short, everything. That instant, M. le Duc d'Orléans
sent Nancré, who came back with word that everything was
exactly as the little girl had described and just as the servant
had whispered into M. le Duc d'Orléans' ear.

M. le Duc d'Orléans never ordinarily spoke to me of such
experiences, because I took the liberty of making him feel
ashamed of them. I tried to do so now, crying down the story
and saying all that I could to prevent his believing in, or diverting himself with such delusions, especially at a time when his
mind should have been filled with much greater matters. 'That
was not the whole of it,' he said. 'I have only told you that much
as a prelude to what followed.' He then related how the child's
success had inspired him to inquire after matters more important for him, namely, the state of affairs after the King's death,
but without asking to know the date, which could not be seen
in the glass. Now the little girl had never heard of Versailles
and knew no one at the Court, but she looked into the glass and
gave them a long description of all that she saw. She depicted
the King's bedroom at Versailles exactly, with all the furniture,
arranged as it was when he later came to die. She saw the King,
lying upon his bed, and the people standing by his side or elsewhere in the room, for example, a little boy wearing the Order
and holding the hand of Mme de Ventadour, at whom she
exclaimed, because she had seen her with Mme de Séry. From
what she said they were able to recognize Mme de Maintenon,
the arresting figure of Fagon, Madame, Mme la Duchesse
d'Orléans, Madame la Duchesse, and Mme la Princesse de Conti.
She exclaimed again when she saw M. le Duc d'Orléans. In a
word, she made known to them everyone she could see,
princes, servants, gentlemen and valets. When she had quite
finished, M. le Duc d'Orléans, who was astonished at her
not describing Monseigneur, Mgr le Duc de Bourgogne,
Mme la Duchesse de Bourgogne, or M. le Duc de Berry, asked
whether she could not see other persons who looked in such

and such a way, but she persisted in saying that she did not, and repeated her descriptions of the rest. This, M. le Duc d'Orléans had failed to understand; he expressed his astonishment to me and tried vainly to discover the reason, which in due course was made plain. The year was 1706, and the four persons he had mentioned were then alive and well. In 1715, when the King died, they were already dead. The same was true of Monsieur le Prince, Monsieur le Duc, and M. le Prince de Conti whom she did not see, although she described the children of the two latter, also M. du Maine and his family, and M. le Comte de Toulouse. But nothing of all this was understood until after the King's death.

This inquiry having been answered, M. le Duc d'Orléans wished to know his own future, but that could not be seen in the glass. The man offered to show it him like a painting on the wall, provided that he did not fear to see himself, and after a quarter of an hour of gesticulating and grimacing, the figure of M. le Duc d'Orléans suddenly appeared before them all, dressed as he then was, life-size, and with a closed-in crown upon his head. It was not the crown of France, nor of Spain, nor of England, nor yet the Imperial crown. M. le Duc d'Orléans stared at it with the eyes starting out of his head, but could not imagine what it was, for he had never seen anything to resemble it. There were only four hoops and nothing at the top. The thought of this crown preyed upon his mind.

Arguing from this and the previous conundrum, I took occasion to point out the vanity of such idle curiosity, a temptation of the devil which God permits in order to punish those who search for forbidden knowledge. I also drew attention to the dissatisfaction and obscurity that had resulted, instead of the light and certainty for which he sought. At that time, he was very far from being Regent of France or from thinking such a thing possible.

All this occurred in Paris, at the house of his mistress and in the presence of their most intimate circle. He told me of it that same evening, and I thought the story so singular that I give it here, not because I approve of it, but merely to put it upon record.

1707

The Kidnapping of Beringhen

A MOST alarming and curious event occurred which caused the King much anxiety and set the whole town agog. On Thursday, March 7th, Beringhen,[1] the first equerry of the royal stables, having followed the King on his excursion to Marly and returned to Versailles with the rest of the suite, set out for Paris at seven in the evening. He was alone in his carriage, that is to say in one of the royal coaches, with two of the King's footmen behind and a postillion with a torch riding in front on the seventh horse. On the plain of Billancourt, between the farm which stands by the roadside near the end of the Sèvres bridge and the tavern called 'Le Point du Jour', he was held up by fifteen or sixteen horsemen, who surrounded his carriage and carried him off. The coachman promptly turned his horses and brought the carriage with the two footmen back to Versailles, where the moment they arrived the King was informed of what had happened. Orders were then given to the four secretaries of state (Pontchartrain, La Vrillière, Chamillart, and Torcy) at Versailles, L'Étang, and Paris, to dispatch couriers to all parts of the frontier warning commanding officers to keep watch on all the fords and bridges, because word had come that a detachment of the enemy had quietly entered Artois and had not yet retreated.

At first it seemed impossible to suppose that the military could be involved, but reflecting that Monsieur le Premier had no private enemies and would not be thought capable of paying a large ransom, also that none of the great financiers had suffered any such mishap, it gradually came to be believed that the kidnapping was indeed the enemy's work. And so it proved.

A certain man named Guethem, a violinist attached to the Elector of Bavaria during the last war that he fought against France on the side of the allies, joined their forces and becoming by degrees a very good and very bold partisan, had risen

---

[1] Jacques-Louis, Marquis de Beringhen, known as Monsieur le Premier. He was master of the Petite Ecurie at Versailles. See p. 66n.

to the rank of colonel in the Dutch army. One evening he laid a wager with his comrades that he would kidnap some important personage on the highroad between Paris and Versailles. He accordingly obtained leave of absence from the enemy generals and with thirty picked companions, most of them officers, crossed the rivers into France. They were disguised as merchants, which made it simple for them to arrange for relays of fresh horses throughout the country. Some of them stayed seven or eight days at Sèvres, Saint-Cloud, and Boulogne, and some even had the temerity to go to Versailles and see the King at his supper. One of the latter was captured on the following day and was not a little insolent when Chamillart questioned him. Another was caught in the forest of Chantilly by one of the guards of Monsieur le Prince, who learned from him that the raiders had horses and a post-chaise ready at La Morlaye for their prisoner. But by that time he had already been conveyed beyond the Oise.

Their great error was in not taking the royal coach itself, with Beringhen inside, as far and as fast as they could manage whilst it was still dark, which would have delayed knowledge of his capture and gained time for their escape. It would also have spared him a long and tiring ride on horseback, for he was fifty-five years old and not robust. Instead, they exhausted him by making him trot and gallop. It seems that they had allowed the chancellor to pass unmolested because they did not dare to stop him in daylight, and they had missed M. le Duc d'Orléans after darkness fell because he was in an ordinary post-chaise. Then they had grown tired of waiting and fearful of detection, and had flung themselves upon Beringhen's coach thinking that they had done marvellously well when by the light of the torches they saw the royal liveries and a man sitting in the carriage with the blue ribbon across his waistcoat, for Monsieur le Premier always wore it. It was not long before he had learned who they were and disclosed his own identity. Guethem showed him every respect and an obvious desire to spare him as much fatigue as possible, in fact he carried consideration so far that his enterprise failed, for they allowed Beringhen to stop and rest twice upon the way and so missed a change of horses at one of their stages, which delayed them much.

Besides the couriers dispatched to the commanding officers on the frontier, others were sent to the provincial administrators and to all the troops in barracks, and after them a detachment of the King's guard went to watch the roads, whilst the entire staff of the Petite Écurie, with whom Monsieur le Premier was very popular, scoured the country in all directions. In spite of the precautions taken to guard the fords, Beringhen, with three officers to whom he had given his parole, was already across the Somme and four leagues beyond Ham, when they were sighted by a cavalry sergeant followed at a short distance by a troop of Livry's regiment, with another close behind. Guethem thus found himself outnumbered, the remainder of his party having gone in search of fresh horses. He surrendered forthwith and became his prisoner's prisoner.

Beringhen was overjoyed at being rescued and exceedingly thankful to his late captors for their consideration. Taking them with him to Ham, he rested for the remainder of the day, and in his turn gave them the best of good treatment. He then sent couriers to his wife and Chamillart, which vastly relieved the King, who read his letters to them aloud after supper.

On Tuesday 29th, about eight o'clock in the evening, Beringhen arrived at Versailles and went straight to the apartment of Mme de Maintenon, where he was admitted at once. The King gave him a wonderfully warm welcome and made him tell all his adventures; but although he had a great liking for Beringhen, he nevertheless took it vastly ill that there should be a holiday and fireworks at the Petite Écurie in honour of his return. He sent at once to forbid all signs of public rejoicing and the fireworks were not set off. The King had his little jealousies, he liked every honour to be his alone, without reserve or division. None the less, the whole Court welcomed that happy return, and in the general goodwill Monsieur le Premier found every cause to forget his weariness.

He had sent Guethem and his officers to await the King's orders at his own house in Paris, where they were entertained far above their station. He even obtained permission for Guethem to see the King, and took him to the review of household troops, which was always held at Marly before the opening of the campaigning season. What is more, he actually presented Guethem to His Majesty, who thanked him for treating his officer so well and added that war should always be waged with chivalry. Guethem was not lacking in intelligence. He said that he felt so overcome at being in the presence of the greatest king on earth and of being honoured by speech with him that he could find no strength to reply. For ten or twelve days he remained in Paris, staying with Monsieur le Premier so that he might see the town. They took him to the Opéra and the Comédie, where he himself provided the greater spectacle. Everyone flocked to see him and even the most distinguished people were not ashamed to applaud him for an act of daring that verged on impudence. Beringhen continued to entertain him at his house, lent him carriages and servants and, at parting, gave him a large sum of money and other valuable gifts. He then rejoined those of his comrades who were on parole at Rheims, where they had the whole town for their prison while they waited for an exchange. Nearly all the rest had managed to escape. Their real project had been nothing less than to kidnap Monseigneur or one of his sons.

This trivial affair gave rise to precautions, so rigorous at first that the passage of fords and bridges became a wearisome business, and a great number of persons were arrested. For a time the princes' hunting parties were restricted, and then things gradually returned to normal. But it was not undiverting to see the ladies so fearful, and even some of the gentlemen could scarcely summon enough courage to walk out in broad daylight and saw marvellous opportunities for kidnapping at every street corner.

1707

The 'Parvulo' at Meudon

BEFORE proceeding to other and more important matters, I observe that I have said nothing of what the Court used to call the 'Parvulo' of Meudon. I must, however, try to explain this code-word in the secret language of the Court if you are to have any understanding of the things which I am about to relate. I have told elsewhere about the actions of Mme la Princesse de Conti, why and how she came to dismiss Mlle Choin, who the latter was, who her friends, and the partiality which Monseigneur felt for her. His fondness was only increased by the difficulty of meeting her after she was dismissed. Almost the only people who knew of the attachment in its early stages were Mme de Lillebonne and her daughters,[1] and in spite of all that they owed to Mme la Princesse de Conti, they fostered it because it made them parties to an intrigue from which they hoped to reap much benefit.

After her dismissal, Mlle Choin retired to the house of her kinsman La Croix, near the Petit Saint-Antoine convent, in Paris, where she lived in complete seclusion. Every time that Monseigneur went to Meudon for the day only, in order to inspect his new buildings and plantations, she was warned beforehand. She would go there in a hired carriage on the previous evening, passing through the courtyards on foot, poorly dressed, like any common woman going to visit one of the servants, and entering Monseigneur's apartments on the entresol by the back way. When he came on the following day, he would spend a few hours in her company. For a long time she continued in this fashion, but later she began to take a maid with a bundle in her pocket, and always stayed from the evening before until the following night, on the occasions when Monseigneur slept at Meudon. Whilst she was there, she remained shut up with her maid, seeing no one but him and never leaving the entresol of the château. One of the pages, the only one whom Monseigneur trusted, brought her meals.

Not long afterwards, Dumont, Monseigneur's equerry and governor of Meudon, was given permission to see her, then the daughters of Mme de Lillebonne came when there were ladies staying at Meudon. Gradually the numbers increased as some of the more intimate circle were included—Sainte-Maure, the Comte de Roucy, then Biron, later, one or two others, a few of the ladies, and M. le Prince de Conti, shortly before he died. Next, Mgr le Duc de Bourgogne and M. le Duc de Berry, and very soon afterwards, Mme la Duchesse de Bourgogne, were admitted to the apartment on the entresol, so that the secret soon became known. The Duc de Noailles and his sisters were occasionally invited. Monseigneur took to dining there with Mme de Lillebonne's daughters, and sometimes with them and Madame la Duchesse, or with a few specially privileged friends. But there it stopped. The same air of mystery always surrounded these parties that were held pretty often. And it was those gatherings that came to be known as the 'parvulo'.

[1] Anne de Lorraine, Princesse de Lillebonne Mlle de Lillebonne, and Mme d'Espinoy.

At this time, Mlle Choin was no longer kept on the entresol solely for Monseigneur's convenience. She now slept in the great bed in the state apartment which Mme la Duchesse de Bourgogne usually occupied when the King came to Meudon, and she always took an armchair in Monseigneur's presence, whereas Mme la Duchesse de Bourgogne had only a tabouret. Mlle Choin never stood up to receive her. When speaking of her, even in the presence of Monseigneur and the whole company, she referred to her simply as 'the duchess', and treated her exactly as Mme de Maintenon did, except that she did not say 'my dear child'. Mme la Duchesse de Bourgogne never would call her 'Aunt', nor was she so familiar and easy with her as with the King and Mme de Maintenon. When Mgr le Duc de Bourgogne visited the entresol, he was exceedingly stiff; his manners and morals did not easily adapt themselves to that kind of society. M. le Duc de Berry, on the other hand, was not so straitlaced and seemed perfectly comfortable. Madame la Duchesse usually monopolized the conversation and occasionally invited some of her cronies, but none the less Mlle Choin never appeared in public. She went to hear mass at six o'clock in the morning on Saints' days, sitting in a quiet corner of the little chapel, alone, well muffled up in hoods and veils. She ate by herself when Monseigneur did not come up to dine with her, which he never did when he stayed at Meudon, except on the first night, and she never set foot beyond his apartments and the entresol. On the way between, the corridor was carefully watched and barricaded so that no one should meet her.

People gradually came to accept her as being to Monseigneur what Mme de Maintenon was to the King, and every courtier had his broadsides trained upon her for future advantage. They intrigued to be allowed to visit her in Paris, and flattered and fawned upon her older friends and acquaintances. Mgr le Duc and Mme la Duchesse de Bourgogne did their utmost to make themselves agreeable by showing her respect and being especially attentive to her friends, but even they were not always successful. She treated Mgr le Duc de Bourgogne as familiarly as a step-mother, which she was not, but her manner was curt and unsympathetic, and it sometimes happened that she took a hectoring, tactless tone with Mme la Duchesse de Bourgogne, which made her cry.

Mlle Choin remained devoted to the daughters of Mme de Lillebonne, for she never forgot that although these ladies owed everything, their livelihood, their friendship with Monseigneur, their position in society, to Mme la Princesse de Conti, they had not hesitated to desert their benefactress for her sake. Moreover it was not from any sense of grievance that they forsook her, but solely because they knew of Monseigneur's fond passion and realized the advantages of enjoying his confidence after Mlle Choin's dismissal. She herself had witnessed Monseigneur's friendship for the two sisters long enough to refrain from annoying them in any way. Thus she remained on cordial terms with them and also with Madame la Duchesse whose gaiety, good humour and perfect health were a welcome refuge to Monseigneur from the constant nagging of Mme la Princesse de Conti.

The four women therefore came to a perfect understanding with regard to Monseigneur and in certain other matters. They never quarrelled but supported one another continually, yet each held herself free at the King's death, should Monseigneur survive him, to supplant the three others and become sole and independent mistress. In the meanwhile, they were united in this common bond and tyrannized over the few men who lived in hopes of the future because of Monseigneur's liking for them, or their own persistent flattery.

As for the King and Mme de Maintenon, they fully realized what was going on, but said nothing, and the Court spoke of it only in whispers. This outline will serve for the present. It will give a clue to many future events. M. de Vendôme and d'Antin were the people best informed.

1707

The Duc du Maine and the Comte de Toulouse

M. DU MAINE realized that Monseigneur detested him. Consequently, the best way of approaching him was through these female confidantes. Vendôme alone did not suffice. The King

MADAME DE MAINTENON
WITH HER NIECE, FRANCOISE D'AUBIGNÉ
From the portrait by Ferdinand Elle at Versailles

(right)
LOUIS-AUGUSTE
DE BOURBON,
DUC DU MAINE

From an engraving by
B. Roger after the portrait
by Troye

(below)
LOUIS-JOSEPH
DE BOURBON,
DUC DE VENDÔME

From the engraving by
B. Roger
after the portrait by
N. de Largillière

Bibliothèque Nationale

Bibliothèque Nationale

was advancing in age and Monseigneur towards the throne. M. du Maine trembled at the thought, I might say, less, like an angel than like the devil whom he so closely resembled in malice, in perversity, in unkindness to all and good to none, in sinister plotting, in sublime vaingloriousness and most subtle falseness, in conceits without number and endless dissembling; yet with much seeming amiability, especially in the arts of pleasing and entertainment, for when he wished he could charm. Being the most arrant coward in heart and mind, he was also most dangerous, for, provided he could manage it unseen, he was ready to go to dreadful lengths in order to escape what he feared, and would lend himself to the meanest and most despicable actions, by which the devil lost nothing.

He was egged on by a wife of the same kidney, whose intelligence, and she too had much, had been spoilt and corrupted by the reading of plays and romances, to which passion she so entirely abandoned herself that for years on end she learned them by heart and acted them in public. This woman was courageous beyond measure, intriguing, bold, quarrelsome, recognizing only her present inclinations and setting them above all else, and despising her husband's subterfuges and precautions, which she called a lamentable want of spirit. She was always taunting him with having married above his station and kept him low and submissive by treating him like a slave. She snubbed him unmercifully and he never dared to protest, for he bore everything from her in terror lest she should go out of her mind. He did manage to conceal a certain amount from her, but her ascendancy over him was beyond belief and she drove him with blows to go her way.

They had no intercourse with the Comte de Toulouse, a man of few words, but the soul of honour, virtue, truth, and honesty, with a manner as gracious as his naturally cold, even icy, disposition would allow. He did his best to make something of himself but used only good means to that end, for he had a sense of justice in everyday affairs, which made up for any want of intellect. Thus, in his rank of Admiral of France, he had been most diligent in learning the affairs of the navy and merchant service, and he understood them very well. A man of this nature was not likely to live on familiar terms with such a brother and sister-in-law, for M. du Maine saw him loved and respected, as he deserved, and was jealous. The Comte de Toulouse, being

F

wise, taciturn, and prudent, realized this fact but appeared not to, although he could not endure the follies of his sister-in-law, as she plainly saw. This made her furious; she, in turn, detested him, and she further alienated the two brothers.

With Monseigneur, the Comte de Toulouse had always been on excellent terms, as well as with M. and Mme la Duchesse de Bourgogne, who treated him with respect and affection. He was nervous with the King, who far preferred the company of M. du Maine, the spoiled darling of Mme de Maintenon, his one-time governess to whom he had sacrificed his mother Mme de Montespan, a fact which neither lady could forget. Du Maine was cunning enough to persuade the King that although extremely intelligent, which no one could deny, he had no opinions, no ambition, but was in fact a fool and an idler with a taste for solitude. He spent his time shut up in his study, eating alone, avoiding society, and hunting alone, and he managed to make this uncivilized life seem meritorious to the King, whom he saw every day at his private times. In short he was a consummate hypocrite, going ostentatiously to mass, and to vespers as well as communion on all Saints' days. He was the life and soul, and also the oracle, of Mme de Maintenon, whom he could twist round his little finger, and who thought only of giving him pleasure and advantaging him, no matter at whose expense.

This is a long digression, but in the end you will see how necessary it is for a full understanding of what I have to tell. These persons stirred up many matters which would make no sense without this clue. I give it here because the need arises and opportunity serves.

1707

Madame de Montespan

A DEATH that caused a great stir, although the victim had long since retired from the world and lost all remnants of her immense influence, was that of Mme de Montespan. She died very suddenly at the watering-place of Bourbon, in the sixty-seventh year of her age, on Friday May 27th, at three o'clock in the morning.

I will not go back beyond my own times to tell of her great days. Let me simply say what is not generally known, that the sin was less hers than her husband's. She warned him when she first suspected that the King was interested in her; she did not leave him in ignorance when she no longer had doubts; she insisted that a certain ball had been given for her; she urged and entreated him to take her to his estate in Guyenne, and to leave her there until the King had forgotten her or engaged himself elsewhere, but M. de Montespan would not be convinced. He soon had reason to regret his obstinacy and suffered for it for the rest of his life, for he died loving her, although he would never consent to see her after the outbreak of the scandal.

Nor shall I tell of many times when fear of the devil almost caused her to leave the Court, and I shall speak elsewhere of the conduct of Mme de Maintenon, who owed everything to her and little by little usurped her place, rising above her, subjecting her to the cruellest indignities, and finally driving her away. What no one else dared to do, what the King himself flinched at, her own son, M. du Maine undertook, and the Bishop of Meaux[1] completed. She left the Court in a storm of tears and never forgave M. du Maine who, by this monstrous service, won for himself the love and perpetual devotion of Mme de Maintenon.

The discarded mistress retired to the convent of Saint-Joseph, in Paris, which she had founded, but she could not be reconciled to her fate. She journeyed restlessly and aimlessly between Bourbon, Fontevrault,[2] and the d'Antin estates, and years passed before she regained possession of her soul. At last God touched her. She had never sinned carelessly, for often in the old days she had left the King to go and pray in her closet. Nothing would ever have induced her to miss a meatless day or a fast. She kept her Lents strictly and was most scrupulous in fasting during the whole time of her evil-living. Generous in alms-giving, respectful to the virtuous, but never showing the least sign of religious doubt or impiety, she was, none the less, imperious, proud, domineering, scornful, with all the faults that perfect beauty and unlimited power bring in their train. At last, however, she resolved to profit by the respite that she had been

---

[1] Jacques-Bénigne Bossuet (1627-1704).
[2] Where her sister was Abbess of the Benedictine convent.

given against her will, and, after seeking for a wise and enlightened counsellor, she placed herself in the hands of the Père de la Tour, general of the Oratoire, who had won a great reputation by his sermons and his talents as a spiritual director.

From that time until the day of her death she never failed to live the life of a practising Christian, and as the years passed her penances increased. First she had to renounce her secret longing to be at the Court and the foolish hopes which she still entertained, for she had persuaded herself that only fear of the devil had caused the King to abandon her, and that this same fear, which Mme de Maintenon had used so skilfully to procure her banishment, had raised the latter to her present high estate. Mme de Montespan also believed that age and ill-health might remove her enemy and that if the King were widowed, nothing would prevent the rekindling of their passion. She imagined that his love would increase because of his affection for their mutual children and his desire to advance them, and that if her husband died he would have no hesitation in setting her up in the place of her rival.

Even her children shared these high hopes and were most diligent in their duty to her. She was passionately fond of them all, with the exception of M. du Maine, whom for a long time she never saw, and afterwards only when decency required. It is too little to say that she influenced the other three; she had power and used it freely. She was unendingly generous to them, not only out of affection and to keep them dependent, but also to preserve this last link with the King, who never communicated with her, not even through their children. As time went on, they became less assiduous and visited her only when she sent for them. Then she devoted herself to her legitimate son, d'Antin, to whom she had hitherto been more like a step-mother, and busied herself with enriching him.

Père de la Tour exacted a dreadful penance when he required her to ask her husband's forgiveness and submit herself to his orders. She wrote to Montespan herself, offering most humbly to return if he would have her, or to live at any place he chose to direct. To those who knew Mme de Montespan, this was heroic self-abasement. She earned the merit but was spared the consequences, for M. de Montespan replied that he would neither see, nor order her, nor hear her mentioned as long as he lived. After his death she went into mourning like

any ordinary widow, but neither before nor afterwards did she
use his arms or liveries. She always bore her own, singly.

Little by little she gave away almost all her possessions to the
poor, and for many hours a day worked in their service, doing
rough sewing, coarse shirts and the like, and her household
was made to work too. In the old days she had been excessively fond of the table, but now her diet was most frugal
and her fasting redoubled. Prayers interrupted her conversations
and the card games with which she amused herself, and often
she would leave the company and retire to her closet to pray.
She mortified her flesh continually, for although her bed-
clothes and nightdresses were made of coarse unbleached calico,
she wore beneath these rough clothes bracelets, garters, and a
belt with iron spikes that wounded her, and her once-dreaded
tongue did not escape punishment. She lived in such constant
fear of death, that she hired women solely for the purpose of
watching by her at night. She slept with the bed-curtains drawn
back and many lighted candles, her watchers round her, and
whenever she woke she liked to find them talking, playing cards
or eating, so that she could be sure that they were not becoming
drowsy.

In spite of this austere life, she never lost the regal manner
which she had assumed in the days of her splendour, and people
became so accustomed to her queenly airs that no one thought
of protesting. Her armchair, the only one in her room, stood
with its back to the foot of the bed; no other might be fetched,
not when her children visited her, not even for Mme la Duchesse
d'Orléans. Monsieur and La Grande Mademoiselle were fond
of her and often went to see her; for them chairs were brought,
and also for Madame la Princesse, but Mme de Montespan never
put herself out for them nor conducted them to the door when
they left. As you may see from all this, she was visited by the
highest society. Here and there about her room small chairs
with backs, and folding stools were placed facing one another
in front of her armchair, to seat ordinary visitors and those who
lived with her, for she housed several nieces and poor gentle-
women, who did the honours.

All France called on her. I do not know how it came to be
considered a social necessity, but the ladies of the Court impressed that duty upon their daughters. Men did not often
appear, unless there were some special motive. She would say a

few words to each guest, like a queen holding court, and was treated by all with the greatest respect. She, herself, never paid calls, not even upon Monsieur, Madame, nor La Grande Mademoiselle, nor even at the Hôtel de Condé; occasionally, she sent notes to those whom she particularly favoured, but not to all, by any means. Until the very day of her death she remained divinely beautiful and always in excellent health, although she often believed herself to be dying. It was this constant anxiety about her health that made her enjoy travelling, always with seven or eight people to accompany her. Her manners were those of a great lady and her graciousness made people forgive her pride. It is hard to imagine anyone more witty or more exquisitely urbane, in particular, she had a special turn of phrase and a gift for selecting the apt word that was all her own. It was enchanting to listen to her, for she had developed what was almost a special language so that her nieces and the other ladies in her household took the habit of it, and even now one recognizes it in those few who are left. It became the natural way of speaking in the families of her brother and sisters.

After she left the Court, she never condescended to ask anything either for herself or others, so that ministers, administrators, and judges heard no mention of her. The last time that she took the cure at Bourbon, as she often did without sufficient cause, she paid two years in advance on the pensions which she gave in great numbers, mostly to the poor nobility, and doubled her other charities. She was in excellent health when she started on this journey, but said that she believed she would not return and hoped that these advance payments would give her pensioners time to seek their livelihoods elsewhere. Indeed, death was ever present with her; she spoke of it as approaching even when she was well, yet in spite of all her fears, her watchers and her prayers, she would never consult any doctor or surgeon.

Mme de Montespan's conviction that she was about to die was comparable to her belief that she might be able to succeed Mme de Maintenon when the latter's death had freed the King. Her children (except M. du Maine who had nothing to gain) shared this delusion; as for the Court, they were used to accepting the most unlikely events as possibilities. It is thought that such an idea lay behind the Noailles' eagerness to marry their daughter to d'Antin's eldest son. Since the Noailles were already related by marriage to Mme de Maintenon, any connection with Mme de Montespan might have seemed most undesirable because the former hated her with a rancour which she showed towards no one else. Such considerations, however, did not deter the Noailles, nor prevent them from fawning upon Mme de Montespan as though they already had expectations.

Their eldest daughter, the Maréchale de Cœuvres, being childless, they seized on the opportunity of her visiting Bourbon to send the younger girl with her and, since they had no house there and no carriage, to use those belonging to Mme de Montespan. The Maréchale set out to flatter the ladies of the household, though they were much beneath her, and showed far more respect to Mme de Montespan than ever she did to Mme la Duchesse de Bourgogne or to Mme de Maintenon. She fairly laid herself out to please. Mme de Montespan queened it over her, played with her like a doll, sent her out of the room when she became tiresome, and scolded her unmercifully, but the Maréchale swallowed every indignity and only fawned on her the more.

All this time Mme de Montespan had been in good health, but she suddenly awoke one night feeling so ill that her watchers sent for help to the other people staying in the house. The first to reach her was the Maréchale who, seeing her choking and congested, ordered an emetic to be given on her own authority, but the dose was so strong and the effects so frightening that they proceeded to give antidotes which may have brought about her death.

There was a brief respite, during which she made her confession and received the sacraments. All the servants were summoned, even the meanest of them, and she made public admission of her sins against the public, humbly asking forgiveness for the scandal which she had caused and for her ill-tempers, with such true-seeming repentance that nothing could have been more edifying. She then received the sacraments with ardent piety. The fear of death, that had so tormented her during her life, was suddenly dispelled and she ceased to be troubled. She then thanked God in the presence of all these people for permitting her to die far from the children of her sin, and that was the only time she spoke of them during her illness. Her mind was set on things eternal although they tried to persuade her that she would recover. Her state was that of a sinner whose fears are soothed by sure confidence in the mercy of God and who dies without regrets, only desirous of rendering her sacrifice agreeable in His sight by gentle and peaceful resignation.

D'Antin had been summoned by courier and arrived as she was dying. She looked at him and said only that he found her in a very different state of mind from when he had last seen her at her Château de Bellegarde. She died soon afterwards, having left orders for her funeral that were either ill-conceived or wrongly interpreted, for her body, which in life had been so beautiful, became the victim of an unskilled country surgeon and the ceremonies were conducted by lower servants, the remainder of the household having immediately deserted her. The Maréchale de Cœuvres lost no time in retiring to the Abbaye de Saint-Menoux, a few miles from Bourbon, taking some of the company with her, while the remainder dispersed in various directions. For a long period the body was left lying at the hall-door, while the clergy quarrelled over matters of precedence in a truly disgusting manner. It was then given into the keeping of the parish, like the corpse of any local townswoman, and only long afterwards was it removed with shameful lack of ceremony to her own family's vault at Poitiers. The poor of the province, on whom she had rained alms, mourned for her bitterly, as did vast numbers of other people who had benefited by her generosity.

Nothing could exceed the grief of Mme la Duchesse d'Orléans, Madame la Duchesse, and the Comte de Toulouse. M. du Maine, on the other hand, could scarcely conceal his joy, for at last he was rid of an embarrassment. Madame la Duchesse's sorrow came as a surprise, seeing that all her life she had prided herself on caring for no one, and love, or what passed for such, had hitherto brought her no regrets. Still more surprising was the intense grief shown by Monsieur le Duc, normally so immovable, who had always seemed ashamed of recognizing her as his mother-in-law. Their reactions confirmed my opinion that Mme de Montespan's death put an end to their most cherished hopes.

Mme de Maintenon might have been expected to feel relief at being delivered from a rival whom she had eclipsed and driven from the Court, but never quite destroyed as a source of fear and jealousy. Not so, however. When she received the news she was overcome with remorse for all that she owed to her former mistress and the way in which she had repaid her kindness. So upset was she that she could not restrain her tears and resorted to her chaise-percée as her only refuge. Mme la Duchesse de Bourgogne, who followed her there, was speechless with amazement, and not less so at the total insensibility of the King, who had loved Mme de Montespan so passionately and for so long. She could not resist expressing her astonishment, but he answered calmly that when he had sent Mme de Montespan away he never expected to see her again, and that thus she was already dead to him. It was plain to see that the grief of their mutual children displeased him, but it took its course nevertheless, and lasted a long time. The whole Court called on them without commenting, and found them a most curious spectacle. Even more remarkable was the, to them, humiliating contrast of the Princesse de Conti, who was wearing mourning for her aunt, Mme de la Vallière, whereas the daughters of the King and Mme de Montespan dared not put on black for their repudiated mother. They could show their sorrow only by wearing no finery or jewels, and by absenting themselves from all pleasures, even from cards, as they all, including the Comte de Toulouse, did for a long time. The life-story and conduct of so famous a mistress after her banishment from the Court has seemed to me sufficiently interesting to warrant enlarging upon, while the effect of her death is entirely characteristic of the life at Courts.

1707

Death of the Duchesse de Nemours

THE death of the Duchesse de Nemours[1] followed very closely upon that of Mme de Montespan and made an even greater sensation, although of a different kind. She was the daughter of the last Duc de Longueville by his first wife, the eldest daughter of that Comte de Soissons[2] who brought and lost the famous suit against the Prince de Condé, his own nephew.[3]

[1] Marie d'Orléans-Longueville, married Henri II of Savoy, duc de Nemours.

[2] Charles de Bourbon (1566–1612), son of the first Prince de Condé.

[3] Here follow three tightly packed pages of genealogy, extending to bastard first cousins with their ancestors, and descendants in several generations. This is part of Macaulay's 'desert road' referred to in the preface to this book.

F*

Mme de Nemours was a very odd shape and had a way of dressing like the most menial lay-sister, which was not less peculiar. She had prominent short-sighted eyes and a habit of twitching one shoulder, but none the less managed to appear dignified. Haughty in the extreme, she was also exceedingly intelligent, with an eloquent and witty tongue which she made no effort to control. She lived in one half of the Hôtel de Soissons and in the other lived the Princesse de Carignan, with whom she frequently quarrelled, notwithstanding that the latter was her mother's half-sister and a Princess of the Blood. To her inherited hatred of the Condé family she joined the rancour which step-children often feel towards their stepmother; indeed, she never forgave the second Mme de Longueville for the ill-treatment which she professed to have received from her. Still less would she forgive the two Princes de Condé for having removed from her the guardianship and property of her young step-brother, nor the Prince de Conti for having succeeded to the family inheritance through a will drawn up in his favour. Her speeches on these subjects were intensely violent and cutting, and often most amusing, for she never lacked words and spared no one, not even the Princes of the Blood. She liked her natural heirs, the Gondys and the Matignons, no better.

She was immensely wealthy and lived in great splendour and state, but quarrels and lawsuits soured her nature so that she became spiteful and unforgiving. She never ceased to talk of her supposed injuries, and when someone once asked her whether she said the Lord's Prayer, she answered that she did, but avoided the clause about forgiving trespasses. It may thus be inferred that her religion did not much incommode her. One of her favourite anecdotes was that on one occasion she went to confession leaving her people outside the church. The priest, who was unfavourably impressed by her clothes and appearance, told her to be quiet when she began to speak of her great wealth and the sins of the Princes de Condé. She, however, believed her case to be so important that she insisted on elaborating in terms of millions and vast estates. The good priest then began to think her crazed and after bidding her be calm and banish such vain imaginings, he told her to think no more of them and to go and drink some good strong broth, if she had the means to make it. Whereupon she flew into such a passion that he shut the slide. She then rose from

her knees and made for the church door, with the priest
following, in his anxiety to see what would become of her.
Imagine his amazement when he saw this lunatic, as he thought,
received by ladies-in-waiting, equerries, and the vast suite of
servants who always attended her. He felt like sinking through
the ground and ran to her carriage door to ask her pardon. She
mocked him and gained one day's dispensation from confession.

A few weeks before her death she became so ill that they
urged her to meditate on her approaching end, and she finally
consented to send her confessor with one of her gentlemen to
ask forgiveness of Monsieur le Prince, M. le Prince de Condé,
and MM. de Matignon[1] on her behalf. They all then returned to
see her and were amiably received. But that was all, it did them
no good, for none of them gained anything. She died at the age
of eighty-six, having left all that she could to the two daughters
of the bastard of the last Comte de Soissons. One of them died
young and unmarried, the other married the Duc de Luynes.

1708

Mishap to Mme la Duchesse de Bourgogne

MME LA DUCHESSE DE BOURGOGNE was pregnant; she felt
extremely unwell. Contrary to his usual custom, the King
wished to go to Fontainebleau at the beginning of the summer
and announced his intention. In the meantime, he wanted to
make the usual Marly excursions. His granddaughter amused
him, he would not go without her, but travelling was bad for
her condition. Mme de Maintenon grew anxious. Fagon put in
a discreet word. This merely irritated the King, who was not
used to being crossed and had been spoiled by his mistresses,
who had always accompanied him on journeys, even when
pregnant or just risen from child-bed, and had always worn
full court-dress. Objections to the Marly visits irritated him
but did not prevent them. The most that he would concede
was to defer twice the one arranged for Low Monday, and
he insisted on going on the Wednesday of the following week
despite all that could be said or done to stop him, or to gain

[1] The Maréchal de Matignon and the Comte de Matignon, her natural heirs.

permission for Mme la Duchesse de Bourgogne to remain at Versailles.

At Marly, on the Saturday, the King went out into the gardens after mass, and was diverting himself with the carp in the ornamental basin between the Château and the long vista when the Duchesse du Lude appeared, walking towards us, although there were no ladies with the King at that time— there seldom were in the morning. He realized that she must have something important to say and went to meet her, and as they approached one another we stopped and left him to join her alone. The conversation was short. The Duchesse returned to the Château, and the King to us and on towards the carp, without uttering a word. Everyone could see what had happened, but no one dared to comment. Eventually, when the King was quite near the basin, he turned to the chief persons present and said crossly, addressing no one in particular, 'The Duchesse de Bourgogne has miscarried!' nothing more. Thereupon M. de La Rochefoucauld actually exclaimed; M. de Bouillon, the Duc de Tresmes, and the Maréchal de Boufflers echoed his words in an undertone, and M. de La Rochefoucauld protested out loud that it was a thousand pities, since she had miscarried before and might well have no other children. 'And if that should happen,' interrupted the King furiously, 'what do I care? She has one son already, has she not? And if he dies, is not the Duc de Berry of age to marry and have children? Why should I mind who succeeds me; are they not all grandchildren of mine?' Then with a sudden rush of impatience, 'Thank God that she has miscarried, since it was bound to happen! Now, perhaps, I shall not be thwarted in my excursions and everything else that I want to do, by doctors' orders and midwives' argufying. At last, I can come and go as I please and they will leave me in peace.' A silence during which you might have heard an ant walking succeeded this outburst. All eyes were lowered, people scarcely dared to breathe. Stupefaction reigned. Even the gardeners and the craftsmen working on the buildings stood still. The silence lasted for fully a quarter of an hour.

It was the King himself who broke it by leaning over the balustrade and speaking of a carp. No one answered him. Thereafter, he addressed his remarks about carp to the gardeners, who were not usually included in his conversation, and then he only spoke to them of the carp. It was all vastly dull and the King went away soon afterwards. As soon as he was out of sight and we dared to look at one another, our eyes met and spoke volumes. For a moment all those present became intimate. They marvelled, were sorry, finally shrugged their shoulders. Although this scene happened so long ago it is as vivid as yesterday to me. M. de La Rochefoucauld was furious and, on this occasion, rightly so. The first equerry[1] was almost swooning with fright. As for me, I was all eyes and ears as I noted these people, and I congratulated myself for having long ago discovered that the King only loved and considered himself, and was his own prime object. His dreadful speech had repercussions far beyond Marly.

1708

Samuel Bernard the Banker

I MUST not omit a trivial affair which I witnessed on this same excursion, when the King was showing his gardens at Marly. It was about five in the afternoon when he came out walking; he proceeded past all the pavilions on the Marly side, and stopped at the one in which Desmarets, then controller-general of finance, was lodging. Thereupon Desmarets came out accompanied by the famous banker Samuel Bernard, whom he had invited to dine and consult with him. The latter was then the richest man in Europe and the owner of the greatest and safest banking business. He was one who knew his own power and required to be treated with respect, so that the controllers-general who usually had far greater need of him than he of them, were always most deferential in their manner towards him.

The King spoke to Desmarets, saying that he was glad to see M. Bernard, then turning to the latter, said, 'You are a nice one never to have seen Marly. Come with me now, and I will show you the gardens and afterwards hand you back to Desmarets.' Bernard accordingly followed him and during the entire walk the King spoke only to him, took him everywhere and showed him everything, with the charm which he knew so

[1] Beringhen.

well how to assume when he had some object in view. I marvelled, and not I alone, that the King, who was usually miserly with words, should so prostitute himself, as it seemed, to a man of Bernard's quality. It was not long, however, before I understood the reason, and then I marvelled at the straits to which the greatest kings sometimes find themselves reduced.

Desmarets had been at his wits' end to find money, which was needed for everything, every fund having been exhausted. He had been to Paris hat in hand to every banker, but so often and so flagrantly had all manner of contracts been dishonoured and firm promises broken that he had met with nothing but apologies and closed doors. Bernard, like the rest, would not lend, indeed there was already much owing to him. In vain Desmarets had urged the pressing need and the enormous profits which he had at times made in the King's business. Bernard was not to be moved. So there were the King and Desmarets sorely perplexed. Finally, the latter told His Majesty that all things being considered, Bernard was the only man capable of extricating him because, as was well known, he had enormous sums at his command. The difficulty would be to persuade him to change his mind and to overcome his stubbornness that verged on insolence. Desmarets added that Bernard was eaten up with vanity and might be more ready to open his purse if the King were to condescend to flatter him. In the critical state to which his affairs had come, His Majesty consented, and Desmarets proposed the expedient which I have already described, so as to give the affair a cloak of seeming respectability and avoid a refusal. Bernard fell for the bait. He returned to Desmarets after his walk with the King so delighted that, of his own accord, he said that he would prefer ruin rather than leave in difficulties a prince who had shown him so much honour, and he proceeded to praise him to the skies. Desmarets took instant advantage of the situation and extracted far more than ever he had intended.

1708

Death of Mansard

MANSARD[1] died very suddenly during that Marly excursion. He was the surveyor of the works, and a character on whom we may well pause for a moment. A tall, well-built man, of very humble origin, he had a pleasant face and exceedingly sharp wits, which he cleverly used to ingratiate himself with his betters, although he never wholly shook off the vulgarity belonging to his earlier condition. First a drummer-boy, then a stone-cutter, then a mason's apprentice, later a groom, he managed to endear himself to the great François Mansard, who left so fine a name in French architecture, who used him on the King's buildings and endeavoured to train and make something out of him. People used to say that he was Mansard's bastard, but he gave it out that he was a nephew of the great man, and took his name after his death in 1666, by which means he hoped to become better known, and he succeeded. Finally, he attracted the King's notice. Thereafter, he proceeded to put his acquaintance with the gentlemen, valets, and masons to such good purpose that His Majesty, who already admired in him the virtues of obscurity and unattachment, endowed him with his uncle's genius and, hurriedly dismissing Villacerf, the then surveyor, put Mansard into his place. None the less, Mansard did not know his work, and De Coste, his brother-in-law, whom he made his head architect, was as ignorant as he. They took all their plans, drawings, and ideas from another architect nicknamed L'Assurance, whom as far as possible they kept firmly under lock and key.

Mansard cunningly enticed the King from small beginnings to embark on long and costly enterprises. He showed him unfinished sketches, especially for gardens, which fired his imagination so that he made suggestions. Then Mansard, exclaiming that he would never have thought of such a thing, would go into raptures, declaring that compared with His Majesty he was no better than a student, so that the King fell

[1] See note, p. 58.

into his trap quite innocently. Drawings in hand, he insinuated himself into the semi-private apartments and then gradually into all of them and at all hours, then often without any plans or business to discuss. Later, he took to sharing in the conversation and accustomed the King to discuss the news and other matters with him. Sometimes, he went so far as to ask questions, but he knew how to choose his moments, for he understood the King to perfection and never mistook the times for being familiar or formal. He liked to show off his privileges during the King's walks and to see people marvelling at the lengths to which he dared to go. Yet he never used his influence to harm anyone, although it might have been dangerous to attack him. In this way he acquired status and induced not only the nobles and Princes of the Blood, but even the bastards and ministers to serve his interests. They and the upper servants were very careful to remain on good terms with him.

The King had precisely the same kind of partiality for Mansard as he had for Fagon.[1] Just as he was greatly vexed when courtiers did not consult the latter when they were ill, and obey his orders, so it was thought most rash for anyone to consider building a house or making a garden without employing Mansard. As a matter of fact, Mansard thought the same himself, but he was not capable. He built the bridge at Moulins and called it a masterpiece of stability and boasted of it in a monstrously complacent way. Four or five months after it was finished, however, Charlus, the father of the Duc de Levis, happened to attend the King's *lever* on returning from his estates near Moulins. Mansard was present at the time and hoping to hear praise of his bridge, after a while asked the King to inquire about it. But Charlus was a clever man, although disappointed and inclined to be cynical, and he made no reply, which the King noticed and asked him again. 'Sire,' said Charlus then, 'I know nothing about it since it went away, but I think that at present it must be somewhere near Nantes.' 'What are you talking about?' said the King. 'I mean the bridge at Moulins.' 'Precisely, Sire,' replied Charlus soberly, 'the bridge at Moulins. It came adrift the night before I left, and went floating off down the river.' The King

---

[1] On one occasion, when walking with Mansard in the sun, Louis XIV told him to put his hat on. He is then supposed to have said to the astonished courtiers, 'I can make twenty Dukes in a quarter of an hour, but it takes centuries to make a Mansard.' Saint-Simon does not record this anecdote.

and Mansard looked astounded, and the courtiers laughed behind their hands. This was indeed exactly what had happened;
and the bridge at Blois, which Mansard built shortly before,
played him the same trick.

He made an enormous deal of money out of his buildings,
contracts, and all other aspects of his work. He was autocratic
in the extreme. No craftsman nor contractor, nor any other
person concerned with his buildings ever dared to argue
with him or make the slightest protest. Since neither he nor the
King had any taste, he never created a thing of beauty, nor even
anything convenient for its purpose, to justify the vast expenses
which he incurred. Monseigneur ceased to employ him at
Meudon after others had convinced him that Mansard merely
led him into extravagances, but the King, instead of being
grateful to Monseigneur and angry with Mansard, did his
best to reconcile them and even offered to defray some of the
costs. None the less, Monseigneur was annoyed at being taken
for a fool; he refused the offer, and remained vexed about the
whole affair. Du Mont told me this as a fact.

The fine chapel at Versailles, for fine it is, so far as craftsmanship and ornamentation are concerned—that chapel that
took so many years to build and cost such millions of francs—is
so badly proportioned that it seems to overpower the palace. It
was designed in that way for a special purpose. Mansard
indeed calculated the proportions solely from the viewpoint of
the royal pew, because he knew that the King was most unlikely to enter the chapel from below. He then deliberately
made that hideous excrescence above the roof of the palace so
as to force the King to raise the whole building one storey in
order to hide it. Had not war broken out at the critical moment,
the work would have been carried out. In the meanwhile,
however, Mansard died.

1709

The Fearful Winter of 1709

IT was a terrible winter, worse than any within living memory.
A bitter frost continued without respite for two months,

freezing the rivers down to their very mouths and making the edge of the sea so hard that heavily laden wagons were driven over it. A false thaw then set in, melting the snow that had covered the land, and this was followed by a sudden renewal of the same hard frost that lasted for another three weeks. It was so cold that bottles of Queen-of-Hungary-water, the strongest elixirs, and the most spirituous liquors burst in the cupboards of rooms in the palace of Versailles, rooms that were heated with fires and surrounded by chimney-flues. I saw this happen with my own eyes, several times. Once, indeed, when I was supping with the Duc de Villeroy in his small bedroom, pieces of ice fell into our glasses from bottles that had been standing on the chimneypiece after being brought from his tiny kitchen where a great fire was burning, and it was on the same level as his bedroom, with only a little ante-chamber between the two. That apartment is the one now occupied by his son.

It was the second frost that proved disastrous. The fruit trees were all killed; no walnuts, olives, apples, nor vines survived, or none worth mentioning. Other kinds of trees perished in great numbers, the gardens were ruined, and the seeds died in the ground. You can form no idea of the destruction caused by this national calamity. Everyone began to hoard their old grain and the price of bread rose, as hopes of a harvest receded. The wisest resowed their wheat fields with barley; others followed suit, and they were the fortunate ones, for it proved to be their salvation. However, the police took it into their heads to forbid it, and then repented too late. Several government decrees were issued about wheat, searches were instituted for hidden stocks of grain, and commissaries were sent into the various provinces three months later than was advertised. Yet all that this policy achieved was to bring poverty and prices to a fatal height at a time when the computations showed there to be enough wheat stored in France to feed the entire nation for two years, independently of the harvest.

Many people began to think that the gentlemen of the finance department were using the opportunity to lay hands on the wheat by sending their agents to buy in all the markets of the kingdom, and then selling to the King's profit, not forgetting their own. It then happened that a very great number of barge-loads of corn purchased by the King went rotten and had to be thrown into the Loire, and this gave weight to suspicion, for they could not hide the circumstances. It is very certain, at any rate, that wheat was sold at the same price in all provincial markets, whereas in Paris, the commissaries kept prices at a higher level and often obliged vendors to raise them against their will. When the people cried out to know how long this dearness would last, some commissaries—and this in a market not two paces from my own house in Saint-Germain-des-Prés— were moved by pity to let slip the revealing answer, 'As long as you choose.' They meant by this, so long as the people suffered no wheat to enter Paris without a permit from d'Argenson, the police-lieutenant, for none was allowed to enter otherwise, and this prohibition was enforced with the utmost severity especially as regards the bakers. What I have been describing soon became the general practice all over France, for the administrators everywhere did what d'Argenson was doing in Paris. Moreover, in all provincial markets, wheat that remained unsold at closing time at the prices they had fixed was forcibly removed, and any dealer with sufficient compassion to sell lower was severely punished.

Maréchal, the chief surgeon, of whom I have spoken more than once, had the courage to tell the King of all this, and to warn him of the dreadful conclusions to which the people were driven, even the more dependable among them and those of better condition. The King seemed moved and was not vexed with Maréchal for speaking, but he would do nothing.

Vast stocks of wheat were stored in many different places and with the greatest possible secrecy, although nothing was more expressly forbidden in the edicts. The people were even enjoined to denounce hoarders, but one unfortunate man who tried to lay information with Desmarets was very roughly handled by the mob. The houses of the Parlement assembled separately on account of the unrest, and then held a meeting of deputies in the great chamber. A resolution was passed that the King should be advised to send counsellors throughout the provinces, at their own expense, to inspect the wheat stocks, instruct the police, and punish those who disobeyed the edicts, and a list was added of counsellors willing to make such tours through the different départements. When the King was informed of this by the president, he became amazingly angry and wished to send back a severe reprimand, bidding them mind their own business and concern themselves solely with adjudicating in lawsuits. The chancellor dared not remind him that what the Parlement proposed was perfectly correct and well within its province, but he emphasized the love and respect with which the advice had been proffered and the ministers' full realization that he was master, to accept or reject it. After some argument the King was sufficiently pacified so that he did not send the reprimand, but he absolutely insisted on the Parlement being informed that he forbade it to concern itself with wheat. This message was given in open council, when only the chancellor spoke. All the other ministers preserved absolute silence. It was very obvious what they were thinking, but they were careful to say nothing in a matter that touched the chancellor's own ministry. Indeed, although like other public bodies the Parlement was well used to snubs, it felt this one deeply and obeyed with great reluctance.

The public, as a whole, were equally distressed. Not a man but believed that had the finance department been forced to give up these cruel practices the resolution might have pleased the King, and served him by interposing the Parlement between him and his people. It would have demonstrated that no chicanery was intended, without diminishing by anything, either real or apparent, that absolute, boundless authority of which he was so acutely jealous.

Without probing into the question of who devised or most profited from the transactions, it may be said that scarcely another age can show a plot more sinister, more brazen, or better organized, or a tyranny more lasting, sure, and cruel. The fortunes it made were countless, and countless were the people who died literally of starvation, or perished afterwards from illnesses caused by extremes of poverty. Infinite numbers of families were ruined and cascades of misfortunes of all kinds followed thereafter.[1]

In the meanwhile, the most sacred trusts began to cease payments; returns from customs duties and the various mortgage and lending establishments, even the hitherto inviolable rentes of the Hôtel de Ville were all suspended. The repayment of the rentes was only delayed but because of the delays and subsequent reductions, most families in Paris and many other large towns were distressed. At this time, taxes were raised and

---

[1] Madame said that while Mme de Maintenon ostentatiously ate black bread in public, she was making a fortune speculating in wheat.

multiplied, and applied with a rigour that completed the ruin of France. Prices reached fantastic heights so that no money was left to buy in even the cheapest market; yet, although through the poverty of their owners cattle were dying for lack of food, still another tax was levied upon them. Very many people who had assisted the poor in previous years found themselves reduced to a bare subsistence and many of these were even driven to receive alms in secret. No one can tell how many others tried to gain admission into almshouses that had been the dread and shame of the poor, nor how many ruined almshouses vomited back their poor upon the public charge (which meant certain death by starvation), nor how many worthy families died of want in their empty granaries.

Again, it can hardly be told how the sight of such misery awakened the zeal for charity, nor how immense were the alms given. Yet at this very time when poverty was increasing day by day, some meddlesome, autocratic philanthropist conceived the idea of new taxes and a levy for the benefit of the poor. These were applied with so little discretion in addition to the other taxes that vast numbers of people were placed in even greater need and some were provoked to curtailing their voluntary alms-giving. Thus apart from the cost of collecting these ill-distributed taxes, the poor were left in a worse state than before. What, however, has proved far more disturbing is that these taxes, which were levied to succour the needy, were appropriated by the King, in a modified but perpetual form. Officials of the finance department collect them openly even today as a branch of the royal revenues and have not even troubled to change their names.

The same is true of the tax levied in each division annually for the maintenance of the highroads. That, too, has been appropriated by the finance department in the same flagrant manner and without changing the name. Most bridges in the kingdom are broken and main roads have become impassable. Trade has suffered immense damage, but the merchants are now alive to what has been happening. In Champagne, Lescalopier, the administrator, devised a scheme for repairing the roads by forced labour, and did not pay even with bread. Other regions copied him and he has been rewarded by being made counsellor of state. Officials employed on these works were enriched by a government monopoly, but the labourers died in gangs. In the end the whole system became impossible and was abandoned, like the roads themselves. None the less, the tax for constructing and maintaining the roads was in existence during the whole time of the forced labour gangs, has continued ever since, and is still collected as part of the royal revenues.

Let us, however, return to the year 1709. At that time, people were constantly wondering what had become of all the money in France, for no one could pay because no one was paid. In the country, people were insolvent on account of extortions and bad debts, commerce brought in no returns, good faith and confidence were shattered. Thus the King was left with no resource but terror and the exercise of his supreme power, but boundless though that was, it often failed for want of anything to act upon. The circulation of money stopped and there was no means of restarting it. The King ceased even to pay his troops, and no one could imagine what became of the vast millions that were entering his coffers.

Such was the dreadful state of affairs when Rouillé, and after him, Torcy, were sent into Holland to negotiate a peace. The description which I have given is exact, faithful, and not exaggerated. For, indeed, I must be accurate if you are to have any understanding of the desperate straits to which we were reduced, the enormous sacrifices which the King was compelled to make in order to obtain a peace, and the evident miracle performed by Him who encompasses the sea with bounds and calls to that which is not and to that which is; by Whom France was delivered from the clutches of a Europe ready and willing to destroy her. In truth, the country was saved with many advantages, considering her condition and the little hope of salvation which she had possessed.

In the meanwhile, the reminting of the currency and its revaluation at a third above its intrinsic value brought the King some profit, but at the same time private persons were ruined and trade was thrown into such confusion that it nearly came to a standstill.

Lyons was destroyed by the unexpected, stupendous bankruptcy of Samuel Bernard and its terrible after-effects although Desmarets supported him as far as he was able. Paper-money and its depreciation were the cause of it. The famous banker had issued notes to the equivalent of twenty millions and owed for almost as much at Lyons. He was given fourteen millions in good assignations in the hopes that with that, added to what he could scrape together from his bank-notes, he would be saved. It has since been suggested that he managed to make a good thing out of his bankruptcy. In fact, whilst no single person of his rank has ever spent or left so much, or possessed anything approaching his credit throughout the whole of Europe until his death thirty years later, he was never able to re-establish himself in Lyons nor the part of Italy adjacent.

1709

Fall of the Duc de Vendôme

ON his return from Flanders, Vendôme had an audience with the King, only one, and that a short one. Nevertheless, he did not forget Puységur[1] and complained of him most bitterly, saying everything bad to which he could lay his tongue, on his usual assumption that his bare word was enough. Puységur, of whom I have spoken more than once, was well known to the King and had a privileged kind of relationship with him, because he reported constantly on the Royal Regiment of Infantry, which the King actually believed himself to command. Puységur had spent most of his life in that regiment, either as major or lieutenant-colonel, and he possessed the King's full confidence.

Puységur was thus quite accustomed to private audiences, and knew that after such an awkward campaign[2] he would be questioned very closely if he arrived hot on the news. He therefore prudently lay low for a couple of months at his house in the Soissonnais, before appearing at Paris or Versailles. By that time interest had begun to cool and he had learned of the Duc de Vendôme's unflattering remarks. He did not care to give the impression that he feared to show himself and thus at last came to Court.

The King, who had always liked him and who had been grieved by M. de Vendôme's aspersions, called him alone into his study a few days later, and asked him, in a kindly way, to

---

[1] Jacques-François du Chastenet, Marquis de Puységur.
[2] The Flanders campaign of 1708, which included the defeat at Oudenarde and the loss of Lille.

explain the many foolish actions of which he had been accused. Whereupon, Puységur enlightened him so vividly that the King was surprised into admitting that M. de Vendôme was his informant. At that name, Puységur was stung into seizing his opportunity. He told the King first, what had kept him so long from the Court, and then described simply and courageously the faults, follies, mulishness, and arrogance of M. de Vendôme, all with so much detail and clarity that the King listened attentively, asking many questions and demanding ever more information.

Puységur answered all that he was asked; then, seeing the King receptive, silent, and at every point convinced, he pressed on to say that since Vendôme had spared him so little, in spite of all his restraint and consideration, he felt it to be both permissible and his bounden duty as a soldier to make him known to the King, once and for all. Thereupon, he gave a complete picture of the Duc de Vendôme, his personal life with the army, his bodily unseemliness, his unsound judgment, his warped mind, the falseness and danger of his military principles, and his total ignorance of proper conduct in wartime. Then reverting to all his Italian campaigns and the two last seasons in Flanders, he exposed him utterly, proving to the King beyond all possible doubt that only by a series of miracles had France not been lost a hundred times under his command.

The conversation lasted for more than two hours. The King, who knew and had proved by long experience not only Puységur's ability but his honesty and exactness, had his eyes suddenly opened to the true character of that man who had so artfully been represented as the hero and guardian angel of France. He was mortified and ashamed of his gullibility. From that instant Vendôme was as dead to his mind and permanently excluded from holding any command—an exclusion that was not slow in becoming known.

Puységur, a naturally humble, modest gentleman, was none the less firm and courageous when roused. He had nothing more to lose with M. de Vendôme, after what the latter had said of him in public and to the King, and moreover he was well content with his audience. He at once repeated everything, word for word, in the great gallery, and nobly braved Vendôme's anger and that of his cabal, of whose existence he was fully aware.

The cabal raged. Vendôme was still more furious. But they could produce only wretchedly unsound counter-arguments that deceived no one. Those most knowledgeable now considered them to be almost out of favour. The rival, and hitherto down-trodden party welcomed Puységur with open arms, and Mme de Maintenon, Mme la Duchesse de Bourgogne and, especially, the Duc de Beauvilliers, finally drove home to the King the truth of what he had first learned from Puységur alone.

The end came swiftly. Vendôme, thrown out of the service, sold his military equipment, dismissed his household, and retired to Anet, where the grass had already begun to grow.[1]

1709

The Silver is taken to the Mint

IN the meantime, especially in Flanders, the armies were lacking in everything. All possible efforts were made during the early part of June to send money and transport wheat by sea from Brittany and by road from Picardy. Nevertheless the money and bread arrived only in small quantities, and for long periods the army was left to forage for itself on a much narrowed frontier.

I have already said that I would not give an account of the peace negotiations, nor of the journeys which Rouillé and Torcy made to Holland. I will merely say that Torcy returned to Versailles on Saturday, June 1st, after being absent for a month. He had nothing good to report and was very coolly received by the King and Mme de Maintenon. The latter, especially, was exceedingly critical, partly because she did not care for him personally, and partly because she had not been informed of his mission in advance.

At this time, when Mme de Maintenon's influence was being so disastrous in great affairs, that nasty woman whom the Duc de Gramont had married was being equally obnoxious in lesser

---

[1] See p. 114. The grass was growing again because courtiers, who had heard rumours of his coming disgrace, had ceased to tread it down.

matters, for such is the way of these unpleasant creatures. The King had compelled her to return from Bayonne, where her habits of looting by trickery and force had become too notorious, but she managed to filch the dowager Queen of Spain's[1] pearls and had shown her want of propriety in every way imaginable. Now that she was back in Paris, she was driven to desperation at being deprived of the honours and privileges which should have been hers on marriage.

While the Court waited for the return of Rouillé, who had been recalled by the King, it was decided to arouse the loyalty of every class in the kingdom by publishing the enemy's monstrous conditions, or rather demands, for a peace settlement. A printed letter was accordingly dispatched to all provincial governors, with orders to spread the facts abroad and make it known to what lengths the King had gone in his efforts to secure a peace, and how unsuccessful those efforts had proved. The results fully came up to expectations. There was an immediate outburst of indignation, a clamour for vengeance, and offers from all manner of people to sacrifice all their possessions so as to continue the war, with many other such extravagant proposals to prove their zeal.

It was in these circumstances that the Gramont woman saw an opportunity of obtaining all that had been denied her and which she so passionately desired. She persuaded her husband to go to the King and offer to give his service of silver plate. She hoped that his example would be followed and that she would gain credit and rewards for procuring so swift, convenient and acceptable a relief. Alas! for her plan. The Duc de Gramont told his son-in-law, the Maréchal de Boufflers, who was so much delighted with the idea that he hastened to offer his own plate, of which he had a great deal and very beautiful. Altogether he made so much noise and fuss in urging others to follow his example, that he was taken for having originated the scheme and no mention was made of the old Gramont, nor even of her husband. They thus became their own dupes, which made her more furious than ever.

All this talk about silver made a great stir. No one dared not to offer, yet everyone greatly disliked the thought. Some people were clinging to their silver plate as a last resource and dreaded parting with it, others feared the uncleanliness of pewter and

---

[1] Mariana of Neuburg (1667–1740), second wife of Charles II. See p. 62n.

earthenware, while others again saw how thankless it would
be to follow where only the first would be given credit. At
the meeting of the Conseil de Finances on the very next day,
the King showed a strong inclination to accept plate from everybody.

This same plan had already been proposed and rejected when
Pontchartrain was contrôleur-général. Now that he was chancellor, he spoke most emphatically against it, pointing out the
smallness of the profit compared with the great sacrifice to the
individuals concerned. He also stressed the shoddiness of the
whole proceeding, for it would mean that the Court and nobility
ate off earthenware, while in the provinces private gentlemen
kept their silver plate, and if that were to be made illegal, the
general discontent and concealment that would result. He
represented the loss of prestige to the government, who might
appear to be using this shift as a last resource, the rumours to
which it would give rise in foreign countries, the contempt of
our enemies, and the encouragement it would be to them.
Finally, he recalled the jests made during the war of 1688, when
the precious silver furniture in the gallery and the great and
little apartments at Versailles, even including the silver throne,
were sent to the Mint. Very little, he said, was gained from that
transaction and, more precious than the metal itself, the loss of
that magnificent craftsmanship, which was then devoted to the
designing of silver plate, had proved irreparable.

Notwithstanding such cogent arguments, the King persisted
in wishing, without using any kind of compulsion, to accept free-
will offerings of all the silver plate which people might choose to
present. This was announced verbally, and patriots were offered
two alternatives. They might give their silver outright by sending it to Launay, the King's goldsmith, who kept a list of names
and of the number of ounces received. For a few days, at least,
the King read the list with care, and promised, again verbally
and in general terms, to return an equal weight to the donors
when his affairs permitted (which no one believed) and to remit
stamp duty from any new plate which they might purchase in
the future. Those who desired repayment might send their
silver for conversion to the Mint, where it would be weighed
on arrival, the names, dates, and ounces written down, and
the owners reimbursed as soon as money became available.
Many were not sorry to be able to sell their plate without

shame, and thus to find some relief in their present need for ready money. Inestimable damage was done, however, for much beautiful work was lost with the moulded, engraved, embossed or carved ornamentations, which once adorned the silver plate of wealthy and tasteful persons.

When the final reckoning was made, there turned out to be fewer than a hundred names on Launay's list and the entire proceeds from the gifts and conversions amounted to less than three millions. The Court, Paris society, and some of the notables had not dared to refuse; a few others, who hoped to gain some immediate relief had followed in their wake, but almost no one else either in Paris or the provinces.

I must admit to having been one of the last to offer, for I was becoming monstrously weary of taxes and felt little inclined to submit to a voluntary levy. When I found myself to be almost the only man of my condition still eating off silver, I sent a thousand pistoles' worth to the Mint and locked away the remainder. I had had a little of my father's old silver, which was unornamented, so I regretted its loss less than the inconvenience and dirt. M. de Lauzun, who had much plate, and all of it very fine, found that his reluctance overcame his loyalty and he did not send. I and several others were present when the Duc de Villeroy questioned him about it. He answered in his low voice, 'Not as yet, I do not know who would favour me by taking it, and besides, how can I be sure that it does not go up the Duchesse de Gramont's petticoat?' I thought that we should die of laughing as he turned sharp about, and left us.

All the nobility had put themselves on porcelain within a week, so that the china shops were emptied and the trade boomed; but the middle classes still continued to use their silver. Even the King began to talk of going onto porcelain. He sent his gold plate to the Mint and M. le Duc d'Orléans sent what little he possessed. The rest of the royal family began to use silver-gilt or silver services, and the Princes and Princesses of the Blood took to porcelain. However, the King soon discovered that most people were cheating, whereupon he expressed himself with a tartness that was unusual with him but had no effect. He would have done better to speak to the Duc de Gramont and his unpleasant old wife, who had caused this shameful, useless sacrifice. They were not duped, for they had locked up their good silver and she, herself, had taken their old plate to the Mint and had seen that she was given good value.

None of the donors enjoyed for long the sensation of having pleased the King. After three months, His Majesty at last realized the futility of this monstrous idea and said that he was sorry he had ever consented to it. That was how they managed things in the Court and kingdom.

1709

Why I wished to Retire from the Court

For a long time I had been realizing the truth in the Bishop of Chartres's warning that someone had spoken ill of me to the King and had made an impression. The change in his manner was most marked and although I still went on all the Marly excursions, I was forced to conclude that I was not being invited for my own sake. This vexed me much because chimney-pots seemed to be falling about my ears and I could not discover the cause nor, consequently, the remedy, and I was weary of the animosity of bitter and powerful enemies whom I had done nothing to provoke, for instance, Monsieur le Duc, Madame la Duchesse, the Vendôme clique, and other jealous, spiteful people such as usually inhabit courts. I had none to set against such enemies but friends like Chamillart, the chancellor, the Maréchal de Boufflers, and the Ducs de Beauvilliers and Chevreuse, who were all without influence or out of favour, and thus, in spite of their good will, unable to help me. In short, my dissatisfaction grew to such a pitch that I seriously desired to leave the Court and abandon all my hopes.

Mme de Saint-Simon, always more prudent than I, argued the sudden changes that continually occur in Court life, those which time might bring, our total dependence on the King, not only for our condition but for my patrimony as well, and many other reasons for delay. Eventually we came to an agreement to go for two years into Guyenne, on the pretext of inspecting a large estate which we owned there but had never visited. In this way we hoped to absent ourselves for a long time without vexing the King and afterwards to proceed as circumstances might direct.

M. de Beauvilliers had asked to be included in our consultations with M. de Chevreuse. He, and the chancellor, to whom we spoke later, approved our plan, since they could not persuade me to remain at Court, but they strongly advised us to speak of the journey well in advance, so as to avoid an appearance of chagrin, and scotch any rumours that I had received a gentle hint to depart.

For so long an absence in a distant place it was necessary to obtain the King's permission, but as in the circumstances I did not care to approach him directly, my good friend La Vrillière, whose département included Guyenne, spoke for me and the King consented. However, for various reasons we were prevented from going to Blaye at that time and therefore decided to stay at La Ferté instead, resolving to spend a year or more at that place, only occasionally returning to the Court, and not always every year, if that were possible without failing in the absolute letter of my duty.

My continued attachment to Chamillart after his downfall had already given offence. I therefore waited to leave the Court until about a month after he had gone into the country in search of some estate where he might live away from Paris. His daughters travelled with us and remained at La Ferté, and he also came there between his excursions, so that I was able to welcome him with the entertainments and pleasure-parties which I could not give for him when he was in favour and office. Now that there was no obligation to court him and nothing to be gained, I had no scruples, and he was clearly touched by my attentions. He stayed with us for a considerable time, and left his daughters with us when he went to Paris to conclude his affairs and the purchase of a property at Courcelles in Maine. In the meanwhile I remained in my own home, as I had intended, but made sure of being fully acquainted with all that happened at the Court.

Let us now return to the situation there both before and after my departure, which was much delayed, although I continued to desire it keenly. Here I find myself without a word to express what I wish to explain, for the Court had become more than ever divided since the downfalls of Vendôme and Chamillart. To speak of cabals is perhaps too strong a word, but without

endless circumlocution no better can be found[1] and I shall therefore use it, adding that although it goes beyond my exact
meaning, the sense can be rendered by no other single term.
Thus I shall say that the Court was split into three different
cabals that included all the principal personalities, very few of
whom allowed their minds to be fully known, while others kept
certain corners secret and had many reservations. Very few
indeed had the country's good solely at heart, although all professed that its precarious state was their chief concern. By far the
greater number thought only of themselves, each man following
his own somewhat indefinite aims to secure fame, influence and,
for the future, power. Some strove for wealth and office. Others,
more cunning or less well placed, adhered to one or other of the
three cabals, forming subordinate cliques that sometimes gave an
impetus to affairs, and ever stimulated the civil war of tongues.

To make matters plain, let us now call these parties by their
proper names and speak of the Cabal of the Nobles, as it was
known at that time, the Cabal of the Ministers, and the Cabal
of Meudon. The first sheltered beneath the wing of Mme de
Maintenon, was on good terms with Monseigneur, alternately
used and was used by Mme la Duchesse de Bourgogne, and
basked in the reflected glory of Boufflers' fame and high reputation. The guiding hand was Harcourt's,[2] even from the Rhine,
and in the second rank was Pontchartrain, the chancellor, in
spite of his exasperation at Mme de Maintenon's aversion to
him and his consequent lack of favour with the King. The second
cabal was united by hopes that sprang from the birth, virtue,
and capabilities of Mgr le Duc de Bourgogne. It included,
bound together by a strong affection, the Duc de Beauvilliers

---

[1] This is how Madame described the situation in a letter to the Duchess of Hanover.
'The entire Court is in a ferment of intrigue. Some try to win the favour of the all-powerful
lady [Mme de Maintenon], others that of Monsieur le Dauphin, others, again, that of the
Duc de Bourgogne. He and his father have no love for one another; the son despises the
father, has ambitions and would like to rule. The Dauphin is completely dominated by his
bastard-sister, Madame la Duchesse. The Princesse de Conti has become the latter's ally,
so as not to lose all her influence with him. All of them are against my son [the Duc
d'Orléans], for they fear that the King may look kindly on him and arrange a match
between his daughter and the Duc de Berry. Madame la Duchesse would much like that
marriage for her own daughter and that is why she monopolises the Duc de Berry. The
Duchesse de Bourgogne, who wants to rule the Dauphin as well as the King, is jealous of
Madame la Duchesse and has accordingly made a pact of friendship with the Duchesse
d'Orléans so as to thwart her. It all provides a vastly pretty comedy of intrigue and
counter-intrigue, and, I might say, in the words of the song, "If we do not die of hunger we
shall laugh ourselves to death." In the meanwhile, the Old Lady sets them all one against
th other so that she may rule all the better.'

[2] Duc d'Harcourt, Marshal of France, not to be confused with the Lorraine d'Harcourts.

the most forthright of them all, the Duc de Chevreuse the centre and strategist of the party, and the Archbishop of Cambrai[1] who directed it from the depths of his exile and disgrace. In the subordinate clique were Torcy and Desmarets, Père Le Tellier, the Jesuits, and Saint-Sulpice. The third cabal, that of Meudon, I have already explained.[2]

The two first held each other at a respectful distance, the second pursued its course quietly, the first, noisily, using every opportunity to injure its rivals. The most fashionable people of the Court and army all belonged to the Cabal of the Nobles; others joined it out of disgust with the government, and many wiser heads were attracted by Boufflers' honesty and the intelligence of Harcourt.

What the world calls chance, which, like everything else, is really an instrument of Providence, has caused me all through my life, in the strangest manner, to become attached to the most opposing personalities. It now played me the same trick with regard to the Cabals of the Nobles and the Ministers. I was in close friendship with the Ducs de Beauvilliers and Chevreuse and with nearly all their families; I was intimate with Chamillart even after his downfall; I stood well with the Jesuits and with Mgr le Duc de Bourgogne, and also with the Archbishop of Cambrai, although I did not know him personally. My real place, therefore, was with this cabal that counted Mgr le Duc de Bourgogne as one of themselves against the whole world.

On the other hand, I was the confidant of the chancellor and his family in almost all their affairs both public and private; I was on friendly terms with the Duc and Duchesse de Villeroy and through them with the Duc de La Rocheguyon. I also had the confidence of Beringhen, and of Du Mont and Bignon who, with his wife, was a friend of Mlle Choin. The latter belonged to the Meudon Cabal, which was still so much alive that I could wish neither of the other two to succumb.

I dare say that the good opinion of these important people and the friendship which many of them felt for me allowed them to speak freely and confidentially of the most secret and serious matters. And although it sometimes happened that they let slip something concerning my friends on the other side, they were not unduly perturbed. It was through the chancellor and

---

[1] Fénelon: François de Salignac de la Mothe (1651–1715).
[2] See page 125.

the Maréchal de Boufflers that I learned most of what went on, for the Ducs de Beauvilliers and Chevreuse were less observant and often ill-informed.

Besides these reliable sources, I had access to one of the inmost circles of the Court through some of the most intelligent ladies, especially those in the entourage of Mme la Duchesse de Bourgogne. Old and young, and of various characters, they perceived many things from their own observation and learned the rest from the princess. Thus, day by day, I received confidential news of the inner workings of that fascinating sphere, and by the same channels I often learned the secret intrigues of Mme de Maintenon's sanctum.

I had still other sources of information regarding a circle no less private. I refer to the confidential valets who, day and night, were in attendance in the King's apartments and by no means kept their eyes and ears tightly shut.

By such means I was regularly informed of all that went on, both grave and trivial, through honest, direct, and sure channels. Thus, apart from my other concerns, my curiosity was satisfied, and you must admit, whether you be somebody or nobody, that that is the only nourishment to be found at Courts, and that without it you would die of boredom.

1711

Death of Monseigneur

In that year, Easter Sunday fell on 5 April. On the following Wednesday, after the meeting of the council, Monseigneur dined *in parvulo* at Meudon, taking Mme la Duchesse de Bourgogne tête-à-tête in his coach. What the *parvulos* were, I have already explained. The Court had asked for this Meudon visit, which was due to last one week, until the Marly excursion announced for the next Wednesday. I myself had been absent since the Monday in Holy Week and intended to go to Marly on the same day as the King. The Meudon parties were now intensely embarrassing to me, feeling, as I did, that the whole place was infested with devils. Mme la Duchesse had returned to queen it there and had brought her daughters. Mlle de

G

Lillebonne and Mme d'Espinoy openly ruled the roost; d'Antin gave the orders, and between them they controlled Monseigneur. They were all my personal enemies and therefore I avoided the visits to Meudon, for although this made me feel ill at ease with Monseigneur and his circle, I might have felt far worse had I risked going there.

Although the present situation disquieted me, other thoughts were still more troubling. Every day, the prospect grew clearer of the future time when Monseigneur would sit upon the throne, and, when the quarrelling of those who now influenced him and aimed at ruling him exclusively had abated, would have raised beside him one or other of the enemies who above all things desired to ruin me. They would only have to express their wish. Failing all other comfort, I lived on my courage, telling myself that one never experiences all the good or all the ill which one has most reason to expect. In this way, hoping against hope, I put my trust in the uncertainty of all earthly things and whiled away my time, calm enough as regards the future, but in the utmost embarrassment where the present and Meudon were concerned.

That was why I had gone to spend the Easter fortnight resting and meditating far from the Court, where at that time, every prospect, with the exception of Monseigneur and some others, was pleasing to me. That sting seemed past all remedy and it plagued me cruelly until suddenly, at the most unexpected moment, it pleased God to deliver me. No one was staying with me at La Ferté, except M. de Saint-Louis, a retired cavalry officer, who for the past thirty years had been living at the Abbaye de La Trappe, and a gentleman of Normandy, a former captain in my regiment, who was much attached to me. I had been walking with them in the garden on the morning of Saturday 11th, and was alone in my study shortly before dinner, when a courier brought me a letter from Mme de Saint-Simon to say that Monseigneur had been taken ill.

That prince, as I have already said, going to Meudon on the day after the Easter festival, was passing through Chaville when he saw a priest bearing Our Lord to a dying man, and got down from his coach with Mme la Duchesse de Bourgogne to kneel and worship. He asked to whom they were taking the Sacrament and heard that it was to a man dying of the small-pox, which was very prevalent at that time. Monseigneur had

had the disease in early childhood, but very slightly, and was mortally afraid of it. He was much alarmed, and said to Boudin,[1] his chief physician, that it would not surprise him if he had taken it. None the less, the rest of that day passed without incident.

On the following day, Thursday 9th, Monseigneur had intended to hunt, but weakness overcame him as he was dressing and he fell over in his chair. Boudin had him put back to bed, but Fagon mentioned the matter so casually to the King that he thought nothing of it and drove out to Marly after his dinner. There he received reports several times from Meudon, where Mgr and Mme la Duchesse de Bourgogne stayed to dine, for they would not leave Monseigneur even for an instant. The princess, so naturally kind, did more than her duty as his daughter-in-law and fed him with her own hands. She cannot have grieved over what her mind told her to think probable, but she never failed in her devoted care and behaved without any affectation or pretence. Mgr le Duc de Bourgogne, so simple, so saintly, always so eager to pay his respects to his father, redoubled his attentions. He had not had the smallpox, which was already strongly suspected, yet neither he nor the duchess would desert Monseigneur until they had to leave him to go to sup with the King.

When the latter had heard their news, he sent such definite instructions to Meudon that he learned of Monseigneur's danger as soon as he woke on the following morning. He had already said that he intended to go to Meudon the next morning and to stay there throughout the whole of the illness, no matter what that might be, and he set off immediately after his mass. Just as he was leaving he forbade his children to follow him and issued a general interdiction to all who had not had the smallpox, which was a kindly and considerate gesture. He said further that those who had had the disease might pay their court to him at Meudon, or stay away if they felt nervous or were discommoded.

Several guests were sent away to make room for the King's suite, whom he strictly limited to personal attendants and ministers, so that he might work as usual. Only the chancellor did not sleep at Meudon. The ladies who remained were Madame la Duchesse and the Princesse de Conti with their maids of

---

[1] Jean Boudin, the King's apothecary, a pupil of Fagon.

honour, Mlle de Lillebonne and Mme d'Espinoy, Mlle de Melun
because she was deeply devoted to Monseigneur, and Mlle de
Bouillon, who did not wish to leave her father, the grand
chamberlain. They all supped with the King, but he dined alone,
as at Marly. I have not yet mentioned Mlle Choin, who had
been there since the Wednesday, nor Mme de Maintenon, who
drove out from Versailles with Mme la Duchesse de Bourgogne.
The King firmly refused to allow the latter to enter Monseigneur's apartments and ordered her rather abruptly to
return. That is how matters stood when Mme de Saint-Simon's
courier arrived at La Ferté.

I shall continue to speak of myself with the same frankness
that I have used in speaking of others, and with all possible
truth. In the situation that I then was regarding Monseigneur
and his circle, you may readily imagine how the news affected
me, for I understood that for better or worse the matter would
soon be decided. I was very comfortable at La Ferté, and therefore, resolving to wait for further reports, I returned the courier
to Mme de Saint-Simon, asking her to send another on the following day. All that day I spent in a state of flux, alternately
gaining and losing ground as I tried to keep the Christian on
guard against the courtier. At this critical time, many other
thoughts occupied my mind, persuading me to foresee a speedy
and unexpected deliverance under the happiest auspices for the
future.

Thus I waited impatiently for the courier to return, which he
did, early in the afternoon of the next day, Low Sunday. I then
learned that the smallpox had declared itself and that things
were going as well as could be expected. This seemed to be
confirmed when I heard that Mme de Maintenon, who never
left her room when she stayed at Meudon, had gone early
that morning to Versailles, had dined with Mme de Caylus,
and had been in no hurry to return. I therefore concluded that
Monseigneur was saved and decided to stay at home; however,
after taking counsel, as I have done all my life and been the
better for it, I regretfully gave orders to leave on the following day, which I did, early in the morning. When I reached La
Queue, fourteen leagues from La Ferté and six from Versailles,
a banker named La Fontaine came up to the door of my coach
as I was changing horses. He had just come from Paris and
Versailles, where he had seen some of Mme la Duchesse de

Bourgogne's people, and said that Monseigneur was better, giving me details that seemed to prove him out of danger. There seemed no longer any reason for fear, except the treacherous nature of that kind of illness in a very stout man of fifty.

The King took counsel and worked with his ministers as usual. He saw Monseigneur every morning and evening and sometimes in the afternoon as well, sitting for long periods by his bedside. He dined early on the Monday when I arrived, and drove out to Marly, where Mme la Duchesse de Bourgogne went to meet him. As he passed through the Versailles gardens, Messeigneurs his two grandsons were waiting to speak to him, but he would not let them approach and only called out, 'Good day,' as he drove by.

The King was never happy except in his own houses. He detested being anywhere else. That is why he paid only short visits to Meudon, on rare occasions and purely out of courtesy. Mme de Maintenon disliked being there still more. Everywhere that she went, her room was kept strictly private, accessible only to the ladies of her intimate circle, yet in spite of this, she always insisted on having some other absolutely inviolable sanctuary, where only Mme la Duchesse de Bourgogne might come occasionally, for a few moments and alone. Thus, when at Versailles and Marly she had Saint-Cyr, at Marly she also had Le Repos, and, at Fontainebleau, a house in the town was reserved for her. Now that Monseigneur was so much better and the visit to Meudon seemed likely to last a long time, the King's decorators were ordered to furnish Chaville as a retreat for her. This was a house which Monseigneur had purchased from the late chancellor, Le Tellier, and had enclosed within the park. At this time things seemed to be going so well that the King decided to hold a review on the Wednesday.

As soon as I arrived at Versailles, I wrote to M. le Duc de Beauvilliers asking him to inform the King that I had returned when I learned of Monseigneur's illness, and that I should have gone to Meudon, only that I had not had the smallpox and felt myself to be included in the general prohibition. He sent word back that my return had been well received, and again told me on behalf of the King that I was not to go to Meudon, either alone or with Mme de Saint-Simon. This personal interdiction did not distress me in the very least, Mme la Duchesse de

Berry had had smallpox and unlike Mme la Duchesse de Bourgogne was forbidden to see the King, and neither of their husbands had ever had it. The interdiction, except as regarded the
two Sons of France, who were very properly included, only
covered the royal family in as far as the King thought it best.

Meudon itself was full of contrasts. The Choin was confined
to her attic. Mlle de Lillebonne and Mme d'Espinoy never
moved from Monseigneur's bedroom, but the recluse was only
allowed there when the King was away and Madame la Princesse
de Conti, who was equally devoted, had gone to bed. This lady,
however, realized that Monseigneur would be cruelly frus-
trated if he were allowed no freedom in that respect and acted
with great kindness. On the very morning after the King's
arrival, the day after she herself had come, she told Monseigneur
that she had known for some time that someone was at Meudon,
that she herself could not stay away from the château in her
present anxiety, but that it was not fair to allow her affection to
inconvenience him. She therefore begged him to send her away
whenever he chose and promised never to enter his room without first discovering whether she might see him without embarrassment. Monseigneur was delighted by her consideration, and
the princess kept her word, quietly accepting hints from Mme
la Duchesse and her daughters when it was time for her to leave
the room, and never appearing disconcerted or ill-humoured.
In all this she deserved true praise.

Of course the someone referred to was Mlle Choin. She and
Père Le Tellier figured at Meudon in the most extraordinary
manner. Both were there incognito, each lived secluded in an
attic, eating their meals alone, seen only when strictly necessary, yet making everyone aware of their presence. There was
this essential difference between them; whereas the lady saw
Monseigneur daily and nightly and never set foot elsewhere, the
confessor went to the King's apartment and all others, excepting
only Monseigneur's room and those adjoining. Mme d'Espinoy
carried polite messages backwards and forwards between Mme
de Maintenon and Mlle Choin. The King did not see her. He
believed that Mme de Maintenon had done so, and when he
later made enquiries and discovered that she had not he did not
approve. Mme de Maintenon then sent Mme d'Espinoy to Mlle
Choin with her excuses, saying that she hoped they might soon
be able to meet, an odd remark considering that the message

was sent from one room to another under the same roof. In fact, they never did meet afterwards.

Versailles presented a very different spectacle. Mgr and Mme la Duchesse de Bourgogne openly held court there, and that Court was like the dawn of a new day. All the courtiers had congregated there, all Paris came flocking and, since prudence and tact are not virtues of the French, all Meudon came as well, and were believed when they maintained that they had not entered Monseigneur's rooms. The times to pay one's court were during the *levers* and *couchers*, dining and supping with the ladies, in the general conversation after meals, or walking in the gardens. The state apartments could not contain the crowds. Couriers arrived every quarter of an hour bringing reminders of Monseigneur. The illness was progressing as well as could be expected; there was every reason for hope and confidence, a general eagerness to please at the new Court, and a stately and soberly cheerful bearing on the part of the young prince and princess, who had a gracious welcome for all and took care to say a few words to each individual. The crowds themselves were full of amiability, there was general satisfaction all round, with the Duc and Duchesse de Berry practically nonentities. Five days passed in this way, each person thinking of the future and trying to adapt his behaviour to suit any eventuality.

On Tuesday, April 14th, the day after my return to Versailles, the King, who was finding Meudon very dull, held the usual Conseil des Finances in the morning and, against his custom, a Conseil des Dépêches in the afternoon. I met the chancellor on his return from the latter and he assured me that Monseigneur's condition was good and that Fagon had actually said that things were going as well as could be wished and beyond what they had dared to hope. The chancellor appeared exceedingly confident and I believed him all the more because he was intimate with Monseigneur and did not banish all cause for anxiety, although he expressed none other than was reasonable in illnesses of that kind.

Monseigneur's devoted friends, the Paris fish-wives, who had figured once before when an acute attack of indigestion was mistaken for apoplexy, again distinguished themselves by arriving at Meudon that morning in several hired coaches. Monseigneur had insisted on admitting them to his room, and they had flung themselves upon the foot of his bed, kissing it repeatedly. Then, overjoyed at the good reports, they had vowed that they would go back to make all Paris glad and to have Te Deums sung in all the churches. Monseigneur, who was never insensible to popular affection, thereupon had given orders that they should be shown the house, entertained to dinner, and sent away with presents of money.

In the meantime, as I was returning from meeting the chancellor and was crossing one of the courtyards at Versailles to go to my own apartment, I saw Mme la Duchesse d'Orléans walking on the terrace of the new wing. She called out to me, but Mme de Montauban[1] was with her so I pretended not to see or hear and continued on my way full of the latest news from Meudon. My rooms were in the upper gallery of the new wing, almost next to those of M. and Mme la Duchesse de Berry, who were giving a supper-party that night for M. and Mme la Duchesse d'Orléans and some of the ladies including Mme de Saint-Simon, but she had excused herself because she was slightly indisposed.

I had been in my study only a very short time when they announced Mme la Duchesse d'Orléans, who had come for an hour's chat before supper. I received her in Mme de Saint-Simon's room, although she happened to be out, but she returned before long and made a third in the conversation. The princess and I had been itching to see one another and gossip about the whole situation, regarding which we thought alike. She had returned only an hour earlier from Meudon and had seen the King. It was now eight o'clock.

In talking to me, she used the very same words as Fagon, when he was speaking to the chancellor; described the confidence that reigned at Meudon, praised the skill and care of the doctors, who neglected nothing, not even the little homely remedies which were usually despised. She expatiated upon the success of their treatment and, to speak frankly, albeit to our shame, both she and I lamented that Monseigneur, with his age and corpulence, should be escaping so dangerous a disease. She reflected sadly in the witty, languishing manner of the Mortemarts, that after such a purging he would not retain even the tiniest little likelihood of apoplexy, and that the chance of

---

[1] Saint-Simon describes her earlier as hunchbacked, lop-sided, hideous, raddled with paint and patches, debauched, avaricious, wicked, 'a kind of monster'. No one would speak to her on the rare occasions when she came to Court.

indigestion was irretrievably ruined now that he had taken fright and delivered his system into the doctors' hands. We concluded even more gloomily that we should now have to resign ourselves to the idea that he might live and reign a very long time. From that point we proceeded to predict the fatal consequences of his reign and the vanity of trusting even the most reliable symptoms regarding Monseigneur's health, which had seemed so desperate, yet had found continuance and new strength in the very heart of death. In short, we fairly let ourselves go, although not without some scruples intervening occasionally to interrupt this fascinating conversation, which Mme la Duchesse d'Orléans, in her drolly plaintive fashion, always brought back to the point. Mme de Saint-Simon, all goodness, tried to check our more outrageous remarks, but the brakes were off, and there ensued the oddest struggle between the expression of sentiments that, humanly speaking, were very natural to us, and the feeling that they were not Christian.

Two hours passed in this way, very quickly as it seemed to us, and then we were interrupted by supper-time. Mme la Duchesse d'Orléans went to her daughter, and Mme de Saint-Simon and I to my room, where company had collected and we supped.

While everything seemed so settled at Versailles and even Meudon, a change was actually in progress. The King had seen Monseigneur several times that day, for such tokens of affection and kindness were much appreciated, but during the visit after dinner he had noticed a great swelling of the face and head, which had shocked him so much that he stayed only a little time and shed a few tears as he left the room. They had done their best to reassure him and after the council was over he had gone for a walk in the gardens. Nevertheless, Monseigneur had already failed to recognize Mme la Princesse de Conti, and Boudin was alarmed. The prince himself had never ceased to be so. Courtiers had been seeing him one after another; some of the more intimate had never left his room, and he had asked them continually whether his sensations were usual symptoms of the disease. At moments, when he believed their reassurances, he had high hopes of recovery, and at one such time he had said to Mme la Princesse de Conti that he had been feeling unwell for a long while but had not liked to say so, and that on Holy Thursday he had been hard put to it to hold his prayer book.

G*

At about four o'clock in the afternoon he grew so much worse that Boudin suggested to Fagon that they should send to Paris for other advice, since, as Court physicians, they themselves never saw infectious diseases and had no experience of treating them. Fagon thereupon flew into a rage, refused to listen to argument and stubbornly refused to send for anyone. He said that nothing would be gained by disputation and conflicting opinions, maintained that they could do as well if not better without outside interference, and although Monseigneur's condition worsened hourly, decided to keep secret the true state of affairs. By seven o'clock even some of the courtiers had noticed the deterioration, but they were terrified of Fagon's presence, and none dared to warn the King and Mme de Maintenon. Mme la Princesse de Conti and Mme la Duchesse de Bourgogne were equally helpless and tried to comfort one another. What was extraordinary was that they decided to let the King sit down to his supper before alarming him with talk of desperate remedies and he finished his meal without receiving any kind of warning. Indeed, on the strength of Fagon's reports and from the general silence he believed that Monseigneur was at any rate no worse, although because of the change and the swelling he had been troubled about him earlier in the evening.

While the King was thus calmly eating his supper, panic had broken out in the bedroom of Monseigneur. Fagon and the other doctors had tried one remedy after another without waiting for any to take effect. The curé of Meudon,[1] who called to inquire every evening, had found the doors standing wide open and the footmen distracted. He entered the room, and when he saw the truth, so belatedly recognized, ran to the bed, took Monseigneur by the hand, spoke of God and, seeing that he was still conscious though almost speechless, extracted some sort of confession (which no one had thought of) and suggested certain acts of contrition. The wretched prince managed to utter a few words distinctly and to mumble some others, touched his breast, clasped the curé's hand, seemed imbued with proper sentiments, and received absolution with apparent eagerness and repentance.

By now the King had risen from table, and almost fell over backwards with astonishment when Fagon appeared before him

[1] Louis de Rond.

completely distraught, crying out that all was lost. You may imagine the horror that seized everyone in this sudden transition from perfect confidence to the last degree of despair. The King had hardly recovered himself before he immediately started towards Monseigneur's apartments, cutting short tactless efforts to restrain him and saying that he wished to make sure that no remedy had been left untried. As he was about to cross the threshold, however, Mme la Princesse de Conti, who had flown to Monseigneur's side in the short interval since the end of supper, appeared to prevent his entering. She even went so far as to press him back with both hands, saying that he must now think only of himself.

After that, the King, almost swooning from this sudden and complete reversal, sank down upon a sofa near the door of the ante-room. He asked for news from all who came out of the bedroom, but few had the courage to answer him. On his way down to Monseigneur he had sent for Père Le Tellier, who had already gone to bed, but hastily redressed and was soon in the bedroom. By then it was too late, at least so all the servants said, but that Jesuit, perhaps to reassure the King, maintained that he had found good and sufficient grounds to give absolution. Meanwhile, Mme de Maintenon had hurried to the King's side and was sitting on the same sofa, endeavouring to weep. She made efforts to take him away, for his coaches were ready in the courtyard, but could by no means persuade him to go until after Monseigneur had expired.

The coma lasted for nearly an hour after the King had entered the ante-room. Madame la Duchesse and Mme la Princesse de Conti divided their attention between the dying man and the King, to whom they often returned. As for the others, the doctors were bewildered, the servants distracted, the courtiers murmured. They jostled against one another so that there was constant movement with scarcely any change of position. At last the dreadful moment came and Fagon left, which allowed it to be generally known.

The King had been profoundly distressed and shocked at the absence of a proper confession, and he lashed out at Fagon before he allowed Mme de Maintenon and the two princesses to lead him away. The apartment was on the ground floor, level with the courtyard. As he came out to get into a carriage he noticed that the one in front of him was Monseigneur's own berline, and he signed for them to bring up another because the sight of that one upset him. Yet he was not too affected to notice Pontchartrain, and he called out, telling him to warn his father and the other ministers to come later than usual to Marly next day, for the Wednesday meeting of the council of state. I shall not comment on his extraordinary self-control, but merely say that the witnesses were astounded, and so were all who heard of it. Pontchartrain answered that since the only questions concerned current affairs, the meeting might well be postponed for a day until the King was less harassed. To this the King consented. He got with difficulty into the coach, supported on either side; Mme de Maintenon got in after him, followed by Mme la Princesse de Conti, who sat on the front seat. A crowd of the officers of Monseigneur's household had flung themselves upon their knees, lining the entire length of the courtyard on both sides of the King's way, imploring him with terrible cries to have compassion on them, for they had lost all and would die of hunger.

Whilst Meudon was thus providing a scene of horror, everything was quiet and peaceful at Versailles. We had finished our supper, the guests had retired some time later, and I was chatting with Mme de Saint-Simon as she undressed to go to bed, when suddenly one of our former footmen, whom she had given to Mme la Duchesse de Berry and who served her at table, entered in a great state of alarm. He said that bad news must have come from Meudon, because Mgr le Duc de Bourgogne had whispered something to M. le Duc de Berry, whose eyes had filled with tears. He had left the table precipitately, and when an urgent second message had come, the entire company had risen and had gone into the drawing-room. So sudden a change amazed me, and I hurried off to Mme la Duchesse de Berry's apartment, where I found no one. They had gone in a body to Mme la Duchesse de Bourgogne and I followed as quickly as I could.

I found all Versailles assembled there, the ladies out of their court-dresses, most of them ready for bed, the doors all wide open, and everything in a turmoil. I soon learned that Monseigneur had received Extreme Unction, that he was now unconscious, his condition regarded as hopeless. I also heard that the King had sent word to Mme la Duchesse de Bourgogne that he was on his way to Marly and that she was to wait for him in the avenue between the two stables as he wished to see her when he passed.

Amid the thoughts and sentiments that came crowding into my mind, I concentrated all the attention that I could spare upon the scene before me. The two princes and the princesses were in the little ante-room behind the alcove, where the toilet accessories had been laid out ready for the *coucher* in Mme la Duchesse de Bourgogne's bedroom. She herself went backwards and forwards between the two rooms, filling in the time until she had to go to meet the King. She bore herself as graciously as usual, but there was a look of compassion and stress about her, which many people mistook for grief. When people spoke to her as she passed, she answered their inquiries or said a few brief words. The expressions on the faces of the bystanders were truly eloquent; one needed only to have eyes, not the least knowledge of the Court, to read the desires of some, whilst the countenances of those who had nothing to gain remained perfectly blank. Some were self-possessed; others seemed cruelly affected, or else highly serious, and careful to reveal nothing of their joy and relief.

My first action was to inquire from several persons, but I did not place much reliance on their words, nor on the spectacle before me, for I feared that there might be all too little cause for so much excitement. Then I brought myself to reflect on the common lot of man and that I too should one day find myself at the gates of death. None the less, joy kept on breaking through these passing thoughts of religion and common humanity, by which I was striving to remember the proprieties. My own deliverance seemed so vast, so unlooked for, that from evidence which boded better than the reality, I believed that the State had everything to gain from this death. Among such reflections, however, I could not help feeling slightly afraid that the patient might still recover, and then I was mortally ashamed of myself.

Deeply immersed, as I was, in my own thoughts, I did not forget to send word to Mme de Saint-Simon that she had better come, nor to keep a surreptitious watch on each face, appearance, and action. Thus I indulged my eager curiosity, confirmed my first impressions (they have never proved wrong) of every important person present, and drew the proper conclusions from those first impulsive movements that are rarely mastered and

are therefore sure signs, to those who know the Court and their
fellow-men, of attachments and sentiments that are invisible in
more settled times.

I saw Mme la Duchesse d'Orléans arrive, but her set, dignified countenance told me nothing. She entered the little ante-
room and shortly afterwards returned with M. le Duc d'Orléans, whose manner, agitated and confused, reflected the general excitement rather than any deeper emotion. They then left
together. A few moments later, I noticed M. le Duc de Bourgogne in the distance, near the door of the ante-room. He
seemed profoundly moved and distressed, but the searching
glance which I shot at him could detect no tender feelings, only
the intense preoccupation of a man absorbed in his own
thoughts.

The footmen and valets were already weeping noisily, their
sorrow showing how much such kind of people stand to lose.
At about half-past midnight news was received from the King,
and I saw Mme la Duchesse de Bourgogne come out of the
little ante-room with Mgr le Duc, who seemed now even more
affected and returned immediately. The princess took her
shawl and hood from the dressing-table; then, erect, purpose-
ful, and almost dry-eyed, she crossed the room, her inner turmoil betrayed only by the furtive questioning glances which she
cast to right and left. Followed only by her ladies, she went
down the grand staircase to her coach.

When she had left, I took the opportunity to go to Mme la
Duchesse d'Orléans, for I was itching to be with her, but as
soon as I entered I learned that they had gone to Madame's
apartment, and pushed my way through the crowd in pursuit of
them. I met her as she was returning and she asked me very
gravely to come with her; M. le Duc d'Orléans was still with
his mother. Having regained her own room she sat down, and
the Duchesse de Villeroy, the Maréchale de Rochefort, and five
or six ladies of her circle gathered round her. I was twitching
with impatience at finding so much company, and Mme la
Duchesse d'Orléans, no less exasperated, took a candle and
stepped into the back of the room. I then wished to say something into the ear of the Duchesse de Villeroy, for she and I
thought alike in the present circumstances, but she gave me a
little push and told me in a whisper to control myself. It nearly
choked me to have to keep silence amid the ladies' conventional

expressions of pity and amazement, but at that moment M. le Duc d'Orléans appeared at the door of his study and called me to come in.

I followed him downstairs to his inner study that leads into the great gallery, he, almost swooning, and I, with my legs trembling because of all that was happening around and within me. By chance we sat facing one another, and I saw at once to my intense astonishment that tears were falling from his eyes. 'Monsieur!' I exclaimed, rising to my feet. He understood at once and answered in a broken voice, now actually weeping, 'You may well be surprised, indeed so am I; but such scenes are moving. He was a good man and I have known him all my life; when they let him alone, he treated me well and was good to me. I know that my grief will be short, and in a few days' time I shall see every cause to console myself, considering the bad feeling that they created between us. At present, kinship, pity, humanity, are all involved, and one does feel moved.' I praised his sentiments, but expressed my intense surprise, on account of his bad relations with Monseigneur. At this he rose, put his head in a corner, nose towards the wall, and began to weep and sob bitterly, a thing I never would have believed had I not seen it with my own eyes. After a short silence, I urged him to control himself, saying that he would soon have to return to Mme la Duchesse de Bourgogne's apartment, and that if he were seen with red eyes everyone would ridicule him for a piece of arrant humbug, for the entire Court knew on what sort of terms he had been with Monseigneur. He then did what he could to patch up his eyes, and was still at that work when word came that Mme la Duchesse de Bourgogne had returned and that Mme la Duchesse d'Orléans was about to go to her apartment. He went to join her and I followed.

Mme la Duchesse de Bourgogne had waited only a short time in the avenue between the two stables before the King drove up. She had stepped down from her coach to greet him at his carriage door, when Mme de Maintenon, who was sitting on her side, called out, 'What are you thinking of, Madame? Do not come near, we are pest-ridden!' I never learned what gesture the King made, but I know that he did not kiss her, on account of the contagion. The princess immediately stepped back into her coach and returned to the château.

The fearful secrecy with which Fagon had concealed Mon-

seigneur's real condition deceived everybody so completely that
the Duc de Beauvilliers, who had been sleeping at Meudon
throughout the illness, actually returned to Versailles after the
Conseil des Dépêches. He usually retired about ten o'clock because he was a very early riser, and that night he had gone to
bed without the least anxiety. It was not long before a messenger arrived summoning him to Mme la Duchesse de Bourgogne's apartment, where he found the two princes and Mme
la Duchesse de Berry waiting in the ante-room.

When the first embraces were over, after Mme la Duchesse
de Bourgogne's return, which, in itself, told all, the Duc de
Beauvilliers noticed that it was stifling in that little room and
persuaded them to go through the bedroom, into the drawing-
room that separates it from the great gallery. The windows
were opened and the two princes, each with his princess by
his side, sat down on a sofa that stood near the windows, with
its back to the gallery. The whole company in this room was
dispersed, standing and sitting in great disorder, and the ladies
of the intimate circle sat on the floor near the foot of the
princes' sofa.

From then onwards in that room and, indeed, in the whole
apartment, countenances might be read like open books. Monseigneur was dead. Everyone knew it, everyone spoke of it;
no one now held back out of deference, and these first moments
revealed first impulses in a true light, and for once free of the
constraints of good manners. Yet people behaved discreetly
amid the anxiety, excitement, shocks, crowding, and general
confusion of that eventful night.

In the outer rooms smothered groans could be heard from
servants in despair at losing a master who had suited them to
perfection and dreading the prospect of inheriting another (the
King) whom they greatly feared. Among them were strangers,
the more intelligent footmen of the chief personages at the
Court, who had hurried to hear the news and plainly showed by
their manner to which clique their masters belonged.

Farther on were crowds of courtiers of every description, the
greater number, the fools, drawing sighs out of their very heels,
while with dry eyes and roving glances they praised Monseigneur with one voice and for one virtue only, kindness, and
pitied the King for losing so excellent a son. The cleverest, or
the most prudent among them, pretended anxiety about the

King's own health, congratulating themselves on remaining cool amid so much confusion, and leaving no one in doubt by their constant repetition. Others seemed truly distressed, and the members of the stricken cabal[1] wept bitterly, or controlled themselves by an effort as obvious as any sobbing. The hardest, or the most cunning, kept their eyes on the ground, or meditated in distant corners on the probable outcome of this totally unexpected event, and still more on their own futures. There was little or no conversation between the variously afflicted; although every now and then someone would let fall a remark which was echoed by his neighbours, words dropping at the rate of one every quarter of an hour. Faces were melancholy or haggard, gestures more frequent than intentional and for the rest, almost absolute stillness. Those who were merely curious or indifferent remained almost impassive; only the fools chattered and asked questions, adding to the distress of the mourners and being an embarrassment to the others. Those who were glad tried in vain to increase their appearance of gravity by looking sad or stern; yet all that they could achieve was a thin veil through which keen eyes might discover their real feelings. Such people stood as motionless as those who were most affected, on their guard against public opinion, curiosity in others, complacency in themselves, or impulsiveness, but nevertheless the excitement in their eyes made up for their bodies' stillness. A change of attitude, as of men sitting uncomfortably or tired of standing, a particular care to avoid one another or even to prevent eyes from meeting, tiny incidents that arose from such encounters, an indescribable hint of release in the whole deportment of these people, shone through their efforts to be calm and controlled. A liveliness, a kind of glitter distinguished them from the rest, making them conspicuous in spite of all their efforts to the contrary.

The two princes with their princesses sitting beside and comforting them were exposed to every eye. Mgr le Duc de Bourgogne wept in all sincerity, quietly shedding tears of compassion, piety, and long endurance. M. le Duc de Berry was equally sincere, but he seemed to be weeping tears of blood, so bitterly he cried; indeed, it was not merely sobs that came from him, but shrieks and howls, even bellowings. Sometimes he was quiet, but only when he was choking, and then his cries

---

[1] Those who had been relying on Monseigneur's accession.

would break out again, so loud, so monstrously loud that it was like the uncontrollable trumpeting of deep despair. Many others joined in these heartrending outbursts, goaded into weeping either by emotion or by a sense of the proprieties. At last, he reached such a pitch that they were forced to undress him there and then, and to have remedies prepared and call for the doctors. Mme la Duchesse de Berry was beside herself; you shall soon discover why. The bitterest despair was imprinted on her face. You could see as plainly as though it were written a perfect paroxysm of uncontrollable woe, not from grief or affection, but from pure selfishness. There were intervals when she was dry-eyed, but sullen-looking and angry. Then came torrents of tears and gestures, involuntary yet restrained, that betrayed deep bitterness of spirit, resulting from her preceding meditations. The cries of her husband often interrupted her, and then she was quick to support and embrace him or to offer him smelling-salts; you could see her eagerness to minister to him. Then, just as swiftly, she would relapse into her own thoughts, then into a storm of weeping that helped her to stifle her sobs. Mme la Duchesse de Bourgogne also comforted her husband, and found it easier to do so than to give any appearance of needing consolation herself. She paraded no false emotion, yet one could see that she did her utmost to produce the tears, which she felt decency required, and which often will not come when they are most needed. A frequent use of her handkerchief reflected the sobs of her princely brother-in-law and a few tears, occasioned by the scene around her and carefully husbanded, were encouraged by artful rubbing to smudge her face and make her eyes red and swollen; but all the time, her furtive glances wandered over the bystanders and scanned the faces of each one in turn.

The Duc de Beauvilliers stood beside them, looking as cool and detached as though nothing were happening, or the scene were an everyday event. He quietly attended to the princes, giving orders to allow few to enter, although the doors stood open, and sending for all that was needed without any bustle or misjudgment, behaving, in fact, as though he were at an ordinary *lever* or *petit couvert*. His composure was unruffled, for since his conscience forbade him either to be glad or to conceal the little grief that he felt, he was able to preserve a truthful appearance to the end.

Madame again put on her full Court dress,[1] and arrived shrieking, not rightly knowing why she did either. She drowned with her tears all whom she embraced and made the palace re-echo with her cries, presenting the remarkable spectacle of a princess putting on formal attire in the middle of the night, and coming to weep among a crowd of women in their night-gowns, or almost in fancy dress.

Mme la Duchesse d'Orléans had left the princes and was sitting near the fireplace with her back to the gallery, among a group of ladies; but she was very silent and they gradually went farther off, which pleased her very much. Only the Duchesse Sforza, the Duchesse de Villeroy, Mme de Castries, and Mme de Saint-Simon remained, who were thankful to be left alone and drew into a little knot beside one of the camp-beds. They pulled the curtains together, and as all were of the same mind regarding the event that had assembled so large a company, they began to talk freely in low voices.

For reasons of security, a number of these camp-beds were set up at night for the use of the Swiss guards and floor-polishers, in all the state apartments, and they had been arranged as usual before the bad news had come from Meudon. In the middle of the conversation, Mme de Castries, who was touching the bed, felt something stir, which terrified her, be-cause she was nervous of everything although she had plenty of courage. The next moment, a great naked arm pulled open the curtains, and the ladies saw a huge Swiss guard between the sheets, only half-awake, yawning, and staring fixedly at the people round him, whom he was very slow to recognize. Then, obviously thinking it unsuitable to get out of bed in such exalted company, he buried himself once more between the sheets and pulled his curtains. The fellow had apparently gone to bed before any news had come and had slept so soundly that he had only just wakened. The most ridiculous incidents do sometimes relieve the most solemn spectacles, and this one made several of the ladies laugh, although Mme la Duchesse d'Orléans

[1] On the following day, April 16th, Madame wrote as follows to her aunt, the Duchess of Hanover, 'Those who imagined that they were harming me by alienating Monseigneur le Dauphin's affections, may perhaps have saved my life, for had he and I been on the same terms as before Monsieur's death I might have died from fright and grief, or have re-mained inconsolable, whereas at present I can support the affliction patiently and grieve only for the King. I do indeed pity Monseigneur le Dauphin, but I cannot be as much distressed at the loss of one who did not love and had entirely forsaken me, as I might have been had he remained my friend.'

feared lest they might have been overheard. On reflection, however, they were reassured by the man's sleepiness and evident
stupidity.

As for myself, I endeavoured to keep an open mind. Although
everything seemed to prove what had happened, I refused to
believe until I had found some responsible person who would
confirm the news, and I happened to see M. d'O, who told me
facts, over which, when I learned them, I tried not to rejoice
openly. I am not sure how far I succeeded, but one thing is certain, that neither joy nor sorrow abated my curiosity, and whilst
I was careful to preserve the decencies, I did not think it necessary to pretend to any grief. I no longer feared repercussions
from Meudon, nor persecution by its relentless garrison, and
since the King was away at Marly, I felt unconstrained and
could study the crowd freely, allowing my eyes to dwell
on those who, from different motives were much or little
affected.

Thus, I followed the movements of certain personages and
endeavoured stealthily to penetrate their inmost thoughts, for
indeed, to one who knows the inner life of a Court, these first
moments after some extraordinary event are intensely gratify-
ing. Each face reminds one of the cares and intrigues, the
laborious efforts to advance a private fortune, or form and
strengthen a cabal, the cunning devices designed and executed
for that purpose, the attachments at varying degrees of intimacy, the estrangements, dislikes, and hatreds, the ill-turns
played and favours granted, the tricks, petty shifts, and baseness of some individuals, the dashing of the hopes of some in
mid-career, the stupefaction of others at the summit, who had
thought their ambitions fulfilled and, at the same blow, the
importance given to their adversaries in the opposing cabals,
the force of the recoil, which in that self-same instant brought
the affairs of some (myself included) to a successful conclusion
and consequently to extreme and unlooked-for joy, and the fury
displayed by the rest, in spite of all their concern to hide it.
At such a time one's glances fly from face to face, trying to
penetrate the very soul, in those first moments of shocked surprise and sudden upheaval. One takes stock of all that one sees,
realizing one's astonishment at not finding expected qualities
in some, for want of intelligence or courage, and in others,
seeing more than one had dared to hope. Such an amalgamation

of ambitious people and critical events is a delight to those who understand and, ephemeral though it may be, it provides one of the greatest pleasures to be enjoyed at Court.

It was to this pursuit, then, that I gave myself wholly up, and with all the more alacrity because whilst I myself had been accorded a very real deliverance by this death, I was closely bound up and embarked with the illustrious personages who could not force tears into their eyes. Thus I rejoiced in the unalloyed gain to them, and their gratification increased my own, raising my hopes and promising me the peace of mind of which, before this sad event, I had had so little prospect, for I had never ceased to mistrust the future. On the other hand, as an opponent of the cabals and almost a personal enemy of their leaders, I realized at my first keen glance and with inexpressible delight, all that was slipping from their grasp and all the troubles that would crush them. I knew so well the affairs of the different cabals, their leaders, and degrees of leadership, their ramifications and sub-divisions, that several days of meditation would not have told me these things half so clearly as that first sight of faces, which reminded me of others, not then seen, but none the less delectable morsels for my mind to feed upon.

I stayed for a little while to consider the scene in that vast and now chaotic state apartment. The tumult had lasted for fully an hour, but the Duchesse du Lude, who was in bed with the gout, did not appear. Finally, it was the Duc de Beauvilliers who decided that it was time to deliver the two princes from their distressingly public situation. He suggested that M. and Mme la Duchesse de Berry should retire to their own apartments and allow the Court to leave those of Mme la Duchesse de Bourgogne. His advice was accepted immediately. M. le Duc de Berry slowly moved forwards, partly alone, partly with the support of his wife. Mme de Saint-Simon attended them with a handful of the officers of their household; I followed, but at a distance, so that my curiosity was not noticeable. The prince wished to go to his own room to sleep, but Mme la Duchesse de Berry would not consent to leave him, indeed, he was so much congested and she also, that a complete faculty of doctors, all furnished and equipped, was asked to remain with them.

The whole of that night they spent in weeping and sobbing. From time to time M. le Duc de Berry asked for news from

Meudon, apparently refusing to understand the reason for the King's departure to Marly. Sometimes he inquired whether there was no longer any room for hope, and then he wished to send for further news. Only much later in the morning was the tragic veil drawn from his eyes, so hard it is for nature and self-interest to accept absolute disaster. I cannot describe his state when final realization came. The condition of Mme la Duchesse de Berry was not much better, but that did not prevent her from taking all possible care of him.

The night of Mgr and Mme la Duchesse de Bourgogne passed more quietly, and they went to bed in reasonable peace. Mme de Levis whispered to the princess that since she had no cause for affliction it would be dreadful to see her make a pretence. She answered, most unaffectedly, that without any pretence she was moved by compassion and by the scenes she had witnessed, and that she was restrained by a sense of the proprieties, nothing more. Indeed, she kept within those limits with sincerity and dignity. They asked that some of the palace ladies should spend the remainder of the night in armchairs in their room. The curtains were left open and before long the room became like the palace of Morpheus. The prince and princess promptly fell asleep and woke once or twice, but only for an instant. As a matter of fact, they rose early and without fuss. The fountains had dried up within them; from then onwards they wept seldom and gently, when occasion demanded. The ladies who had watched and slept in their room told their friends what had occurred. No one was surprised, and since Monseigneur was no more, no one was scandalized. Mme de Saint-Simon and I then spent two hours alone together. Finally, it was common sense rather than a desire to sleep that persuaded us to go to bed, and we slept so little that I was up and dressed by seven in the morning. Nevertheless some insomnia is sweet and such awakenings are delectable.

At Meudon, in the meanwhile, horror reigned. When the King left, such attendance as remained with him followed, piling themselves into whatever vehicles came to hand. In a moment Meudon was a desert and Mlle de Lillebonne and Mlle de Melun went up to Mlle Choin, who, isolated in her garret, was only beginning to feel the transports of despair. She knew nothing, for no one had thought of bringing her the bad news, and she had only realized her misfortune from the sound of lamentations. Her two friends bundled her into a hired coach that happened to be available and took her away with them to Paris.

A crowd of officers and servants of Monseigneur's household, and many others, spent the night wandering about in the gardens. Some of the courtiers slipped away singly and on foot. There was a complete dispersal. One or two valets, at the most, stayed by the body, which was a most laudable action, and La Vallière,[1] the only courtier who had not abandoned him in life, remained with him in death. He had much difficulty in finding anybody to send to fetch the capuchins to pray beside the corpse. Decomposition set in so suddenly and so violently that it was not enough to open the doors and windows wide upon the terrace; La Vallière, the capuchins, and the few remaining servants were forced to spend the night outside.

Everything had seemed so quiet before the crisis that no one dreamed of the King's going to Marly that night. Nothing, therefore, was ready to receive him, the door-keys were missing and there were only a few night-lights and no candles at all. In these circumstances the King and Mme de Maintenon were forced to sit for an hour or more in the ante-room to her apartment, with Madame la Duchesse, Mme la Princesse de Conti, and Mmes de Dangeau and de Caylus, the latter having hurried from Versailles to be with her aunt.[2] The last two ladies, however, stood discreetly here and there, and only for short intervals; others, who arrived later, stayed in the salon in spite of the disorder, for they did not know where else to go. For a long time they groped about in the dark, without even a candle, and when at last the servants did manage to find the keys they were so distraught that they mixed them up. Gradually the boldest of those in the salon began to show their faces in the ante-room, and then all made an appearance, partly out of curiosity, partly from a desire to show zeal. The King sat in a far corner between Mme de Maintenon and the princesses and wept for long stretches at a time; but at last Mme de Maintenon's door was opened and he was relieved from that uncomfortable situation. He entered the room with her alone and remained for another hour. He then went to bed—it was nearly four o'clock—

[1] Charles-François de la Beaune-le-Blanc, Duc de La Valliére. He was a nephew of Louis XIV's mistress and first cousin of the Princesse de Condé.
[2] Mme de Maintenon.

and left her a breathing-space in which to recover. After his departure, the rest of the company were free to find lodging for themselves. . . .

Summing up the details of Monseigneur's character, it appears that he was a man without vice or virtue, knowledge or understanding, and totally incapable of acquiring any. He was vastly lazy, with no imagination or creative ability, without taste, decision or discernment. He was capable only of being bored and infected others with his ennui. Nature fashioned him to be like a ball that is rolled hither and thither at the will of others. Stubborn, and in all things very mean, incredibly gullible and easy to prejudice, a prey to most pernicious influences, yet unable either to escape from them or to realize their vileness, immersed in his fat and his gloom, albeit with no desire for wrong-doing, he would have made a most abominable king.

He died of the smallpox, but the purples and the rapid decomposition that resulted therefrom made it useless as well as dangerous to open his body. Some say that he was prepared for burial by the grey sisters, others, by the floor-polishers of the château, or perhaps by the workmen who made the coffin, over which was thrown an ancient pall, belonging to the parish church of Meudon. There was no other retinue except the few who had remained, that is to say, La Vallière himself, some junior officials, and the capuchins of Meudon, who took turns to pray by the coffin, without funeral hangings or any lights, except for a few candles.

It was about midnight that he died, between Tuesday and Wednesday. On the Thursday, he was taken to Saint-Denis in one of the royal coaches, not in mourning, and with the front window removed to allow room for the foot of the coffin. The curé of Meudon and the chaplain-in-residence travelled in the same coach, which was followed by another, also out of mourning, in which sat the Duc de la Trémoïlle and M. de Metz, the lord high almoner, on the back seat; and in front, Dreux, the grand master of ceremonies, and the Abbé de Brancas, who afterwards became Bishop of Lisieux. These two carriages, with footmen and twenty-four of the royal pages carrying torches, formed the whole of the very short procession that left Meudon at six or seven in the evening, crossed the bridge at Sèvres and through the Bois de Boulogne, and arrived at Saint-Denis by way of the Saint-Ouen plain. The body was then lowered into the royal vault without ceremonial of any kind.[1]

Such was the end of a prince who for nearly fifty years allowed others to plan, whilst he, who stood upon the steps of the throne, led a life that was private, not to say obscure, so much so, indeed, that nothing in it was remarkable except the estate of Meudon and what he did to beautify it. He hunted without pleasure in the chase, he was a near-voluptuary, but without discrimination. At one time he gambled heavily in order to win, but after he began to build, he used to stand in a corner of the salon at Marly, whistling through his teeth, drumming on his snuff-box, staring vacantly around him without really seeing anything, without conversation or amusements, I am inclined to say without either thoughts or feelings. Yet, because of his high estate, he was the head and centre, the soul, the very life of one of the strangest, most sinister, most secret, and, in spite of its ramifications, most united cabals that have emerged since the Peace of the Pyrenees put an end to the revolt of the King's minority. I have dwelt too long on this prince, whose character is almost beyond definition, because only the superficialities of it are known. It would take an eternity to describe them all. Nevertheless, the subject is interesting enough to have warranted my enlarging on this so little known Dauphin, who himself was nothing, who counted for nothing in his long, vain expectation of the crown, and with whom, at last, that cord was broken, on which had depended so many hopes and fears and schemes.

1712

Death of Mme la Duchesse de Bourgogne

On Monday, January 18th the King went to Marly. The Dauphine had arrived there early in the morning with a face hugely swollen and had immediately retired to bed. She rose again at seven o'clock because the King wished her to preside

---

[1] In fact, the King requested 3,000 masses from Cardinal de Noailles, and two hundred from the Quinze-Vingts (the famous hospital for the blind of Paris, founded by Louis IX in 1260), not to mention public prayers.

in the drawing-room, but she played cards in morning dress and with her head muffled in a hood. She went to see the King in Mme de Maintenon's apartment shortly before his supper and then returned to bed, where she ate her own meal. On the 20th the swelling had subsided, she was somewhat prone to inflammation of the gums, for her teeth were badly decayed, but she felt better and for the next few days was able to lead her ordinary life.

On Friday February 5th, the Duc de Noailles presented her with a beautiful snuff-box filled with fine Spanish snuff, which she tried and thought excellent. This occurred towards the end of the morning and afterwards she placed the box on a table in her private boudoir, where no one ever went. That same evening she was seized with a feverish chill, retired to bed, and did not get up again, not even to go to the King's room after supper. She had a bad night, but rose at her ordinary time on the following day and went about her business as usual. That evening, however, the fever returned. She was unwell during the whole of the night, but slightly better on the Sunday. At six that evening she was seized with a sudden pain below the temples, not greater in size than a six-sous piece, but so violent that she implored the King not to enter her room when he came to visit her. This maddening pain lasted without intermission until Monday the 8th, and was not relieved by smoking and chewing tobacco, nor by quantities of opium and two bleedings from the arm. When the pain grew less the fever increased. She said that she suffered more even than in childbirth.

The violence of the illness gave rise to rumours about the snuff-box which the Duc de Noailles had given her, for she had spoken of it to her ladies when she went to bed on the first day of her illness, and had praised both the box and its contents; but when Mme de Levis went to fetch it from the table in her boudoir it was not there and, to make a long story short, it was never seen again. The disappearance seemed strange enough when it was first discovered, but the long and fruitless search, followed by such sudden and terrible events aroused the darkest suspicions.[1] They did not actually point to the giver of the box, or were so carefully generalized that they did not reach his understanding. The rumour, indeed,

---

[1] Saint-Simon suspected that the Duc and Duchesse de Bourgogne were poisoned. It is now believed that they and later their eldest son died of the measles.

was minimized even in that small circle, where so many hopes were fixed on that adored princess, on whose life depended the fortunes of her small group of intimates. The fact that she took snuff was unknown to the King, but this did not make her nervous because Mme de Maintenon knew; nevertheless, there would have been a dreadful to-do had he discovered, and that was why they were afraid to mention the strange disappearance of the snuff-box.

On the Monday night, the Dauphine was very drowsy. All that day, during which the King came often to her bedside, she had been in a high fever with short periods of delirium. Some spots began to appear on her skin, which made the doctors hope that the disease might turn out to be measles, which was very prevalent at that time and many people had had attacks, both at Versailles and Paris. The Tuesday night was harder to bear because by then the hope of measles had faded. Early the following morning, the King came to see her and found that she had been given an emetic, but although the result was everything that could be desired, it brought her no relief. At this point they persuaded the Dauphin, who had never left her side, to go into the garden for the fresh air, but he was so anxious that he returned almost at once. Towards nightfall she became worse and about eleven o'clock the fever increased. It was a very bad night. The King came to the Dauphine at nine o'clock in the morning of February 11th, and Mme de Maintenon was with her the entire time, except during his visits. By this time, the princess was so bad that they decided to speak to her of the Sacraments, but although so weak, she seemed surprised and questioned them about her condition, and they reassured her as best they could, but continued gently to press the suggestion, urging her not to delay. She thanked them for their frankness and said she would prepare herself.

A little later, they feared that there might be a sudden change, and her confessor, Père La Rue,[1] a Jesuit, whom she had always appeared to like, came up to the bed and urged her to wait no longer. She looked at him, answered that she understood him perfectly, but did no more, and when La Rue proposed to hear her there and then, she did not answer. Being a man of intelligence, he realized that something was amiss and tactfully changed his manner of approach. Saying that she might perhaps

---

[1] Charles de La Rue, one of the most fashionable preachers of that day.

have some personal reasons for not wishing to confess to him, he bade her not to be afraid but to name a priest and he would take all responsibility upon himself and go himself to fetch him. She then said that she would like M. Bailly, priest of the mission of the parish of Versailles, a man of high reputation, who confessed the more orthodox members of the Court, and was not free of all suspicion of Jansenism, although that was a rare thing among those missioners. Unfortunately Bailly had gone to Paris. The Dauphine seemed distressed when she heard the news and desired to wait until his return, but Père La Rue told her that she had better not waste precious time, which the doctors could profitably use after she had taken the Sacraments. She accordingly asked for a Franciscan friar, Père Noel, whom Père La Rue immediately went to fetch and brought to her.

You may imagine the excitement that was caused by this sudden change of confessor at so dreadful a moment, and all the suspicions that were aroused. I shall return later to the subject, for I cannot now interrupt a tale of such tragic interest. The Dauphin was by this time overcome with grief. He had hidden his distress as long as possible in order to remain by the bedside, but the fever could no longer be concealed, and the doctors wished to spare him the dreadful scenes which they foresaw. With the King's approval, they therefore did everything to persuade him to stay in his own room and sustained him with lying reports of his wife's true condition.

The Dauphine's confession was a very long one, and immediately afterwards Extreme Unction was administered and she partook of the Last Sacraments, which the King went out to greet at the foot of the grand staircase. An hour later, she asked for the prayers for the dying, but they told her that the time had not yet come, and comforted her, urging her to try to sleep. Throughout all this time, the King and Mme de Maintenon remained in the drawing-room, where the doctors were summoned to consult in their presence. There were seven of them altogether, some attached to the Court, others sent for from Paris. They unanimously recommended that she should be bled from the foot before the fever returned and that an emetic should be given in the early hours of the morning if the bleeding did not produce the desired effect. When the fever returned it was less violent than before, but the night was cruel. Next morning, the King came very early and the Dauphine was given an emetic at nine o'clock, but with very small result. As the day went on, new symptoms appeared, each more distressing than the last, and she was conscious only at rare intervals. Towards evening, her servants became distraught, so that many strangers were admitted to the room even although the King was present. He left only a few moments before she died and, stepping into his carriage at the foot of the grand staircase, was driven away to Marly with Mme de Maintenon and Mme de Caylus. Both of them grieved so bitterly that they could not summon up strength to visit the Dauphin.

No princess coming so young to a foreign Court was ever better prepared and instructed. Her wise father had known the modes of our Court and had described them perfectly to her, teaching her the only way in which she could be happy with us. He was greatly assisted in his task by her natural quickness and intelligence, and she had many lovable qualities which won people's affection. Moreover, her personal relationships with her husband, the King, and Mme de Maintenon caused her to be regarded with respect and approval by men of ambition. From the moment of her arrival, she strove to achieve this end, and throughout her whole life she persisted in this useful labour, from which she reaped continual benefits. Gentle, shy, but none the less shrewd, she was so kind that she dreaded causing the slightest pain to anyone, and though she was lively and pleasure-loving, she was capable of forming her own opinions and could act upon them consistently and for long periods at a time. The constraints, which bordered on torture, of the Court life, bore down upon her with all their weight, but they seemed not to affect her. Kindness came naturally to her, and she showed it to all, even to her own household.[1]

In appearance she was plain, with cheeks that sagged, a forehead too prominent for beauty, an insignificant nose, and thick sensual lips, but the line of her chestnut hair and eyebrows was well marked, and she had the prettiest, most eloquent eyes in all the world. Her few remaining teeth were badly decayed, which she was the first to laugh at and remark on. She had, however, a fair complexion, a beautiful skin, a small but

[1] Other people took a less kindly view of her character. In 1698, the Venetian ambassador wrote, 'The little Duchesse de Bourgogne is sly and spiteful. She has a deadly hatred, for no good cause, for her lady-in-waiting, the Duchesse du Lude, mimics her and makes her look ridiculous. On the other hand, she fawns most abjectly over Mme de Maintenon and, when they are in private, calls her "Grandmamma".'

admirable bust, and a long neck with the suspicion of a goitre, which was not unbecoming. The carriage of her head was noble; she was very stately and gracious in her manner and in the expression of her eyes, and she had the sweetest smile imaginable. She was long-waisted, slender but not angular, very supple. Altogether, she had a beautiful figure and she walked like a goddess upon clouds. Her charm was beyond description; it showed in her impulsive ways and gestures and coloured her most ordinary remarks. She always appeared natural and unaffected, sometimes a little childish, but with a touch of wit. She delighted all who met her because through her own graciousness she had the knack of putting everyone else at their ease.

She loved to be pleasant, even to the most ordinary and undistinguished people, but seemed to make no effort to be popular. When you were with her, you were tempted to believe that she was wholly and solely on your side. The whole Court was enlivened by her youth and high spirits, she flitted hither and thither like a nymph, like a summer breeze, she seemed to have the gift of being in many places at once and brought life and gaiety wherever she passed. Every entertainment was graced by her presence, for she was the life and soul of all the balls and plays and fêtes, besides enchanting everyone by the elegance and neatness of her dancing.

She enjoyed playing cards, even for low stakes, for she was easily amused, but she preferred playing high; she was quick and clear-headed, the finest gambler imaginable, and could see through her opponent's game in a moment. But she was as cheerful and as much pleased to spend an afternoon in quiet reading, sewing, and conversation with her 'serious ladies', as she called the older palace ladies. She never spared herself, not even for her health's sake, and never forgot the least little thing that might please Mme de Maintenon and, through her, the King. In that respect her versatility was amazing; it never flagged for a moment, although she tempered it with the caution which long experience had taught her, for she knew exactly when to be discreet, and when bold. Her personal wishes, her pleasures, even, I repeat, her health, she sacrificed for them and thus she became familiar with them in a way that none of the King's children nor even his bastards was able to approach.

Her manner in public was serious, reserved, reverential

towards the King, and shyly formal with Mme de Maintenon, whom she called 'Aunt', in a pretty mingling of affection and respect. When they were in private, she chattered, skipped, and frolicked around them, sometimes perching on the arm of their chairs, sometimes upon their knees. She used to fling her arms around their necks, kissing and hugging them, rumpling them and taking hold of them by the chin. She would rifle their writing-tables, rummaging among the papers, unsealing their letters and sometimes, when she saw that it would amuse them, insist on reading them aloud, commenting on what she read. The King's private apartments were open to her at all times, even when couriers brought important dispatches or during the meetings of the council, and she was always ready to oblige, to assist by smoothing away difficulties or to do a kindness, except to someone for whom she had taken a violent antipathy, as she did for Pontchartrain, whom she sometimes spoke of to the King as 'your one-eyed villain'. She was so bold, indeed, that one evening when the King and Mme de Maintenon were speaking affectionately of the English Court—it was at a time when they hoped to make peace with Queen Anne—she said, 'Aunt, you say that the queens in England are better than the kings, but do you know why?' and skipping all the time about the room, she continued, 'It is because when there is a king, the women rule, but under the queens men do so.' The wonder was that they both burst out laughing and agreed that she was perfectly right.

Were these Memoirs more solemn, I could scarcely bring myself to relate the following anecdote, but it does serve to illustrate to what point she was free to say and do as she pleased with them. I have already described how she shared the informal private life of the King and Mme de Maintenon. One evening there was to be a play at Versailles and she was chattering about this and that when Mme de Maintenon's old nurse, Nanon, came into the room. Instantly, arrayed as she was in full Court dress, with her jewels, she went and stood with her back to the fireplace and leaned on a little screen, placed between two tables. Nanon, who seemed to have one hand in her pocket, slipped quietly behind her and went down on her knees, whereupon the King, who was nearest to them, asked what they were doing. The princess burst out laughing and said that she was only doing what he often did before a play, but the

King persisted. Then she said, 'Must I really tell you, since you have not seen for yourself? The truth is that I am having an enema.' 'What?' said the King, in an explosion of laughter. 'You are not seriously telling me that you are having an enema at this moment?' 'Indeed, I am,' she said. 'But how?' asked the King, and they all four laughed until their sides shook. And in very truth, Nanon had brought the syringe all prepared, hidden under her petticoats, and had lifted up the princess's skirts while she pretended to warm herself. Then she had inserted the nozzle, the skirts were pulled down, and Nanon carried the syringe away underneath her own petticoats. In this way everything was discreetly hidden. The King and Mme de Maintenon paid no particular attention, thinking that Nanon was rearranging some part of the princess's dress. Thus they were completely taken by surprise and found the whole episode intensely amusing. What is extraordinary is that she used to go to the play holding the *lavement*, and in no hurry to be quit of it. Sometimes she held it throughout the entire time of the King's supper and afterwards. She said that she found it refreshing and that it prevented her from getting a headache in the stuffy theatre. After being found out, she did not alter her ways, for she knew them through and through, and could not help realizing what Mme de Maintenon and Mlle Choin had been.

One evening, when she was about to join Mgr le Duc de Bourgogne in bed, and was sitting on her chaise-percée, where she often talked confidentially, she told Mmes de Nogaret and du Châtelet, who repeated it afterwards to me, that she marvelled at the good fortune of those two sirens. She then added, laughing, 'I should like to die before M. le Duc de Bourgogne, so as to see what happens afterwards. I am sure that he will marry a grey sister, or the portress of the Filles de Sainte-Marie.' She tried as hard to be charming to him as to the King himself, but she often went too far, and was over-confident of his passion for her, although she was greatly concerned to uphold his rank and personal honour. As for the King, he could not bear to be without her. When her pleasure parties, which in his affection for her he encouraged, drove her from his side, his life was empty, and even at his public suppers when she was absent, as rarely happened, a cloud seemed to descend upon him and he was more solemn and silent than usual. Consequently, although she enjoyed her parties, she was very quiet about them,

Louis Duc de Bourgogne

L'ETAT GLORIEUX ET FLORISSANT
DE LA FAMILLE ROYALE
Par le nombre et le merite
des PRINCES ET PRINCESSES qui la composent

Bibliothèque Nationale

LOUIS XIV AND HIS FAMILY

and only arranged them when expressly bidden to do so. She always made a point of visiting the King when she left and returned, and if she happened to be kept late at night by a ball in winter, or a picnic in summer, she always arranged to be there to kiss him when he woke and to amuse him with her tittle-tattle.

I have said enough already of her disapproval of Monseigneur and the members of his private court. I shall say no more now, except that she took care to hide her feelings from the Court, in general, for she masked them under an appearance of being on pleasant terms with him, and perfectly serene among them all whenever she was at Meudon. Nevertheless she felt deeply embarrassed by the situation, and promised herself that she would be revenged after Monseigneur's death.

One evening, at Fontainebleau, when the princesses and their ladies were with the King in the drawing-room after supper, and she had been diverting him by pretending to chatter in half a dozen different languages, and other such nonsense, she suddenly noticed that Madame la Duchesse and Mme la Princesse de Conti were eyeing one another and contemptuously shrugging their shoulders. As soon as the King rose and went into his inner study in order to feed his dogs, the Dauphine seized Mme de Saint-Simon and Mme de Levis by the hand, and pointed to Madame la Duchesse and Mme la Princesse de Conti, who were only a few feet away. 'Did you see them? Did you see them?' she cried. 'I know as well as they that I behave nonsensically, that it is all very silly, but he has to have a bustle about him and that kind of thing diverts him.' And then, swinging on their arms, she began to dance and sing, 'Oh! it makes me laugh, oh! I can jeer at them, because I am going to be their queen. I need not care for them now nor ever, but they have to reckon with me, for I'm going to be their queen,' and she shouted and jumped and laughed as loud and as high as she could. Mme de Saint-Simon and Mme de Levis whispered to her to be quiet because the princesses would hear her and the entire company think that she had taken leave of her senses, but she skipped and sang the more, 'What do I care for them, for I'm going to be their queen!' and she only ceased when the King returned.

Alas! sweet princess, she believed what she said, and who could have thought otherwise? But for our sins, it very shortly

H

afterwards pleased God to arrange matters differently. So far
was she, indeed, from imagining her approaching end, that on
Candlemas Day, when she was alone with Mme de Saint-Simon
in her bedroom, the other ladies having gone before her into
the chapel, she had begun to speak of the numbers of people
about the Court whom she had known and who were now dead,
of what she would do when she grew old, and how no one but
Mme de Saint-Simon and Mme de Lauzun would be left from
the days of her youth, and she had run on in this way until it
was time to go to hear the sermon.

In spite of so many good and agreeable qualities, however,
there was another side to her character, both as a princess and
a woman; not, indeed, where the keeping of secrets or loyalty
to friends was concerned, for in that she was like a deep well,
nor in her care for the interests of others; but she had small
failings that marred her perfection. She gave her friendship to
acquaintances, when she saw them continually, because they
amused her, or merely because she happened to need them
(indeed, so far as I am aware, Mme de Saint-Simon was the
only exception), and she confessed to this dangerous weakness
with a grace and candour that made it almost seem tolerable in
her. As I have already said, she liked to please everyone, and
she could hardly be blamed if some pleased her in return. When
she first came to the Court, she had been kept strictly apart,
and had then been surrounded by ancient gallants, whose roman-
tic inclinations were no whit reduced because decrepitude prevented their enjoyment. Then, as time went on and she came
more into the world, she chose companions of her own age less
for their virtues than for their good looks. She was naturally
adaptable and apt to like the people whom she saw day by day,
although (and this was never made sufficient use of) she took
as much pleasure in serious reading and conversation with the
elder ladies of her household, as in the lighter, less proper gossip
of the rest, who often led her further than she cared to go—for
shyness and some remains of modesty still restrained her.
Nevertheless, she did go to very great lengths, and a princess
less lovable and less beloved might have found herself in serious
trouble on several occasions. The manner of her death revealed
some of these mysteries and showed, too, the extreme tyranny
which the King exercised over the members of his family. Both
he and the Court received a shock when, in those awful moments

when the present vanishes and only the future is feared, she desired to change her confessor and repudiated the entire Order to which he belonged, before receiving the Last Sacraments.

With her death, all joy vanished, all pleasures, entertainments, and delights were overcast and darkness covered the face of the Court. She was its light and life. She was everywhere at once, she was its centre; her presence permeated its inner life, and if, after her death, the Court continued to subsist, it merely lingered on. No princess was ever so sincerely mourned, none was ever more worth regretting. Indeed, mourning for her has never ceased, a secret, involuntary sadness has remained, a terrible emptiness that never can be filled.

1712

Death of Mgr le Duc de Bourgogne

THE King and Mme de Maintenon were pierced with sorrow, the only real sorrow that had ever entered into his life. As soon as they arrived at Marly, he went straight to Mme de Maintenon's apartment, then dined alone in his own room and stayed only a short while afterwards in the study with M. le Duc d'Orléans and his natural children. The Duc de Berry, who was full of his own sincere grief, and felt even more deeply for that of Monseigneur his brother, had stayed at Versailles with Mme la Duchesse de Berry. She was beside herself with joy at being thus delivered of one who was greater and better loved than herself, and to whom she owed everything; but she forced her mind to rule her feelings, so far as she was able, and managed to keep up the appearances. On the morning of the following day they went to Marly in time for the King's *lever*.

The Dauphin, ill, and stricken as he was with the most bitter personal suffering, did not leave his room at Versailles and would see no one but M. le Duc de Berry, his confessor, and the Duc de Beauvilliers. The latter had been lying ill for the past week at his town house, but he made the effort to leave his bed and go to his pupil, and so was able to admire the great qualities which God had given him, for the Dauphin never appeared so noble as in that last terrible day and throughout all those that followed until his own death. This must certainly have been the last occasion on which they met in this world.

On the morning of February 13th, they managed to persuade the Dauphin to go to Marly, so as to spare him the anguish of hearing noises in the room above, where the Dauphine had died. He left at seven in the morning by the back door of his apartment and flung himself into one of the blue chairs[1] in which they carried him to his coach. A few courtiers, more lacking in tact than curious, were standing beside it and he courteously acknowledged their bows. When he reached Marly, he stopped at the chapel and heard mass, and was then carried to a window of his private apartments, through which he entered, and Mme de Maintenon went at once to visit him. You may imagine the anguish of that interview, indeed, she could not endure it for long and returned quickly to her own rooms. He was also obliged to see the princes and princesses, but they were considerate and stayed only for a few moments. Even Mme la Duchesse de Berry called on him, attended by Mme de Saint-Simon, to whom he gave a look expressive of sorrow shared. Afterwards he spent some time alone with M. le Duc de Berry.

It was then nearly time for the King's *réveil*, and when the three pages went in to announce it, I ventured to enter with them, and the Dauphin let me perceive that he had noticed me, turning on me so gentle and loving a glance that I was deeply moved. None the less, I was horrified at his appearance, for his eyes looked wild and glazed, and his face was changed, and there were spots upon it, livid rather than red in colour. I noticed a fair number of them, some large, and other people in the room also perceived them. At that time he was standing, but when, a few moments later, they came to announce that the King was awake, the tears which he had held back for so long brimmed over his eyelids. He turned away without saying anything but did not move otherwise. With him were only his three pages, myself, and Du Chesne; they suggested once or twice that he should go to the King, but he neither moved nor answered. Then I approached him and motioned to him to go; I also spoke to him in a low voice, but seeing that he still did nothing, I dared to take him by the arm, saying that he would

---

[1] A fleet of chairs with carriers dressed in the blue of the royal liveries, which were at the service of the courtiers in the gardens of Versailles.

have to see the King sooner or later, for he was waiting and certainly longing to see and embrace him, and that it would be gracious in him to delay no longer. Then, gently urging him on, I took the liberty of giving him a little push. He gave me such a look as nearly broke my heart and left the room. For a little way I followed him and then went to recover myself. I never saw him again. God grant that I may meet him in that eternal life to which His mercy will surely have called him.

The whole company at Marly, very few at that time, were assembled in the great drawing-room, and the princes and princesses and those who had the grand entrée were in the small room between the King's apartments and those of Mme de Maintenon. She was in her bedroom, but when they announced the King's *réveil* she went in to him alone, passing through the little room and the people gathered there, who shortly afterwards followed her. The Dauphin, who had entered by way of the offices, found all this company in the King's bedroom, but the King, as soon as he saw him, called him and kissed him long, lovingly, and repeatedly. These first touching moments were interrupted by broken sentences, tears, and sobs.

After a while, when the King had had time to look well at the Dauphin, he, too, was alarmed by the same symptoms which we had observed in the other room, and all who were present were equally dismayed, and the doctors more than anyone. The King ordered them to take his pulse, which was very bad, or so they afterwards said, although at that time they were content to say that it was not quite normal but that all would be well if he would go to bed. The King then embraced him again, urged him very affectionately to take good care of himself, and told him to go to his bed, which he did, and never rose again.

By this time it was late in the morning. The King had spent a wretched night and his head ached; while he was dining he saw the few great nobles who presented themselves, and afterwards went to visit the Dauphin, whose fever had increased and whose pulse was worse than ever. He then went to Mme de Maintenon, supped in his own room, and spent only a very short time in his study with those who were accustomed to be there. From then onwards, the Dauphin saw no one but his pages and the doctors, his brother for short periods, his confessor for rather longer, M. de Cheverny, for a little while. His day was spent in prayer and sacred reading. The list for Marly was made up on the spot and the company was notified, as had been done at Monseigneur's death so short a time before.

The next day, Sunday, the King spent as he had the previous day. Anxiety for the Dauphin increased. He did not disguise from Boudin, in the presence of Du Chesne and M. de Cheverny, that he had no expectation of recovery and that by what he felt, Boudin's information would prove to be correct. He repeated this more than once with the utmost unconcern, showing much contempt for the world and its vanities and an inestimable love and fear of God. It would be impossible to describe the general dismay.

On Monday the 15th, the King was bled and the Dauphin was no better. The King and Mme de Maintenon saw him separately more than once, but no one else was admitted, except M. le Duc de Berry for a few moments only, his pages scarcely at all, M. de Cheverny occasionally. He continued to read and pray.

On Tuesday the 16th, he was worse. He complained of a consuming fire which did not correspond with the external appearance of the fever, although the pulse was hard to find, most abnormal, and very alarming. As the day wore on, there was a deterioration in his condition and also a disappointment, because the spots spread from his face over his entire body and were mistaken for measles. This gave rise to some hope, but the doctors and the more thoughtful members of the Court remembered that similar marks had appeared on the Dauphine's body, although this was not generally known until after her death.

By Wednesday the 17th, the illness had increased considerably. I received news continually through Cheverny, and also through Boulduc, who came to speak to me whenever he found it possible to leave the bedroom. This Boulduc was an excellent apothecary, attached to the King, and after his father died he had become ours and was devoted to us. He knew quite as much as the best doctors, as we had discovered for ourselves, and, moreover, had much courage, honour, discretion, and wisdom. He hid nothing from Mme de Saint-Simon and myself, had already told us what he suspected about the Dauphine, and had spoken very plainly to me from the second day of the Dauphin's illness. Thus I no longer hoped, but some people, it seems, will go on hoping to the end, against all expectations.

The pains that were like a devouring flame increased during the day, becoming more and more violent. Late in the evening, the Dauphin sent to ask the King's permission to take communion very early in the morning, with no ceremonial and without spectators at the mass, which would be said in his bedroom. But no one heard about this on that night, it was only generally known in the course of the next morning. On that same Wednesday evening, I went quite late to visit the Duc and Duchesse de Chevreuse, who had their lodgings in the first pavilion, and we were in the second, both on the side of Marly village. I was by then in a state of utter misery; I saw the King scarcely once a day and went out only to hear news, and then only to M. and Mme de Chevreuse, for thus I could be sure of seeing none but those who were as much affected as myself, with whom I could be perfectly frank. Mme de Chevreuse had no more hope than I, but M. de Chevreuse, always calm, ever optimistic, ever seeing life through rose-coloured glasses, tried to prove to us, with talk of good constitutions and remedies, that there was more reason to hope than fear, all with an equanimity that exasperated me and caused me to round upon him somewhat uncivilly, but it gave some relief to Mme de Chevreuse and the few who were with us. I then returned and spent a very wretched night.

Early in the morning of Thursday, February 18th, I learned that the Dauphin had waited impatiently for midnight to come, had taken the Sacrament immediately afterwards, had then spent two hours in close communion with God, and that his head was now much confused. Mme de Saint-Simon told me later that he had received Extreme Unction, and had died at half-past eight o'clock. These Memoirs are not intended to be a record of my personal sentiments; if ever, long after I am dead, they should be published, readers will understand only too well my feelings and the state that I was in, and Mme de Saint-Simon also. Suffice it now to say that we could scarcely bring ourselves to appear in public, even for a moment, during those first days, that I wished to give up everything and retire from the Court and society, and that it was only the wisdom and good guidance of Mme de Saint-Simon that prevented me. Even so she had a hard task.

That prince, first the presumptive, then the apparent heir to the throne was born with a violent temper and in his early youth was alarming. Hard and choleric to the last degree, subject to transports of rage even against inanimate objects, wildly impetuous, unable to brook the slightest opposition, even from time or the weather, without flying into such a passion that one feared his whole body would break, stubborn beyond measure, mad for pleasures of every kind, he was a woman-lover and at the same time, which is rare, had an equally strong fancy in another direction. He loved wine and good eating just as well, was passionately fond of hunting, and listened to music in a kind of ecstasy. Cards he delighted in, but so hated to be beaten that it was dangerous to play against him. In sum, he was subject to all the passions and loved all the pleasures.

Often tyrannical and naturally inclined to cruelty, he was ruthless in sarcasm and exposed fools with a devastating realism. From his celestial height, he thought of other men, no matter who they were, as of atomies bearing no resemblance to himself, and although he and his brothers were supposed to have been brought up in perfect equality, he regarded them, at best, as go-betweens twixt himself and the human race. He was extremely intelligent and quick-witted, and even in a rage his replies were astonishing, for when most angry his arguments were reasonable and well-founded. Acquiring abstract knowledge was child's play to him, but his varied and lively interests prevented him from concentrating on any one subject at a time, so that he never became efficient. They were forced to allow him to draw during his lessons, otherwise he would not learn, but although he had great taste and aptitude, this practice may have contributed to ruining the shape of his body.

He was short rather than tall, with a long, brown face, the upper part of which was exceedingly handsome, and he had the finest eyes imaginable. His look was alert, moving, memorable, very aristocratic, usually rather kind, always penetrating; his expression was pleasant, noble, sensitive, and so intelligent that it inspired others. The lower part of his face was less good, for it was too pointed, and the nose, long, high-bridged, but not well shaped, did not become him. His chestnut hair was too thick and curled so tightly that it frizzed. The mouth and lips were pleasant enough when he was not talking, and his teeth were not decayed, but the upper jaw jutted out so far that it almost enclosed the lower, which gave a most unhappy effect. Apart from the King himself, he had the finest legs and feet that I have seen in any man, but they and his thighs were too long in proportion to the rest of his body.

When he left the nursery, his back was straight, but it was soon noticed that it had begun to curve, and they made a collar and cross of iron, which he wore at all times in his apartments, even when there was company, and neglected none of the games and exercises designed to straighten such deformities. Nature, however proved to be stronger and he grew hump-backed, and so much more so in one shoulder that he limped, not because his legs and thighs were unequal, but because when the shoulder dropped there was no longer the same distance between his hips and the ground, so that instead of standing upright he leaned to one side. This did not make him walk less comfortably, nor less far, nor less quickly or gladly, for he still enjoyed going for walks and riding, although he did that very ill. What was surprising was that for all his clearsightedness and intelligence, and in spite of all the virtues to which he later attained and his real and notable piety, the prince never learned to see his body as it really was, or would never acknowledge it. This was a failing that caused great anxiety to others lest they should be thoughtless or indiscreet, and a great deal of trouble to his valets when they dressed him and arranged his hair, for they had to try to conceal the defect as much as possible and yet be very careful not to appear to see what was visible to all. From this we must conclude that it is given to no man to reach perfection here below.

The prince never completely mastered his intellectual capacity, but like the bee, he gathered his honey from the finest and sweetest blossoms. He endeavoured to meet men of learning and to extract from them the knowledge and ideas for which he sought. Occasionally, he would confer with some of them, but as it were casually and on some special topic or, more rarely, he would see them in private to obtain necessary information, but such interviews were never repeated nor habitual. I have never heard, and surely it would not have escaped me, that he ever worked continuously with any one person, excepting with the ministers, including by that term the Duc de Chevreuse and certain prelates. Apart from them, I was the only person to have free and frequent access to him, either at my request or his, and when I was with him, he spoke his mind about the present and the future confidently, with restraint, yet discreetly. He would expatiate on the plans he thought necessary and on general topics, but was more reserved about

H*

private matters and individuals. At the same time he would try
to extract everything that he could from me. I adroitly gave
him the opportunity for such outpourings, and often successfully, for he came to feel more and more confidence in me.

A whole volume would not suffice to recount all the conversations that took place between the prince and myself. What
love of goodness! What unselfishness! What learning! What
fine results! What detachment! Dare I say it? what a clear reflection of the Divinity appeared in this pure soul, so strong, so
simple, so candid, who, so far as is permitted here below, retained the image of its Creator! In him one saw the shining
marks of an education that was laborious, active, virtuous, wise
and Christian, exemplified in a brilliant pupil, who was born
to command.

The debasement of the nobility was odious to him, for he
thought it intolerable that all should be considered equal. This
latest innovation, only waived for holders of offices, which
ranked noblemen, gentilhommes, and seigneurs on the same
level, seemed to him to be the final injustice, and the resulting
lack of degrees an immediate danger to a military State. He
remembered that at the times of greatest peril, under Philippe
de Valois, Charles V, Charles VII, Louis XII, François I, his
grandsons, and Henry IV, France owed her salvation entirely
to the old nobility, who knew their places and acknowledged
their different grades. They were thus able and willing to
march to their country's aid by companies and provinces, because no one stepped out of his place or objected to obeying
those greater than himself. He saw that this defence had been
destroyed, for there was not a man who did not now claim
equality with all others, and consequently there was no organization, no commanding, no obedience.

In the present situation he was deeply moved at the ruina-
tion of the aristocracy and shocked at the steps, which had
already been taken and still continued, to bring them to destruction and to hold them down. He saw the degeneration in
courage, character, morals, and humanity, which had been
brought about by poverty and mixed blood, for more and more
low marriages had become necessary in order to avoid starvation. He was indignant that the French nobility, once so famous,
so illustrious, should have been reduced to a class almost in-
distinguishable from the common herd. For indeed, the only

difference is that commoners have the right to work in every profession, including arms, whereas the nobility must choose between a deadly, destructive idleness that renders them unfit for anything, mocked and censured by all, or death in the wars, after being exposed to insults from secretaries of secretaries of state and secretaries of intendants. Even the very greatest among the nobles, whose birth and dignities alone should place them above the rest, cannot avoid unemployment, or humiliation from the quill-drivers when they serve with the armies. Above all, he could not stomach the wrongs done to the profession of arms, on which this' kingdom has been founded and maintained; for example, that a veteran officer several times wounded, a lieutenant-general, perhaps, retiring from the army with honours, reputation, possibly with a pension, should, unless he belongs to the nobility, be subjected to the same taxes as all the peasants in his parish and be classed in every way on a level with them. This I have seen happen to aged knights-captain of Saint-Louis, pensioners, and they had no hope of exemptions, whereas exemptions are granted by the score to the lowest grades of pettifogging bank clerks.

That noble and Christian maxim that kings are made for their peoples, not peoples for their kings was so firmly imprinted on his heart that splendour and warfare were hateful to him. That was why he sometimes argued too warmly against war; he was carried away by truths too hard for the ears of worldly men, and people often said maliciously that he did not care to fight. His justice was blindfolded with the completeness that is her only security. He took great trouble to study the various cases that came up for the King's decision at the Conseils de Finance and Dépêches, and if any great matter were concerned, he worked with specialists, consulting their expert knowledge but not slavishly adopting their opinions. Every fortnight, at least, he took communion with most notable quietness and reverence, and always wore the collar of the Order of the Holy Spirit, with the mantle and bands. He saw his Jesuit confessor once or twice a week, sometimes for long periods at a time, but later, although he went more often to communion, he did not stay with him so long.

He perfectly understood the King, respected him and, towards the end, loved him as a son. He paid homage to him as a subject, but always with a proper sense of his own position.

Mme de Maintenon he cultivated with all the civility that their
respective situations required. While Monseigneur lived, he
was careful to render him his due, but one felt the constraint,
still more so with Mlle Choin, and his entire disapproval of the
inner life of Meudon. I have so often described the reasons for
his embarrassment that I shall not repeat them now. The
prince, like most other people, failed to understand how Monseigneur, who for all his sensuality had plenty of pride, who
never learned to tolerate Mme de Maintenon and only visited
her out of politeness when he could not avoid so doing, should
yet keep his own Maintenon in Mlle Choin and force his children to accept her just as the King subjected his to Mme de
Maintenon. He loved his brothers tenderly and his wife passionately. His sorrow at losing her broke his heart and only by
the most prodigious effort did his religion survive. It was a
sacrifice which he made without reservation; it killed him, yet
in that terrible affliction he showed nothing mean or common,
nothing unworthy. Onlookers saw a man, driven frantic with
grief, who still wrung out of himself the strength to preserve a
calm exterior but died in the struggle. His days were soon
brought to a premature close.

It was the same throughout his last illness, for he never
believed that he would recover and maintained that opinion
against his doctors, not concealing the reasons on which it was
based. Indeed, what he felt from first to last confirmed them.
What an appalling thing to have reached such a conviction
regarding his wife's death and his own! But, Great God! what
an example Thou has given us in him! The inmost, most
sublime secrets may not yet be revealed, and Thou alone
knowest the price which he had to pay! What an imitation he
gave of Jesus Christ upon the Cross! I speak not only of death
and suffering, but of his gentle tolerant outlook, his supreme
unselfishness! What thankfulness that he was not called on to
reign and to render an account of his kingship! How humble
he was; how excellent! How dearly he loved God; how clearly
saw his own unworthiness and sins! How wonderful his sense
of the divine mercy! How holy his fears! How temperate his
hopes! What peace of mind! How continually he read and
prayed! How eagerly he longed for the Last Sacrament! How
deep his self-communion! How invincible his patience; how
good he was; how thoughtful for all who came near him! How

pure the love that urged him to go to God! In his death, France suffered her final chastisement, for God showed her the prince whom she did not deserve. Earth was not worthy of him; he was ripe already for the joys of Paradise.

1712

The King is Bored

THE King grew bored at Mme de Maintenon's apartment in the intervals of working with his Ministers, for the void left by the Dauphine's death could scarcely be filled by the diversions of that very small circle of elderly ladies who were occasionally admitted. Musical entertainments were given increasingly often, but they had begun to pall for that very reason, until someone thought of enlivening them with short scenes from Molière's comedies, acted in costume by the King's musicians.

Mme de Maintenon then had the Maréchal de Villeroy recalled for no better reason than that he amused the King with old tales of their past youth. He alone was allowed into the intimate circle at these modest entertainments, in order to animate them with his tittle-tattle, but he was well under her thumb at all times and knew that he owed his return to favour to her. She made him useful in many ways, for instance in broaching certain subjects that did not come within the scope of the ministers and about which she wished the King to consult with her. Thus she was able to urge her views in some matters with greater delicacy and assurance because the topic did not seem to originate with her.

The Princes of the Blood had died leaving only children, the two Dauphins and the Dauphine were dead, M. le Duc d'Orléans had been reduced to nothing by black and subtle calumny, and the agonies of fear which M. le Duc de Berry already felt in the King's presence were being carefully fostered. Thus a vast new field lay open to the limitless ambition of M. le Duc du Maine and the mad partiality of his one-time governess. The Maréchal de Villeroy, a vile courtier, no more, was the finest possible instrument to serve their object, and Mme de

Maintenon made sure of having him at hand in case he should
be needed.

1713

Brissac Plays a Prank

OLD Brissac,[1] who had been living in retirement for several
years, was another who died at a great age. He was a lieutenant-
general, governor of Guise, and had been adjutant of the Gardes
du Corps for a long time. A gentleman of very small standing
he had risen through all the ranks by attracting the King's
notice for his keenness, his attention to detail, and his devotion
to the King and none other. He gained such a reputation for
knowing everything about the Gardes du Corps that even the
captains, all of them great nobles and general officers, felt that
he needed to be handled with care and tact, and how much more
so the junior officers. To speak truth, he was a coarse, common
man, exceedingly disagreeable and abominably spoilt by the
King, but he was a man of honour and good principles, honest
and worthy, and was esteemed as such. At the same time many
people hated him, and everyone, even the courtiers, even the
great ones, dreaded having dealings with him, for he was dangerous. He was the only man who ever dared to attack Fagon
about medicine, and barked at him in the King's presence in a
way that put Fagon into a rage, and made the King and the
bystanders laugh until their sides ached. Fagon, himself a man
of no little wit, and fiery-tempered, gave back as good as he got
and caused much amusement; but at the same time, he could not
endure to see Brissac or even to hear him mentioned without
losing his temper.

One anecdote about this adjutant of the Gardes du Corps will
give a little sketch of the Court. Every evening at Versailles
there were public prayers at the end of the day, followed by
evening service, and benediction on Sundays and Thursdays.
In wintertime, the service was at six o'clock, and at five in
summer, so as to allow time for going out of doors afterwards.
The King always attended on Sundays, and rarely missed on
Thursdays during the winter. At the end of prayers, one of the

[1] Albert de Grillet, Marquis de Brissac.

blue footmen on duty in the tribune, would run to warn him, so that he arrived a moment before benediction. But whether he was expected or not, the service always began at the proper time, and guards were always posted in the tribune, where the King stood. The ladies made a point of filling the bays between the tribunes, and in wintertime they took care to make themselves conspicuous by holding the little candles, which they carried to light their prayer books, in such a way as to throw a beam full upon their faces. Regular attendance was accounted a merit; thus all the ladies, young as well as old, endeavoured to be seen by the King and Mme de Maintenon.

Brissac grew tired of seeing so many ladies present who had no reputation for eagerness to hear benediction, and one day he laid a plot with the officers of the Gardes du Corps. Towards the end of prayers, he entered the royal tribune, rapped with his staff, and cried out with a loud voice, 'Gardes du Corps, you may withdraw! The King is not coming to benediction.' Everyone obeyed the order, the guards went away, and Brissac hid himself behind one of the pillars. Then a great whispering began in the other tribunes, which were full of ladies, and a moment afterwards, each one snuffed out her candle and vanished, leaving only Mme de Dangeau and two others of no great standing.

All of this occurred in the old chapel. The officers, having been forewarned, posted the guards on the staircase to Blouin's[1] room and in the back passages, where they were well hidden, and when Brissac had given the ladies ample time to get out of earshot, the guards were reposted. It was all timed to perfection, so that the King appeared and benediction was begun only a moment afterwards. He always ran his glance around the tribunes to see who was there, and being used to seeing them filled to capacity he was extremely surprised to discover no one but Mme de Dangeau and the two other ladies. When he came away he spoke about it and expressed his astonishment. Then Brissac, who always walked near him, began to laugh and told the whole story of the joke he had played on those pseudo-saints, because he was tired of seeing the King duped. The King laughed heartily, and his courtiers still more. They soon found out who the ladies were who had blown out their candles when they heard that the King was not coming, and some of them

---

[1] The King's head footman.

were so furious that they would have liked to scratch out
Brissac's eyes. Indeed, he almost deserved it for the scathing
remarks that he made about them.

1714

The King's Will

IT is now time to speak of the King's will, which made its
appearance amid the most extraordinary precautions to keep
the entire contents secret and the document itself inviolably
secure.

The King was at last showing his age; not that there was
any change in his way of life, but those nearest him were beginning to fear that he had not long to live. This is not the place
to give details of a constitution that for so long a time had been
remarkably strong; suffice it to say that there had been ominous
signs. For very many years, he had been accustomed to master
his fate, but lately he had suffered a series of bitter defeats and
his family tragedies had wounded him still more. His legitimate children had all died before him, leaving him a prey to the
most sinister suspicions, and every moment he expected to meet
the same fate himself. Yet instead of receiving comfort from
the intimate circle whom he saw every day, he found there only
fresh cause for anxiety.

Maréchal, the chief surgeon, was the only one who strove to
allay his fears. All the rest, Mme de Maintenon, M. du Maine,
Fagon, Blouin, and the confidential servants who were all
creatures of the bastard and his former governess, endeavoured
only to increase his doubts, and to speak truly, they had no
great difficulty. Everyone suspected poison, no one could
seriously think otherwise. Maréchal was equally certain of it,
although he said otherwise because he wished to save the King
from useless worry. M. du Maine and Mme de Maintenon
(because she hated the Duc d'Orléans and wished to serve one
whom she loved better) had too many interests at stake not to
endeavour to increase the King's alarm by allowing suspicion
to fall on the one remaining royal prince who was old enough to
oppose them. Indeed they had determined to ruin him. You **may**

imagine the mental state of the King who daily, at his meals and in his study, was confronted by that prince who, so they assured him, had committed such appalling crimes.

Besides the loss of his own children he had suffered the death, in the same cruel manner, of an irreplaceable princess, the life and light of his Court, his joy, his darling, his great delight at the times when he was not engaged with public business. Never, since he first entered the world, had he felt at ease with anyone but her, and I have already described to what lengths he went in his relaxation. Nothing could fill so vast an emptiness, and his sorrow was all the greater because he could find no other distraction. In this wretched state he took what comfort he could find, and abandoned himself more and more to Mme de Maintenon and M. du Maine. He found their seemingly unending devotion and their restraint a reassurance. They had long since managed to persuade him that M. du Maine, although sufficiently intelligent to be consulted over the final details of public business (and final details were the King's foible), was without aims and ambitions and incapable of having any. The King pictured him as engrossed in family affairs and only interested in grandeur in so far as it reflected that of a monarch whom he loved simply, honestly, transparently, and above all else. He imagined him after a day spent dutifully working to please the King, and after giving much time to his prayers and meditations, going off to hunt alone, or exercising his charm and wit in the bosom of his family, often quite ignorant of the affairs of the Court.

Such an opinion pleased the King immensely and made him feel perfectly at ease with M. du Maine who, in any case, was his favourite constantly beside him, amusing him with jokes and anecdotes. Indeed, of all the good conversationalists I have ever known, M. du Maine was the most accomplished. He could be charming and so easy that one was almost tempted to trust him; yet at the same time he was clever at being spiteful and could mock absurdities most cruelly. His words were always carefully considered; he suited the occasion and the King's humour, which he understood to perfection.

He and Mme de Maintenon being thus firmly established in the King's heart and confidence, it had become merely a question of making the best use of a precious time which they thought could not endure long. If the crown itself were not

their immediate objective, which seems hard to believe in
view of the edict[1] that had made the bastards capable of the
succession, they were at least determined to keep what they had
gained, to make sure of greatness in the future, and to force the
future Regent to reckon with them.

Fortune seemed to smile upon their atrocious designs. They
themselves had prepared and smoothed the way for success by
abominable slanders, most artfully and perseveringly sustained,
in order to blacken the reputation of the one prince whose right
to the regency was incontrovertible. With great skill and cunning manœuvres, they convinced the ignorant and put doubts
into the minds of others, thus rendering M. le Duc d'Orléans suspect in Paris and the provinces, and especially at
the Court, where no one cared or dared to approach him.
How could a friendless prince defend himself in that deplorable
situation to which they had reduced him? How could he dis-
prove a negative, especially not one of that particular kind?
And what could he do to clear himself in the eyes of a king
whose mind was thus bedevilled? M. du Maine could scarcely
have held better cards, and he felt this so strongly and Mme
de Maintenon also, that they determined there and then to
reap all the benefits that they desired for the present and the
future.

For them it was no longer a matter of appointments, high
office, governorships and reversions, still less one of rank
and honours. What they now wanted was something far greater,
to make themselves what no man can become, to take what no
subject, although crowned, can assume, namely, the Divine
Right. They wished to defraud the Princes of the Blood of that
sublime birthright that distinguishes them from all other kinds
of men, to introduce the most tyrannical and pernicious of
precedents, to destroy the holiest and most ancient law, thus
making a mockery of the crown and trampling upon the nation.
Worst of all, to perform this dreadful act, they chose a man who
could not change nature, nor make that which is not become
what is, a man who, as head of a unique line, should have been

---

[1] Edict of July 1714, registered in the Parlement on August 2nd of the same year. It
admitted to the succession of the crown of France, M. le Duc du Maine, M. le Comte
de Toulouse, and their male descendants should there be no Princes of the Royal Blood
available. It also laid down that the bastards and their descendants should enjoy the
same ranks, honours and privileges as the Princes of the Blood, and rank immediately
after them.

doubly anxious to preserve its sanctity, since he was King solely by right of inheritance. They caused the King of this most loyal and obedient nation to dishonour and overthrow its most sacred laws in order to make possible the crowning of the off-spring of a double adultery. Louis XIV was the first King of France to raise from nothingness what all other nations, including the savages, have kept hidden from the beginnings of time. The plot was vast enough, but it would have ended in failure, for had it even been mooted, its authors would have perished amid the general ruin and have lost all that they had gained.

As they thought then, however, their only concern was to have a will drawn up by the King at their dictation. By this means, because of the respect paid to the wishes of that testator, they hoped to establish their new position and gain more far-reaching powers in the future. M. du Maine had so successfully convinced the King and the bulk of the nation of the criminality of M. le Duc d'Orléans that it only remained for him to gather his fruit. This was to persuade the King for conscience's sake, for the safety of his one remaining legitimate heir and the security of his kingdom, to reduce as far as possible the power of the prince who had become suspect, by dividing his power as future Regent and making M. du Maine the keeper and absolute governor of that precious infant, the future King.

One other no less difficult point remained, how to ensure the safety of the will once the King had been brought to make it, for it must be secured beyond all doubt and such extraordinary precautions taken that would increase the respect ordinarily felt for such a document. It must, moreover, be so arranged that the executing of it should become a proper matter for the Parlement, and some means be found to overcome the King's dislike for that body. To those who knew him, his obstinate clinging to his principles, his never broken habits, and his extreme sensitiveness regarding his absolute authority even in the distant future, made the task seem impossible. But Providence decreed otherwise. In punishment, perhaps, for the scandal offered to the world by the double adultery, the King, fully realizing the wickedness of the act in all its shame and significance, was yet driven to perform it, step by step, against his will, and came at last, groaning in bitterness of soul and despair at his weakness, to crown his crime with this most terrible apotheosis.

We have already seen from the King's unguarded words when he told M. du Maine what he had done to include him in the line of succession, and from his tone and manner of speaking, how unwillingly that outrageous concession had been wrung from him.[1] We shall now see how that monarch, who was usually a master of self-control, betrayed his true feelings no less plainly in the matter of his will.

A few days before the news broke, when the King was still full of that monstrous thing, he was in his study with the two bastards, d'O, d'Antin, and some of the confidential servants. He turned to M. du Maine, and speaking with a sour, resentful air, said sternly, 'You would have it so, but remember, however great I make you in my lifetime, when I am dead you are nothing. It is for you to make good use of what I have done, if you can.' All present trembled at this thunder-clap, so sudden so totally unexpected, so foreign to the King's nature and habits. It clearly revealed M. du Maine's ultimate ambitions and the violence which he had done to the King in his weakness, for the latter obviously reproached himself for his own failing and the bastard for his ambition and arrogance.

Then it was that the curtain began to be raised before that small circle of the inner household, who had been so troubled and baffled by the changes that were taking place. M. du Maine's dismay at the outburst, for which he had been quite unprepared, was so intense that the spectators held their breath and gazed fixedly at the floor. A long silence ensued that lasted for an appreciable time. It was only broken when the King had gone into his dressing-room and everyone could breathe again.

The King's heart was very heavy because of what he had been made to do, but that was only the beginning. Like a woman who gives birth to twins, he had produced one monstrosity, but still had to be delivered of a second, and he felt all its anguish without any relief from the suffering caused by the first. Two days later, a second event completed the raising of the curtain.

The Court was at Versailles at that time. On Sunday, August 26th, after the *lever*, the King sent for Mesmes, the premier

---

[1] In his study, surrounded by the courtiers and officers of his household, the King had said, sighing deeply, that he had now done everything in his power for M. du Maine and his brother the Comte de Toulouse, but that the higher he raised them the more they had to lose. They must try to make themselves worthy of their new rank, which after his death could be sustained only by their merits.

président, and Daguesseau, the procureur général, who had already seen the chancellor[1] and agreed upon a means of safeguarding the precious document. You may be sure that as soon as M. du Maine became certain of it, he had discussed it thoroughly with his tool, the premier président. When they were alone, the King unlocked a drawer and took out a large packet sealed with seven seals—I do not know if M. du Maine, when he so sanctified it, was thinking of that mysterious Book with the Seven Seals that is mentioned in the Apocalypse. This he handed to them saying, 'Messieurs, this is my will. No one but myself knows its contents. To your care I consign it for safe keeping by the Parlement, to whom I can show no higher proof of my trust and esteem. The fate of the wills of earlier kings and of my royal father makes me well aware what may become of it. But they would have it so. They have pestered me. They have allowed me no peace, no matter what I said. Now I have purchased my rest. Here it is! Take it away! Come what may, I shall at least have peace and quiet and hear no more about it.' Then, turning on his heel with a curt nod, he went into another room, leaving them almost petrified with fright. They looked at one another terrified by what they had just heard and by the King's glance and expression, and as soon as they had come to their senses they withdrew and went back to Paris.

It was not generally known until after dinner that the King had made a will and given it into their keeping. As the news spread, the whole Court was filled with dismay, although the toadies, who at heart were as much shocked as the rest, surpassed themselves in praises and congratulations.

On the following day, the Queen of England,[2] who as usual was staying at Chaillot, came to visit Mme de Maintenon. The King went in to see her, and as soon as he caught sight of her, exclaimed in an exasperated tone, 'Madame, I have made a will, they badgered me into so doing. I know how futile it is. We do what we choose whilst we are alive, but after we are dead we have less power than ordinary individuals. You have only to think of what became of my royal father's will, and that immediately after his death, and of the wills of many other Kings. I am well aware of all this, but they have insisted on it. They gave me no peace nor rest until it was done. Well!

---

[1] Daniel François Voysin (1654–1717). He became Chancellor of France in 1714.
[2] Mary of Modena, wife of James II.

Now it is done, Madame. Perhaps it may have some influence. At least they will stop pestering me!'

Such words, so expressive of outraged feelings and a long and bitter struggle before he yielded, are so plain and so momentous that they require equally clear proof of authenticity. Here it is! What the King said to the premier président and the procureur général, I learned from the former who could never forget it. It is also true, for I must be accurate, that he told me a long time afterwards, but he repeated the speech word for word, exactly as I have written it down. What the King said to the Queen of England was much more direct and emphatic, partly because he was more familiar with her and partly, perhaps, because he was in the presence of Mme de Maintenon, on whom he intended his reproaches to fall. I heard it two days later, from M. de Lauzun, to whom the Queen told it in her first astonishment, and she did not need pressing, so full was she of the King's dreadful speech. She repeated it to M. de Lauzun, word for word, as he reported it to me, and just as I record it here.

As soon as the premier président and the procureur général reached Paris, they sent for workmen and took them into a tower behind the robing-room of the great chamber and the former's office. There they bade them hollow a large hole out of the wall, which is very thick in that place, and in that hole they placed the will. They then closed the opening, first with an iron door, then with an iron grille, and finally walled it in. The door and the grille were fitted each with three locks, in such a way that three keys each opened two of the locks. The premier président and the procureur général each kept a key and the third they gave to the chief clerk, so as to prevent jealousy between the second président à mortier and the doyen. The Parlement happened to be sitting at that time, and the premier président at once gave a most flattering account of the King's respect and esteem, and his confidence that the will would be kept safe and its provisions put into effect when the time came.

I have already said that consternation was very great when the existence of a will became known. It was always M. du Maine's fate to obtain what he wished, but with public abhorrence, and this was so in the matter of the King's will. When he realized the general opinion he became frantic, Mme de

Maintenon was furious, and both redoubled their efforts to prevent any whispers reaching the King. They set themselves more than ever to keep him happy and amused, and saw to it that he heard nothing but praise, joy, and general congratulations for his great, wise, generous, and necessary gesture, one that was calculated, so they said, to maintain order and extend the glories of his reign beyond the span of his lifetime. It was indeed natural that the public should feel dismayed; but M. du Maine himself had been deceived and found himself in difficulties. He himself was fully persuaded of having prepared and smoothed his path by making M. le Duc d'Orléans hated and suspect. He had, in fact, partly succeeded, but not so well as he believed, for his own desires and his spies had exaggerated his success, and when instead of applause he received the opposite, he became utterly discomfited.

People saw very clearly that the will must be aimed against M. le Duc d'Orléans, for had there been no desire to hinder him, there had been no need to make a will, matters would have taken their normal course. The doubts and suspicions so carefully cultivated were not diminished, but whatever people may have thought privately, or however much they disapproved, no one was so blind that he did not realize that the Duc d'Orléans must become the Regent because of his incontestable birthright. No provisions in any will could weaken that right, unless some new power were set up equal to his own. But to do that would be to create two parties, which the rival leaders would support by every possible means. Everyone would then be forced to choose a side, and in such choices lie a thousand dangers and no good hopes.

What the people desired was that the King, during his lifetime, should establish the government that he wished to continue after him, bring into his councils and businesses those whom he intended to leave in power, and at once give them their functions and offices. Thus, whilst still retaining authority, he would train the future Regent and those who served under him in a new administration. In fact, the King would be executor of his own will, so that after his death there would be no sudden change, but all continue smoothly as he had directed and arranged.

M. le Duc d'Orléans was stunned by the blow. He felt how nearly it touched him, but saw no remedy in the King's life-time.

A deep, respectful silence seemed to him the only possible course, for any other would have led to precautions being redoubled. I shall leave the matter there. This is not the time to enter into the prince's ideas and plans for the future. The King avoided all speech with him on the subject, except for a bald statement after the event. M. du Maine the same. M. le Duc d'Orléans therefore contented himself with a monosyllable of acquiescence, like a good courtier who never comments, and even refrained from discussing it with his wife. I was the only one to whom he dared to speak openly. With all others he took pains to appear as usual and avoided looking displeased or laying his mind open to prying eyes. His utter isolation at the Court and in society saved him from overhearing casual remarks, for nobody came near him.

1715

Character of M. le Duc d'Orléans

THE reign of Louis XIV has now been brought almost to its close and nothing more remains to tell, or only the events of the final month. These are so very important that they must be recorded with the utmost exactness and clarity and in their proper order, for they are closely linked with all that followed immediately after the monarch's death. It is no less essential, however, to describe the plans, thoughts, and problems that were revolving in the mind of that prince who, in spite of the endeavours of Mme de Maintenon and the Duc du Maine to strip him of all but the bare title of Regent, would inevitably become head of the State during the minority of the future King. Now therefore the time has come to disclose many things, after which I shall return to the events of the last month of the King's life.

Before venturing upon that thorny path, I think it best to describe, if I can, the nature of the leading figure, his private and official difficulties, and his personal characteristics. I say 'if I can', for never in all my life have I met a man so perfectly inconsistent as M. le Duc d'Orléans. I knew him intimately for very many years, during which time he never tried to conceal his nature from me, indeed, during the latter part of that time I was his only friend, the only one to whom he could speak freely, and he did so speak, openly, trustingly and, indeed, of necessity. Yet, in spite of this, I never learned to know him; neither did he fully know himself.

M. le Duc d'Orléans was, at the very most, of medium height, stout, without being gross, with an easy aristocratic bearing, a large pleasant face, red complexion, black hair and a black wig.[1] He always was an abominable dancer, and had not succeeded at the Academy, but he possessed such natural charm of manner and expression that it coloured and enhanced all his actions, even the most commonplace. When nothing crossed him, he could be gentle, cordial, frank, easily approachable, with an agreeable voice and a most original turn of phrase. He could converse clearly and fluently on any subject, never hesitating for words, and always surprisingly interesting. What is more, he could talk just as sensibly and eloquently on the abstract sciences, government business, finance, the law, military matters, and the affairs of the Court, as engage in polite conversation or discuss the arts and engineering. He knew the histories and memoirs of great men and could put them to good use. He was familiar with the lives of leading personalities in other periods and the intrigues of ancient courts as well as those of his own time. To hear him speak you would have thought him vastly well-read. Not so indeed, for he was a skimmer; but his memory was so good that he forgot nothing, not even names and dates, which he could quote accurately. His understanding was so admirable that in glancing through a book he took in as much as though he read it carefully, and he excelled in impromptu speeches, being very witty with his sallies and repartees. I never flattered him, for which he used to reproach me, as others did, but I did praise him often for a quality which few possess and which he had abundantly, namely great intelligence combined with excellent good sense. Had he followed his first instincts in every matter he would have made no mistakes. He sometimes took this praise of mine as though it were meant in

---

[1] Madame described him as follows: 'When my son was only about fourteen or fifteen years old he was not ill-looking, but the suns of Spain and Italy so bronzed his skin that his complexion turned to a dark red. He is not tall, but in no way gross. His bad sight causes him sometimes to squint a little, and he carries himself badly. I love him with all my heart, but I can understand that women should not be attracted by him, for he is ungallant with them and has no tact.'

reproach, but although he was not always wrong, it was none the less true. With all these talents, he never gave himself airs or paraded superior knowledge, but argued with each man as an equal and often surprised scholars by his cleverness. In society he was never pompous or overbearing, but retained a proper sense of his rank and position so that no one forgot himself in his presence, yet everyone felt at ease because he placed himself on their level.

He was particularly careful to keep his place with the Princes of the Blood. No one was more respectful in speech and bearing, no one more dignified in his attitude towards the King and the Sons of France, for he inherited through Monsieur inordinate pride in his royal ancestry. Although not prone to say ill-natured or spiteful things he was a dangerous critic of other men's courage. He never boasted of his own, and, indeed, was unusually modest and silent about events in which he had played a leading part. He gave others due credit, but found it hard not to round upon those whom he described as not pulling their weight (*franc du collier*) and made his dislike and scorn very evident.

Another of his weaknesses was to believe that he greatly resembled Henri IV and to imitate his ways and sayings. He even managed to convince himself that he looked like that monarch in face and figure, and no flattery pleased him more. But this I would never stoop to, for I was too much assured that he tried to copy that great king's vices as well as his virtues and that he admired both equally. As a matter of fact, he did re-semble Henri IV in being by nature good, kind, and compassion-ate. They have accused him of most inhuman crimes, yet I never met a man more violently opposed to murder, none more averse even to causing pain. You might reasonably say that he carried humanity and tolerance too far, for I maintain that he made a vice of the sublime virtue of forgiving enemies, and that his indiscriminate generosity verged on carelessness and caused him much annoyance and trouble in later years, as will be seen.

I remember, for example, that about a year before the King died I was at Marly and went up soon after dinner to pay a call on Mme la Duchesse d'Orléans, whom I found in bed, suffer-ing with a migraine. M. le Duc d'Orléans was with her alone, sitting in an armchair by the bedside. No sooner had I seated myself than Mme la Duchesse d'Orléans began to tell me of the Cardinal de Rohan's part in the plot against the duke, and of his support of Mme de Maintenon and M. du Maine in their efforts to substantiate the abominable imputations which were then so fashionable. I exclaimed all the more emphatically because M. le Duc d'Orléans, for some unknown reason, had always favoured the Cardinal and his brother and thought of them as friends. 'What do you think of M. le Duc d'Orléans?' she continued. 'He knows that this is true beyond dispute, yet he goes on treating them with the same kindness.' I looked at the duke lolling in his chair and saying nothing beyond a word or two in confirmation, and I said, 'To speak truth, Monsieur, I think that since Louis the Meek (*le Débonnaire*), there has never been anyone as meek as you.' At these words he leapt up, scarlet with rage to the very whites of his eyes, and began to splutter angrily at me, accusing me of spite and malice, while the duchess egged me on and laughed at him. 'Well done, Monsieur,' I said. 'Go on scolding your friends and making much of your enemies. I am delighted to see you so angry. It shows that I have put my finger on an abscess; when I press it the patient screams. I wish I could squeeze all the poison out of your system, you would be a better man and better respected.' He growled at me a little longer and then subsided. This was one of the only two occasions when he was really vexed with me, the other I shall proceed to relate.

It occurred two or three years after the King's death, when I was talking one day in a corner of the long gallery at the Tuileries, waiting for the Conseil de la Régence to begin, and M. le Duc d'Orléans was speaking to someone in one of the window recesses at the other end of the room. I heard my name called from one to another and was told that he wished to speak to me, as often happened before the meetings. I accordingly went to the window, where I found him looking grave, thoughtful, and angry, which surprised me much. 'Monsieur,' he said abruptly, 'I have much to reproach you with; I had hitherto thought of you as my friend.' 'I, Sir!' I exclaimed, still more astonished. 'Pray, what have I done?' 'What you have done,' he answered, 'is something which you cannot deny, verses, Sir, which you have written against me.' 'Verses!' said I. 'Who on earth has been telling you such nonsense? You have known me for forty years and must be aware that I cannot string two lines together, let alone write verses.' 'Disgraceful,' he said. 'but you cannot deny these,' and bursting into laughter, he there and then began to sing a street-song with the refrain, '*Notre Régent est débonnaire, la la, il est débonnaire*'. 'What!' I exclaimed, 'you have not forgotten that incident? Well, since you have had your revenge, remember to make good use of it.' And I, too, laughed heartily. He was still laughing when he sat down at the council table. I do not hesitate to record this trifling incident, because it describes him so well.

He truly loved liberty, as much for others as for himself. One day he praised the English to me because they had no exiles and no *lettres de cachet*, and because their King could forbid no one anything but the entrée to his palace and could keep no one imprisoned. He then told me with great relish (all our princes were alive at that time) that King Charles II had had many lesser mistresses besides the Duchess of Portsmouth, and that the Grand Prieur,[1] young and charming in those days, once went into England when banished for some foolishness, and was given a warm welcome by the English king. By way of showing his gratitude, he managed to seduce one of those little mistresses, to whom the king was so passionately devoted that he begged for mercy, offered bribes of money, and promised to smooth matters so that his rival might return to France. The Grand Prieur refused to yield up the lady. Charles forbade him the palace, but he cared nothing for that and took his conquest every night to the play, sitting opposite to the King. Finally, the King of England, not knowing how to get rid of him, so pestered King Louis for his recall that that was ordered. But the Grand Prieur still stayed on, pretending that he was very comfortable in England and pursuing his love-affair openly. Then, in indignation, King Charles went so far as to tell the King in confidence of the situation in which the Grand Prieur had placed him, which procured so swift and peremptory an order to return, that back he went forthwith. M. le Duc d'Orléans seemed to admire him for this episode, and I am not sure that he himself would not have liked to have been in the Grand Prieur's shoes. I said that for my part it astonished me that the grandson of a King of France should have lent himself to so insolent a manœuvre and that speaking as a subject who, like him, had no claim to the throne, I thought it more than scandalous and most worthy of punishment. But the Duc d'Orléans would not have it so, and went on telling the story with enormous gusto.

[1] Philippe de Vendôme, brother of the duke.

He had no desire himself to reign or govern, and although he did do a very foolish thing in Spain,[1] it was solely because some-one else put it into his head. As a matter of fact he had never seriously considered ruling the country until forced to choose between exercising his birthright or being dishonoured, and as for reigning, I can truthfully say that he never aspired to it. Had the necessity arisen, he would have been troubled and em-barrassed. What did he want? you will say. To command the armies so long as the wars lasted, and for the rest of the time, to find amusement, without restraint on himself or others.

That was really what suited him best. By nature he was calm and courageous, able to foresee difficulties and apply the proper remedies. He had great aptitude for campaigning, making plans and executing them, mustering his resources, taking full advantage of them, and making prompt use of any good opportunities that might occur. It is not too much to say that he was a most able commander, engineer, and commissary-general. He knew the effective strength of all the troops under his command, the names and capabilities of the officers and the particular merits of the different regiments. The troops adored him; he kept them under strict discipline and inspired them to fulfil the most difficult tasks although they lacked for every-thing. Both his military and his governmental plans were re-markably wise and practical. It was really amazing to see how well he could grasp the details of different courses of action, never confusing the issue, but weighing the advantages and disadvantages and explaining them most lucidly to others. In short, he had fine and varied capabilities and knowledge, but never paraded them, for truly he had no very great opinion of himself.

What a man! So superior, so well-informed! So fit to bring happiness to France when he came into power! Moreover he had one other excellent qualification for ruling; he was more than thirty-six years old when the two Dauphins died and nearly thirty-eight at the death of the Duc de Berry. During the whole of that time he lived as a private individual, an ordinary subject, with no idea of ever taking the helm. Like the other courtiers, he was buffeted by all the storms and tempests and learned to know all those who were leading

---

[1] In 1708 the Duc d'Orléans, commanding the French army in Spain, was accused of attempting to dethrone Philip V in order to succeed to the Spanish throne.

personalities and many who were not. Thus he had the advantage of leading a private life, and gained a knowledge of the world which he would not otherwise have acquired. That is the good side of him, and very good it is, no doubt, and very rare. Unfortunately there is another, which must be mentioned at the risk of repeating what has already been said.

The prince had been intended to be the fruit and perfect example of a good education, but he was not lucky in his masters. When he gained his freedom, he was young, healthy, and virile, but resentment at his marriage, lack of employment, and inevitable boredom bred in him an admiration for men of fashion and that desire to copy them which is so often fatal at an early age. Tempted into promiscuous love-affairs, influenced by bad companions who pleased their vanity or ambition by encouraging him to live like them, he grew so accustomed to debauchery and excitement that eventually he could not exist without them and found pleasure only amid noise, turmoil and licentiousness.

After Monseigneur died he came more frequently to the Court, where he was bored to tears. He then plunged into those scientific experiments which I have mentioned earlier and which were used so spitefully against him. It is difficult to realize how incapable he was of gathering a circle of friends, how totally unsuited to hold his Court, even before the fiendish plots of Mme de Maintenon and the Duc du Maine had isolated him entirely. In spite of his apparent unconcern, society embarrassed and wearied him,[1] yet in his own home he was without resources, although his many talents should have provided him with endless interests. He was born bored and by this time had become so accustomed to outside amusements that he found his own company intolerable and would not even try to distract himself. He lived only amid the hustle and bustle of affairs, when, for instance, he was with the army supplying the needs of a campaign, or amid the excitement of some debauch. As soon as the noise and tumult ceased he began to flag and found it hard to pass the time. When his passion for chemistry was exhausted or destroyed by the unkind things that were said, he flung himself into art. He painted during nearly the whole

[1] Madame wrote: 'I wish that my son would take more pleasure in the company of men of quality, and less with actors, artists and doctors. When he is with the latter he will talk, whereas when men of quality visit him he hangs his head, bites his nails, and does not utter, so that they are vexed when they leave him.'

of every afternoon when he was at Versailles or Marly, knew a good deal about pictures, loved them, and made a collection as fine and as large as that of the King. He also liked compounding strong perfumes, but there I used to discourage him because the King hated them, and he nearly always smelt of them. Never was any man so gifted, yet no man's life was ever so flat, vain, and empty.

Madame, who loved fairy-stories, used to tell how all the fairies were invited to his christening and how each gave him the present of a talent so that he possessed them all. Unfortunately, one old fairy had lived in retirement for so long that she was forgotten. She arrived late, in a fury, leaning on her little stick, but when she heard what had been done and that the fairies had already made their gifts she became even angrier, and nullified them all by decreeing that although he might possess all the talents he should be incapable of making use of any. In truth, I must admit that the portrait is on the whole a speaking likeness.

One of the prince's chief misfortunes was to have so little perseverance that he scarcely knew the meaning of the word. Another of his weaknesses, as I have already mentioned, was his insensibility to affronts, even dangerous or deadly slanders, and, since the instinct and origin of love and hatred, gratitude and revenge, are one and the same, and since he lacked that instinct, the consequences were many and pernicious. He was by nature undecided, and he knew it and was ashamed, so that he pretended to the contrary and boasted of his firmness. The truth is, however, that as everyone realized when he came into power, nothing could be gained from him, neither favour nor justice, without importuning him or acting on his fears. He would try to escape by making promises, with which he was very liberal, but only the strongest could force him to keep his word. At last, he broke so many pledges that his word ceased to mean anything, for he often promised to several people what he could grant only to one. There was much discontent and he ceased to be respected. In the end he was not believed even when he spoke in good faith and his glibness of speech weakened his actions. Finally, the low company that he sought, and from among whom he chose those boon companions whom he openly referred to as his 'rascals', drove better men from his side and did him infinite harm, even after he had risen to power.

We often spoke of religion, for so long as I had any hope of reclaiming him I took great pains to discuss it with him from different angles so as not to weary him. I never could discover what convictions he held, if any, and I ended by deciding that he remained uncertain, having formed none. Like his boon companions, he longed to persuade himself that God did not exist, but was too intelligent to be an atheist, a far rarer type of lunacy than most people imagine. This glimmer of enlightenment worried him; he did his best to extinguish it, but was never entirely successful. It would have comforted him to have believed that he had no soul, but he could not be convinced in spite of all his efforts. The idea of a living God and an immortal soul greatly distressed him, yet he was unable to blind himself to the fact that both do exist. I was only able to discover what he was not; I never found in him any positive feelings towards religion. Yet I do know his extreme discomfiture regarding that great mystery, and I think that had he incurred some dangerous illness and been given time, he would have required no urging to put himself into the hands of all those priests and friars whom he made such a parade of despising and ridiculing. His besetting sin was to pride himself on irreligion and to try to out-mock the most brazen scoffers.

I remember one Christmas Eve at Versailles when he accompanied the King to matins and the three midnight masses and astonished the Court by appearing to be absorbed in a book that looked like a prayer book. Mme la Duchesse d'Orléans' head ladies' maid,[1] who was devoted to them both and like all old retainers very free in her speech, was so much overcome with delight that she congratulated him on his piety in public, before Mme la Duchesse d'Orléans and a large company. M. le Duc d'Orléans was pleased to indulge her for a time, and then said, 'You are a great ninny, Mme Imbert. Do you want to know what I was reading? It was my Rabelais. I brought it with me for fear of being bored.' You may imagine the effect of this answer. And it was a fact, but done out of sheer bravado, for beyond all comparison of subjects and places, the music in the chapel was far beyond any at the opera, or indeed anywhere else in Europe. Moreover, as matins, lauds, and the three Christmas masses lasted a very long time, the music was even finer than usual. In any case nothing could have been lovelier

---

[1] Henriette Prieur Imbert, wife of Pierre Imbert, the duke's family-doctor.

than the decoration of the chapel and the way in which it was
lighted. It was always crowded, even the bays between the
tribunes were filled with the ladies of the Court, not indeed in
full court-dress, but none the less glamorous for that. The spectacle was therefore as beautiful as could be and the music enchanted the ears. M. le Duc d'Orléans loved music. He composed a little himself, and even wrote a short opera for which
La Fare supplied the libretto, and it was sung before the
King. Listening to the music in the chapel would have been
quite enough to occupy his mind most delightfully; he would
not have needed his Rabelais. But he had to make a show of
being a mocker and free-thinker.

1715

Character of Mme la Duchesse d'Orléans

MME LA DUCHESSE D'ORLÉANS was quite another kind of
person. She was tall and in every way dignified, with an admirable complexion, bosom, and arms, fine eyes, a mouth that
was not ill-formed, and beautiful if rather long teeth. Full,
pendulous cheeks spoiled her a little, but did not prevent her
from being a woman of beauty. The most unbecoming feature
was the arch of her eyebrows, for there the skin looked red and
as though it were peeling, and the hairs were scanty. On the
other hand, she had good eyelashes and her hair grew prettily.
Although neither lame nor in any way misshapen, one of her
sides was bigger than the other, which made her walk crab-
wise, and this physical defect matched another that was more of
a handicap in society and troublesome even to her, as I shall
describe.

She had as much intelligence as M. le Duc d'Orléans, and
even better, for she possessed a greater sense of continuity.
Words came easily to her, with a gift for choosing the apt and
unexpected phrase that always came as a delightful surprise.
What is more, she used that enchanting idiom to which none but
Mme de Montespan, her sisters, and those brought up in her
household possessed the key. Mme la Duchesse d'Orléans was
capable of saying what she pleased and how she pleased with

I

point, tact, and charm. She could also speak without uttering a word and could make her meaning plain to the precise degree that she chose. But her speech itself was so thick and hesitant, so hard upon unaccustomed ears that this disability, although she seemed not to regard it as such, took much of the charm from what she said.

Reserve, propriety, good manners were innate in her. She was the very essence of pride and fastidiousness. You will scarcely believe me when I tell you, what is no more than the exact truth, that at the bottom of her heart she felt that she had conferred a great honour upon M. le Duc d'Orléans by marrying him, and often let slip an almost imperceptible hint to that effect. She had too much sense not to perceive that such an attitude would not be tolerated but too much pride to discard it entirely. She was relentless, even with her own brothers, in keeping the rank into which she had married and remembered that she was a Granddaughter of France even upon her chaise-percée. M. le Duc d'Orléans used often to laugh about it, and when he was alone with her called her Mme Lucifer, which she allowed she did not mind. Moreover, she was fully conscious of the advantages and favours which, at the time of Monsieur's death, had accrued to M. le Duc d'Orléans on account of his marriage. Her annoyance at his behaviour towards her, although in public he was most punctilious, came not from jealousy but from resentment that he would not treat her like a goddess. On the other hand, she never made a step towards him, nor did anything to please him or win his affection, nor did she ever refrain from doing what she saw he disliked. Never did she show him any kindness, nor those little liberties which women take who live happily with their husbands. She received any advances from him coldly, with a kind of patronizing superiority. This was one of the main causes of their estrangement, and after their reconciliation all the endeavours of M. le Duc d'Orléans counted less with her than politics.

As for her Court, for that is how one had to speak of her household and the company who went to her, she preferred to be worshipped rather than courted. Indeed, I think I can truthfully say that in all her life she found only the Duchesse de Villeroy and myself, who were not ready to bow down before her, but always did and said to her as we thought right. Yet at the same time Mme la Duchesse d'Orléans was painfully nervous.

The King needed to look at her only a little sternly and she felt ill at once; possibly Mme de Maintenon had the same effect upon her. At any rate she trembled before them both, and even in public on the most banal subjects could only stammer her answers and look terrified. I say answers because it would have required more courage than she possessed to speak to them first, especially to the King.

For the rest, although she enjoyed excellent health, her life was very boring—solitude and reading until dinner-time, needlework for the rest of the day, and company between five and six in the evening, but there was neither amusement nor relaxation because she did not know how to put people at their ease. She had no intercourse, except very formally, with Mme la Duchesse du Maine, and M. du Maine visited her seldom and almost never during her visiting hours. As for me, I never saw her when she had company, but nearly always tête-à-tête, or with M. le Duc d Orléans, sometimes, but very occasionally, with M. le Comte de Toulouse, never with M. du Maine. Neither of the latter ever set foot in M. le Duc d'Orléans' apartments except on state occasions, for they did not care for him. Self-interest apart, M. du Maine had very little inclination to care for anyone. He afterwards adopted Mme de Maintenon's likes and dislikes, and you have seen what endeavours he later made to steal away M. le Duc d'Orléans' birthright and seize the sovereign power. The Comte de Toulouse, unfeeling by nature, led a different life and disapproved of that of M. le Duc d'Orléans; he sympathized with his sister's vexations, and held aloof because of the King's displeasure. Yet in the events that followed, I never found him otherwise than truthful, honourable and prudent, fulfilling his duty towards M. le Duc d'Orléans, although never becoming friendly nor affectionate.

When the Court entirely abandoned M. le Duc d'Orléans, leaving him in the wilderness, his wife, whose pride and laziness were extreme, was disinclined to make the slightest approach towards anyone. She seemed perfectly prepared to wait for society to pay her homage, without herself taking any trouble, and thus their lives became wearisome, ignominious, unsuited to their rank and despised. That was one of the first conditions which they had to remedy. Both of them realized this, but it must be allowed that once her mind was made up, Mme la Duchesse d'Orléans set herself to the task with much more courage and perseverance than her husband. I say courage advisedly, because her pride had to suffer many hurts in the long struggle to extricate herself from that unhappy situation.

The ladies whom she invited to her dinner-parties were fertile in inventing excuses. They dreaded being seen in company with M. le Duc d'Orléans, and the most cunning among them waited for one of his excursions to Paris in order to dine with his wife, and then considered themselves exempt for several months to come. They also feared the King, which is to say Mme de Maintenon and, for those most in the know, the Duc du Maine. For a long time it was fashionable to refuse at first and then to be persuaded into going, on the excuse that continual invitations gave one no further grounds for escape. Men were a more difficult problem for her than women, because her rank as a Granddaughter of France allowed her to invite only noblemen to her table.

Once Mme la Duchesse d'Orléans had convinced herself of the need to break down this most unseemly barrier that separated her from society on account of her husband, she did not flinch. Realizing that she could not entice people to her unless they were also reconciled with him, she assumed, so far as she was able, an amiable and gracious manner in order to melt the ice and make her apartments and table alluring. The labour was odious to her and very hard, but she persisted and finally succeeded. People began to grow bolder, following the example of others, and little by little the numbers increased after the manner of a snowball.

The food and wine at her table were delicious, and after a while the constraint became less obvious although respect for rank and the proprieties was strictly observed. M. le Duc d'Orléans became more guarded in his speech and gradually began to converse on general topics, such as public affairs, in a way that did not embarrass others or himself. Card-tables were often arranged after the meal, so that the company were detained until it was time for the King's salon. After a while people began to praise these dinner-parties and to express surprise that they should ever have been shunned. The lack of interest shown by the King and Mme de Maintenon reassured them and they began to feel ashamed of having feared their disapproval. None the less, those who frequented the King's salon did not soften towards M. le Duc d'Orléans. At the dinner-parties one dined in the apartment of the King's bastard-daughter, her husband only happened to be there in the position of a guest. In the King's salon, where most of the gentlemen had not been to the dinners, he was still kept at a distance and was even avoided by many who had just left his table. This state of affairs did not change until the King's last illness.

Mme la Duchesse d'Orléans was well aware that M. le Duc d'Orléans confided in me and that I had much influence in his thoughts and plans for the present and the future. This she had known for a long time, and realized more clearly than outsiders could do that I was the only man to whom he could speak frankly on matters of importance. She also knew that I had my own opinions and ideas of the changes that would follow after the present reign, and she was very anxious to learn them and tried to lead me on about people and future events in the course of our many conversations. I was careful about both, less so perhaps about people, for she already knew my mind in most cases. As regards events, I escaped into generalities, and as time went on I emphasized the carelessness, irresponsibility and idleness of M. le Duc d'Orléans, who acted as though the present situation would last for ever. Perhaps I may have exaggerated somewhat in my complaints to her, but indeed, it was only too true, for as you will see my criticisms were well-founded.

1715

A Highly Dubious Ambassador from Persia

AN ambassador from Persia arrived at Charenton, all expenses having been paid from the time when he disembarked. The King made a great occasion of his coming and Pontchartrain used the opportunity to press his court. Indeed, he has been accused of manufacturing this embassy in which there seems to have been nothing genuine, for the envoy's behaviour was as discreditable as his wretched following and miserable presents. In any case he produced no credentials nor letters of authority from the King of Persia or his ministers. He would appear to have been merely a provincial administrator, charged by the governor of his province with business to transact in France, and Pontchartrain had him enlarged to ambassadorial rank. Only the King was duped.

He entered Paris in state, riding between the Maréchal de Matignon and the Baron de Breteuil, head of the protocol; but his manners were so vulgar and he made so many difficulties about procedure that they left him as soon as the procession arrived at the Hôtel des Ambassadeurs, and did not accompany him to his room as is the custom. They then went straight to Versailles to complain to the King, who approved their action and thought the ambassador exceedingly ill-bred.

The King's interpreter of oriental languages had recently died so that they had to send for a priest, living near Amboise, who had spent several years in Persia.[1] He did his work well and was very poorly paid for it. I came to know this man and conversed with him. He was gentlemanly, very sensible, and well acquainted with the manners and customs of Persia as well as with the government and language. He told me that from all that he had seen of this supposed ambassador, he felt sure that the embassy was bogus and the man himself a merchant in a small way of business, who was much discomfited at having to maintain a position for which he was totally unfit. Nevertheless they always spoke to the King as though he were genuine and, almost alone of the Court, he believed in him and felt highly flattered that the Persians should have sent him an ambassador without invitation. He often spoke of it with satisfaction and desired the entire Court to appear in great splendour on the day of the audience, which was fixed for Tuesday, February 19th. He himself set the example, which was most extravagantly followed.

The long gallery and all the state apartments were superbly decorated, and they placed a magnificent throne at the end of the gallery with tiers of seats set at different levels along both sides. The rows nearest the throne were reserved for the ladies of the Court and the rest were for gentlemen and sightseers, but no one was allowed in without full Court dress. The King lent a set of pearl and diamond ornaments to M. le Duc du Maine for the occasion, and one of coloured stones to M. le Comte de Toulouse. M. le Duc d'Orléans wore a blue velvet coat,

---

[1] He was the Abbé Gauderau, the curé of Notre-Dame-en-Grève. He received a permanent appointment as interpreter to the head of the protocol.

embroidered in a mosaic pattern, overlaid with diamonds and pearls, which was a triumph of magnificence and good taste.

The courtyards, roofs, and avenue swarmed with onlookers, which delighted the King as he looked out of the palace windows. He vastly enjoyed waiting for the arrival of this ambassador, who appeared at eleven o'clock in one of the royal carriages, escorted by the Maréchal de Matignon and the Baron de Breteuil. They stopped in the avenue to mount their horses and, preceded by the ambassador's suite, rode into the great courtyard and up to the door of the apartment of the colonel of the guards, as is customary. The suite seemed miserable in every way, and the supposed ambassador highly embarrassed and very ill-dressed. The presents were beneath contempt.

The King, followed by all those who had been with him, then entered the long gallery and showed himself to the ladies in the seats, those nearest the throne being occupied by the Princesses of the Blood. He wore a dress of black and gold with the order outside, a fashion that was copied by those few knights who usually wore it beneath their coats. The coat itself was embroidered with all the finest diamonds in the crown jewels, to the tune of more than 12,500,000 livres. He stooped with their weight, and looked worn-out, thin, and vastly ill-favoured, as he seated himself upon the throne, with the Princes of the Blood and the bastards standing uncovered beside him. A low step and a space had been arranged behind the throne for Madame, Mme la Duchesse de Berry and their ladies-in-waiting, who were in the first year of their mourning. They were incognito and few noticed them, but they heard and saw everything, and it was planned so that they entered and left by the Queen's apartment, which had been closed since the death of Madame la Dauphine. On the King's right stood the Duchesse de Ventadour,[1] holding the little future king by his leading strings, while on the second tier was the Elector of Bavaria with the ladies of his suite, the Comte de Lusace (the Prince-Elector of Saxony),[2] and the Princesse de Conti. Coypel, the painter,[3] and Boze, secretary of the Académie des Inscriptions, were at

[1] She was governess to the little Dauphin, Louis XV, and saved his life by hiding him from the doctors when he had the measles, of which his father, mother and brother had all died.
[2] Frederick Augustus, Electoral Prince of Saxony (1696–1763), became King of Poland as Augustus III in 1733.
[3] Antoine Coypel (1661–1722). The painting is at Versailles.

the foot of the throne to paint and describe the spectacle. Pont-chartrain had forgotten nothing that could pander to the King's vanity or delude him into believing that this embassy was a revival of his glorious past. In short, he most shamelessly hoodwinked him in order to give him pleasure, for by this time no one else was deceived.

The envoy mounted the ambassadors' grand staircase, crossed the state apartments, and entered the long gallery by the salon at the end opposite to the throne. He seemed completely nonplussed by the magnificent scene and more than once lost his temper with the interpreter, allowing it to be seen that he knew at any rate some French. After the audience was over he was entertained to dinner by the household, as is the custom, and then visited the future King in the apartments of the late Queen, which were also richly decorated. From thence he called upon Pontchartrain and Torcy, got into his coach and returned to Paris. The presents were as shaming to the King of Persia as they were to King Louis, consisting, in all, of four hundred very commonplace pearls, two hundred exceedingly poor tur-quoises, and two gold boxes full of mumia, which is a precious balm that issues from a rock enclosed within another, and which congeals after a certain time. It is said to be marvellous for wounds. The King ordered that nothing should be moved in the gallery and the state apartments, for he intended to hold the final audience in the same spot and with the same ceremonial as at the reception of this bogus ambassador. He commanded Torcy, Pontchartrain, and Desmarets to superintend the arrange-ments, which caused Pontchartrain a good deal of embarrass-ment.

1715

Death of the King

ON Friday August 9th, Père Tellier instructed the King at some length on the registration in the Parlement of the Bull *Unigenitus*,[1] entire, as it stood. Then the King saw the premier

---

[1] The Bull issued by Pope Clement XI in 1713 condemning Jansenism. It caused a fierce struggle between the Jansenists and the Jesuits, during the early part of the eighteenth century.

président[1] and the procureur général,[2] whom he had summoned on the day before. After dinner, he went stag-hunting, driving his own calash himself for the last time in his life, and returned home exhausted. That evening there was *grande musique* in Mme de Maintenon's apartment. On the Saturday, he walked before dinner in his gardens at Marly, and about six o'clock returned to Versailles for the last time in his life, never again to contemplate that monstrous work of his creation. In the evening he worked with the chancellor in Mme de Maintenon's rooms. Everyone thought him looking gravely ill. On Sunday August 11th, he held the council of state, and in the afternoon walked to the Trianon. He never went out again.

On the following day he took physic in the ordinary way and led the life to which he was accustomed in those days. It was reported that he complained of sciatica in the leg and thigh. He had never before suffered from sciatica, nor from rheumatism; he had never had even a cold and for a long time past had had no attacks of gout. That evening they had *petite musique* at Mme de Maintenon's, and that was the last time he ever walked.

On Tuesday August 13th, he made a last effort, on returning from mass in his chair, to give the final audience, standing without support, to that dubious ambassador from Persia. His weakness did not allow him to repeat the splendours of the first audience and he had to be satisfied with receiving him in the throne room, where nothing happened out of the ordinary. This was the last of the King's public engagements, one in which Pontchartrain played vilely upon his vanity in order to press his court. Indeed, he was shameless enough to conclude the farce with the signing of a treaty, whose results amply demonstrated the fraudulence of the whole affair. The audience was long and tiring, but after it was over the King would not rest although he must have longed to do so. He held the Conseil des Finances, dined in private, and was carried to Mme de Maintenon's rooms, where there was *petite musique*. As he was leaving his study, he stopped to allow the Duchesse de La Rochefoucauld to present her daughter-in-law, the Duchesse de La Rocheguyon, the last lady ever to be presented to him. She took her tabouret that night at the King's supper, the last time that he ever ate in public. Afterwards he worked alone with the chancellor, and on the following day he sent gifts, including some jewels,

---

[1] M. de Mesmes.   [2] Henri François Daguesseau.

I*

to that fine ambassador, who, two days later, was escorted to
the house of a merchant at Chaillot and shortly afterwards
left for Hâvre-de-Grace, where he re-embarked.

The King's health had been failing for more than a year. The
personal valets had been the first to notice it, and had observed
every symptom without daring to speak. Then the bastards,
especially M. du Maine, also perceived it and with the assistance
of Mme de Maintenon acted with all dispatch. Fagon, now weak
in body and mind, was the only one in all that great household
who noticed nothing. Maréchal, the chief surgeon, often reminded him, but was harshly rebuffed. At last, out of duty and
attachment to the King, Maréchal was driven to go to Mme de
Maintenon to warn her how completely Fagon was mistaken.
He assured her that the King, whose pulse he had often taken,
had for a long time been suffering from a slow internal fever,
that his constitution being so robust there would be no danger
with proper care and remedies, but that if it went unchecked,
the evil might soon prove fatal. Mme de Maintenon lost her
temper, so that what his loyalty led him to tell her only served
to make her angrier still. She said that only Fagon's personal
enemies believed such tales about the King's health, and that
the chief physician's skill, wisdom and experience could not
be deceived. Maréchal told me indignantly that he felt there
was nothing more that he could do. From that moment he
began to mourn for the death of his master. Fagon had indeed
once been the first physician in all Europe, but for a long time
past his health had prevented him from broadening his experience, and his unlimited authority and favour with the King
had spoilt him. He would brook neither argument nor discussion,
continued to treat the King's health as in earlier days and, by
his stubbornness, killed him.

Because the King had once suffered from prolonged attacks
of gout, Fagon continued to swaddle him every night in a
great mass of feather pillows, so that he had to be changed and
rubbed down every morning before the grand chamberlain
and first gentlemen of the bed-chamber could enter. Instead of
the champagne to which he had been accustomed all through his
life, they had of late years made him drink watered-down burgundy, so old that it had lost its potency. He sometimes said
laughingly that foreigners felt swindled when they asked to be
allowed to taste the royal wine. Never at any time did he drink

his wine unwatered, and he had never been accustomed to take sweet wines, nor even tea, coffee, nor chocolate. When he rose, instead of eating a little bread with wine and water, he had for a long time past been used to having two cups of sage and veronica. Between meals, and always at bedtime, he drank more than one pint-size glass full of water flavoured with orange-flowers, and all his drinks were iced. Even on days when he took physic he drank, and always at his meals, and he never ate anything between meals except for a few cinnamon lozenges, which he used to put into his pocket at dessert, with many dry biscuits for the setter-bitches in his dog-room.

When during the last years of his life he became increasingly constipated, Fagon made him begin his meals with iced fruit, such as mulberries, melons, and figs, often half-rotten with over-ripeness, and he ate still more fruit for dessert, with an astonishing number of sweetmeats. He ate an immense deal of salad for his supper, all the year round. His soups, of which he drank several different kinds morning and evening, taking a full cup of each regardless of what was to come, were made of strong meat juices, exceedingly rich, and all that was served to him was highly spiced, at least twice the normal quantity, and very hot. Fagon did not approve of the spices and sweetmeats and often made a face when he saw the King eating them, but he dared not say anything, except once in a way to Livry and Benoist, who told him that it was their business to make the King eat and his to purge him. He never touched venison nor water-fowl, but with those exceptions he ate everything, on feast and fast days alike, apart from Lent, which he kept the last twenty years, although only for a few days. In that last summer he had increased his consumption of fruit and drinks.

In the end, so much fruit taken after soup flooded his stomach and took away his appetite, which never before had failed in the whole of his life, although he never felt hungry, even when his meals were unavoidably delayed. At the first spoonful of soup his appetite came, as I have many times heard him say, and he ate prodigiously of solid meals each morning and evening, and so steadily that one never grew accustomed to watching him.[1] So much water, so much fruit, unrelieved by any alcohol,

---

[1] Madame wrote: 'I have often seen the King consume four full plates of different kinds of soup, a whole pheasant, a partridge, a large dish of salad, two great slices of ham, mutton, served with gravy and garlic, a plate of sweet cakes, and on top of that, fruit and hardboiled eggs.'

turned his blood gangrenous by lowering the vital spirits, and weakened his digestion by nightly sweating. They finally caused his death, as was proved when his body was opened, for all the vital parts were found to be so perfectly healthy and strong that he might well have lived more than a century. His stomach and bowels were particularly remarkable because their size and capacity were double that of any ordinary man, which explains why he was so huge and regular an eater.

No one had thought of applying remedies until it was too late, because Fagon refused to admit that the King was ill, and Mme de Maintenon also, although she took care to safeguard her own future at Saint-Cyr, and M. du Maine's as well. The King himself was one of the first to realize his condition and sometimes spoke of it to his personal valets, but Fagon always reassured him and did nothing. The King listened to what he said but remained unconvinced, nevertheless his friendship for Fagon and more especially Mme de Maintenon's influence restrained him from taking action.

On Wednesday August 14th they carried him to mass for the last time, and he afterwards held the Conseil d'État, ate a full meal, although it was a fast day, and went to the *grande musique* at Mme de Maintenon's apartment. He supped alone in his room and was seen by the Court at his dinner-time. He stayed only a short time in his study among his family and retired to bed soon after ten o'clock. . . .

On Saturday 17th he had another bad night. He remained in bed for the Conseil des Finances, received the company at dinner, rose immediately afterwards, and went to Mme de Maintenon, where he worked with the chancellor. That night was the first when Fagon slept in his room.

Sunday August 18th was like other days, Fagon still pretending that the King had no fever. He held a Council of State, afterwards worked as usual with Le Peletier[1] on the fortifications, and then went to Mme de Maintenon for the music. It was clear, however, that he could not be expected to last for more than a few days in that condition, about which Maréchal told me more truly than Fagon. I then remembered Chamillart, who was receiving a retirement-pension of 60,000 livres from the King and immediately went to M. le Duc d'Orléans to beg for its continuance. I received his promise with permission to write to

---

[1] Peletier de Souzy, directeur général des fortifications.

Chamillart to that effect, which I accordingly did. The latter was much moved at hearing of the King's illness, but showed very little emotion at my other news. None the less, he was agreeably surprised at my having written to him and very grateful for my thought; he had had none for himself. He also sent me a formal letter of thanks to be transmitted to M. le Duc d'Orléans. Nothing that I have ever done has given me greater pleasure. The thing remained a secret until after the King's death, but as soon as the Regency had begun, I lost no time in publishing the news.

The night and the morning of Friday 23rd were as usual. The King worked with Père Tellier, who was trying unsuccessfully to persuade him to appoint nominees for the many important benefices then vacant. Père Tellier was secretly hoping to have the disposal of them himself, so as not to leave them to M. le Duc d'Orléans, indeed, it cannot be denied that as the King grew worse he pressed him ever more urgently. He feared to lose these rich prizes and with them the chance of securing a loyal following, for he made his bargains with intrigues, not with money. None the less, he failed. The King declared that seeing he was so soon to appear before God, he had enough accounts to settle without further burdening himself with appointments and he forbade Père Tellier to mention them again. He then dined standing in his room, wearing a dressing-gown, and afterwards went into the study with the two bastards (M. du Maine very assiduous), Mme de Maintenon, and some ladies of the circle. The evening was as usual.

Here I must pause to describe the arrangements in the King's apartments now that he no longer went out. The entire Court spent the whole day in the great gallery. No one remained in the ante-chamber nearest the bedchamber except the personal valets and the dispensers, who heated whatever was necessary. People merely passed quickly through the room from one door to another. Those who had the entrée entered the private apartments by the mirror-door that gave on to the gallery and was kept shut. It was only opened when one scratched at it and was closed again immediately. Ministers and secretaries of state also entered by that door and waited in the study adjoining the gallery. Not even the Princes of the Blood nor the King's daughters were allowed nearer, unless the King asked for them, which never happened. The Maréchal de Villeroy, the chancellor, the two bastards, M. le Duc d'Orléans, Père Tellier, the curé of Versailles,[1] also Maréchal, Fagon, and the first valets (when they were not required in the bedroom) waited in the council chamber between the King's room and that other room where the Princes and Princesses of the Blood, the entrées, and the ministers were assembled.

The Duc de Tresmes, whose year it was as first gentleman, stood by the open door between the two rooms and never entered the King's bedroom unless his duty made it absolutely necessary. During the daytime, no one entered except those in the council chamber, the valets and dispensers who waited in the first ante-room, Mme de Maintenon, and the ladies of the household, and, for dinner and supper, such officers and courtiers as were permitted. M. le Duc d'Orléans carefully limited his appearances to, at the very most, twice a day, once when the Duc de Tresmes entered the bedroom, and once again at the door leading into the council chamber, where the King could see him from his bed.

On Saturday 24th, the night was scarcely more distressing than usual, for it was always a bad time, but the leg seemed much worse and gave him more pain. Mass was said as usual, dinner was served in bed, where he was seen by the principal courtiers who did not have the entrée. Then the Conseil des Finances, after which he worked alone with the chancellor. Mme de Maintenon and the ladies later came to him and he supped standing in his dressing-gown in the presence of the Court for the last time. I noticed that he swallowed only fluids and that it annoyed him to be stared at. He was unable to finish and asked the courtiers to go on, that is to say, to leave the room. He then desired to be put to bed. They examined the leg and found black spots. He sent for Père Tellier and confessed. By now confusion reigned among the doctors. They had tried milk, and quinine with water, now both were discontinued and no one knew what to do next. They admitted that he had had a slow fever since Whitsun, but excused themselves on the grounds that he disliked remedies, and that they had not thought him very bad.

Sunday August 25th was the feast of Saint-Louis and the night was much worse. No secret now was made of the danger, which

1 Claude Huchon.

was suddenly realized to be great and critical. Nevertheless, the King would allow no change to be made in the order of the day.[1] The drums and fifes stationed beneath his windows still struck up as soon as he woke, and the four-and-twenty violins played in the ante-room as usual during dinner. He then spent some time alone with Mme de Maintenon, the chancellor and, for a little while, with the Duc de Maine. Paper and ink had been sent in to him on the previous evening when he was working alone with the chancellor, and they were again ordered when he was closeted with Mme de Maintenon. It therefore must have been on one of those two days that the chancellor wrote the codicil at his dictation. Mme de Maintenon and M. du Maine, who never ceased thinking of themselves, had decided that not enough was being done for them in the King's will and were determined to remedy this by a codicil, which shows the wicked advantage taken of the King in his extremity and the lengths to which inordinate ambition can lead. Under this codicil, the King's entire establishment, both civil and military, were to be subjected to the Duc du Maine forthwith, without reserve, and under him to the Maréchal de Villeroy. These two would thus become absolute masters of the King's households and residences, of the city of Paris (because two regiments of guards and two companies of Musketeers were quartered there), and of all the service departments, bedchamber, wardrobe, chapels, kitchens, and stables. Thus no shadow of authority would remain to the Regent. He would be at their mercy, in constant danger of arrest, or worse, should he happen to displease the Duc du Maine.

Soon after the chancellor left, Mme de Maintenon, who had remained with the King, sent for the ladies of the household and for the orchestra, which arrived at seven o'clock. But he fell asleep during the general conversation and woke confused, which frightened the ladies and caused them to summon the doctors. In the meanwhile the King recovered his senses, but the pulse was so weak that they did not hesitate to advise him to take the Last Sacraments without delay. Père Tellier was accordingly summoned, and Cardinal de Rohan, who was at home with company, his thoughts quite otherwise occupied.

---

[1] He is supposed to have said: 'I have lived among the people of my court and I desire to die among them. They have followed the whole course of my life; it is only right that they should witness my end.'

The orchestra, who had already arranged their books and instruments, were dismissed, and the ladies left.

It chanced that I was walking through the great gallery at that precise moment, on my way to Mme la Duchesse d'Orléans's apartment from my own rooms in the new wing. I noticed some of the remaining musicians and thought that the rest had entered the ante-room, but one of the ushers came up and told me what had occurred. I found Mme la Duchesse d'Orléans in bed with the remains of a migraine, surrounded by ladies making conversation and suspecting nothing. I went up to the bed and told her the news, but she would not believe me, saying that the orchestra was playing at that very moment and that the King was no worse. Then, after I had whispered to her, she asked the ladies whether they had heard anything; but they knew nothing and Mme la Duchesse d'Orléans was reassured. I told her the facts a second time, insisting that I was certain of them and thought that she should at least send to inquire and, in the meantime, dress. Then she did believe me and I went in to M. le Duc d'Orléans and warned him also, but he rightly thought it more prudent to remain where he was since no one had sent for him.

In a quarter of an hour all was prepared. Père Tellier confessed the King whilst Cardinal de Rohan went to the chapel for the Host and sent for the curé of Versailles and the Holy Oils. Two of the King's almoners walked before the Cardinal, together with eight of the blue footmen carrying torches, two lackeys belonging to Fagon, and one in Mme de Maintenon's service. This very small escort accompanied the Cardinal up the narrow staircase into the King's chamber, while Père Tellier, Mme de Maintenon and about a dozen of the household, lords and valets alike, went out to greet or follow the Holy Sacrament. The Cardinal said a few words to the King about this tremendous final act, during which he seemed to be resolute and much moved. When he had received Our Lord and the Holy Oils, everyone left the room in procession, either before or following the Host; only Mme de Maintenon and the chancellor remained. Then, immediately, and this was most dreadful in the circumstances, they put a book or small table upon the bed and the chancellor laid the codicil upon it, after which the King added four or five lines in his own hand, and it was removed.

The King then asked for a drink, called to the Maréchal de

Villeroy, who was standing by the door leading into the council chamber, and spoke with him for nearly a quarter of an hour. He sent also for M. le Duc d'Orléans and spoke with him privately, expressing his esteem, confidence, and affection and, what was most terrible, with Jesus Christ still upon his lips, assured him that he would find nothing in the will but what would content him, and recommended to his care the State, and the person of the future King. Not half an hour had elapsed between his receiving Extreme Unction and this conversation. He cannot have forgotten the vile provisions which they had extracted from him with so much difficulty, moreover, in that short interval he had added words in a codicil, which placed a knife at the throat of M. le Duc d'Orléans and its handle in the grasp of the Duc du Maine. One strange result of this interview was the rumour that the King had already given the Regency to M. le Duc d'Orléans.

The night of Monday August 26th was no better. The King dined in bed in the presence of the household. As the meal was being cleared away, he bade them approach and said these words, which were written down within the hour. 'Gentlemen, I ask your pardon for the bad example which I have set you. I have much to thank you for the manner in which you have served me and for your constant devotion. It grieves me that I have not done all I could have wished for you; the fault lies in the hardness of the times. I shall ask you to show the same attachment to my great-grandson; that child may right many wrongs. Let your example be a guide to my other subjects. Obey my nephew's orders, for he will govern the kingdom. I trust that he will do it well. I also trust that you will remain united, and that should one of you break away the rest will endeavour to reclaim him. I feel that I begin to be moved to tears and that I am moving you, I ask your pardon. Gentlemen, farewell, I hope that sometimes you will remember me.'

Shortly afterwards he desired the Duchesse de Ventadour to fetch the Dauphin. He made the child come to him, and said these words before Mme de Maintenon and the closest of the household, who later repeated them. 'My child, you are about to become a great King. Do not imitate my love of building nor my liking for war, but try, on the contrary, to live at peace with your neighbours. Render to God all that you owe Him; recognize your duty towards Him; see that He is honoured by your subjects. Always follow good counsellors; try to comfort your people, which it grieves me that I was unable to do. Never forget the debt of gratitude which you owe to Mme de Ventadour.' 'Madame,' said he, turning to her, 'let me kiss him,' and as he did so, he said, 'My dear child, I give you my blessing with all my heart.' As the little prince was being lifted from the bed, the King again asked for him, embraced him once more and, raising his hands and eyes to heaven, blessed him again. It was a most moving spectacle. Mme de Ventadour then hastened to remove the Dauphin and took him back to his apartment.

On Tuesday August 27th, the King said to Mme de Maintenon that he had heard how hard it was to reconcile oneself to dying, but now that he himself approached that awful moment he did not find it difficult to submit. She replied that it was always exceedingly painful when people retained old attachments or hatreds, or had reparations still to make. 'Oh!' said the King, 'as for debts to individuals, I have none; as for what I owe the State I put my trust in the mercy of God.' The night that followed was most distressing. He was seen many times to clasp his hands, and they heard him recite the prayers to which he had been accustomed when he was well, and he beat his breast at the *Confiteor*.

On Wednesday August 28th, he made an affectionate remark to Mme de Maintenon which she did not at all relish and did not answer. He said that he was consoled at leaving her by the thought that at her age the parting would not be for long.[1] Then he sent for Père Tellier. As they were speaking of God, he saw reflected in the mirror above the chimney-piece two of the pages who were weeping at the foot of the bed. He said to them, 'Why do you weep? Did you think that I was immortal? I have never thought so, and considering my age, you should have been prepared to lose me.'

A very rough, common sort of peasant from Provence learned of the King's illness as he was on his way from Marseilles to

---

[1] Mme de Maintenon thus describes the King's three farewells to her: 'The first time, he assured me that his only regret was in leaving me; "But," he said, sighing, "we shall meet again before long." I entreated him to think only of God. The second time, he asked my forgiveness for not having lived better with me and for not having made me happy, but said that he had indeed always loved and esteemed me. Then, feeling that he was near weeping, he asked me to see that we were not overheard, and added, "But no one could be surprised at my loving you." On the third occasion, he said, "What will become of you? You have nothing." I exhorted him again to think only of God; then, reflecting that I did not know in what manner the princes would treat me, I begged him to recommend me to M. le Duc d'Orléans.'

Paris, and appeared that same morning at Versailles with a remedy which he said was a certain cure for gangrene. By this time, the King was so ill and the doctors so desperate that they accepted it without demur, in the presence of Mme de Maintenon and the Duc du Maine. Fagon did try to make an objection, but the peasant, whose name was Le Brun, turned upon him so fiercely that Fagon, who usually bullied everyone until they were terrified of him, was struck perfectly dumb. They gave the King ten drops of the medicine in a glass of alicant at eleven in the morning. For a little while he felt stronger, but the pulse weakened and nearly failed entirely; then they offered him a further dose at about four o'clock, saying that it would revive him. As he took the glass, he said, 'For life or death, as God pleases.'

In the meantime, Mme de Maintenon left the King's room with her hood drawn down, and was conducted by the Maréchal de Villeroy past her apartments, which she did not enter, as far as the foot of the grand staircase. There, raising her hood, she embraced him dry-eyed, said, 'Adieu! M. le Maréchal,' stepped into the King's coach, which she always used, and where Mme de Caylus awaited her, and drove away to Saint-Cyr, followed by her own coach, containing all her women. That same evening in his apartment, the Duc du Maine made a thoroughly good story of Fagon's encounter with Le Brun. But I shall find other opportunities to describe his conduct and that of Mme de Maintenon during those last days.

The day and night before Thursday August 29th were very bad, but the removal of those who had nothing more to do beyond what had already been done left room for the high officers who until then had been excluded from the King's bedroom. No mass had been said on the previous evening and there seemed no prospect of any in the future, but the Duc de Charost, a captain of the guard, who had stolen in with the others, rightly thought this very bad, and directed one of the valets to ask the King if he would not like to hear one. When the King answered that he did so desire it, they sent for the necessary priests and objects, and thus it continued during the following days. He had seemed stronger that morning and there was a ray of hope which was immediately exaggerated. Good news flew in all directions. He had even been able to take two small biscuits in a glass of alicant, and had seemed to enjoy them.

At about two o'clock in the morning I went to M. le Duc d'Orléans's apartments, which had been so swarming with courtiers for the past week at every hour of the day and night that, truthfully speaking, you could scarcely have dropped a pin between them, and I found no one. As soon as M. le Duc d'Orléans saw me, he burst out laughing, telling me that I was the first person he had seen that entire day, for his rooms had been utterly deserted. That is society!

I seized upon this quiet moment to speak to him of many things, and it was then that I realized for the first time how he had changed his mind about summoning the États Généraux, and that except for what had been agreed concerning the councils, he had not given the matter another thought. Nor had he considered many other matters, about which I had taken the liberty of speaking my mind strongly.

The late evening of the 29th did not fulfil the earlier hopes and the King said to the curé of Versailles, who came to tell him that all the people were praying, that it was no longer a question of his life, but of his salvation, and for that he urgently needed prayer. On that same day, when he was giving some orders, he chanced to refer to the Dauphin as 'the young King', and noticed the sudden movement in his entourage. 'Why do you start?' he said. 'That does not trouble me.' At eight o'clock he took more of the medicine of the man from Provence, and afterwards seemed confused, saying that he felt very ill. At about eleven, they examined the leg and found gangrene in the foot and knee; the thigh was much inflamed. He fainted during the examination. It was then that he noticed with dismay the absence of Mme de Maintenon, who had not intended returning. He asked for her several times that day, until it was no longer possible to hide the fact that she had gone. He then sent to Saint-Cyr for her and she returned during the evening.

Friday August 30th was as bad as the previous night. A coma set in and in the intervals his mind wandered. From time to time they gave him a little jelly in fresh water; he could no longer take wine. No one went into his room except his personal valets, the doctors, Mme de Maintenon and, on very rare occasions, Père Tellier if Blouin or Maréchal sent for him. Few people waited, even in the ante-rooms; M. du Maine was not among them. The King responded readily to thoughts of religion when Mme de Maintenon or Père Tellier seized on moments when his mind was clear, but such intervals were short and rare. At five in the evening, Mme de Maintenon went to her apartments, distributed what furniture she possessed there among the members of her household and left for Saint-Cyr, never to return.

The day and night of August 31st were very dreadful. There were only short moments of consciousness at rare intervals. The gangrene spread over the knee and the whole of the thigh. They gave him a medicine of the late Abbé d'Aignan,[1] which had been suggested by the Duchesse du Maine, an excellent remedy against the smallpox, but by this time the doctors were consenting to any suggestion because they no longer had any hope. At eleven o'clock, the King was seen to be so ill that they said the prayers for the dying. The service brought him back to consciousness, and he recited the prayers in so strong a voice that it could be heard clearly above the many priests and all the other persons who had entered the room. At the end of the prayers, he recognized Cardinal de Rohan and said to him, 'These are then the last favours of the Church.' The Cardinal was the last person to whom he ever spoke. Several times he was heard to repeat the words, '*Nunc et in hora mortis*,' also, 'Oh! God help me. Haste Thou to succour me.' Those were his last words. All the rest of that night he lay unconscious. His long-protracted agony ended at a quarter past eight in the morning of Sunday 1st September 1715, just three days before his seventy-seventh birthday, in the seventy-second year of his reign.

1715

Character of Louis XIV

HE was a prince in whom no one would deny good and even great qualities, but he had many others that were petty or down-right bad, and of these it was impossible to determine which were natural and which acquired. Nothing is harder to find than

---

[1] François d'Aignan (nick-named 'Le Père Tranquille'), who travelled in the East as a mendicant monk and brought back the recipes for many remedies, including one called 'La Baume Tranquille' a narcotic ointment, perhaps the first mention of a 'tranquilliser'.

a well-informed writer, none rarer than those who knew him personally, yet are sufficiently unbiased to speak of him without hatred or flattery, and to set down the bare truth for good or ill.

This is not the place to tell of his early childhood. He was king almost from birth, but was deliberately repressed by a mother who loved to govern, and still more so by a wicked and self-interested minister, who risked the State a thousand times for his own aggrandisement. So long as that minister lived the King was held down, and that portion of his life should be subtracted from his reign. Nevertheless, he throve beneath that yoke, for he learned to know love, and discovered that idleness is the enemy of glory. He made feeble excursions in both directions. After Mazarin's death, he had enough intelligence to realize his deliverance, but not enough vigour to release himself. Indeed, that event was one of the finest moments of his life, for it taught him an unshakable principle namely, to banish all prime ministers and ecclesiastics from his councils. Another ideal, adopted at that time, he could never sustain because in the practice it constantly eluded him. This was to govern alone. It was the quality upon which he most prided himself and for which he received most praise and flattery. In fact, it was what he was least able to do.

Born with an intelligence rather below the average, his mind was very capable of development with training and education, for he could learn easily from others and not parrot-wise. He profited immensely from having always lived among people of the highest quality with the widest knowledge of life, men and women of vastly different ages and characters, but all of them personalities.

Indeed if I may say so of a King of twenty-three years old, he was fortunate in entering the world surrounded by brilliant people of every kind. His Ministers at home and abroad were the strongest in Europe, his generals the greatest, and all were men whose names have been handed down to posterity by common consent. The disturbances that rocked the very foundations of the State after the death of Louis XIII produced a Court full of famous men and polished courtiers. The house of the Comtesse de Soissons[1] was the vastly select centre of the life of

---

[1] Olympe Mancini (1639–1708). In 1657 she married Eugène Maurice de Savoie-Carignan, Comte de Soissons. She was the mother of Prince Eugène.

that Court. As superintendent of the Queen's household, she lodged in Paris at the Tuileries, where she reigned supreme by virtue of the remnants of her late uncle Cardinal Mazarin's splendour and her own skill and cunning. There, all the most distinguished men and women foregathered every day, making her drawing-room the centre of the Court love-affairs, the gallant intrigues and manœuvres for ambition's sake—schemes in which birth counted for much, for at that time rank was as much prized and respected as it is now despised. Into this brilliant vortex the King was first launched, and there he first acquired that polite, chivalrous manner which he retained all through his life and knew so well how to combine with stateliness and propriety. You might say that he was to the manner born, for he stood out like a king bee amid all that crowd of people because of his height, grace, and beauty (even in the tone of his voice), and because of his princely bearing which was better than good looks. Had he been born into private life, he would still have had a genius for entertainments, pleasures, and flirtations, and would have caused innumerable broken hearts. It would have been better for him had all his mistresses resembled Mme de La Vallière, who truly loved him, was ashamed of being what she was, and still more ashamed at seeing the fruits of her love elevated and acknowledged against her will. One must allow, therefore that the King was more to be pitied than blamed when he yielded to love and that he deserved credit for having at intervals torn himself away in the pursuit of glory.

Let me repeat. The King's intelligence was below the aveage, but was very capable of improvement. He loved glory; he desired peace and good government. He was born prudent, temperate, secretive, master of his emotions and his tongue—can it be believed?—he was born good and just. God endowed him with all the makings of a good and perhaps even of a fairly great king. All the evil in him came from without. His early training was so dissolute that no one dared to go near his apartments, and he would sometimes speak bitterly of those days and tell how they found him one night fallen into the fountain at the Palais Royal. He became very dependent on others, for they had scarcely taught him to read and write and he remained so ignorant that he learned nothing of historical events nor the facts about fortunes, careers, rank, or laws. This lack caused him sometimes, even in public to make many gross blunders.

You might imagine that as king he would have loved the old nobility and would not have cared to see it brought down to the level of other classes. Nothing was further from the truth. His aversion to noble sentiments and his partiality for his Ministers, who, to elevate themselves, hated and disparaged all who were what they themselves were not, nor ever could be, caused him to feel a similar antipathy for noble birth. He feared it as much as he feared intelligence, and if he found these two qualities united in one person, that man was finished.

His ministers, generals, mistresses, and courtiers learned soon after he became their master that glory, to him, was a foible rather than an ambition. They therefore flattered him to the top of his bent, and in so doing, spoiled him. Praise, or better, adulation, pleased him so much that the most fulsome was welcome and the most servile even more delectable. They were the only road to his favour and those whom he liked owed his friendship to choosing their moments well and never ceasing in their attentions. That is what gave his ministers so much power, for they had endless opportunities of flattering his vanity, especially by suggesting that he was the source of all their ideas and had taught them all that they knew. Falseness, servility, admiring glances, combined with a dependent and cringing attitude, above all, an appearance of being nothing without him, were the only means of pleasing him. Once a man left that path there was no return for him, as Louvois found out to his cost.

The poison gradually spread until it reached a degree almost unbelievable in a prince who was not unintelligent or without experience of the world. For example, although he had no voice nor ear for music, he could often be heard in his private rooms singing the verses written in his praise in the prologues of the plays and operas. You could see that he revelled in them, and sometimes even at State suppers he hummed the words under his breath when the orchestra played these tunes.

Flattery fed the desire for military glory that sometimes tore him from his loves, which was how Louvois so easily involved him in major wars and persuaded him that he was a better leader and strategist than any of his generals, a theory which those officers fostered in order to please him. All their praise he took with admirable complacency, and truly believed that he was what they said. Hence his liking for reviews, which he carried to such lengths that he was known abroad as the 'Review King', and his preference for sieges, where he could make cheap displays of courage, be forcibly restrained, and show his ability to endure fatigue and lack of sleep. Indeed, so robust was his constitution that he never appeared to suffer from hunger, thirst, heat, cold, rain, or any other kind of weather. He greatly enjoyed the sensation of being admired, as he rode along the lines, for his fine presence and princely bearing, his horsemanship, and other attainments. It was chiefly with talk of campaigns and soldiers that he entertained his mistresses and sometimes his courtiers. He talked well and much to the point; no man of fashion could tell a tale or set a scene better than he, yet his most casual speeches were never lacking in natural and conscious majesty.

He had a natural bent towards details and delighted in busying himself with such petty matters as the uniforms, equipment, drill, and discipline of his troops. He concerned himself no less with his buildings, the conduct of his household, and his living expenses, for he always imagined that he had something to teach the experts, and they received instruction from him as though they were novices in arts which they already knew by heart. To the King, such waste of time appeared to deserve his constant attention, which enchanted his ministers, for with a little tact and experience they learned to sway him, making their own desires seem his, and managing great affairs of State in their own way and, all too often, in their own interests, whilst they congratulated themselves and watched him drowning amidst trivialities.

Pride and vanity, which tend always to increase, and with which he was fed continually without even his perceiving it, even from preachers in the pulpits in his presence, were the foundations on which his ministers raised themselves above all other ranks. He was cunningly persuaded that their rank was merely an extension of his own, supreme in him, in them capable of increase (since without him they were nothing), and useful to him, because it gave them as his instruments greater dignity and made them more readily obeyed. That is why secretaries of state and ministers gradually left off their cloaks, then their bands, then their black gowns and simple seemly dress, and finally came to clothe themselves like gentlemen of quality. They then began to adopt the manners and later the

privileges of the nobility, rising by stages to eat with the King,
their wives assuming, as by right, the same prerogatives as
their husbands, dining at the royal table, riding in the royal
coaches, and in every way appearing equal to ladies of the
highest rank.

Personal vanity of another kind led the King to encourage
this behaviour. He was well aware that though he might crush
a nobleman with the weight of his displeasure, he could not
destroy him or his line, whereas a secretary of state or other
such minister could be reduced together with his whole family
to those depths of nothingness from which he had been elevated.
No amount of wealth or possessions would avail him then. That
was one reason why he liked to give his ministers authority over
the highest in the land, even over the Princes of the Blood and
all others who held no office under the crown, and to grant
them rank and privileges to match. That is why any man of consequence who possessed anything which the King had no power
either to destroy or maintain was carefully kept from the
ministry; he would have been a source of danger and a continual anxiety. The sole exception to this rule was the Duc de
Beauvilliers. During the whole course of the King's long reign,
from the death of Mazarin to the King's own death fifty-four years
later, he was the only nobleman to be admitted to the council.

Therein lay the reason for the watchful, jealous attitude of his
ministers, who made it difficult for the King to hear any but
themselves, although he pleased to think that he was easy for
any man to approach. Indeed, he considered that it enhanced his
majesty and the respect and fear with which he was regarded,
and which he used to snub the most noble, that all men should
have access to him only as he passed. Thus great lords and
underlings alike might speak freely to him as he went from one
room to another on his way to or from mass, or stepped into his
coach. The more distinguished might wait at the door of his
study, but none dared to follow him inside. In fact, approach to
him was limited to those moments. Any matters whatsoever
had to be explained to him in a few words, very awkwardly, and
always within hearing range of his entourage, or, if one knew
him well, one might whisper into his wig, which was scarcely
more convenient. His almost invariable answer was, 'We shall
see' (*Je verrai*), very useful no doubt as a means of gaining
time, but often bringing little comfort.

Private audiences in his study were rarely if ever granted, even when the matter concerned State affairs. Never, for example, to envoys returning or going abroad, never to generals, unless in extraordinary circumstances, and private letters written to the King always passed through the hands of some minister, except on one or two most rare and special occasions.

Nevertheless, in spite of the fact that the King had been so spoiled with false notions of majesty and power, that every other thought was stifled in him, there was much to be gained from a private audience, if it might be obtained, and if one knew how to conduct oneself with all the respect due to his dignity and habits. I, indeed, can speak from experience, for I have described already how I obtained, even compelled him to grant me one when he was most angry, and how I each time managed to over-persuade him and leave him satisfied with me, and he said as much to me and others afterwards.

Once in his study, however prejudiced he might be, however much displeased, he would listen patiently, good-naturedly, and with a real desire to be informed. You could see that he had a sense of justice and a will to get at the truth, even though he might feel vexed with you, and that quality he retained all through his life. In private audience you could say anything to him, provided, as I have already remarked, that you said it respectfully, with submissiveness and proper deference, for without that you would have been in a worse plight. With the proper manner, however, you could interrupt him when it was your turn to speak, and bluntly deny his accusations, you could even raise your voice above his without vexing him, and he would congratulate himself on the audience and praise the person he interviewed for ridding him of prejudices and the lies he had been told; moreover, he would prove his sincerity by his subsequent attitude.

It is therefore enough to make one weep to think of the wickedness of an education designed solely to suppress the virtue and intelligence of that prince, and the insidious poison of barefaced flattery which made him a kind of god in the very heart of Christendom. His ministers with their cruel politics hemmed him in and made him drunk with power until he was utterly corrupted. If they did not manage entirely to smother such kindness, justice, and love of truth as God had given him, they blunted and obstructed those virtues to the lasting injury of himself and his kingdom.

From such alien and pernicious sources he acquired a pride so colossal that, truly, had not God implanted in his heart the fear of the devil, even in his worst excesses, he would literally have allowed himself to be worshipped. What is more, he would have found worshippers; witness the extravagant monuments that have been set up to him, for example the statue in the Place des Victoires, with its pagan dedication, a ceremony at which I myself was present, and in which he took such huge delight. From this false pride stemmed all that ruined him. We have already seen some of its ill-effects; others are yet to come.

1715

Louis XIV and the Court

THE Court was yet another device to sustain the King's policy of despotism. Many things combined to remove it from Paris and keep it permanently in the country. The disorders of the minority had been staged mainly in that city and for that reason the King had taken a great aversion to it and had become convinced that it was dangerous to live there. He believed that with the Court residing elsewhere, even though the distance were not great, cabals with Paris would be less easy, and harder to conceal because absences would be more noticeable. He would never forgive Paris for his flight on the eve of the Epiphany,[1] 1649, nor for having witnessed, despite all his efforts, his tears at the first retirement of Mme de La Vallière.[2]

The awkward situation of his mistresses and the dangers involved in conducting such scandalous affairs in a busy capital, crowded with people of every kind of mentality, played no small part in deciding him to leave, for he was embarrassed by the crowds whenever he went in or out or appeared upon the streets. Other reasons for departure were his love of hunting and the open air, so much more easily indulged in the

[1] The Court had to escape to Saint-Germain-en-Laye during the night of January 5–6, 1649, when the Fronde took Paris.

[2] Mme de La Vallière fled from the Tuileries on February 4, 1662, and sought refuge at a convent, near Chaillot, to the west of Paris.

country than in Paris, which is far from forests and ill-supplied with pleasant walks, and his delight in building, a later and ever-increasing passion, which could not be enjoyed in the town, where he was continually in the public eye. Finally, he conceived the idea that he would be all the more venerated by the multitude if he lived retired and were no longer seen every day. All these considerations led him to take up his residence at Saint-Germain soon after the Queen-Mother's death,[1] and it was then that he first began to attract society to him with fêtes and diversions and to let it be known that he wished often to be visited.

The liaison with Mme de La Vallière, which was at first kept secret, occasioned many excursions to Versailles, then a little pasteboard house erected by Louis XIII when he, and still more his courtiers, grew tired of sleeping in a low tavern and old windmill, after long, exhausting hunts in the forest of Saint-Léger and still further afield. They used to cover great distances in those days, even by present standards, when the speed of hounds and the great numbers of mounted grooms and huntsmen have made hunting so short and easy. Louis XIII never, or very rarely, slept there for more than one night, and then only when it was unavoidable. His son used it to be more private with his mistress, a pleasure unknown to that most upright monarch, that worthy son of Saint-Louis, who first built the little château at Versailles.

Gradually, those quiet country excursions of Louis XIV gave rise to a vast building project, designed to house a large Court more comfortably than in crowded lodgings at Saint-Germain, and he removed his residence there altogether, shortly before the death of the Queen.[2] Immense numbers of suites were made, and one paid one's court by asking for one, whereas, at Saint-Germain, almost everyone had the inconvenience of lodging in the town, and those few who did sleep at the château were amazingly cramped.

The frequent entertainments, the private drives to Versailles, and the royal journeys, provided the King with a means of distinguishing or mortifying his courtiers by naming those who were or were not to accompany him, and thus keeping everyone eager and anxious to please him. He fully realized that the

[1] Anne of Austria died on January 19, 1666.
[2] Maria Theresa died on July 30, 1683.

substantial gifts which he had to offer were too few to have any continuous effect, and he substituted imaginary favours that appealed to men's jealous natures, small distinctions which he was able, with extraordinary ingenuity, to grant or withhold every day and almost every hour. The hopes that courtiers built upon such flimsy favours and the importance which they attached to them were really unbelievable, and no one was ever more artful than the King in devising fresh occasions for them. In later days, he made great use of the Marly excursions for that purpose, and Trianon, too, for although every man had the right to go there to pay his court, only the ladies ate with him, and they were specially selected for every meal. Another of his contrivances was the ceremony of the candlestick,[1] which he allowed some courtier to hold every evening at his *coucher*. He always chose from among the most distinguished persons present and called his name aloud as he went out from prayers.

Still another device was the granting of the *justaucorps à brevet*, blue, lined with scarlet, with scarlet facings and waistcoat, embroidered with gold thread and a little silver in a particular pattern. Only a certain number of these jackets were made. The King and the members of the royal family and the Princes of the Blood each possessed one, but the latter had to wait, like the other courtiers, until a vacancy occurred. The greatest persons at the Court used to beg one for themselves or another, and it was considered an enormous privilege to obtain one. Originally, they were designed for the very select few who had the right to go with the King on his excursions to Saint-Germain or Versailles without a special invitation. When these outings ceased, the jackets no longer had any special significance, but they might be worn for Court or family mourning, unless it were full mourning, or at those periods when it was forbidden to wear gold or silver. I never saw the King wear his, nor Monseigneur nor Monsieur, but Monseigneur's three sons often wore theirs, and so did the other princes. Until the King's death, there was always great rivalry among the courtiers as soon as one became available, and if some young nobleman received one it was thought to be a great distinction.

But there would be no end to describing all the different expedients that followed one after another as the King grew

[1] See p. 83.

older and the entertainments increased or diminished in number, or to telling of the methods he employed to keep so large a Court always about him.

He not only required the constant attendance of the great, but was also aware of those of lower rank. He would look about him at his *lever* and *coucher*, at meals, and while walking through the state apartments or the Versailles gardens, where none but courtiers might follow him. He saw and noticed every one of them, marked very well the absences of those usually at Court and even of those who attended more rarely, and took care to discover the reason, drawing his own conclusions and losing no opportunity of acting upon them. He took it as an offence if distinguished people did not make the Court their home, or if others came but seldom. And to come never, or scarcely ever, meant certain disgrace. When a favour was asked for such a one, the King would answer haughtily, 'I do not know him at all,' or, 'That is a man whom I never see,' and in such cases his word was irrevocable.

Another crime was not to go to Fontainebleau, which he regarded as a second Versailles, and if certain people did not beg for an invitation to Marly, even though he might have no intention of taking them, they needed, man or woman, a pretty good excuse to save them from disgrace. Above all, he could not bear people to go to Paris for their amusements. He did not so much mind the absences of those who loved their estates, but none the less, one needed to be moderate, or else take precautions before making a long visit.

Louis XIV took enormous pains to be well-informed about all that went on in public places, in private houses, society, family business, or the progress of love-affairs. He had spies and reporters everywhere and of all descriptions. Many of them never realized that their reports reached the King, others wrote directly to him, sending their letters by secret channels of his own devising. Their letters were seen by him alone and he always read them before proceeding to other business. There were even some who spoke privately with him in his study, entering by the back way. Through such secret informants, an immense number of people of all ranks were broken, often most unjustly, and without their ever discovering the reason, for the King, once suspicious, never trusted again, or so rarely that it made no matter.

One other fault he had, that made him highly dangerous to others and, indeed, to himself, for it often deprived him of loyal subjects. Although his memory was so good that he could recognize some common man, whom he had seen perhaps once, twenty years earlier, and could learn things easily without confusing them, he could scarcely be expected to remember everything. But if he chanced to have only a vague recollection of some person, there remained imprinted upon his mind the idea that he had something against that man, and that alone was enough to exclude him. Nothing could persuade him to change his mind. No matter what his ministers, generals, or even his confessor might argue, he always answered that he could not clearly remember what there was against the man, but that he would feel more secure in choosing some other.

It was owing to the King's curiosity that the lieutenants of police assumed their dangerous power, which went on steadily increasing. These officers were more dreaded, more delicately handled, more respected during his reign even than the ministers, and even by the ministers themselves. No one in France, not even the Princes of the Blood, thought it politic to treat them disrespectfully; for apart from the official reports which they sent to the King, they amused themselves by knowing all the intrigues and the latest scandals in Parisian society.

But the cruellest of all the King's methods of obtaining information was the opening of private letters. Years passed before this practice was generally suspected; and even afterwards, many ignorant and foolish people continued to feed him, for it was almost incredible how swiftly and skilfully the letters were dealt with. He read extracts of those containing any matter which the postmasters or their minister decided that he should see, and entire letters, when their contents or the importance of the persons addressed made it appear worth while. Thus it came about that the chief postmasters were in a position to impute whatsoever they chose to whomever they chose, and since it needed very little to ruin a man irretrievably they had no need for plots or forgeries. A single word of abuse or disparagement of the King or the government, one jest, one sarcastic remark, one plausible fragment cut out of a letter was enough to finish a man's career without further inquiry. Rightly or wrongly accused, it is almost unbelievable how many people of all sorts and conditions were broken to a greater or lesser extent by such means. The veil of secrecy was impenetrable, for nothing came more easily to the King than absolute silence or dissembling. Indeed it was a talent which he carried to the verge of deceit, but never to actual falsehood, for he prided himself on keeping his word, once given. That was why he almost never gave it, and he guarded other people's secrets as scrupulously as he did his own. It even pleased his vanity to receive confidences and to be trusted, and neither mistresses, ministers, nor favourites could drag them out of him, not even when they themselves were implicated.

There is one story in particular of a certain noble lady, whose identity has never yet been discovered, who found that she was pregnant just as her husband was returning after a year's absence with the army. At last, when all other expedients had failed, she besought the King to grant her an absolutely secret audience on the most urgent business in the world. She obtained her interview and told the King that, in her extreme necessity, she had come to the man whom she could best trust in the whole of France. He advised her to let this great trouble be a lesson to live more wisely for the future, and promised her instantly to send orders to keep her husband on duty at the frontier in such a way and for so long that he would have no suspicions, and to refuse him home-leave on any pretext whatsoever. What is more, he sent Louvois instructions that very moment, and forbade him also to leave the fortress which he was to command throughout the winter, even for a single day. The husband, an officer of high rank, had never expected, and had certainly not asked to be employed at that season on the frontier, neither had Louvois, and both were equally vexed and astonished. None the less, they could do nothing but obey and ask no questions, and when the King finally told the story many years later, he made sure that none of the people concerned would be identified, as indeed they never have been, not even by the vaguest hint.

No man ever distributed his favours with a better grace than the King, and in so doing he enhanced their value. No one ever put his words, his smiles, his very glances, to better advantage. Everything that he did, he made to appear precious because of his exquisite tact and majesty. When he stopped to ask a man some question on general matters, everyone turned to look at the person he addressed; it was considered a marked distinction, a cause for congratulation, and so it was with all the courtesies,

K

favours, and preferences, which he showed by different degrees. He never allowed himself to say anything ungracious to anybody, and if he needed to check, reprove, or punish, which very rarely occurred, he always did so in a more or less kindly manner, scarcely ever harshly, and never in a rage—except for that one incident with Courtenvaux,[1] which I described in its proper place. None the less, he could be angry when he chose, and sometimes looked very severe.

There never lived a man more naturally polite, nor of such exquisite discrimination with so fine a sense of degree, for he made distinctions for age, merit and rank, and showed them in his answers when these went further than the usual '*Je verrai*', and in his general bearing. Such fine gradations were perfectly displayed in his manner of giving and acknowledging salutations when one approached or left him. He was admirable for the different ways in which he took the salute at the head of the army or at reviews. But above all, he was unrivalled in his courtesy to women, for he never passed a petticoat without raising his hat, even when, as often happened at Marly, they were housemaids, whom he knew to be such. For ladies, he took his hat quite off, but more or less far, as occassion demanded. For noblemen he would half-remove it, holding it in the air or against his ear, for a few moments, or longer. For landed gentlemen, he only touched his hat. Princes of the Blood he greeted in the same way as the ladies, and if he joined a group of ladies, he replaced his hat only after leaving them. But such things occurred only out of doors, for inside the house he was never covered. All these different degrees of courtesy were easy and relaxed, but incomparably graceful and stately, even down to his manner of half rising from his chair at dinner for each 'sitting-lady'[2] as she arrived, and for no one else, not even for Princes of the Blood. Towards the end of his life, this custom tired him, but he would never give it up, and so the ladies who had the right to tabourets avoided entering after he was seated.

In the same way, he made distinctions when Monsieur, M. le Duc d'Orléans, or the Princes of the Blood served him at his *lever* or *coucher*. To the latter he simply made a civil gesture,

---

[1] Michel François le Tellier, Marquis de Courtenvaux. He was the son of Louvois and colonel of the Swiss Guard. Louis XIV turned upon him in a fury one day at Fontainebleau, or a blunder that exposed the King's system of spying on the Court.

[2] Only Princesses of the Blood, duchesses, and foreign princesses had tabourets, all the rest stood.

and the same to Monsieur; to his sons, some affectionate movement. The high officers he treated with graciousness and consideration.

If they happened to keep him waiting for something when he was being dressed, he was invariably patient. He was punctual to the minute[1] on his daily round and absolutely clear in his orders, but very occasionally, in bad winter weather, he could not go out and would then go to Mme de Maintenon a quarter of an hour or so before his usual time; it was a most rare event. If the captain of the bodyguard had not yet arrived, the King never forgot to tell him afterwards that it was his own fault for not warning him in time. Such unfailing punctuality made him all the better served and was vastly convenient for his courtiers.

His valets he treated with kindness, especially his bodyservants, for with them he felt most at ease and could talk intimately. Their likes and dislikes had much influence so that they were for ever able to do people good or ill turns. They put one in mind of the imperial freedmen of the old Roman Empire, who were fawned upon and courted by senators and other great men. Throughout the whole of his reign, Louis XIV's valets were not less considered and spoiled. The most powerful ministers openly humoured them and so did the Princes of the Blood and even the bastards themselves, not to mention the ordinary courtiers. The duties of the gentlemen of the bedchamber were quite taken over by the head valets, and their high offices were esteemed according to how much the servants and lower officials in their departments had access to the King. Most of them were intolerably insolent; one had to make up one's mind to escape or else bear their rudeness patiently.

The King protected them all. He sometimes told us, with obvious pleasure, how when he was a young man he had had occasion to send a footman with a letter to the Duc de Montbazon, then governor of Paris. The fellow arrived just as the Duke was going in to dinner, but he had insisted that this footman should eat with him and had walked with him into the courtyard, when he left—because he came from the King. Because of this, the King never forgot to ask how his gentlemen

---

[1] Saint-Simon says elsewhere that if you had a calendar and a watch, you could tell exactly what he was doing at any time even though you might be three hundred leagues away.

had been received, when they had conveyed his compliments or condolences to some nobleman, and would have taken it very ill if they had not been asked to sit down and escorted for some way on their return, if they were men as far as the door of their coach.

There was nothing to equal his bearing at reviews or, indeed, anywhere graced by the presence of ladies. I have already said that he had learned his gracious manner at his mother's Court and in the drawing-room of the Comtesse de Soissons. The company of his mistresses had encouraged it. He was sometimes gay, but never undignified, and never, at any time, did he do anything improper or indiscreet. His smallest gesture, his walk, bearing, and expression were all perfectly becoming, modest, noble, and stately, yet at the same time he always seemed perfectly natural. Added to which he had the immense advantage of a good figure, which made him graceful and relaxed.

On state occasions such as audiences with ambassadors and other ceremonies, he looked so imposing that one had to become used to the sight of him if one were not to be exposed to the humiliation of breaking down or coming to a full stop. At such times, his answers were always short and to the point and he rarely omitted some civility, or a compliment if the speech deserved one. The awe inspired by his appearance was such that wherever he might be, his presence imposed silence and a degree of fear.

He loved the open air and exercise so long as strength was given to him. In his youth, he had excelled in dancing, at pall-mall,[1] and at the jeu de paume, and all his life he was a superb horseman. He liked men to acquit themselves well in such past-times; gracefulness or clumsiness in them he regarded as a virtue or discredit, for he used to say that such pursuits were unnecessary and it were better not to do them at all than do them badly. Shooting he loved and was better than the average. He liked beautiful setter bitches and always had seven or eight in his rooms and fed them with his own hands so that they learned to know him. He also loved stag-hunting, but after he broke his arm he rode in a carriage. He drove himself in a small open carriage, drawn by four ponies with five or six relays, and went alone, going full tilt with a skill that few professionals could equal and all the elegance which he habitually displayed. His

[1] A game like croquet.

postillions were children between nine and fifteen years of age, whom he trained himself.

In everything he loved magnificently lavish abundance. He made it a principle from motives of policy and encouraged the Court to imitate him; indeed, one way to win favour was to spend extravagantly on the table, clothes, carriages, building, and gambling. For magnificence in such things he would speak to people. The truth is that he used this means deliberately and successfully to impoverish everyone, for he made luxury meritorious in all men, and in some a necessity, so that gradually the entire Court became dependent upon his favours for their very subsistence. What is more, he fed his own pride by surrounding himself with an entourage so universally magnificent that confusion reigned and all natural distinctions were obliterated.

Once it had begun this rottenness grew into that cancer which gnaws at the lives of all Frenchmen. It started, indeed, at the Court but soon spread to Paris, the provinces, and the army where generals are now assessed according to the tables that they keep and the splendour of their establishments. It so eats into private fortunes that those in a position to steal are often forced to do so in order to keep up their spending. This cancer, kept alive by confusion of ranks, pride, even by good manners, and encouraged by the folly of the great, is having incalculable results that will lead to nothing less than ruin and general disaster.

No other King has ever approached him for the number and quality of his stables and hunting establishments. Who could count his buildings ? Who not deplore their ostentation, whimsicality and bad taste ? He abandoned that lovely Saint-Germain and did nothing to improve or embellish Paris, except out of sheer necessity, as when he built the Pont Royal. Even so, for all its splendid prospect, Paris remains inferior to many towns in other parts of Europe.

When, for instance, the Place de Vendôme was first built, it was square. M. de Louvois, himself, superintended the erection of the four façades. His plan was to provide house-room for the King's Library, the Cabinet of Medals, the Mint, the various academies, and the grand council, which even now holds its sessions in a rented house. On the day of Louvois's death, the first thing that the King did was to stop the work, and give orders to cut off the corners of the square so as to reduce its size. Nothing that had been planned was done; nothing was constructed but private houses, as we see them today.

Saint-Germain he abandoned; unique Saint-Germain, with its combination of superb vistas and the vast stretches of forest that lie close beside; Saint-Germain, with its fine views, trees, soil and situation, its abundance of springs, its lovely gardens, its hills and terraces, its capabilities that might have been extended to include the beauties and convenience of the Seine. There was a city ready-made, whose site alone provided it with all that man could desire. All this, I say, he abandoned for Versailles, that most dismal and thankless of spots, without vistas, woods, or water, without soil, even, for all the surrounding land is quicksand or bog, and the air cannot be healthy.

It diverted him to ride roughshod over nature and to use his money and ingenuity to subdue it to his will. At Versailles he set up one building after another according to no scheme of planning. Beauty and ugliness, spaciousness and meanness were roughly tacked together. The royal apartments at Versailles are beyond everything inconvenient, with back-views over the privies and other dark and evil-smelling places. Truly, the magnificence of the gardens is amazing, but to make the smallest use of them is disagreeable, and they are in equally bad taste. To reach any shade one is forced to cross a vast, scorching expanse and, after all, there is nothing to do in any direction but go up and down a little hill, after which the gardens end. The broken stones on the paths burn one's feet, yet without them one would sink into sand or the blackest mud.

Who could help being repelled and disgusted at the violences done to Nature? Numberless springs have been forced to flow into the gardens from every side making them lush, overgrown and boggy; they are perceptibly damp and unhealthy and their smell is even more so. The fountains and other effects are indeed incomparably fine, although they require a great deal of attention, but the net result is that one admires and flies.

On the courtyard side, the constriction is suffocating and the vast wings recede quite pointlessly. On the garden front, one is able to appreciate the beauty of the building as a whole, but it looks like a palace that has been destroyed by fire because the upper story and the roofs are still missing. The chapel towers above it because of Mansard's attempt to force the King to add an entire upper storey. As it now is, it presents the distressing appearance of some vast hearse. Everywhere in the chapel the craftsmanship is exquisite, but the design is nil, for everything was planned from the point of view of the tribune, because the King never went below.

But one might be for ever pointing out the monstrous defects of that huge and immensely costly palace, and of its outhouses that cost even more, its orangery, kitchen gardens, kennels, larger and smaller stables, all vast, all prodigiously expensive. Indeed, a whole city has sprung up where before was only a poor tavern, a windmill and a little pasteboard château, which Louis XIII built so as to avoid lying on straw.

The Versailles of Louis XIV, that masterpiece wherein countless sums of money were thrown away merely in alterations to ponds and thickets, was so ruinously costly, so monstrously ill-planned, that it was never finished. Amid so many state rooms, opening one out of another, it has no theatre, no banqueting-hall, no ballroom, and both behind and before much still remains undone. The avenues and plantations, all laid out artificially, cannot mature and the coverts must continually be restocked with game. As for the drains, many miles of them still have to be made, and even the walls, whose vast contours enclose a small province of the gloomiest, most wretched countryside, have never been completely finished.

In the park at the gates of Versailles, Trianon was originally a little porcelain house designed for picnics, and was later enlarged to contain bedrooms. Finally, it was converted into a marble palace of jasper and porphyry, with an enchanting garden. The zoo, that stands opposite, on the further side of the canal, is an exquisite miniature, stocked with the rarest species of beasts and birds. Clagny,[1] also at the end of the park was built as a present for Mme de Montespan, and was inherited by the Duc du Maine after her death. It, too, is a beautiful château, with gardens, fountains, and parklands. Aqueducts, not unworthy of the Romans, brought water into it from every side. Not Asia, nor antiquity, could show anything more vast, grandiose, and elaborate than these gardens, which were full of precious works of art of every age, marbles, bronzes, paintings, sculptures, all of them perfect in their several ways.

But water lacked. No matter what was done, the great

[1] Pulled down by Louis XV

fountains dried up (as they still do at times) in spite of the oceans of reservoirs that cost so many millions to engineer in that sandy or boggy soil. Who would ever credit it? That same lack of water brought about the destruction of the French infantry, for peace reigned at that time and M. de Louvois conceived the notion of changing the course of the Eure between Chartres and Maintenon, so as to bring that river bodily to Versailles. Who could count the gold and the men lost in an attempt which was continued for several years? They made a camp at the site of the works, and in the end it was forbidden under heavy penalties to mention the sick, or still worse, the dying, whom the hard labour and exhalations from the turned earth were taking off day by day. How many soldiers wasted long years in trying to recover their health? How many more never did recover? During the whole of that time, not only junior officers, but colonels, brigadiers, and even generals employed there, were forbidden to absent themselves a quarter of an hour, or miss so much as a quarter of an hour's duty on the site. The enterprise finally came to an end with the war of 1688. It has never been restarted. Nothing remains but shapeless mounds to perpetuate the memory of a barbarous piece of folly.

At last the King, growing weary of splendour and crowds, decided that he needed sometimes to have smallness and solitude, and began to search in the neighbourhood of Versailles for a site where he could satisfy this new caprice. He looked at various places, especially among the slopes that lead down from Saint-Germain to the great plain, where the winding Seine waters the meadows and rich pastures after leaving Paris. They tried to persuade him to settle on Luciennes, where Caroye[1] has since built his house, for the view there is bewitching, but he answered that a site so full of capabilities would be the ruin of him. He wanted a mere nothing, and must therefore choose the kind of site that would give him no ideas.

In the end, he lit on a narrow valley with steep and rocky sides that lay behind Luciennes. It was difficult to approach because of the marshes, had no view, was hemmed in by hills on every side, and was exceedingly constricted. On the side of one of the hills was a wretched little hamlet, known as Marly. The fact that this valley was so much enclosed, without any vista or

[1] Louis d'Oger, Marquis de Caroye (1640–1716).

means of making one, was its chief merit in the King's eyes. The narrowness, which would not allow for spreading, was also greatly in its favour. In fact, he was moved by exactly the same motives as when he chose a minister, a favourite, or a general. It turned out to be an enormous labour to dry up this sewer of a valley, into which all the surrounding country drained itself, and to train the earth to form a new kind of soil. But the King's hermitage was made none the less. It was originally intended for visits of three nights, from a Wednesday to a Saturday two or three times a year, with, at the very most, a dozen courtiers to perform the necessary offices.

Gradually, the retreat was enlarged. Piece by piece, the hills were cut away to allow room for building, and a hill at the end of the valley was almost completely levelled so as to give at least one very moderate vista. Finally, with its buildings, fountains, gardens, and aqueducts, so famous, so fascinating under the name of 'La Machine de Marly', with its forests improved and enclosed, its parklands and statues, its precious ornaments of all kinds, there arose Marly, as we now see it, although it has been much despoiled since the King's death.

To provide the forests, many were the tall trees brought from Compiègne and from even greater distances. More than three-quarters of them died and were immediately replaced by others. Great stretches of thick woodland and dark alleyways were transformed with lightning speed into broad lakes, where people were rowed about in gondolas, and were then changed back to forests so dense that daylight was banished as soon as the trees were planted. I speak of what I saw myself in six weeks, during which time fountains were altered a hundred times, and waterfalls redesigned in countless different ways. Goldfish ponds, decorated with gilding and delightful paintings, were scarcely finished before they were unmade and rebuilt differently by the same artists, and such things were done over and over again. The monstrous machinery for supplying water, which I have already mentioned, with its immense aqueducts, conduits and reservoirs, was intended solely for the needs of Marly, and not to serve Versailles. It is a modest estimate to say that Versailles, such as we see it, did not cost as much as Marly.

It you reckon the expense of continual journeys backwards and forwards, for Marly excursions became quite as frequent

K*

and almost as crowded as those to Versailles, until, at the end of the King's life, it was his usual residence, it would not be too much to say that Marly alone cost several thousand million.

Such was the development of a haunt of snakes and vermin, toads and frogs, that was selected solely on the ground that it would entail no expense. Marly was typical of the King's bad taste[1] in everything, and of the proud pleasure which he found in subduing Nature, from which diversion neither the most pressing needs of war, nor religious zeal could ever turn him.

1715

Mme de Maintenon

WE must now pass on to a different kind of love-affair, which astounded foreign nations no less than the earlier ones had shocked them.[2] This time, it was a love which the King carried with him to the grave. From these few words everyone will recognize the famous Françoise d'Aubigné, Marquise de Maintenon, whose reign continued uninterrupted for no less than thirty-two years. She was born in the American Isles,[3] where her father, who may have been of gentle birth, had taken her mother in order to seek their fortunes, and wherein all traces of them have been lost. She returned to France alone, an adventuress, and, landing at La Rochelle, was given asylum out of charity by Mme de Neuillant, mother of the Maréchale-Duchesse de Navailles. Through her poverty and the old lady's avarice, she was there reduced to guarding the keys of the granary and measuring out corn for the horses, until, with the rest of Mme de Neuillant's household, she came to Paris, young, clever, witty and beautiful, but without family or

---

[1] Boislisle, however, comments: 'From everything that we know of Marly, its decorations and its wonderful gardens, it must have been a model of good taste and true magnificence. Its disappearance is an irreparable loss.'

[2] In a passage on the King's early love-affairs, Saint-Simon discusses some of the ladies concerned in what he calls the King's 'passades' (his passing fancies). M. Gonzague Truc says that he once began to make a list of them, but found them as numerous as they were unedifying. They included Anne Lucie de la Mothe Houdancourt, later marquise de La Vieuville, the Princess of Monaco, the Comtesse de Brancas, and many others.

[3] Not true. She was born in the gaol at Niort, where her father was a political prisoner. When she was four he emigrated to Martinique, where he died six years later. His family then returned to France.

fortune. Some happy chance then brought her to the notice of the famous poet Scarron.[1] He thought her amiable, his friends, in all probability, still more so, while she, for her part, thought it a wonderful and unexpected stroke of good luck to have the possibility of marrying that merry, learned, incapable cripple. Certain people, who may have had more use for a wife than Scarron, incited him to marry, and gained their object by persuading him to rescue from her misfortune this charming damsel in distress.

The marriage accordingly took place, and the bride charmed all the many and varied guests who came to Scarron's house, for he received much company, including some of the very best people in every walk of life. It was the fashion to visit him. Indeed, so many of the most brilliant and distinguished members of the Court and Parisian society came to him that he had no need to go outside his own home for company. His wit, his delightful conversation, the merry way in which he bore his pain, his imagination and pleasant humour, always in the good taste which can still be enjoyed in his works, attracted a continual stream of visitors.

Mme Scarron thus made the acquaintance of a great number of people of all kinds, although, after her husband died, this did not prevent her from being reduced to the charity house[2] of

[1] Paul Scarron: comic writer and poet, author of *Virgile Travesti, Le Roman Comique*, and other witty and amusing comedies, which paved the way for Molière. During most of his life, he was twisted and crippled with rheumatism, as he described in his famous epitaph:

> Celui qui cy maintenant dort
> Fit plus de pitié que d'envie,
> Et souffrit mille fois la mort
> Avant que de perdre la vie.

> Passant ne fais ici de bruit;
> Garde bien que tu ne l'éveilles,
> Car voici la première nuit
> Que le pauvre Scarron sommeille.

> He who lies sleeping here
> Aroused more pity than envy,
> And suffered death a thousand times
> Before he lost his life.

> Oh! passer-by be quiet here,
> Take care not to wake him,
> For this is the first night
> In which poor Scarron sleeps.

[2] Les Charités: convents run by nursing-sisters to which many poor young widows retired.

her parish of Saint-Eustache, where she took a room for herself and her maid,[1] on one of the staircases and lived at first in very straitened circumstances. Her charms, however, gradually relieved her discomforts. Villars, father of the Maréchal, Beuvron (Harcourt's father), and Villarceaux were three permanent supporters, and there were many others. Gradually, they set her up again, introducing her to the d'Albret family, the Richelieus, and elsewhere, and so she was passed from one to another. In these homes Mme Scarron was certainly not treated as a guest. She did odd jobs, sending for more wood when required, asking the servants when the meals would be coming, or whether so-and-so's carriage had arrived, in fact, all those small services which the use of bells (introduced much later) has rendered unnecessary. It was in such houses, especially in the Hôtel de Richelieu and the Hôtel d'Albret, that Mme Scarron made most of her acquaintances, some of whom were of great service to her, and others whom she afterwards benefited.

The Maréchal d'Albret was of the highest society and party to all the intrigues of the Court, for he was tutor to Monsieur le Prince and M. le Prince de Conti. He lived on terms of intimate friendship with his cousin, M. de Montespan, and his wife, but when the latter became the King's mistress, he abandoned her husband and became her adviser, by which means he retained great influence until he died at the age of sixty-two. It was to this close relationship between M. d'Albret and M. de Montespan that Mme Scarron owed the introduction which led, fourteen or fifteen years later, to her incredibly high position.

M. and Mme de Montespan were almost continually at the Hôtel d'Albret, where the Maréchal kept great state, and an open house to which flocked all the most brilliant and exclusive society of the Court and Paris. Mme Scarron's respectful civility, her desire to please, intelligence, and attractions delighted Mme de Montespan, who took a fancy to her. When, therefore, her eldest children by the King (M. du Maine and Mme la Duchesse) were born and concealment became necessary, she suggested making Mme Scarron their governess. This was accordingly done, and a house in the Marais and sufficient means were provided so that the governess might live with them and bring them up with the utmost secrecy. From time to time, the children were taken to Mme de Montespan and shown

[1] Nanon Balbien.

to the King, until eventually they were brought into the open and acknowledged. They were then established at the Court with their governess, who pleased Mme de Montespan more and more, so much so, indeed, that on several occasions she persuaded the King to make her presents of money. He, however, could not abide her, and what he gave, which was little enough, was done to satisfy Mme de Montespan and with a very bad grace which he did not attempt to conceal.

The estate of Maintenon coming up for sale, Mme de Montespan was tempted by its nearness to Versailles, and gave the King no peace until she had extracted from him a sufficient sum to buy it for that woman, who took the name of Maintenon then, or shortly afterwards. She also obtained funds to repair the château, and teased the King again until he had given enough to restore the garden, which had been left in a bad state.

All this took place during Mme de Montespan's toilette, and was witnessed only by the captain of the guard attending on the King. He happened to be M. le Maréchal de Lorges, my father-in-law, the most truthful man imaginable, who often described the scene to me. At first the King pretended not to hear, then refused, growing impatient because Mme de Montespan, instead of giving up, continued to importune him. Finally he lost his temper, saying that he had done more than enough for that hussy and could not understand Mme de Montespan's partiality, nor her determination to keep her when he had so often requested her dismissal. He then said again that he could not abide her, but provided that he never saw nor heard mention of her, he would give once more, although he considered that already far too much had been done for that sort of trollop. M. le Maréchal de Lorges never forgot those words, and always repeated them in exactly the same order. He was deeply impressed by them at that time, and much more so later when he witnessed so much that was astonishing and contradictory. He used to say that Mme de Montespan was silent, and appeared distressed at having vexed the King.

M. du Maine was very lame because, or so they said, he had fallen from the arms of one of his nurses. When nothing served to cure him, it was arranged to send him to various bone-surgeons of Flanders and in other parts of the kingdom, and then to certain spas, Barèges among others. Mme de Montespan showed the governess's letters describing their journeys to the King, who thought them well-written, enjoyed them, and gradually lessened in his aversion.

Mme de Montespan's bad temper did the rest, for she was naturally ill-humoured and had never learned to control herself. What is more, her furies were most often directed towards the King himself, who minded them because he was still in love. Mme de Maintenon used sometimes to reproach her for her bad behaviour, and in so doing served him. Others then told him of her good work in soothing his mistress, so that little by little he grew into the habit of telling Mme de Maintenon what she should say, and in the end came to confiding all his sufferings to her ear and asking her advice.

Thus she gradually became the direct confidante of the King's intimate elations with his mistress and laboured so well, turning the position to such good advantage, that by degrees she supplanted Mme de Montespan, who discovered too late that the governess had become a necessity. This having duly been accomplished, Mme de Maintenon began to complain to the King on her own account, telling him of all that she herself had to bear from the mistress who spared him so little. By dint of this mutual complaining about Mme de Montespan, Mme de Maintenon ousted her entirely and made no mistake about securing the situation for herself.

Fate, for I dare not name Providence in such a connection, now prepared the deepest, most flagrant, enduring, unparalleled shame for that proudest of monarchs, by increasing his fancy more and more for that clever woman, so expert in her wiles, which were assisted by the continual jealousy of Mme de Montespan and her frequent, violent outbreaks of bad temper. This is what Mme de Sévigné has described in pretty riddles in her letters to Mme de Grignan, whom she often entertained with the Court gossip.[1]

Fate, I say, the absolute mistress of times and seasons, so ordered things now that the Queen lived just long enough to allow the King's new love to reach its climax, but not so long as to let it cool. The greatest misfortune that could have befallen the King and, as events proved, the State as well, was the sudden death of the Queen at the height of this new attachment,

---

[1] For example, she referred to Mme de Montespan as 'Quanto' or 'Quantova'; to the King as 'our friend', or the 'lord of all'; to the Queen as 'the lady of the house', and to Mme de Maintenon as '*l'enrhumée*' ('Sniffy').

when the ill-temper of his mistress was making her intolerable to him.

The first days of his widowerhood he spent with Monsieur, at Saint-Cloud, and from thence went to Fontainebleau, where he remained throughout the autumn. It was while he was there that absence made his heart grow fonder, until he could no longer bear the pain of separation. On his return, or so they say (for I must distinguish between truth and tittle-tattle), they say, I repeat, that the King spoke more frankly to Mme de Maintenon, and that she dared to test her power over him, intrenching herself most adroitly behind religion and the impropriety of her present situation. When she saw that the King was not indignant, she preached into him such a fear of the devil, and played on his love and his conscience with so much art that she attained to what our eyes have seen and to what posterity will never credit.

However that may have been, what is very certain and very true is that a few months after the King returned to Fontainebleau, in the middle of the winter following the Queen's death (and again, posterity will scarcely believe it), Père la Chaise, the King's confessor, said mass at midnight in one of the King's studies at Versailles. Bontemps, governor of Versailles and chief and most trustworthy of the four personal valets, served that mass, and there and then the King and the Maintenon were married, in the presence of Harlay, Archbishop of Paris, acting as diocesan, and Louvois, both of whom extracted the King's solemn promise that the marriage would never be acknowledged. A third witness was Montchevreuil, cousin and friend of Villarceaux,[1] to whom in earlier days he had lent his country house each summer, without removing either himself or his wife. There, Villarceaux entertained that 'queen', as he did in Paris, and paid all the expenses because his cousin was miserably poor. He was ashamed to bring his concubine to Villarceaux and the notice of a wife, whose patience and virtue he respected.

The boredom of respectability, which is so often fatal to marriages of this kind, only served to increase the King's fondness for Mme de Maintenon. Very soon after the wedding, the affair became common knowledge, for she was suddenly provided with

---

[1] The Marquis de Villarceaux was supposed to have been the lover of Mme de Maintenon when she was Mme Scarron.

an apartment at Versailles, at the head of the grand staircase, opposite to the King's private rooms and on the same level.

Mme de Maintenon was an exceedingly able woman, who had acquired polish and a knowledge of the world from the high society where she was at first tolerated and later cherished. Her love-affairs had taught her the arts of pleasing, and in the different positions which she had occupied she had learned to coax and flatter, to be civil, and always to be agreeable. She was of necessity a schemer, but the various intrigues of one kind and another, which she either witnessed or originated on her own or other people's behalf, gave her a taste for plotting and sharpened her wits. Every action of hers was performed with incomparable grace and ease, for long years of servitude had made natural in her a reserved and modest bearing which marvellously enhanced her own good qualities. When she spoke, it was quietly and correctly, using excellent French, always brief and eloquent. She was three or four years older than the King, so that her best time had coincided with the fashion for witty conversations and elegant gallantries, *Les Ruelles*,[1] as they used to be called. These had so much enchanted her that she never afterwards lost their flavour, nor her pleasure in them. Primness and preciosity added to that old-fashioned air, which had been covered, first with a veneer of self-importance, and later with a thicker veneer of a piety that eventually became her chief characteristic and seemed to absorb every other quality. Piety was, indeed, her greatest asset; she used it to maintain herself upon the heights and, above all, as a means to power, which was her life's ambition, to which she would gladly have sacrificed all else. Truth and frankness ill become such an aim and such success in achieving it; you may well imagine that she could preserve only the outward semblance of those virtues. None the less, she was not so false-hearted as to prefer lies to the truth, but necessity had long since forced the habit upon her, so that, being fickle by nature, she appeared twice as false as she was in reality.

There was no stability in her, except by constraint or force of circumstances. Her natural inclination was to be as changeable in her friends and acquaintances as in her diversions,

---

[1] It was in *Les Ruelles*, the spaces between the bed and the wall, that the arts of elegant conversation and elegant flirtation were born. They were, in fact, the birthplace of French Wit.

excepting always one or two faithful old friends of earlier days, whom I have already mentioned. Those she never forsook, and she also clung to some newer friendships that became necessary to her as time passed. As regards diversions, after she began to think of herself as queen, she varied them hardly at all. Where her fickleness was most apparent was in more important matters, and there it did great harm, for she easily became enthusiastic, even to excess, and was just as easily disenchanted. Infatuations, with her, often changed to disgust without rhyme or reason.

The poverty and the abject situation in which she had lived for so long had narrowed her mind and debased her heart and sentiments. She thought and felt so very meanly about most things that as Mme de Maintenon she was actually less of a personality than she had been as Mme Scarron, and was always the same on every occasion. Nothing could have been more boring than such baseness in her glorious position, and nothing more stultifying to any good that might have arisen from it than this fatal weakness for changing friends and advisers.

She had one other deceiving trick. If one had an audience with her and something about one's appearance chanced to please her, she would greet one with amazing warmth that seemed to promise great things, yet a moment afterwards, she might be excessively short and snubbing. One might rack one's brains to discover the causes for her favour and displeasure, both so suddenly displayed, but it would be sheer waste of time. Caprice was her only motive, and her flightiness was unbelievable. You may imagine how thorny was the road to her favour; but, in any case, she was almost inaccessible, by her own desire and the King's preference.

She was so weak as to be influenced by opinions, and welcomed confidences that almost amounted to confessions, but she was easily duped because the life that she led was so narrow and confined. Yet she had an evil passion for administration that cost her what little freedom she might otherwise have retained. It was incredible how much time she wasted over Saint-Cyr, and the affairs of a hundred other convents occupied as much of her leisure. She saw herself as a kind of universal mother superior, especially in spiritual matters, which led her to undertaking the management of the entire diocese. That was her favourite pastime, for she loved to weigh the respective merits of the higher clergy, superiors of seminaries and other schools, as well as those of convents. Thus she developed a host of trivial businesses, all unreal, burdensome, and falsely conceived. There were endless letters to receive and answer, orders to be given to her favourites, and all manner of other such nonsense, mostly ending in nothing, but occasionally leading to important decisions and deplorable mistakes in selection and the appreciation of events.

Mme de Maintenon's heart's desire was always the public announcement of her marriage with the King, and at one point that wish was almost realized. But the King, remembering in time what had happened on that occasion, consulted the famous Bossuet, Bishop of Meaux, and Fénelon, Archbishop of Cambrai, both of whom so earnestly dissuaded him that he put the matter aside for ever. The Archbishop was already in bad odour with Mme de Maintenon, but Bossuet escaped her wrath because he had once unintentionally done her a very great service.[1]

Bossuet was a man in whom honour, virtue, and integrity were inseparable from vast erudition. His office as tutor to Monseigneur brought him into contact with the King, who more than once consulted him on matters of conscience. Bossuet had then spoken out with a freedom worthy of the first centuries of Christianity and the first bishops, and had more than once stopped the King in his immoralities, even venturing to pursue when the King tried to evade him. In the end, he succeeded in preventing all adulterous practices, and crowned his great work by dealing the final blow that drove Mme de Montespan for ever from the Court. Even at the height of her triumph, as she then was, Mme de Maintenon could not have rested easy while her late employer still remained in residence receiving daily visits from the King, for she resented them as so much time and attention stolen from herself. What is more, she could not, with propriety, have avoided treating Mme de Montespan, if not with the respect of earlier days, at least with great civility and the outward semblance of devotion. Such courtesies reminded her only too well of past servitude, as did Mme de Montespan herself, with barbed and exceedingly well-phrased darts, aimed to hurt. Nevertheless, when the King paid

---

[1] When he persuaded the King to leave Mme de Montespan. By so doing he paved the way for Mme de Maintenon, which he surely did not intend.

his daily semi-public visits to the former mistress, he went between mass and dinner, so as to cut them decently and necessarily short, which provided a most absurd contrast to the lengthy sessions held, also daily, with the former governess, now supposedly neither mistress nor wife, whose apartment had become the stew-pot of the affairs of Court and State. Mme de Montespan's final departure was thus an immense relief to Mme de Maintenon, who realized that she owed it entirely to the Bishop of Meaux.

That also was the period of the perfect harmony and understanding between M. du Maine and Mme de Maintenon, and of her virtual adoption of him, a relationship that became increasingly close and opened the way for him to incredible grandeurs. It would, indeed, have brought him to the throne, had that been within the power of his devoted '*Mie*'.[1]

Having secured the great victory of Mme de Montespan's perpetual banishment, Mme de Maintenon had a further triumph. After failing for the second time to declare her marriage, she realized that nothing would be gained by reviving the subject and decided to accept her disappointment sweetly, showing no chagrin at the refusal to make her queen, which made the King feel vastly relieved and grateful to her, and increased his affection, consideration, and trust. In point of fact, she might well have failed under the crushing weight of the rank to which she aspired, whereas in those circumstances, she became ever more firmly established by sustaining the transparent pretence of her position.

It must not, however, be supposed that she needed no skill to maintain herself in power. On the contrary, her life was one long campaign, and that of the King a perpetual delusion. She never received visits, and paid none; there were few exceptions to that rule although she sometimes called on the Queen of England and was visited by her, and sometimes went to see Mme de Montchevreuil, her dearest friend, who came often to her. She never called on the Princesses of the Blood, nor on Madame; but when she had something to say to the King's daughters, which was not often, and almost never except when she wished to give them a good dressing-down, she had them sent for. They used to arrive trembling and nearly always left in tears.

---

[1] The Duc du Maine's pet-name for Mme de Maintenon.

Audiences with her were nearly as hard to obtain as with the King himself, and what few she did grant were mostly at Saint-Cyr, and one had to go at a given day and hour. People would wait outside her apartments when she was leaving or returning to Versailles, those of no account, the poor, and men of quality, all alike. There was not a moment to lose, and a race to catch her eye. The Maréchaux de Villeroy, Harcourt, Tessé, and, in later days, M. de Vaudémont spoke to her at such times, and if she were returning, they would follow her only as far as the ante-room, where she very quickly broke off the conversation and left them. As for me, I never spoke to her anywhere, except as I have described elsewhere.[1] One or two ladies whom the King knew and liked sometimes saw her when he was not present, and very occasionally a few of them dined with her.

Her mornings, which she began very early indeed, were filled by interviews with obscure persons concerned with charities or religious administration. Sometimes she saw one or two ministers or, more rarely, generals, when they had something special to report. Fairly frequently, at eight in the morning, or even earlier, she would go to see some minister or other, and very occasionally stayed to dine with them, their wives, and some carefully selected guests. That was a great favour, and made news, but led to nothing but jealousy and a certain amount of deference. The ministers for war and finance were those with whom Mme de Maintenon had most to do, and their acquaintance she cultivated. She seldom went to others, except for business, very early in the morning, and never dined with them.

Usually, as soon as she rose, she went to Saint-Cyr and dined there alone in her room, or with some favourite nun, gave as few audiences as possible, presided over the convent's internal affairs, ruled the Church outside, read and answered letters, directed the convent schools in all parts of France, received reports from her spies, and returned to Versailles almost exactly at the time when the King habitually visited her. When she grew old and infirm, she used to arrive at Saint-Cyr between seven and eight o'clock in the morning, and at once go to bed and rest or take some remedy or other.

[1] In 1710 when Mme de Saint-Simon was made lady-in-waiting to the Duchesse de Berry, Mme de Maintenon congratulated and praised her in public. Saint-Simon was unwillingly obliged to pay a duty-call and never went again.

At Fontainebleau, she had a house in the town, where she often went for the same purposes. At Marly, she had a little room with a window looking into the chapel. She used it as she did Saint-Cyr, but called it 'Le Repos'. It was inaccessible to all, without exception, except to Mme la Duchesse de Bourgogne.

At nine in the evening two maids used to come to undress Mme de Maintenon and, directly afterwards, her butler and a footman brought in her supper—soup and something light to eat. As soon as she had finished, her women put her into bed. All this took place in the presence of the King and the minister in attendance, if one were on duty, or the ladies of the intimate circle. Voices were not hushed and work or conversation continued uninterrupted. By that time it was usually ten o'clock, when the King went to his supper and Mme de Maintenon's curtains were drawn.

It was the same on excursions. She would leave early in the morning with some favourite friend, always Mme de Mont-chevreuil while she lived, then Mme d'Heudicourt, Mme de Dangeau, or Mme de Caylus. A royal carriage was at her disposal at all times, even for journeys from Versailles to Saint-Cyr, and the equerry in charge of the smaller stables handed her into the coach and rode beside her on horseback. That was his daily duty. On the Court journeys, Mme de Maintenon's own coach took her women and followed behind. She always arranged matters so that when the King arrived he found her comfortably established.

In private, she behaved exactly as though she were indeed the Queen, remaining seated in the presence of the King, Monseigneur, Monsieur, and the English Court. Elsewhere, she was simply a private person, and one of low rank. I have seen her at Marly, sitting at the lower end of the King's table with the rest of the ladies and, in full court-dress, at the Queen of England's apartment at Fontainebleau, yielding up her privileges, drawing back to allow titled, and even otherwise distinguished women to pass. She never allowed herself to be obliged to do so, but did all willingly, courteously, and in all situations was polite, affable, conversational, without pride or ostentation. She seemed intent only on giving consideration to those about her, but for all that, her presence made itself felt.

At all times, she was richly and neatly dressed, in good taste, but very simply, and in a style rather older than her years. On the rare occasions when she appeared after her retirement nothing was to be seen but a black bonnet and shawl. To the King's bedroom she never went, unless he were ill, or on the mornings of days when he took physic, and for much the same reasons she went to the room of Mme la Duchesse de Bourgogne, but never otherwise, not on any account. When the King came to her, they sat each in their armchair on either side of the fireplace with tables before them, she on the side where the bed stood, and the King with his back to the wall, on the side of the ante-chamber door. Two stools were placed in front of his table, one for the minister and the other for his portfolio. On working-days, the King and Mme de Maintenon were alone together only for the short time before the minister entered and the even shorter time after he had gone.[1] The King then went to his chaise-percée, and returned to the bedside, where he stood for a little while, said good night to her, and went to table. Such was the daily life of Mme de Maintenon.

While the work was in progress, she read or did her embroidery, hearing everything that passed between the King and his ministers, for they spoke aloud. Very occasionally, she put in a word, more seldom still, something of importance. Often, the King asked her opinion, and then she would answer with great caution and restraint, never or hardly ever, showing any concern for the matter, still less any interest in individuals. All the while, however, she was secretly in agreement with the minister who not having dared to oppose her in their private interviews, could still less do so in the King's presence. When the matter concerned some favour or appointment, it was arranged between them before ever it was brought to the King for his decision. Thus long delays occurred, for which neither the King nor anyone else guessed the reason.

She used to send word to ministers when she desired to speak to them, and they dared not mention any subject to the King without knowing her wishes, or until the revolving machinery of times and seasons had given them leisure to come to an

---

[1] In a letter to Mme de Brinon, Marquise de Villacerf, Mme de Maintenon wrote: 'When the King returns from hunting he comes to me. They close the doors and no one enters. I have to sympathize with his troubles, if he has any, his sorrows, and his vapours. Sometimes he is overcome by tears which he cannot master, or he feels uncomfortable and there is no conversation. Then one or other of the ministers arrives. . . .'

agreement. Only then did the minister present his proposals and lists to the King. If the latter paused at the name chosen by Mme de Maintenon the matter ended there, but if he chanced to stop at some other name, the minister would suggest examining the rest, encourage the King to criticize and thus contrive to have them excluded. He scarcely ever directly proposed Mme de Maintenon's choice, but mentioned several other persons, balancing them so nicely against one another that the King would become confused. He would then ask the minister's advice, and he, in turn, would repeat the arguments in favour of a few, finally coming to rest on their nominee. At this point, the King usually demurred, and turned to Mme de Maintenon for her opinion. The lady would smile, play the simpleton, say a word for one of the others and then, as though it were her first thought upon the matter, name the one the minister had suggested, and so it would be settled. Thus, the three-quarters that had to do with favours and appointments, and three-quarters of the remaining quarter of all that took place in her presence between the King and his ministers, were decided as she wished.

In great affairs of state, if Mme de Maintenon desired to make some proposal succeed or fail or go otherwise (which was much rarer for her than interference with favours and appointments), she had the same kind of understanding with the minister, and matters proceeded in much the same way. From this description, you will perceive that that capable woman did almost all as she pleased, but not all that she pleased, nor when and how she pleased.

There was another ruse for when the King was stubborn. They would prevent his coming to a decision by complicating and prolonging the affair, or changing the subject to some other matter that seemed to arise from it, so that the King became confused and the minister could propose obtaining further information. Thus the first determination would be forgotten, and when they later returned to the charge, they usually succeeded. By such methods or others similar, they made faults to seem greater or less; letters from spies or the secret police were given weight, or glossed over, and ruin or riches might be the result.

That was why working in Mme de Maintenon's apartment was so immensely important for the individuals concerned, and why it became so necessary for her to make the ministers her slaves. It gave them powerful assistance in rising to high rank and continually increased them in reputation and authority—them and their families, because Mme de Maintenon was ready to cast honours on any dunghill in order to attach such persons to her.

In the short time before they came to work, or after they left her apartment, she took the opportunity to sound the King on their behalf, to excuse or praise them, pity them for their hard labours, extol their merits and, if there were something to be gained for them, to prepare the way, sometimes breaking the ice on the pretext of their modesty, saying that the King's interest demanded that they should be encouraged to further efforts. Thus there arose between Mme de Maintenon and the ministers a chain of reciprocal wants and services, of which the King had no suspicion whatsoever.

If Mme de Maintenon could achieve nothing without them, however, the ministers could do nothing without her, much less against her. Directly she saw that it was impossible to retrieve them when they strayed from her ideas, or if they fell out of her favour, their ruin was assured. She never miscarried, although she sometimes needed time, double-dealing and cunning to a great degree, as when she ruined Chamillart, and Louvois before him. Pontchartrain only escaped her because his wit amused the King, because of the thorny financial situation during the war, and because his wife was clever enough to stay in Mme de Maintenon's good books for a very long time. Even he, in the end, was got rid of by the golden gate of the chancellery, that opened for him only just in time. The Duc de Beauvilliers thought that he would be wrecked on two different occasions,[1] and only escaped by a miracle, as I have described elsewhere.

Since the most outstanding ministers and the most distinguished men were on such terms with Mme de Maintenon, you may judge how it was with other sorts of persons, less able to defend themselves or even to realize what was happening Very many people who had their heads broken were at a loss to understand the cause, and went to much trouble to find out and seek a remedy. But all was useless.

The King's short, very occasional sessions with the generals usually took place in the evening, in her presence and that of

---

[1] In 1698, Mme de Maintenon had tried to remove the Duc de Beauvilliers from being governor to the Duc de Bourgogne, and in 1709, from the King's council.

the secretary of state for war. Those with Pontchartrain, filled, as they were, with reports from spies, and tittle-tattle of every kind about Paris and the Court, gave her opportunities for doing much good and harm. Torcy never worked at her apartment and she almost never saw him to speak to, which made her positively dislike him, especially as he was head of the post office and had many private interviews with the King over intercepted letters. The King often brought snippets for Mme de Maintenon to read, but there was no continuity; she only learned things by scraps, whenever the King remembered to tell or show her some matter.

As for foreign affairs, they were dealt with at the council of State or, if anything pressed, Torcy took it straight to the King at any hour; there were no fixed times for him. Mme de Maintenon would dearly have loved to have had these conferences held in her apartment, but Torcy was too wise to fall into that trap. He always avoided it by saying modestly that no business of his warranted so much inconvenience to her. It was not as though the King did not tell her everything afterwards, but it was not the same. She felt the difference between hearing regular discussions which she could influence and prepare for at leisure, and having to argue with the King herself on the basis of what he alone had told her, or stand up to him alone if she preferred one course to another.

At the same time the King was very watchful. It sometimes happened, if they had been less subtle than usual, that he realized when some minister or general favoured a relation of Mme de Maintenon. Then he would say, half angrily, half-mocking, 'So-and-so has paid his court well. It appears that because he is Mme de Maintenon's cousin, he need not prove loyal service.' Such snubs made her very nervous and cautious when she was driven to speak openly to the King about someone or something, and she always publicly professed that she never interfered on any account, not even in the littlest things.

Le Tellier, in very early days, long before he was Chancellor of France, understood the King's reactions perfectly. One of his friends once asked him to assist in some matter that was coming under discussion, and Le Tellier promised to do his best. This answer did not please the friend, who said frankly that with his position and the King's favour, he might do much better. 'You do not know the circumstances,' said Le Tellier. 'Out of twenty matters which we bring before the King, we are sure that nine-teen will go as we wish, but equally surely, the twentieth is decided against us. The trouble is that none of us can foresee which the twentieth will be, and very often it is the one that most concerns us. This is a trick which the King keeps up his sleeve to show us that he is master, and should it occur on some matter so important that we continue to press our opinion, although that rarely happens, we are sure of an out-burst. But in truth, after the reprimand, the King rests content with having put us in our places, and is sorry for vexing us. That is the time when he becomes most gentle and reasonable, and then we can do as we please.'

That, indeed, was how the King behaved all through his reign towards his ministers. He was entirely ruled by them, even by the youngest and most mediocre, even by those whom he liked and trusted least. Always, he was on guard against influences, and always believed that he had been completely successful in avoiding them.

He was the same with Mme de Maintenon, and from time to time flew into terrible passions with her, afterwards congratu-lating himself for so doing. Sometimes she burst into tears in front of him, and lived on tenterhooks for several days. When she had planted Fagon as chief physician in place of d'Aquin, because she liked to have near her that clever man, to whom she had become attached when she had journeyed to different spas with M. du Maine, she sometimes pretended illness after such scenes and usually ended by turning them to her advantage.

Not that any tricks of that kind, nor even real illness had power to move the King, for he was supremely self-centred and considered others, no matter whom, only as regarded him-self. His hardness was extraordinary. In the times when he was most ardent for his mistresses, discomforts that made travel and tight Court dresses most awkward for them (for until Marly, ladies never appeared otherwise clothed in coaches or at Court) earned them no dispensations. Pregnant, sick, less than six weeks after labour, otherwise indisposed, no matter, they had to be fully dressed, bejewelled, tight-laced into their bodices, ready to travel to Flanders or further, to dance, be lively, attend the fêtes, eat, be cheerful and good company, move about, seem not to notice heat or cold or draughts or dust, and all punctual to the moment, giving no trouble of any kind.

He treated his daughters in the same way. You have already seen how little he was concerned for Mme la Duchesse de Bourgogne,[1] in spite of all that Fagon and Mme de Maintenon could say. Yet for Mme la Duchesse de Bourgogne he felt all the love of which he was capable.

When he travelled, his coach was always full of women, his mistresses, and after their time, his bastard-daughters, his daughters-in-law, sometimes Madame, and some of the ladies when there was room for them. But it was only to meets of the hunt, on journeys to Fontainebleau, Chantilly, Compiègne, and on long journeys that such was the arrangement. When he went shooting, or drove out, or slept at Marly or Meudon, he travelled alone in a lighter carriage. He did not care to listen to the conversation of the high officers who might otherwise have accompanied him; they say that Charost, who used to take such opportunities to tell him many things, persuaded him to adopt that attitude more than forty years earlier. The arrangement suited his ministers, who might otherwise have had fresh cause for nervousness every day, about the exact amount of formality which they must maintain, for the King was most meticulous. As regards women, the mistresses of early days, the daughters who followed them, and the small circle of ladies allowed in his coach, except that attendance was obligatory, the occasions were few and far between and the chatter not greatly to be dreaded.

On longer journeys there was always a vast store of provisions of many different kinds in the King's coach, cold meats, cakes and fruit, for example. They were never more than a quarter of a league on their way before the King asked whether the ladies did not care to eat something. He himself never ate between meals, not even fruit, but it amused him to watch others eat, and eat to bursting point. They had to appear hungry, gay, and had to set to with good appetite, and good grace, or else he became displeased and showed his resentment, saying that they were being pettish, nice, or trying to appear refined. Yet those same ladies or princesses who supped at his table on such days, were obliged, under threat of the same reprimands, to produce as much eagerness as though they had not eaten all day. As for the needs of nature, they could not be mentioned, and in any case, it would have been very embarrassing for the ladies, with detachments of the household cavalry and the King's escort

[1] Pp. 139–142.

riding before and after the coach, and officers and equerries
by the doors, raising a dust that covered everyone within. The
King liked fresh air, and would have all the windows lowered;
he would have thought very ill of it, had any lady drawn one of
the curtains against the sun, wind, or cold. One had not to
notice that, nor any other kind of discomfort, and he always
drove exceedingly fast, and usually with relays of horses. To
feel sick was an unforgivable crime.

I have heard the Duchesse de Chevreuse, whom he liked and
took with him in his carriage so long as she was able to travel,
tell how once, driving with him from Versailles to Fontainebleau, she had been overtaken before they had gone two leagues
by one of those pressing emergencies which one feels powerless
to resist. The journey was continuous and the King did not leave
his coach when he stopped to dine. Her need became even
greater, but did not make itself felt at any convenient time, when
they dined, for instance, and she might have got down and gone
into the house opposite. Unfortunately the meal, although she
ate as little as she decently could, brought her to an even worse
pass. At moments she thought that she would be forced to
confess and stop the coach, and at others she felt near swooning,
but her courage kept her up until they arrived at Fontainebleau, where she could hold out no longer. As she set foot to
the ground, she happened to see the Duc de Beauvilliers, standing at the King's entrance, and instead of following with the
suite, she took his arm and told him that she would die if she did
not relieve herself. They crossed the end of the oval courtyard,
and entered the chapel, which, luckily, happened to be open, for
mass was said there each morning. Necessity knows no law!
Mme de Chevreuse relieved herself then and there in the chapel,
behind the back of the Duc de Beauvilliers as he guarded the door!
I repeat this misfortune to show the discomforts that daily beset
those who approached the King most nearly, and those whom
he most favoured, for that incident happened in the hey-day of
the Duchesse de Chevreuse. Such things may appear the merest
trifles, and so indeed they are, but they are too much characteristic to be omitted. The King himself sometimes felt the
needs of nature, and then he did not hesitate to get down from
the carriage, but the ladies at such times might not move.

Mme de Maintenon, who detested fresh air and other discomforts, gained no privileges in such matters. All that she

obtained, on the pretext of modest reserve and for other reasons, was to travel alone in the manner which I have described. To travel she was obliged, in whatever state of health, and to arrive at the destination as arranged, and be settled and in good order before the King came to her. She made many excursions to Marly in a state in which one would not have sent even a servant, and on one occasion when she went to Fontainebleau, they really thought that she would die upon the road. No matter how badly she might be feeling, the King went to her at his ordinary time, and did whatever he had planned; at the very most, she was allowed to lie in bed. Often she lay there sweating great drops, but the King, who, as I have said, liked fresh air and hated hot rooms, would be amazed at finding everything shut, and would order the windows to be opened, and none left closed, although he saw her state. And this would continue until ten o'clock, when he went to dinner, without consideration for the dampness of the night air. If music had been arranged, neither fevers nor headaches might serve to prevent it, and a hundred candles flared in her eyes. So the King went his own ways, and never inquired whether she might be inconvenienced.

1715

After the Death of the King

THE King's death appeared to take the slothful mind of M. le Duc d'Orléans as much by surprise as though it were unexpected, for he remained in precisely the same state as when I had left him.[1] He made no progress towards settling the urgent

---

[1] In the will which Louis XIV had made, the Duc d'Orléans was named Regent. The Duc du Maine, however, became guardian of the five-year-old King, Louis XV, who, according to the will, was to be taken from Versailles to the fortress of Vincennes, as though to protect him from a possible murderer. If d'Orléans had submitted to this clause, du Maine could very easily have seized the power and ousted him from the Regency. Furthermore, the Regency Council, as named by Louis XIV, was composed of friends of the Duc du Maine. D'Orléans, lazy and unambitious, would quite likely have let matters slide, had he not been pushed and prodded by Saint-Simon. The latter, however, complicated the issue for d'Orléans by insisting that the rights of the dukes in Parliament, which had been allowed to lapse under Louis XIV, should be restored to them. These rights were symbolized by the 'affair of the bonnets', in other words, the privilege of remaining covered when addressing the assembly, whereas the Premier Président had to speak bareheaded.

questions concerning businesses in hand or new appointments and, just as I had foretold, was so inundated, in those first days, with orders to give and decisions to take over a thousand trivial matters, each more petty than the last, but all most pressing, that he had no time to think of what was really essential.

I myself received the news of the King's death when I awoke, and went at once to make my bow to the new monarch, whom I found almost alone, the first flood of courtiers having already departed. Thence I went straight to M. le Duc d'Orléans, whose apartments were so beseiged with callers that you could scarcely have dropped a pin between them. I managed, however, to draw him apart into his study to make one last effort, which proved useless, for the summoning of the Etats Généraux, and reminded him of the promise made to me in the presence of ten or twelve other peers that we should remain covered when called upon to speak, and of our complaints at other encroachments by the Parlement,[1] to all of which he assented.

I saw him again at dinner-time, when he was somewhat less overwhelmed with visitors, and he then confessed to me that he had drawn up no lists, made no appointments and, in fact, had made up his mind about nothing whatsoever. This was no time for scolding and reproaches. I merely shrugged my shoulders and besought him to be on his guard against petitioners and ministers, and I made certain of the absolute exclusion of Pontchartrain and Desmarets from the new councils. I then confronted him with the affair of the late King's will and codicil and asked him how he proposed to deal with the matter when we attended the Parlement on the following day for the reading of these two documents.

Tête-à-tête in his own study he had the firmest character imaginable; elsewhere, the weakest. He promised miracles, and I again stressed the vital importance, to him, of the occasion and all that might result from it. I was with him nearly two hours. After leaving him, I went to Mme la Duchesse d'Orléans, whom I found behind her curtains with many ladies sitting silently around. Thence back to my own apartments, where I had company awaiting me for dinner, immediately after which I had intended going to Paris. It grew very late, for we

---

[1] A further cause for aggravation in the affair of the bonnets was that Premier Président de Novion had got into the habit of removing his hat in Parlement when addressing the Princes of the Blood and the other presidents, but keeping it on when he spoke to dukes.

had much to discuss, but just as I was about to leave, M. le Duc d'Orléans sent for me and the other dukes who were with me.

As soon as we reached his apartment he made us a flowery speech, urging us to start nothing new on the following day (although he had previously given permission), saying that we should distract attention from great and pressing affairs of State, such as the Regency and the future administration, and bring indignation upon ourselves for interrupting and delaying vital public matters for our private purposes.

Many of us were astounded at this sudden reversal of what he had said only that morning. d'Antin, M. de Metz,[1] and some of the others pointed out how awkwardly we were now placed in an affair which we had been asked to undertake against our inclinations. M. le Duc d'Orléans appeared upset. He said several times that the affair of the bonnets was indeed an intolerable infringement of our rights, and the other matters of which we complained not less so, but that we should choose a better occasion. So momentous a session was, he said, not the time to air a private quarrel. 'But, Monsieur,' I said, 'when these great affairs are settled, you will not care for us or our rights, and if we do not seize this opportunity, you will put us off time after time and we shall have sacrificed our interests in vain.' He then gave his word most emphatically, promising to give judgment in our favour on all disputes in the Parlement about encroachments, bonnets, councillors upon the bench,[2] etc., just as soon as the state matters had been concluded. I implored him to remember that he had given us a solemn undertaking and not to promise more than he meant to fulfil.

Everything having been settled in this way, we very reluctantly had to decide how best to inform our absent colleagues of the sudden change, for they had to know before they went to the Parlement. Finally it was agreed that we should each send word to his nearest neighbour to meet at five o'clock next morning, in parliamentary robes, at the house of the Archbishop of Rheims, on urgent and important business. It was ten o'clock before we reached Paris, and we all immediately acted as had been arranged.

[1] Henri Charles du Cambout, Duc de Coislin, Bishop of Metz.
[2] Once again, it was Président de Novion who had thought of getting a councillor to sit on the dukes' bench in Parlement so as to reduce the latter in rank.

Between five and six o'clock on the following day, we accordingly assembled at the Archbishop's house, at the end of the Pont Royal, behind the Hôtel de Mailly. There was a good deal of grumbling, but since nothing could be done everyone was obliged to submit. I then made one last attempt to shift the responsibility of making the formal protest onto some other person's shoulders. But it was useless. It was argued that what had been agreed must stand, that nothing could be changed without the consent of M. le Duc d'Orléans, who had always insisted that I should be the speaker, and that there was neither time nor good reason to ask him to change his mind. They ended by exhorting me to proceed with good courage and not be too accommodating towards M. le Duc d'Orléans, since he cared so little about accommodating us.

These last remarks made me feel it desirable to recall them to a better frame of mind, and I spoke of the awkward situation in which M. le Duc d'Orléans found himself, between the Parlement, as the guardian of the late King's will and codicil, and the bastards, whose powers and privileges these documents were intended to increase, as no one could doubt for a moment. I pointed out how all-important it was for M. le Duc d'Orléans, for the State, and for ourselves, that the bastards should not be allowed to profit by the King's intentions, and that M. le Duc d'Orléans's promise, which he had given and reiterated, was a proof of his sincerity and goodwill. I added further that we could not reasonably blame him for being loath to put the Parlement on the side of the bastards at this critical juncture when the Regent's powers were to be decided, or to provoke a quarrel and a delay in settling grave and pressing matters in which he had everything to lose.

My little speech seemed to have the desired effect. It was now nearly seven in the morning, and we went all together straight to the Parlement, with our coaches and retinues following after.

1715

The Session of the Parlement

LESS than a quarter of an hour after we had taken our seats, the bastards entered. M. du Maine was bursting with joy. That is a terrible expression, but I can find no other to describe his appearance. A veneer of smiling satisfaction overspread his look of complete self-assurance, which was plainly visible at times, in spite of his seemingly polite efforts to restrain himself. He advanced bowing to left and right, scanning the faces with a piercing glance. He then saluted the bench with an air of triumph, which was clearly reflected in the bow of Mesmes, the premier président.[1] Towards the peers, the gravity, indeed, the respect, the slowness and profundity of his inclination to all three sides were truly eloquent. His head remained bowed even after he had straightened himself, so heavy is the weight of wickedness, even when victory is within grasp. I never took my eyes from him, and I noticed that from all three sides the bows returned to him were very stiff and short.

Hardly were we reseated, before Monsieur le Duc arrived and, immediately afterwards, M. le Duc d'Orléans. I let the noise of their entry subside a little and, seeing that the premier président was about to uncover before speaking, I raised my hand, removed my own bonnet, instantly replaced it, and spoke myself. I said that I was charged by the peers to announce to the assembly that only in consideration of the urgent and vital nature of the matters now to be discussed would they tolerate the shameless usurpation of the privilege of the bonnet and many other abuses of which they had to complain. In so doing they showed their very proper regard for the vital importance of state affairs. Nevertheless, I here made the strongest possible protest in the most formal manner and in the name of the whole body of peers and with the consent of M. le Duc d'Orléans.

The deep silence in which I was heard bore witness to the amazement of the entire assembly. M. le Duc d'Orléans un-

---

[1] Jean-Antoine III de Mesmes, Comte d'Avaux. He was a great friend of the Duc du Maine.

L

covered to signify his assent, bowed his head rather low, looked embarrassed, and immediately put back his bonnet. I glanced towards M. du Maine, who appeared rather relieved at having been let off so lightly, although my neighbours assured me that he had looked very vexed when I began.

After a short silence, I saw the premier président turn to M. le Duc d Orléans and say something in a low voice. Then in loud tones he summoned the deputation from the Parlement to fetch the King's will and the codicil, which had been stored together in the same place. A silence lasted throughout these long and short periods of waiting, each man looked at his neighbour without moving. We peers were seated upon the lower seats, and the doors were supposed to be kept shut, but the great chamber was crowded with sightseers of all sorts and conditions, and with the many followers of those who were taking part in the session.

The deputation was not long in returning. The will and codicil were placed in the hands of the premier président, who presented them to M. le Duc d Orléans without relinquishing his hold upon them. They were then passed from hand to hand along the rows of magistrates to Dreux,[1] one of the counsellors of the Parlement, who read them loudly and clearly so that they could be heard by all from his place in the high seats behind the premier président, near the lantern window of the robing-room. You may imagine how attentively he was listened to, and how all eyes and ears were turned towards the reader. M. du Maine looked troubled, for in spite of his jubilation, he knew that this was the overture to a crucial battle. M. le Duc d'Orléans appeared merely politely interested.

I shall not pause here to describe the contents of these two documents, which related solely to the powers and dignities of the bastards, Mme de Maintenon, and Saint-Cyr, the education of the young King, and the composition of the Regency Council, all to the detriment of M. le Duc d'Orléans, whom they delivered up, deprived of all authority into the all-powerful hands of the Duc du Maine.

I noticed a shade of gloom and indignation overspread the faces of the audience as the reading proceeded. This changed to a kind of silent anger when the codicil was reached. The Du

---

[1] Thomas II Dreux de la Gallissonnière. He was the doyen of the Parlemen , age seventy-five at that time.

du Maine grew pale, for all his attention had been fixed upon the faces, and my eyes followed him closely as he listened, and I also cast a glance from time to time at the face of M. le Duc d'Orléans.

When the reading was over that prince prepared to speak. Looking round the assembly, he removed and replaced his bonnet and said a few words in praise and mourning for the late King. Then raising his voice, he declared that he had nothing but praise for the clauses relating to the education of the present King and the maintenance of so handsome and beneficial an establishment at Saint-Cyr. Regarding those clauses in the will and codicil that concerned the government of the kingdom, he would prefer to take each document separately. He found them, he said, difficult to reconcile with the assurances which the King had given him in the last days of his life, that nothing in his will would displease him, after which the King had referred the ordering of all public business and the ministers concerned to him. The King, therefore, could not have understood what he had been made to do (here M. le Duc d'Orléans stared hard at M. du Maine), for by the terms of the will the Council of Regency was already appointed and the Regent's personal authority so circumscribed that no real power was left to him. Such an insult to his birth, to his devotion to the King and love for his country, he could not bear without dishonour, and he felt sufficiently confident of the esteem in which he was held by the present assembly to be sure that his Regency would be declared what it should be, namely, absolute, independent, and with full authority to select the members of his Council, whose right to deliberate he would not question. His address seemed to make a deep impression.

At this point M. du Maine seemed to wish to speak, but as he was removing his bonnet. M. le Duc d'Orléans put his head round in front of Monsieur le Duc, and said dryly, 'Monsieur, you shall speak when your turn comes,' and a moment afterwards the matter began to turn in M. le Duc d'Orléans's favour. The selection of the Council of Regency was offered to him as Regent of the kingdom, endowed with full authority; its decisions were to be subjected to the vote of a majority, with the Regent's vote counting as two, in cases where the votes were evenly cast. Thus, all favours and penalties would lie with the Regent alone. The applause was such that M. du Maine dared not say a word. He reserved his efforts for the codicil which, had it been declared valid, would have rendered null and void everything that M. le Duc d'Orléans had gained.

After a short pause M. le Duc d'Orléans spoke again. He expressed his astonishment that to those who had inspired it the will alone had not seemed enough, although it made them masters of the kingdom. They had apparently thought some of its terms so outrageous that in order to make themselves safe they needed to control the young King's person, himself, the Court, and Paris. He added that whilst the will wounded his honour to an extent which the assembly seemed to feel as deeply as he, the codicil injured it still more, for it left him secure in neither life nor liberty, and placed the King in the absolute power of those who had not scrupled to take advantage of the weakness of a dying monarch in order to wring from him privileges which he had never intended to grant. He ended by declaring that he could not act under such limitations, and that he did not doubt but that the assembly would annul a codicil that was indefensible since its conditions would throw the whole of France into great and certain disaster.

The Duc du Maine, who had turned all the colours of the rainbow, began again to speak and this time was permitted to do so. He said that the education of the King having been entrusted to him, and consequently the care of his person, it was only natural that he should be given entire authority over the civil and military establishments, otherwise he would be unable to discharge his task. He then took the opportunity to boast of his loyalty, which the late King had recognized by giving him his entire confidence.

Here M. le Duc d'Orléans interrupted, taking exception to these last remarks, and M. du Maine attempted to soften them by praising the Maréchal de Villeroy, who had been associated with him, under his authority. M. le Duc d'Orléans replied that he thought it strange indeed that the trust had not been placed solely in the hands of M. du Maine, and stranger still that he should think it impossible to live near the King without the protection of those who had made themselves absolute rulers of the household inside and out, of Paris, and even of the Guards regiments.

The dispute grew hotter as the speakers interrupted one another in broken sentences, until, fearing that the argument

might become unseemly, I made a signal to M. le Duc
d'Orléans to leave the assembly and finish the discussion
in the fourth Chambre des Enquêtes, which was empty and
which had a door leading into the great chamber. What led
me to this action was that I noticed that M. du Maine was
beginning to mumble something about sharing the responsibility, and that M. le Duc d'Orléans was not appearing at his
best. The latter, however, was very shortsighted and so much
occupied with attacking and answering that he did not see
my sign. A few moments later, therefore, I rose and said,
'Monsieur, if you would care to step into the next room with
M. du Maine you could speak more freely,' and leaning forward I made a gesture with my hand and eyes, which he did
see. He nodded to me, and I had hardly reseated myself before
I saw him step forward in front of M. du Maine, and they
both left the chamber. I did not observe who followed them,
for the whole assembly rose as they went out and then sat
in perfect silence and did not move again. After a time, the
Comte de Toulouse also entered the other room, followed
by Monsieur le Duc and shortly afterwards, by the Duc de la
Force.

The latter was not long gone. Returning to the chamber, he
passed along the row of dukes and put his head between the
Duc de Sully and myself so as not to be overheard, saying, 'For
God's sake go in to them. Things are going abominably and
M. le Duc d'Orléans is weakening. Go and stop the discussion
and bring him back. Tell him to say that it is time to adjourn
for dinner, and let us use the interval to summon the King's
lawyers to the Palais Royal and to canvass the doubtful peers
and the bell-wethers among the magistrates.'

This advice seemed good to me, and I accordingly went into
the next room, where I found a large circle of onlookers standing at a respectful distance from the fireplace, where M. le Duc
d'Orléans and the Duc du Maine stood apart arguing in low
voices but looking very angry. I stayed to watch for a moment
or two and then went forward looking as though I wished to
speak. 'Well, what is it? said M. le Duc d'Orléans impatiently.
'Just one word, sir, for your private ear.' But he went on talking to M. du Maine with myself almost making a third in their
discussion. I continued to insist, however, until at last he
listened to me. 'Not here, sir,' I said, taking him by the hand

and drawing him towards a corner of the hearth. At that, the Comte de Toulouse, who was standing near, took a long step backwards, and the Duc du Maine stepped back also.

I whispered quietly into M. le Duc d'Orléans's ear that he had no hope of obtaining anything from M. du Maine, for he would not relinquish the codicil to any arguments, and that it would be dangerous, unbecoming and futile to prolong the discussion. 'You are quite right,' he said, 'I shall end it.' 'Do so now,' I said, 'do not let yourself be diverted.' He then left me, said two words to M. du Maine to the effect that it was getting late and that it would be better to finish after dinner.

I remained where he left me, so that I saw M. du Maine make his bow and retire, and at the same time Monsieur le Duc stepped forward and spoke to M. le Duc d'Orléans. Then, as it was necessary to pass the spot where I stood in order to re-enter the great chamber, they both came up to me. That was how I was the first to know that Monsieur le Duc had asked to be made chairman of the new Council of Regency, and that M. le Duc d'Orléans had granted his request. I believe that although he had not dared to tell me so, M. le Duc d'Orléans had already promised him the appointment. At any rate, he now told me quickly that he intended to inform the Parlement before the session ended. I bowed with an air of congratulation and approval, and we forthwith returned to the chamber.

When the noise of their entrance had subsided, M. le Duc d'Orléans announced that it was time to adjourn for dinner. He added that he desired Monsieur le Duc to join the Regency Council as chairman, and that since the assembly had done him the honour due to his birth and office as Regent, he would explain the forms which he thought most suitable for the administration, and hoped to profit by the wisdom and experience of the present company. His words were greeted with loud and unanimous applause, and the assembly rose.

I had been invited to dine with Cardinal de Noailles that day, but thought it best to spend the short time of the recess with M. le Duc d'Orléans. I therefore approached him as he left, saying, 'Time is precious, I shall follow you to the Palais Royal.' Then going back to my place to go out with the other peers, I sent a gentleman with my excuses to the Cardinal. I drove in my coach to the Palais Royal, where a great crowd of people were waiting, with everyone asking me for news, but I answered only that everything was going well, according to the proper forms, but that all was not yet over.

When I arrived, I found M. le Duc d'Orléans closeted in his study with Canillac, who had been waiting for him. We made our plans there and then, and he sent for d'Aguesseau, the procureur général, who afterwards became chancellor, and Joly de Fleury, the chief avocat général. It was then two o'clock. They served dinner at a small table laid for four, and I sat down to eat with the prince. I should mention in passing that this was the last meal I ever ate in his company, except for one at Mme la Duchesse d'Orléans' country house at Bagnolet.

In the meanwhile, the Maréchal de Villeroy had remained at Versailles, where he had been kept posted with the latest news. Three couriers, coming swiftly one after another, filled him with such joy and hope that he and his former mistress, the Duchesse de Ventadour, never doubted but that the codicil would be accepted and the will proved. The pair could hardly contain their delight and spread the good news of a complete victory for M. du Maine. Paris was equally deceived by Villeroy's messengers, but his triumph was not of long duration.

We returned to the Parlement about four o'clock—I alone, and slightly ahead of M. le Duc d'Orléans—and found everyone already in their seats. People looked at us curiously, or so I thought. I do not know whether they guessed where I had been, but I took care to allow my face to betray nothing.

M. le Duc d'Orléans began by saying that he would take up the business where it had been left that morning, for he was obliged to confess that he had been unable to come to any agreement with M. du Maine. He would therefore call their attention to the vile terms of the codicil that had been wrested from a dying monarch, for they were even more abominable than those of the will which had already been set aside. That will having been annulled, the Assembly could not rightly allow M. du Maine to be master of the young King, the Court, Paris, and, consequently of the government of the kingdom, with power over the life and liberty of the Regent, whom he could arrest at any time, once he had become absolute master of the King's households both civil and military. The Council realized the disasters that must follow from such a revolutionary change, and he relied upon the wisdom, prudence, and justice of

the present company, as well as upon their love for their
country, to speak their minds openly.

At this stage, M. du Maine showed himself as despicable
upon the field of battle as he had been formidable in the tents.
He looked like a condemned man. He who was always so ruddy
now appeared deathly pale, and he mumbled something in a
low voice, very humbly and respectfully, in striking contrast to
his bold demeanour of earlier in the day. They took the vote
without waiting for him to finish. It was given unanimously for
the total annulment of the codicil.

Seeing himself thus completely denuded, M. du Maine
made one final desperate effort. He claimed, more vigorously
than might have been expected and yet with moderation, that
since the authority given to him by the codicil had been removed he would ask to be relieved of the guardianship of the
King's person, retaining only the supervision of his education.
M. le Duc d'Orléans answered, 'Right willingly, Monsieur,
that will be quite sufficient,' Whereupon, Mesmes, the premier
président, who looked as crushed as M. du Maine himself,
called the vote.

While this was being done, and for the rest of that session,
he remained with his eyes cast down, looking more dead than
alive and apparently unable to move. There was loud and prolonged applause, when the judgment was delivered, from the
great crowd of spectators that had filled the entire building as
the news spread.

After waiting for the noise to subside, the Regent made a
short, courteous and dignified speech of thanks to the Assembly.
He then said that it was now time to inform the Parlement of
the measures which he considered it necessary to take in order
to govern the State, adding that he felt all the more confident
of what he proposed because they were the plans of M. le Duc
de Bourgogne (so he referred to him), as they had been discovered among his papers. His words were received with
acclamations from the magistrature, which were echoed by the
crowd. The session was closed with a brief compliment to M. le
Duc d'Orléans from the premier président, who then rose with
the rest of the company, and all departed.

August 26, 1718

The Bed of Justice[1]

AT last the members of the Parlement arrived in procession and, like children, we all went to watch from the windows. They came walking two by two in their scarlet robes through the great gate of the courtyard and into the Salle des Ambassadeurs, where the premier président and the Président d'Aligre waited for them. The latter came by coach and entered through the smaller courtyard so as to have less far to walk. While most of the spectators crowded into the two windows, I was careful to lose nothing of what happened inside the chamber, for fear of intrigues or evasions. Several times, Desgranges, the master of ceremonies, came up to tell me how matters were proceeding, and I walked about watching everyone closely. A few people, either from actual necessity or merely because it was forbidden, asked the Regent's permission to leave the room, and he readily gave his consent, on condition that they should keep silence and return at once. He even told La Vrillière to caution the Maréchal d'Huxelles and some other suspects, but he meant not to lose sight of them, which La Vrillière understood and did very well. I acted in the same way with the Maréchaux de Villars and de Tallard, and when I saw Effiat opening the King's private door for the Maréchal de Villeroy, I ran ostensibly to help him, but really it was to prevent him from talking through the door and sending a message to the bastards. For the same reason, I stayed near Effiat until the Maréchal returned and I saw that the door was shut securely after him, but I must say that the alertness of mind and body required to invigilate over that vast chamber and crowd of people was both fatiguing and laborious.

When at length the Parlement were assembled, the peers seated, and the presidents had been in two relays to fetch their furs from behind the screens in the adjoining room, Desgranges came to announce that all was prepared. There had been some discussion as to whether the King should dine while he was waiting, but I had managed to prevent this, fearing that coming

[1] The ceremony during which a French King imposed his will upon a Parlement.

to the Bed of Justice after an unusually early meal, he might be
unwell, which would have been vastly inconvenient. As soon
as Desgranges had made the announcement, the Regent told
him to warn the Parlement to send their deputation to greet the
King at the further end of the guardroom of the Swiss guards;
then, turning to the council, he said in a loud voice that it was
time to go for the King.

When he said these words, I felt a sudden thrill of joy as I
thought of the momentous drama that was about to be enacted
before my eyes, and I remembered to pay great attention to my
own deportment. I tried to fortify myself with the strongest
possible dose of calm, seriousness and modesty as I followed
M. le Duc d'Orléans through the private door into the study.
As we processed, the Duc d'Albret and others were con-
spicuously civil to me in their eagerness to learn what was
afoot. I repaid them with equal courtesy, complaining of the
crush and the discomfort of my coat, and so we reached the
King.

He was in ordinary dress, without robes or bands. After M.
le Duc d'Orléans had spent a little while with him, he asked
whether it would please him to start and a passage was cleared
at once. The few courtiers, who were there because they could
find no room in the audience chamber, drew to one side, and I
gave the signal to the Maréchal de Villars, who slowly led the
way towards the door. The Duc de La Force followed behind
him, and then myself, making sure that I walked immediately
in front of M. le Prince de Conti. Monsieur le Duc came behind the latter and after him M. le Duc d'Orléans. Then followed the gentlemen ushers with their maces and the King, himself, escorted by four captains of the royal bodyguard, the great
chamberlain the Duc d'Albret, and his governor the Maréchal de Villeroy. After them came the keeper of the seals,
because he was not a member of the Parlement, and the Maréchaux d'Estrée, d'Huxelles, Tallard and Bezons, who could
enter the assembly only as members of the King's suite. They
were followed by the chevaliers of the Order, and by such of the
provincial governors and lieutenant-generals as it had been
possible to notify. It had already been arranged for these officials to sit below on the bailiff's bench, uncovered and voteless.
That was the order in which we processed by way of the terrace to the hall of the Swiss guards, at the end of which the

deputation from the Parlement, headed as usual by four judges and four counsellors, waited to greet the King.

As the deputation moved forward, I said to the Duc de La Force and the Maréchal de Villars that we had best go to our seats before the King entered the chamber, and they followed me in solemn procession, single file, and in order of seniority. We three were the only ones who had the right to enter in this way, because d'Antin was absent, the Duc de Guiche had retired, Tallard was not a peer, and the four captains of the bodyguard always attended on the King at state ceremonies.

Since the Parlement was already assembled and the King about to appear, I used the same door when I made my entrance. There was room to pass, but nevertheless, the officers of the bodyguard cleared the way for me and for the Duc de La Force and the Maréchal de Villars, who processed after me. As I crossed the threshold, I paused for a moment, overjoyed at the sight of this noble spectacle and the thought of the precious moments that were about to pass. Indeed, I had need to do so, in order to recover myself sufficiently to take stock of what I saw, and furnish my appearance with a fresh veneer of seriousness and becoming modesty. Well was I aware that I should be scrutinized attentively by that assembly which had been so well trained to dislike me, and by the curious bystanders, who eagerly waited to learn the secret reason why that momentous session had so hastily been convened. Everyone realized that I must know the truth, if only because they had seen me that instant leave the Council of Regency.

Indeed, I was not mistaken. The moment I appeared all eyes turned in my direction. I slowly advanced towards the table of the clerk of the Parlement, then turning back between the two benches I crossed the whole width of the chamber, passing in front of the King's counsellors who saluted me cordially, and mounting the three steps to our high seats, where the peers I have mentioned were already in their places. They all rose as I reached the steps. I bowed very low towards them from the top of the third step. As I slowly moved along the row, I took La Feuillade by the shoulder and whispered into his ear to mark me well and to show no sign of surprise, for he was about to hear a proclamation on the Parlement, followed by two others. Then, at last, we should be touching on affairs of the most joyful and unlooked-for nature, for the bastards were to be reduced to the bare level of the seniority of their peerages. Only the Comte de Toulouse would be reinstated, but without entail, even for his own children. La Feuillade could not understand for the first moment; then he was so overcome with joy that he was speechless. He pressed against me, and as I left him, said, 'But how about the Comte de Toulouse?' 'You will see,' I answered, and passed on. . . .

When the votes had been counted and the keeper of the seals was announcing the result, I observed a commotion on that 'High Bench', as they call it in the jargon of the Palais Royal in order to annoy the presidents who sit upon it. The premier président was insisting upon speaking, and he made that protest which has been published, full of the most subtle malice, of impudence to the Regent and insolence to the King. Yet all the time the scoundrel was trembling. His broken voice, the nervousness in his eyes, his shocked and troubled air gave the lie to this last remnant of his spite, although he could not bear to deny himself or his party this last libation. Then it was that I was able to savour with inexpressible rapture the spectacle of those proud jurists, who had dared to deny us our rightful salutations, humbly kneeling to render at our very feet their homage to the throne, whilst we, seated and covered, remained in our high place beside the King. Such postures, such situations, so utterly dissimilar, were visible signs of the justice of our cause who, verily and indeed, are *laterales Regis* in contrast to the *vas electum* of the third estate. My eyes, fixed, nay riveted, upon those arrogant citizens, traversed that whole 'High Bench' of kneeling or standing figures, their fur robes billowing out at each long, ever more subservient genuflection, until the King himself, through the mouth of the keeper of the seals, gave them permission to rise. Miniver trying to pose as ermine! Their heads, uncovered and humbled, were on a level with our feet.

That protest made, the keeper of the seals again mounted the three steps to the King, and without pausing for further instructions went back to his place. Then, casting a glance at the premier président, he proclaimed in a loud voice, ' *Le Roi veut être obéi, et obéi sur-le-champ.*' This tremendous announcement, falling, as it did, like a bolt from the blue, annihilated presidents and counsellors alike. They bowed their heads and in many cases it was a long time before they raised them. With the exception of the Marshals of France, the spectators seemed very little moved by their discomfiture.

None the less, this was a petty triumph compared with what was to follow. After a short interval, the keeper of the seals once again mounted the steps and, returning to his place, stood in silence. Then everyone present clearly perceived that the business of the Parlement having been terminated, something more still remained to do. Each man tried anxiously to think what it might be. It has since been learned that most of the Parlement expected that a decision in the matter of the bonnets was to be given in our favour. Others, who had noticed the absence of the bastards, rightly decided that the matter would concern them; but none guessed the truth, still less the full scope of it.

At last the keeper of the seals opened his mouth to speak, and in his first sentence proclaimed the downfall of one brother[1] and the other's[2] preservation. It would be impossible to describe the effect of his words upon the faces of his hearers; but although I was fully occupied in controlling my own feelings, I lost nothing of what was going on around me. Amazement seemed the prevailing emotion. Many appeared to be glad, whether from a sense of justice or because they hated the Duc du Maine and loved the Comte de Toulouse. Some were aghast. As for the premier président, he was completely put out of countenance, his face, usually so arrogant and self-satisfied, began to twitch convulsively; only extreme anger prevented him from falling down in a faint. For him matters became far worse as the reading continued, for each word was law and each brought fresh disaster. The remainder of that audience listened intently; all sat motionless for fear of losing a word, and all eyes were turned upon the reading clerk. Towards the middle, the premier président, grinding the few teeth that remained to him, leaned his forehead upon the baton, which he held with both hands, and in this strange and most revealing attitude heard the rest of that reading, so devastating for him, so life-giving for us.

In the meantime, joy was nearly killing me. I truly felt as though I were going to swoon, for my heart seemed to swell within me and could find no room in which to expand. I did violence to my feelings in order not to betray them, yet the

---

[1] The Duc du Maine.   [2] The Comte de Toulouse.

very torment was a delight. I remembered the long days and years of servitude, those unhappy times when, like a victim, I was dragged to the Parlement to witness the triumphs of the bastards, as they rose by degrees to a pinnacle above our heads. Then I thought of this day of law and justice, this dreadful retribution, which had elevated us by the force of the recoil. I re-savoured with even more exquisite pleasure the words I had dared to use to M. du Maine on the day when the scandal of the bonnets had been announced under the tyrannic rule of his father. Now, at last, my eyes could see the fulfilment of my prophecy. I could rightly congratulate myself that all this had been brought about by me, and that I enjoyed the shining splendour of that hour in the presence of the King and all that august assembly. I triumphed, I was avenged, I rejoiced in my vengeance, I delighted in the satisfaction of my strongest, most eager and most steadfast desires. I was even tempted to feel that now nothing else mattered. Yet I never ceased to give my attention to those reviving words, each of which vibrated on my heart-strings like the bow upon an instrument, or to notice their effect upon every other hearer.

At the first words spoken by the keeper of the seals my eyes met those of the two bishop-peers. Never have I seen surprise to equal theirs, nor joy so unmistakable. I had not been able to forewarn them because our seats were separated by some considerable distance, and they could hardly contain their sudden access of emotion. My eyes took in one delicious draught of their delight and then I turned away for fear of being overcome. I dared not look at them again.

While the registration was in progress I let my glance travel around me on all sides, but although I was most careful to control myself, I could not resist the temptation of giving vent to some of my feelings upon the premier président. A hundred times, during the session, I annihilated him with a long and withering look. Mockery, contempt, scorn, triumph darted from my eyes into the very marrow of his bones. Sometimes he shifted his glance when it encountered mine, once or twice he met my gaze steadily, and then I delighted to insult him with a stealthy and malicious smile, which eventually confounded him. I basked in his rage and revelled that he should know it. I sometimes mocked at him with my two neighbours, pointing him out with a sly wink when I thought that he would perceive it. In a word,

I bore down upon him without mercy to the utmost limit of my capabilities.

When the registrations were over, the King descended from his throne and left by the door through which he had entered. Then the two bishop-peers, moving in front of the throne, placed themselves at our head, and as they passed me they pressed my hands and embraced me in mutual rejoicing. We followed them, returning two by two in order of precedence along the rows of benches, down the three steps, and out by the door opposite. The Parlement then began to process out of the chamber by the other door, which was the one by which the King had entered and left. The way was cleared for us as far as the steps. The crowd of onlookers, the company, the place restrained our conversation and our joy, and I was bitterly disappointed. I entered my coach at once, for it was close at hand, and had little trouble in leaving the courtyard. In less than a quarter of an hour I was back in my own home.

Index

For background of the life of the Court and accounts of Louis XIV and members of his family, see Preface.

Abrantès (Augustin d' Alencastro, duc d'), 59, 60

Aignan (François d', abbé) called Le Père Tranquille, 245

Alberoni (Jules, abbé, later cardinal) (1664–1752), 111, 112, 113

Albret (Charles Amanieu, marquis d') introduces Mme Scarron to Mme de Montespan, 268; 298

Aligre (Etienne IV d', Premier Président) (1660–1725), 297

Anjou (Philippe de France, duc d'). See Philip V King of Spain

Anne of Austria (The Queen-Mother) (1601–66), 99, 100, 253

Antin (Louis Antoine de Gondrin de Pardaillon, marquis, later duc d'), 105, 128, 132, 136, 162, 212, 287, 299

Aquin (Antoine d') Chief Physician to the Queen, 1667. Chief Physician to the King, 1672, 56, 57, 282

Argenson (Marc René de Voyer, marquis d'), 147

Argenton (Comtesse d') Formerly Séry, Mlle de 74; mistress of le duc d'Orléans 118–120

Assurance (Pierre Cailleteau, architect, called l'), 143

Auneuil (Nicolas de Frémont, seigneur d'). See Frémont, N.

Balbien (Nanon), 191, 192

Bavaria (Maxmilien, Elector of) (1662–1726), 231

Baville (Nicolas de Lamoignon, marquis de), 97, 100

Beauvilliers (Paul, duc de) (1648–1714), 14, 36, 61, 65, 66, 69, 81, 105, 106, 113, 153, 157, 158, 159, 160, 161, 165, 176, 178, 181, 250, 280, 284

Benoist (Georges). The King's Taster, 235

Beringhen (Jacques-Louis, marquis de) (1651–1723). Le Premier Ecuyer, called Monsieur le Premier, 160; his kidnapping, 122–3; rescue, 124; hospitality to Guethem, 125

Bernard (Samuel) (1651–1739). The famous banker; conversation with Louis XIV at Marly, 141–2; bankruptcy, 150–1

Berry (Charles of France, duc de) (1685–

1714). See genealogical table of the Royal family. See preface ix, xii, xiii; 36, 68, 120, 126, 127, 140, 167, 181, 195, 205, 221; grief at Monseigneur's death, 177

Berry (Marie Elisabeth d'Orléans, duchesse de) (1695–1719); formerly called Mlle de Valois, Daughter of the Regent. M. 1710 Charles, duc de Berry. See genealogical table of the Royal family. See preface xiii, 166, 167, 178, 181, 231

Blécourt (Jean Denis, marquis de), 62; French ambassador in Madrid, 59–60

Blois (Mlle de). See Orléans (duchesse de). See genealogical table of the Royal family

Bontemps (Alexandre) (1626–1701). The King's head valet, 14, 56, 271

Bossuet (Jacques Bénigne, bishop of Meaux) (1627–1704), 131, 274, 275

Boudin (Jean). The King's apothecary, 163, 169, 170, 198

Boufflers (Louis François, marquis, later duc and maréchal de) (1644–1711), 157, 159, 161; at manoeuvres at Compiègne, 43–52; offers his plate to the mint, 154

Bouillon (Cardinal de), 10; at the marriage of the duc de Chartres, 9

Boulduc (Gilles François). The King's apothecary, 198

Bouligneux (Louis de la Palu, marquis de), 96

Bourbon (Marie Anne de). See Conti (la princesse douairière de)

Bourbon (Marie Thérèse de Bourbon-Condé). See Conti (la princesse de)

Bourgogne (Louis de France, duc de) (1682–1712). See genealogical table of Royal family. See preface ix, xii, 10, 46, 50, 63, 68, 107, 120, 126, 127, 159, 163, 182, 187, 188, 196; betrothal and marriage, 33–46; holds court at Versailles, 167; grief at Monseigneur's death, 177; illness and grief at wife's death, 195; death, 199; character, 200–205

Bourgogne (Marie Adélaide of Savoy, duchesse de) (1685–1712). See genealogical table of the Royal family. See preface viii, xii, 9, 46, 49, 51, 63, 68,

M

85, 86, 87, 89, 120, 126, 127, 137, 153, 159, 162, 163, 166, 172, 173, 174, 175, 178, 182; arrival in France, 32; betrothal and marriage, 33–36; miscarriage, 139–140; holds court at Versailles, 167; illness and death, 185–9; character, 189–95

Bracciano (Duchesse de). See Ursins (la princesse des)

Brancas (Henri Ignace de Brancas-Céreste, abbé de). Later Bishop of Lisieux, 184

Breteuil (François le Tonnellier de) (1638–1743); his ignorance, 52–3

Breteuil (Louis Nicolas le Tonnellier, baron de), 230, 231

Brissac (Albert de Grillet, marquis de) (1627–1713); plays prank on ladies of the court, 206–8

Budos (Diane Henriette de), See Saint-Simon (duchesse de)

Bury (Anne Marie d'Eurre d'Aiguebonne, Comtesse de), aunt of Mlle Choin, 18

Callières (François de) (1645–1717). The King's private secretary 1701, 104

Cambrai (Archbishop of). See Fénelon

Canillac (Philippe de Montboissier Beaufort, marquis de) (1669–1725), 50, 295

Castel Dos Rios (Marquis of). The Spanish Ambassador, 62

Castries (Marie Elisabeth de Rochechouart-Mortemart, marquise de), 179; lady-in-waiting to the duchesse de Chartres, 36–7

Caumartin (Louis Urbain Lefèvre de) (1652–1720), 52

Caylus (Marthe Marguerite le Valois de Villette de Mursay, marquise de), 164, 183, 189, 243, 277

Chaise (François d'Aix, le Père de la) (1624–1709), 29, 271

Chamillart (Michel) (1652–1721). Contrôleur Général des Finances, 1699; ministre d'Etat, 1700; secrétaire d'Etat à la Guerre, 1701; retired 1708–09, 83, 84, 87, 88, 93, 105, 106, 114, 122, 123, 124, 157, 158, 236, 237, 280

Chancellor (The). See Pontchartrain

Charles (The Archduke Charles Francis Joseph, archduke of Germany) (1685–1740), 59

Charles I, King of England (1600–49), 38

Charles II, King of England (1630–85), 39, 220

Charles V, King of France (1364–85), 202

Charles VII, King of France (1422–61), 202

Charles II, King of Spain (1665–1700). See preface xii; death of, 59

Charles V, King of Spain (1516–55), 69

Charlus (Charles Antoine de Levis, comte de), 144

Charlus (Marie François de Paule de Bethisy, comtesse de Levis, marquise de); death of, 91; behaviour, 92

Charost (Armand II de Béthune, duc de) (1663–1747), 243, 283

Chartres (Philippe d'Orléans, duc de). See Orléans (le duc d')

Chartres (Françoise Marie de Bourbon, duchesse de) (formerly known as Mlle de Blois). See Orléans (La Duchesse d')

Chastre (Edmé de la), comte de Nancay, 101

Chesne (M. Colin du). The Duc de Bourgogne's head valet, 196, 198

Chevreuse (Charles Honoré d'Albert, duc de), 157, 158, 160, 161, 199, 201

Chevreuse (Jeanne Marie Colbert, duchesse de); wife of the above, 84, 199, 284

Choin (Marie Emilie Joly, mademoiselle de); see preface xi; 125, 128, 160, 164, 166, 204; dismissed by Princesse de Conti, 18–21; visits Monseigneur at Meudon, 126–7; grief at Monseigneur's death, 182

Choiseul (Claude, comte et maréchal de) (1632–1711), 81, 102

Clement X (Pope) (1670–1676 P), 58

Clermont-Chaste (François Alphonse de) (1661–1740); love affair with Mlle Choin 18–20

Cleveland (Barbara Villiers, Duchess of) (1640–1709), 39

Coeuvres (Lucie Félicité de Noailles, comtesse d'Estrées, later maréchale d'Estrées). See Estrées. Lady-in-waiting to the Duchesse de Bourgogne

Coislin (Armand du Cambout, duc de), 54, 55

Coislin (Charles César du Cambout, chevalier de), his revenge, 53–5

Coislin (Henri Charles du Cambout, duc de) (1664–1732). Bishop of Metz, 53, 73, 184, 287

Coislin (Pierre du Cambout de) (1636–1706), bishop of Orléans and Cardinal, 35, 54

Condé (Henri I de Bourbon, prince de), 138

Condé (Henri II de Bourbon, prince de) (1588–1646), called Monsieur le Prince, Father of Le Grand Condé; see preface xiv, 138

Condé (Henri-Jules de Bourbon, prince de) (1643–1709). Called Monsieur le Prince. Son of Le Grand Condé; see preface xiv, 42, 138; conflict with Rose, 71–2

Condé (The house of Bourbon-). See Soissons, Prince (Monsieur le) Duc (Monsieur le)

Conti (Louis Armand de Bourbon, prince de) (d. 1685). See genealogical table of Royal family

Conti (Marie Anne de Bourbon, princesse douairière de) (1666–1739). Wife of the above. See genealogical table of Royal family; see preface ix, xi, 3, 17, 30, 31, 33, 37, 120, 125, 128, 163, 169, 171; takes Mlle Choin as maid-of-honour, 18; mistress of Clermont, 19; dismisses Mlle Choin, 20

Conti (François Louis de Bourbon, Prince de) (1664–1709), 26, 117, 126

Conti (Marie Thérèse de Bourbon-Condé, princesse de) (1666–1732). Formerly called Mlle de Bourbon. M. 1688 the above, her cousin, 49, 231.

Coypel (Antoine) (1661–1722). Court painter, 231

Daguesseau (Henri François) (1668–1751), le procureur général; chancellor of France 1717, 213, 295

Dangeau (Sophia Maria of Bavaria, gräfin von Loewenstein, marquise de), 87, 183, 207, 277

Dauphin (Le Grand). See Monseigneur

Dauphine (Maria Anne Christine Victoria of Bavaria, called Madame la) (d. 1690). See genealogical table of the Royal family; see preface xi

Desgranges (Michel Ancel). The master of ceremonies, 69, 297, 298

Desmarets (Nicholas) (1648–1721). Contrôleur général des Finances 1708, 147, 150, 160, 232, 286; at Marly with Bernard the banker, 141–2

Dreux (Thomas II, marquis de) (1640–1731), 184, 290

Dronero (Charles Philippe d'Este, marquis de), 32

Dubois (Cardinal) (1656–1723), later Prime Minister to Louis XV; succeeds Saint Laurent as tutor to the duc de Chartres, 4

Duc (Louis III de Bourbon-Condé, known as Monsieur le) (1668–1710). Son of Monsieur le Prince. See genealogical table of the Royal family, 3, 26, 157, 289

Duchesse (Louise Françoise de Bourbon, Madame la) (1673–1743). See genealogical table of the Royal family, 3, 17, 30, 120, 126, 127, 157, 161, 163, 166, 171; reprimanded by the King, 31; grief at Mme de Montespan's death, 136

Duras (Jacques Henri de Durfort, maréchal de) (1626–1704), 72, 73, 80, 81

Effiat (Antoine Coiffier-Ruze, marquis and maréchal d'). See preface x, 5

Elbeuf (Henri de Lorraine, duc d') (1661–1748), 29, 30

Espinoy (Elisabeth de Lorraine-Lillebonne, princesse d') (1664–1748), daughter of Mme de Lillebonne; M. 1691 le Prince d'Espinoy, 126, 162, 164, 166

Estrées (Lucie Félicité de Noailles d'Ayen, comtesse d'), maréchale de Coeuvres, later maréchale d'Estrées, 87, 135, 136

Eugène (Eugène Francis of Savoy, called Prince) (1663–1736), 111

Fagon (Guy Crescent) (1638–1718). Chief Physician to the Royal family, 89, 93, 120, 139, 144, 167, 170, 171, 206, 208, 234, 235, 236, 238, 243, 282, 283

Fargues (Balthasar de), his hospitality, 98; treatment by the King, 99–100

Fénelon (François de Salignan de la
Mothe—) (1651–1715). Archbishop of Cambrai. See preface viii, 160, 274

Ferdinand V, King of Spain (1452–1516) (K. 1468), 69

Ferreiro (Thomas Félix de), 45

Francis I, King of France (1494–1547), 2, 202

Frémont (Nicolas de Frémont, seigneur d'Auneuil) (1622–96). Father of the Maréchale de Lorges, 21

Frémont (Geneviève Damond de), wife of the above. Mother of the Maréchale de Lorges

Fronde (La) (1648–53). See preface vii, 99

Gesvres (Bernard François Potier, marquis de). See Tresmes (duc de)

Gramont (Antoine Charles, duc de) 1645–1720), 153, 156

Gramont (Elisabeth Hamilton, comtesse de) (1641–1708), 84, 156, 157; her unpleasant character, 153, 154

Grand (Louis de Lorraine, comte d'Armagnac, called Monsieur le) (1641–1718). Grand Ecuyer de France, 55; engineers the marriage of the duc de Chartres, 4

Grignan (François Adhémar de Monteuil, comte de). Son-in-law of Mme de Sévigné, 94

Grignan (Louis Adhémar de Monteuil, marquis de). Grandson of Mme de Sévigné, 94

Grignan (Françoise Marie de Sévigné, comtesse de). Wife of F.A. de Monteuil, comte de Grignan, 94

Guethem (P), 122; kidnaps Beringhen, 123; is captured and entertained, 124–5

Harcourt (Henri, marquis de Beuvron, duc de) (1654–1718), maréchal 1706; 159, 160, 276

Harcourt (Marie Françoise de Brancas-d'Oise, princesse d'), 90, 91

Harrach (Louis Thomas, comte d'), 62, 63; Austrian envoy in Madrid, 59–60

Hautefort (Marie d') duchesse de Schonberg. Maid of Honour to the Queen-Mother, Marie de Médicis and later to Anne of Austria, 16

Henry II, King of France (1547–1559), 119

Henry IV, King of France (1589–1610), 202, 218

Huxelles (Nicolas de Laye du Blé, marquis and maréchal d'), 297, 298

Imbert (Henriette Prieur), 224

Innocent XI (Pope) (P1676–89), 104

Isabella, Queen of Spain (b. 1451–1504), 69

James Stuart (The Old Pretender) (1688–1766), 12

James II, King of England (1633–1701). See preface viii, 35, 36, 39, 66, 67; at the marriage of the duc de Chartres, 10

Janson (Toussaint de Forbin, Cardinal de).

Bishop of Beauvais. Le Grand Aumônier (1630–1713), 104

La Feuillade (François III d'Aubusson, maréchal, duc de), 299, 300

Lamoignon (Guillaume de) (1616–77); 1658, premier président du parlement, 97, 99, 100

La Rochefoucauld (François VII, duc de) 1634–1714). Le Grand Veneur. Son of the author of the Memoirs, 41, 42, 81, 95, 140, 141

La Rue (Le père Charles de) (1643–1725), the celebrated preacher, confessor of the Duchesse de Bourgogne, 187, 188

La Tour (Le père Pierre François d'Arères de). Général de l'Oratoire, 132

La Trémoïlle (Joseph Emmanuel, abbé, later Cardinal de) (1658–1720), 104, 107, 108, 104

L'Aubespine D'Hauterive (Charlotte de). See Saint-Simon (duchesse de)

Launay (Nicolas de) (1647–1727). The King's jeweller, 155, 156

Lauzun (Antonin Nompar de Gaumont, marquis de Puyguilhem, later duc de) (1632–1723), 42, 46, 47, 93, 98, 156, 214; lover of La Grande Mademoiselle, 11–12; rescues the Queen of England, 12

Lauzun (Geneviève Marie de Lorges, duchesse de) (1680–1740) M. 1695 the above. Formerly Mlle de Quintin, 194

La Vallière (Louis de la Beaume-le-Blanc, duchesse de) (1644–1710), 183, 184

Le Brun (Le sieur), a quack doctor, 243

Ledran (Henri) a surgeon, 93

Le Nôtre (André, contrôleur-général des bâtiments et jardins) (1613–1700), death of, 57; his character and achievements, 58–9

Le Nôtre (Jean) father of the above, 58

Leopold I (Archduke of Austria) (1640–1705). Emperor 1658, 64

Lescalopier (Charles), 149

Le Tellier (Charles Maurice, Archbishop of Rheims) (1642–1710), 92

Le Tellier (Le Père Michel) (1643–1719) S.J. the King's confessor 1709, also of Monseigneur 1711. Expelled after the King's death, 160, 166, 171, 232, 237, 238, 239, 240, 242, 244, 281

Lillebonne (Anne de Lorraine, Princesse de) (1639–1720). Natural daughter of Charles IV and the Comtesse de Cantecroix. M. F.M. de Lorraine (Prince de Lillebonne), 126

Lillebonne (Béatrice Hiéronyme de Lorraine, called Mlle de) (1662–1738). Probably married the Chevalier de Lorraine q.v., 126, 162, 164, 166, 182

Livry (Louis Sanguin, marquis de) (1648–1723). The King's chief butler, 46, 56, 57, 235

Lorges (Guy de Durfort, comte, later duc de Quintin-Lorges) (1630–1702). Maréchal de France 1676. Father-in-law of Saint-Simon, 2, 21, 22, 23, 81, 269

Lorges (La maréchale de) (1658–1727) M. 1676. Formerly Geneviève de Frémont. Mother-in-law of Saint-Simon

Lorges (Mlle de). See Saint-Simon (duchesse de)

Lorraine (Henri de). See Elbeuf (duc d')

Lorraine (Louis de). Comte d'Armagnac et de Brionne. See Grand (Monsieur le)

Lorraine (Philippe de Lorraine-Armagnac, called Le Chevalier de) (1643–1702). Brother of the above. Engineers the marriage of the duc de Chartres, 4

Lorraine (The house of). See Elbeuf, Vaudémont, Marsan

Louis XII, King of France (1498–1515), 202

Louis XIII, King of France (1601–43), 1, 80; fondness of hunting, 15; erected original Versailles, 253

Louis XIV, King of France (1638–1715). K. 1643. M. 1660 Maria Theresa of Spain (1638–83). See preface vii, viii, ix, xii, xiii, xv, xvi, 2, 12, 14, 16, 17, 19, 20, 21, 27, 28, 54, 120; and the marriage of the duc de Chartres, 3–10; approves Saint-Simon's marriage, 23–5; beats waiter, 29; meets future duchesse de Bourgogne, 33; and the Prince of Orange, 37–8; receives English ambassador, 39; at Compiègne manoeuvres, 43–51; robberies at Versailles, 55–7; with Le Nôtre, 58; accepts Spanish throne for duc d'Anjou, 63–7; bids farewell to latter, 68; and Rose his secretary, 69–74; quarrel with Monsieur and grief at his death, 74–7; annoyed with Saint-Simon, 83–4; annoyed over offertory affair, 86–91; conversation with Puysieux, 95–6; punishes Fargues, 99–100; and the duc de Vendôme, 113–15; alarm at Beringhen's kidnapping, 122; jealousy of Beringhen, 124; and Mme de Montespan, 131–7; callousness, 139–141; meeting with Bernard, 141–2; fondness for Mansard, 143–5; concern at economic position, 145–50; interviews and dismisses Vendôme, 151–3; supports and later regrets plan to send silver to mint, 155–7; alarm at Monseigneur's illness, 163; shock at his death, 171; grief at duchesse de Bourgogne's death, 189; sympathy for duc de Bourgogne, 197; boredom, 205–6; at Mass, 207; will, 208–16; receives Persian ambassador, 231; illness and death, 233–45; character, 245–52; his court, 252–66

Louis XV, King of France (1710–74). K. 1715. See preface xv, 120, 211, 231, 244; at Louis XIV's deathbed, 241–2; bed of justice, 297–303

Louis I, King of France (814–40). Called Louis le Debonnaire, 219

Louvois (François Michel Le Tellier, marquis de) (1641–1691). Ministre d'Etat 1672; surintendant des bâtiments 1683, 11, 12, 54, 95, 102, 248, 257, 261, 264, 271, 280

Lude (Marguerite Louise de Béthune-Sully, duchesse du) (1643–1726). Lady-in-waiting to the Queen, to the Duchesse de Bourgogne 1696, 10, 33, 34, 35, 36, 45, 63, 84, 86, 89, 90, 140, 181

Madame (Henrietta of England) (1644–1670), so-called. M. Philippe, duc d'Orléans 1661. See preface viii, x.
Madame (Elisabeth Charlotte of Bavaria) (1652–1722), so-called. M. 1671 Monsieur (Philippe d'Orléans) as his second wife. See genealogical table of the Royal family. See preface viii, xi, 68 179, 223, 231; at the duc de Chartres' marriage, 4–10; at the death of La Grande Mademoiselle 11; at Monsieur's death, 78
Mademoiselle (Anne Marie Louise d'Orléans, duchesse de Montpensier, called La Grande) (1627–93). See genealogical table of the Royal family. See preface viii, 133; death of, 11–13
Mademoiselle (Elisabeth Charlotte d'Orléans, called) (1676–1744). Daughter of Monsieur, Sister of the Regent. See genealogical table of the Royal family
Mailly (Marie Anne Françoise de Sainte-Hermine, Comtesse de) (1667–1734), 34, 36
Maine (Louis Auguste de Bourbon, duc du) (1670–1736). See genealogical table of the Royal family. See preface ix, xi, xiv, xv, xvi, 121, 134, 208, 209, 212, 213, 222, 227, 234, 237, 243, 289, at the front, 25–30; detested by Monseigneur, 128; character, 129; popularity with the King, 130; favourite of Mme de Maintenon, 131; dislike for his mother Mme de Montespan, 131–2; ambition, 205; schemes to be governor of future Louis XV, 211; dissatisfied with the King's will, 239; hostility to duc d'Orléans, 291–6
Maine (Anne Louise Bénédicte de Bourbon Condé, duchesse du) (1676–1753). Sister of Monsieur le Duc; formerly called Mlle de Charalois. See genealogical table of the Royal family, xiv; see preface xiv; her character, 129–30
Maintenon (Françoise d'Aubigné, marquise de) (1635–1719). M. 1651 the poet, Paul Scarron; W. 1660; Marquise 1674; M. secretly C. 1684 Louis XIV. See preface viii, ix, x, xiii, xiv, 120, 127, 159, 165, 187, 188, 190, 191, 192, 205, 209, 222, 234, 237, 242, 243; meets future duchesse de Bourgogne, 34; at Compiègne manoeuvres, 49–51; advises acceptance of Spanish throne, 62; dislike of Monsieur, 76; friend of Ninon de l'Enclos 102; her debt to Mme de Montespan, 131; remorse at the latter's death, 136; her disastrous influence, 153; hatred for duc d'Orléans, 208; reproached by the King, 214; dissatisfied with the King's

will, 239; at the King's deathbed, 244; leaves Versailles, 245; origins and first marriage, 266–88; governess to Royal children, 268; marries the King, 271; character and behaviour, 272–85
Mansard (François) (1598–1666), architect, 143
Mansard (Jules Hardouin) (1646–1708); architect; son of the above, his origins and character, 143; relationship with the King, 144; his lack of taste, 145; death 145
Maréchal (Georges) (1658–1736). The King's chief surgeon; appointed 1703, 93, 147, 208, 234, 238, 244
Mariana of Neuburg (Queen of Spain) (1667–1740), 154
Maria Theresa of Spain (Queen of France) (1638–83). M. Louis XIV 1660. See preface ix, xii, 61, 253
Marly. See preface xix; lay-out of, 75; constructed as residence of the King, 265–6
Marsan (Charles de Lorraine-Armagnac, comte de) (1648–1708), 93, 94
Mary of Modena (Queen of England) (1658–1718), M. James II 1673, 12, 35, 36, 66, 67, 213; at the marriage of the duc de Chartres, 10
Massillon (Jean Baptiste) (1663–1742); see preface viii
Matignon (Charles Auguste Goyon, Comte de Gracé, maréchal de) (1647–1739), 139, 230
Mazarin (Cardinal) (1602–1661). See preface xii, 99, 246, 247
Mesmes (Jean Antoine III de) (1661–1723). Premier Président du Parlement, 212, 289, 296
Metz (Bishop of). See Coislin (H.C. de Cambout)
Michelet (Jules) (1798–1874). Historian, see preface xii
Mohammed Riza Beg (Doubtful Persian Ambassador), arrival in France, 229; reception by the King, 230–1; presents to the King, 232
Monseigneur (Louis, Dauphin of France, called Le Grand Dauphin) (1661–1711). See genealogical table of the Royal family. See preface ix, xi, 18, 19, 31, 33, 40, 41, 50, 63, 66, 77, 120, 125, 128; at the marriage of the duc de Chartres, 7; renounces succession to Spanish throne in favour of his son, 61; meets Mlle Choin at Meudon, 126–7; ceases to employ Mansard, 145; death and character, 161–85
Monsieur. See Orléans (Gaston, duc d'). See also genealogical table of the Royal family.
Monsieur (Philippe, duc d'Orléans, so-called) (1640–1701). See genealogical table of the Royal family. See preface ix, xi, 17, 31, 33, 63, 66, 68, 133; and the marriage of the duc de Chartres,

3-10; at the death of La Grande Mademoiselle, 11; quarrels with the King, 74-76; death and character, 77-80

Montbazon (Louise Jeanne de la Tour d'Auvergne, Princesse de). M. 1698 François Armand de Rohan (Prince de), 86, 90

Montespan (Louis Henri de Pardaillon de Gondrin, marquis de) (d. 1702), 131, 132, 268

Montespan (Françoise Athénais de Rochechouart, marquise de) (1641-1707). See preface ix, 11, 263; death of, 130; mistress of Louis XIV, 131; her devotion to religious life and her character, 132-137; introduced to Mme Scarron, 268-269; supplanted by Mme de Maintenon, 274-5

Montpensier (A.M.L. d'Orléans, duchesse de). See Mademoiselle (La Grande)

Mortemart (the family of). See Castries (Mme de), Montespan (Mme de) Rochechouart (M.M.G. de)

Nancré (Marie Anne Bertrand de la Bazinière, comtesse de), 119, 120

Nanon. See Balbien (Nanon)

Nemours (Henri II de Savoie, duc de) (d. 1657), 137

Nemours (Marie d'Orléans-Longueville, duchesse de) (1625-1707), daughter of Henri II d'Orléans. M. the above 1657. Her death, strange appearance and character, 137-9

Ninon de L'Enclos, her character, 100-3

Noailles (Anne Jules, duc et maréchal de) (1650-1708). Formerly Comte d'Ayen, 65, 66, 69, 186

Noailles (Marie Françoise de Boumonville, duchesse et maréchale de) (1656-1748), 85, 86, 87

Noel (Le Père), 188

O (Gabriel Claude, marquis de Villiers d') (1698-1734), 180, 212

Orange (William, Prince of). See William III, King of England.

Orléans (Jean Philippe, Chevalier d') (1702-48). Le Grand Prieur de France, 1719. Bastard son of the Regent and Mme d'Argenton, 118

Orléans (Gaston, duc d') (1608-60). Called "Monsieur". See genealogical table of the Royal family, 11

Orléans (Philippe, duc de Chartres, later duc d') (1674-1723). Regent of France 1715. See genealogical table of the Royal family. See preface x, 2, 26, 33, 74, 75, 76, 77, 78, 123, 156, 205, 230, 237, 240, 244, 297, 298; marriage 3-10; reconciled with the King, 79; relationship with Saint-Simon, 116-21; in love with Mlle de Séry, 118; denigrated by duc du Maine, 210-11; to be Regent after the King's death, 215; character, 216-225; speaks with the King, 241; antipathy to duc de Maine, 291-6; triumph, 296

Orléans (Françoise Marie de Bourbon, duchesse de Chartres, later duchesse d') (1677-1749). Formerly Mlle de Blois. See genealogical table of the Royal family. See preface ix, 17, 36, 117, 120, 168, 174, 218, 219, 240, 286, 287, 288, 289; marriage of, 3-10; reprimanded by the King, 31; grief at Mme de Montespan's death, 136; character, 225-9; Regent, 285

Orléans (Bishop of). See Coislin (Pierre de)

Parma (The bishop of) (Alexandre, Comte di Roncoveri). Wrongly described as bishop of Parma, he was bishop of Borgo San Donnino, 111, 112

Parma (Francisco II Farnese, Prince, later duke of) (1678-1727), 111, 112

Persia (Bogus Ambassador from). See Mohammed Riza Beg

Persia (The King of), 229, 232

Philippe VI de Valois, King of France (1338-50), 202

Philip II, King of Spain (1527-98). K. 1555, 69

Philip IV, King of Spain (1605-65). K. 1621, 69

Philip V, King of Spain (Philippe de France, duc d'Anjou) (1683-1746). King of Spain 1700. See genealogical table of the Royal family. See preface ix, xii, becomes King of Spain, 61-7; leaves for Spain, 68-9

Pontchartrain (Louis II Phélypeaux, comte de) (1643-1727). Chancellor of France 1699, 52, 61, 81, 105, 114, 122, 159, 172, 191, 229, 230, 232, 280, 281, 286

Pontchartrain (Marie de Maupéon, comtesse de), 52, 53

Portail (Antoine IV, seigneur de Vandreuil) (d. 1736), 73

Portland (John William Bentinck, Earl of) (1647-1709). English Ambassador to France, 39-42

Portsmouth (Louis Renée de Penancoët de Kérouaille, duchess of) (1649-1734), mistress of Charles II, 39, 220

Premier (Monsieur le). See Beringhen (marquis de)

Prince (Monsieur le). See Condé (Henri Jules de Bourbon, Prince de). See also Condé (Henri II de Bourbon, Prince de)

Procureur-Général (le). See Daguesseau (Henri François)

Puységur (Jacques François de Chastenet, marquis de) (1655-1743), 153; hated by the duc de Vendôme, 151; conversation with the King, 152

Puysieux (Roger Brulart, marquis de) (1640-1719). Sketch of, 95-6

Queen (The). See Maria Theresa, Queen of France.

Queen-Mother (The). See Anne of Austria

Quintin (Mlle de). See Lauzun (duchesse de)

Regent (The). See Orléans (Philippe, duc d')

Rheims (Archbishop of). See Le Tellier, Mailly

Richmond (Charles Lennox, Duke of) (1672–1723), 39

Rohan (Armand Gaston, cardinal de) (1643–1749), 218 219, 239, 240, 245

Rond (Louis le). Curé of Meudon, 170

Rose (le président Toussaint) (d. 1701), the King's private secretary, death of, 69; character and duties, 70–4; quarrel with M. de Duras, 73

Rouillé de Marbeuf (Pierre) (1657–1712), 150, 154

St. Albans (Charles Beauclerc, duke of) (1670–1726), special envoy from England, 38–9

Saint-Hérem (A. Le Gras, marquise de). See preface xix

Saint-Laurent (Nicolas François Parisot de). Tutor of the duc de Chartres, 4

Saint-Mauris (Charles-Cézar, marquis de), 80, 81, 82

Saint-Simon (Claude de Rouvroy, duc de) (1607–93). Father of the writer, death of, 13–17

Saint-Simon (Louis II de Rouvroy, duc de) (1568–1645). Grandfather of the writer

Saint-Simon (Charlotte de l'Aubespine d'Hauterive, duchesse de) (b. 1645; M. 1672). Mother of the writer, 1

Saint-Simon (Diàne Henriette de Budos, duchesse de) (d. 1670; M. 1640 Claude de Rouvroy) duc de), 1

Saint-Simon (Marie Gabrielle de Lorges, duchesse de) (1678–1743). Formerly called Mlle de Lorges. M. the writer 1695, 84, 85, 88, 89, 91, 105, 106, 107, 108, 157, 162, 165, 169, 172, 173, 179, 193, 194, 198, 199

Savoy (The little Princess of). See Bourgogne (duchesse de)

Scarron (Paul) (1610–60). Poet, first husband of Mme de Maintenon, 267

Scarron (Françoise d'Aubigné, dame). See Maintenon (marquis de)

Séguier (Charlotte). See Verneuil (duchesse de)

Séry (Marie Louise Madeleine le Bel de la Boissière, Mlle de). See d'Argenton (comtesse de)

Soissons (Olympe Mancini, comtesse de) (1639–1708). M. Eugène Maurice of Savoy (comte de), 246, 247, 260

Spain (Kings of). See Charles II, Ferdinand V, Charles V, Philip II, Philip IV, Philip V

Spain (Queens of). See Isabella, Mariana of Neuburg

Spanish Ambassador (The). See Castel dos Rios (marquis of)

Tallard (Camille d'Hostun de la Baume, maréchal, duc de) (1652–1728), 297, 298, 299

Tessé (René III de Froullay, comte et maréchal de)(1650–1725). Maréchal de France 1703, 276; trick played on him at manoeuvres, 46–7

Torcy (Jean Baptiste Colbert, marquis de) (1665–1746), 40, 61, 62, 63, 95, 105, 106, 107, 114, 122, 150, 153, 160, 232, 281

Toulouse (Le Comte de) (1678–1737). Louis Alexandre de Bourbon, legitimised son of Louis XIV and Mme de Montespan. See genealogical table of the Royal family. See preface ix, xiv, 28, 121, 227, 294, 300; character, 129; grief at Mme de Montespan's death, 136

Tresmes (Bernard François Potier, marquis de Gesvres. Later duc de) (1655–1739), 76, 77, 238; his ignorance, 53

Trévou (Pierre du) (1649–1729). (Le Père du) confessor of Monsieur, 77

Turenne (Henri de la Tour d'Auvergne, maréchal de) (1611–75), 115

Ubilla (Antonio), marquis de Rivas, 60

Ursins (La Princesse des)(1640–1722). Anne Marie de la Trémoïlle M. 1675 (Flavio degli Orsini, Duca di Bracciano, grandee of Spain) W. 1698, took the title of 'Princess des Ursins'. 45

Vaudémont (Charles Henri de Lorraine, Prince de) (1649–1723), 25, 26, 27, 276

Vendôme (Louis Joseph, duc de) (1654–1712), 128; character and behaviour, 109–16; hatred for Puységur, 151–2; dismissed by the King, 153

Vendôme (Philippe de) (1655–1727). Grand Prieur de France 1678–1719, 220; character, 115–16

Ventadour (Charlotte Eléonore de la Mothe-Houdancourt, duchesse de)(1661–1744). Lady-in-waiting to Madame, later governess of the future Louis XV, 118, 120, 231, 242

Verneuil (Henri de Bourbon, duc de). Son of Henri IV and the Marquise de Verneuil, 10

Verneuil (Charlotte Séguier, duchesse de Sully, later duchesse de) (1623–1704), at the marriage of the duc de Chartres, 10

Versailles, the Curé of. See Huchon (Claude)

Versailles. See preface vii, ix, 7, 55, 237, 253; gardens, 58; chapel, 145; description of, 262–4

Victoria (Queen); resemblance to Louis XIV. See preface viii

Vienne (François Quintin de la), the King's masseur, 28

Villarceaux (Louis de Mornay, marquis de) (1619–91), 268, 271

Villacerf (Édouard Colbert, marquis de) (1628–99) replaced by Mansard, 143

Villeroy (François de Neufville, duc et maréchal de) (1644–1730), 25, 26, 27, 28, 41, 109, 115, 117, 146, 156, 160, 238, 239, 243, 276, 297

Villeroy (Marie Marguerite de Cossé-Brissac, maréchale et duchesse de) (1646–1706), 160, 174, 179, 205, 226

Voysin (Daniel François) (1654–1717). Minister 1709; Chancellor of France and Keeper of the Seals, 1714

Wartigny (César de Brouilly, marquis de), 97

William III, King of England (1650–1701) (K. 1688), 39, 40; relations with Louis XIV, 37–8

Zinzendorf (Philip Louis, Count von). The Emperor's envoy, 64–5; 67